ABORIGINAL PEOPLES OF CANADA: A SHORT INTRODUCTION

Aboriginal Peoples of Canada: A Short Introduction provides the first comprehensive overview of Canada's First Nations peoples. Drawn from the highly successful *Encyclopedia of Canada's Peoples*, it offers extensive coverage of the Algonquians/Eastern Woodlands, Algonquians/Plains, Algonquians/Subarctic, Inuit, Iroquoians, Ktunaxa, Metis, Na-Dene, Salish, Siouans, Tsimshian, and Wakashans, as well as the many nations within these larger groupings.

With a new preface by Paul Robert Magocsi and an introduction by well-known historian J.R. Miller, the collection has chapters on each main group written by scholars such as Janet Chute, Olive Dickason, Louis-Jacques Dorais, and Eldon Yellowhorn. Each chapter covers the economics, culture, language, education, politics, kinship, religion, social organization, identification, and history of each nation, among other topics, and ends with suggestions for further readings. Readable, and suitable for the student, casual reader, or expert, the book is an excellent introduction to Canada's aboriginal peoples.

PAUL ROBERT MAGOCSI, a Fellow of the Royal Society of Canada, holds the Chair of Ukrainian Studies at the University of Toronto.

ABORIGINAL PEOPLES OF CANADA

A Short Introduction

Edited by Paul Robert Magocsi

UNIVERSITY OF TORONTO PRESS
Toronto Buffalo London

© University of Toronto Press Incorporated 2002
Toronto Buffalo London
Printed in Canada

ISBN 0-8020-3630-9 (cloth)
ISBN 0-8020-8469-9 (paper)

Printed on acid-free paper

National Library of Canada Cataloguing in Publication

Main entry under title:

Aboriginal Peoples of Canada : a short introduction /
edited by Paul Robert Magocsi.

Essays which originally appeared in Encyclopedia of Canada's
peoples.
ISBN 0-8020-3630-9 (bound)   ISBN 0-8020-8469-9 (pbk.)

1. Native peoples – Canada.   I. Magocsi, Paul R.   I. Title:
Encyclopedia of Canada's peoples.

E78.C2A149 2002   971'.00497   C2002-901740-8

All of the present work appeared in a slightly different version in
Encyclopedia of Canada's Peoples (Toronto: University of Toronto Press,
1999), edited by Paul Robert Magocsi, pp. 1–114. ©University of
Toronto Press Incorporated 1999.

University of Toronto Press acknowledges the financial assistance to
its publishing program of the Canada Council for the Arts and the
Ontario Arts Council.

University of Toronto Press acknowledges the financial support for
its publishing activities of the Government of Canada through the
Book Publishing Industry Development Program (BPIDP).

CONTENTS

PREFACE

This book is an outgrowth of a major project for which I served as editor-in-chief, the *Encyclopedia of Canada's Peoples*. Published in 1999 by the University of Toronto Press, the encyclopedia contains information about 119 peoples that have lived at some time within the boundaries of what today is Canada.

Pride of place in the encyclopedia is given to the aboriginal peoples, who received the first and longest entry. There were, of course, various ways in which the aboriginals could have been treated in a reference work dealing with all the peoples of Canada. For instance, there could have been entries for each tribe / band, or articles based on larger regional or linguistic groupings, or a single essay covering all aboriginal peoples. The entry itself could have carried one or another of various names: aboriginals, First Nations, Indians, natives, perhaps even Siberian Canadians.

In the end, it seemed most useful to have a single entry titled "Aboriginals," which we divided into twelve discrete sections based for the most part on major linguistic groupings. We presented these sections alphabetically: Algonquians / Eastern Woodlands, Algonquians / Plains, Algonquians / Subarctic, Inuit, Iroquoians, Ktunaxa, Metis, Na-Dene, Salish, Siouans, Tsimshian, and Wakashans. Within each of these sections various peoples / tribes / bands are discussed. Such a conceptual approach provides a sense both of the unity and of the individual distinctiveness of Canada's many aboriginal peoples. In order to provide an overview of the topic, we asked Professor J.R. Miller to write an introduction for the entry in the encyclopedia.

This present book fulfils in part one of the original goals of the *Encyclopedia of Canada's Peoples*: to provide easily accessible information to as many readers as possible about the richness and variety of Canada's population in the past and present. However, the size of the encyclopedia (over 1,400 pages) and its price limited its accessibility. It is with great pleasure therefore that we present this first portion of the encyclopedia – containing appropriately the entry on the First Nations – in a format that is much more accessible than the original work. We hope that other volumes will follow, drawn from the encyclopedia's entries on, for example, Caribbean peoples, East Asians, Latin Americans, Muslims, Scandinavians, Slavs, and South Asians, among others. In this way, all Canadians (not to mention readers in other countries who are interested in Canada) will be able to learn about and better appreciate the various cultures and peoples living in their midst.

Paul Robert Magocsi, FRSC
University of Toronto
July 2001

ABORIGINAL PEOPLES OF CANADA: A SHORT INTRODUCTION

INTRODUCTION

J.R. Miller

Aboriginal peoples – also known as First Nations, Indians, and native peoples – once played a central role in Canadian society but over time were shunted to the background as Europeans, from the late eighteenth century onwards, confiscated native lands for agriculture, mining, forestry, and other forms of natural-resource extraction. During this long period, the economic marginalization of aboriginal peoples was exacerbated by horrific loss of life to disease and by systematic efforts of the state and Christian churches to remake natives culturally while also controlling them politically. Then, in the 1940s, aboriginal peoples began to emerge from the shadows, taking advantage of their increasing numbers and better political organization as well as the growing economic importance of the lands many of them still controlled. Their demands for justice became more insistent, and, in the 1980s and 1990s especially, their political leaders made them a formidable force in protracted disputes over land claims, constitutional renewal, and recognition of minority rights. By the last decade of the century, aboriginal peoples were once again at the forefront of Canadian life.

Aboriginal Peoples in Historical Writing

Most writing about aboriginal peoples was done not by academics but by private citizens, usually self-trained amateurs, who had a personal, often nostalgic, interest in the communities they saw in disarray around them. A pioneer in this field was Peter Jones, or Sacred Feathers. In the early nineteenth century Jones, a mixed-blood of Mississauga origin and a Methodist cleric, produced several volumes about the Ojibwa whom he was trying to help through religion and schooling from the 1820s to the 1850s. Later in the nineteenth century, Jones's work was taken up by non-native amateurs such as Horatio Hale in Ontario, who produced much of the early ethnographic writing on the Iroquois. Hale and others like him were anxious to salvage some record of peoples who were obviously in a weakened state and might be destined for extinction. Other examples of the non-specialist approach to this brand of ethnography could be found among missionaries who ministered to First Nations communities across the country at a time when most Canadians were uninterested in native peoples. The Anglican Edward Francis Wilson in Sault Ste Marie, Ontario, and Charles M. Tate in British Columbia reported in considerable detail on several First Nations, and the Oblate missionary Adrien-Gabriel Morice produced an enormous body of literature on the languages of aboriginal peoples in western Canada.

Father Morice, a missionary from France, typified another feature of the early writing about aboriginal peoples: there was greater interest in the subject abroad than within Canada itself. With the distinguished exception of anthropologist Daniel Wilson of the University of Toronto, most of the scholars in this field were from Europe. Franz Boas of Germany made the study of the northwest coast peoples his life's work, producing an enormous volume of scholarship. Diamond Jenness, a New Zealand anthropologist, started around World War I to study and record his observations of a number of aboriginal groups. He began with studies of the Inuit but went on to investigate the Ojibwa in Ontario and the Carrier in British Columbia. Towards the end of his career he was pronouncing on all manner of native-policy issues before parliamentary committees and in print. Unlike Boas and Jenness, both of whom spent lengthy periods in Canada, the French ethnographer Marcel Giraud produced a monumental work on the Metis of western Canada after only a few years' field research in the 1930s. Boas, Jenness, Giraud, and others such as the Canadian Marius Barbeau of l'Université Laval laid the foundation for studies by numerous twentieth-century anthropologists.

Indeed, anthropology has dominated the scholarly approach to recording information about aboriginal peoples in this century. Anthropologists began their work in the spirit of the inventory science that prevailed in the middle of the nineteenth century: they sought to classify the peoples they observed according to social, political, economic, and religious practices and structures. As universities slowly developed throughout Canada, especially from the 1960s onwards, more researchers began to devote themselves to the study of First Nations. Although the classification method still prevailed, anthropology was also pursuing other approaches by the 1970s and 1980s. Long before other scholars showed any interest in such aspects of aboriginal life, anthropologists were paying attention to native medicine, and they were also the first to catalogue the destructive impact of government policies on Inuit and Indians in the north and elsewhere.

The first scholars from other fields usually employed investigative techniques and questions developed by anthropologists. For example, in his 1937 study, *The Conflict of European and Eastern Algonkian Cultures, 1504–1700*, New Brunswick historian Alfred G. Bailey produced an early form of ethnohistory, which can be described simply as the product of research in historical sources such as European documents interpreted through the lens of anthropological knowledge of native peoples. Several decades later ethnohistory would emerge as the pre-eminent investigative tool for scholars working on aboriginal subjects. Another import was military history, exemplified in George F.G. Stanley's landmark 1936 book *The Birth of Western Canada*, which focused on what Stanley termed the "Riel rebellions" of 1870 and 1885. Marrying an interest in military history to American-inspired notions about the influence of the frontier on institutions and human actions, Stanley's work paralleled, undoubtedly unintentionally, another American scholarly emphasis, a preoccupation with the role of aboriginal peoples in European-inspired diplomacy and war. On the whole, this approach, with a few distinguished exceptions such as Robert Allen's *His Majesty's Indian Allies*, has not taken hold north of the border. Indeed, until well into the 1970s historians in Canada still had their face resolutely turned away from the First Nations. It took brilliant practitioners from other disciplines, such as McGill archaeologist-anthropologist Bruce Trigger, to demonstrate the potential fruitfulness of historical studies on aboriginal peoples.

The last quarter of the twentieth century has witnessed the flowering of historical writing on aboriginal peoples and their relationships with European newcomers. Some of the best early work, such as Cornelius Jaenen's *Friend and Foe*, focused on New France, while an interest in regional approaches to Canadian history led to such outstanding studies as Robin Fisher's *Contact and Conflict*, a treatment of native-newcomer relations in British Columbia to 1890. Also important were new examinations of fur-trade history, such as Daniel Francis and Toby Morantz's *Partners in Furs* and studies on the place of women and families in the fur trade by Jennifer S.H. Brown (*Strangers in Blood*) and Sylvia Van Kirk (*"Many Tender Ties"*). These revisionist fur-trade studies were reinforced by the important work of a historical geographer, A.J. Ray, whose two-volume *Indians in the Fur Trade* placed native traders in the centre of the story rather than on the margins to which they had been consigned by earlier writers. The same forces and fashions that stimulated Brown and Van Kirk persisted to produce a steady volume of articles and books on native women, especially in interaction with Europeans. In contrast to the preoccupation of the pioneering studies by Brown and Van Kirk, however, writing on this theme in the 1980s and 1990s concentrated on native women in relation to Christian missionaries and fur-trading companies. The other important development that emerged by the 1980s was increasing attention to government policy towards aboriginals and the latter's response. Among the works emerging from western Canada were Gerald Friesen's *The Canadian Prairies: A History* and Brian Titley's *A Narrow Vision*, an analysis of the influential bureaucrat D.C. Scott. In the 1990s other works from the same region included Sarah Carter's *Lost Harvests*, an examination of misguided agricultural policy, Katherine Pettipas's *"Severing the Ties That Bind,"* which explores attempts to suppress summer ceremonials on the prairies, and Douglas Cole and Ira Chaikin's *An Iron Hand upon the People*, a study of the campaign in British Columbia against the potlatch (a sharing and redistributive winter ceremonial). The 1990s also witnessed the publication of syntheses of aboriginal history by J.R. Miller (*Skyscrapers Hide the Heavens*) and Olive P. Dickason (*Canada's First Nations*) as well as efforts by writers of Canadian history textbooks – now usually teams rather than individuals – to integrate the origins and experiences of First Nations into the national story. Whereas texts written before the 1980s generally started with the Vikings, those that emerged in the 1980s and 1990s almost always began with the origins and pre-contact experience of First Nations.

However, just as historical writing on the aboriginal peoples produced clear signs of maturity in the 1990s, historians began to be supplanted by authors from other fields. Part of the reason for this development was historians' preoccupation with new forms of social history that emphasized microscopic studies of groups and classes. But a more important explanation involves the constitutional and social issues that dominated the national agenda in the 1980s and early 1990s. The political soap opera of attempted constitutional reform, from Prime Minister Pierre Trudeau's initiatives following the election of the Parti Québécois government in 1976 to the failures of the Meech Lake and Charlottetown accords in the 1990s, cast First Nations as political debaters and constitutional lobbyists. The result has been that lawyers, political scientists, and even some sociologists have become the academic interpreters favoured by the literate public. Simultaneously, a growing preoccupation with the social pathology that had emerged in many native communities by the 1980s attracted the vulture-like attention of journalists, who produced a series of works as notable for their prurience and sensationalism as for their insight.

Recent fashions in writing on aboriginal peoples symbolize, in a perverse way, the historical and contemporary role of natives in Canadian society. Historically, natives were taken seriously by Euro-Canadians when they had something the newcomers wanted, such as furs, military muscle, agricultural lands, or mineral resources. Today, when non-native observers comment on aboriginal issues, they are most likely to focus on incarceration, family breakdown, substance abuse, violence in defence of native lands, and aboriginal leaders' insistence that their communities be heeded in debates on constitutional reform or Quebec's potential secession. The sheer strength of aboriginal communities in the last decade of the twentieth century has forced non-natives to pay more attention. Yet, on the whole, non-native observers of native society are inclined – understandably, perhaps, if unfortunately – to pay attention to aboriginal issues only when they intersect with their own priorities, such as energy production, forestry expansion, or constitutional change.

Questions of Terminology

Much of the language used in relation to aboriginal peoples is as likely to obscure as to clarify what and whom is under discussion. For a long time, most of these peoples were known as Indians or Eskimos, even though the former term was a misnomer and the latter an epithet used by opponents. "Indian" was adopted because Columbus thought that he had reached south Asia; "Eskimo" derived from an Algonquian description of a northern enemy who were dismissed as "eaters of raw meat." Currently, the latter are usually referred to by the term they use themselves, Inuit (singular Inuk), which means "the people." Further confusion is found in the terminology for people of mixed aboriginal and European ancestry. Originally, "Metis" and "halfbreed" were used to distinguish between those of French or British and native background, but "halfbreed" is now considered offensive and unacceptable. More common in academic circles is the use of "country-born" to describe those whose parentage was Scottish or English and native. In this chapter, as in Olive P. Dickason's essay that follows, the word "Metis" refers to both francophone and anglophone mixed-blood populations.

Selecting appropriate nomenclature for those previously known as "Indians" is also difficult. For some time, the federal government has preferred to refer to them as aboriginal peoples, but the explicit definition of aboriginal peoples in the 1982 Charter of Rights and Freedoms includes status Indians (those recognized as Indian under various pieces of federal legislation), non-status Indians, Metis, and Inuit. On the whole, "First Nations" (as in the Assembly of First Nations) is the preferred form for peoples who used to be described as status Indians, this stylization serving to distinguish them from mixed-blood communities. Whatever term one uses, there will almost certainly be someone who takes exception to it. In this entry, the terms aboriginal peoples, indigenous peoples, and natives are inclusive of Indians, Metis, and, depending on context, Inuit. Where possible, more specific terminology is employed to minimize confusion.

More specific terminology for aboriginal peoples is of two types: ethnic group or nation, and linguistic grouping or family. This chapter organizes the subject matter along linguistic lines, the approach long taken by anthropologists. Accordingly, what follows will deal with the Algonquian (subdivided into Eastern Woodlands, Subarctic, and Plains), Iroquoian, Siouan, Ktunaxa (Kutenai), Salish, Wakashan, Tsimshian, and Na-Dene linguistic families, along with the Inuit and Metis. In reality, most of these groupings contain within them many collectivities that are often regarded – and frequently see themselves – as distinctive nations. Patrick Moore points out that the Na-Dene linguistic family includes at least forty Athabaskan or Dene languages. Similarly, the Algonquian linguistic family embraces the Maliseet, Cree, and Blackfoot; the Iroquoian encompasses the Iroquois Confederacy, the Huron (Wendat), and the Neutral; the Wakashan includes the Nootka or Nuu-chah-nulth and Kwagiulth; and the Na-Dene consists of the Haida, Tlingit, Tagish, Tutchone, Carrier, Chilcotin, and more. Although to some degree these linguistic groupings are artificial constructs crafted by academic researchers, they nonetheless reflect actual language patterns and often comprise peoples with similar economies and social organizations. The more specific terms of the particular groups, such as Ojibwa or Metis, are used to provide as much precision as possible without rendering the overall portrait incomprehensible because of its immense detail.

The Pre-Contact Era

Origins
The origins of these many human communities are the subject of a bewildering number of explanations on the part of natives themselves. Perhaps the most straightforward is that of the Metis, whose genesis as a distinct people is the product, as Olive P. Dickason shows, of the interaction in recent centuries between natives and non-natives in the western fur trade. More complicated are the origins of the First Nations. While each of these peoples has its own creation story, many of the explanatory legends overlap and possess similarities. Strikingly different, however, are the creation stories of the Haida on the Queen Charlotte Islands (or Haida Gwaii, as they call their lands) in the Pacific and of the Onondaga, one of the six nations of the Iroquois League or Confederacy, located south of Lake Ontario when the Europeans came to North America.

According to the Haida version, in the time of Raven a god by the name of Quautz encountered a crying woman who lived entirely alone and was miserable. When the woman saw Quautz, she was so startled that she sneezed. In the stuff she spewed out, Quautz noted, was a tiny man, perfectly formed. Quautz instructed the woman to house the little one in clam shells until he was grown.

The Iroquois, on the other hand, believe that humans came to earth after the pregnant wife of a chief fell from Skyland through the hole created by the uprooting of a Great Tree. When the creatures below saw her fall, they decided to try to rescue her. Swans caught the woman and began to lower her slowly towards the water, and the others decided to dive below the surface to bring up some earth they had heard existed there. Several failed in the attempt, but, finally, a little muskrat dove into the water and brought some mud up in its tiny paw. When the animals cast about for a place to put the mud, the Great Turtle volunteered to have it on his back. Once placed on Turtle, the earth expanded rapidly until it became the world. The swans brought the woman down to earth, which the Iroquois nations to this day call Turtle Island.

The obvious contrasts between the Haida and Iroquois accounts should not obscure certain underlying similarities in aboriginal peoples' understanding of their origins, as Eldon Yellowhorn remarks of creation stories among the Plains Algonquians. The Cree of northwestern Ontario, for example, have a creation story involving a flood, a muskrat who dove into the waters in search of clay and retrieved earth that expanded to be the entire world, and a human figure – in this case baked out of clay by the trickster figure Wee-sa-kay-jac. The latter had to try three times before he got the clay figure just right. The first attempt was black, and Wee-sa-kay-jac flung it across the waters to an unknown land; the second, which was an unhealthily pale figure, he also tossed across the flood; the third was an olive-brown being, and Wee-sa-kay-jac decided that this version, obviously an Indian, was perfect. In the Blackfoot account, the being corresponding to Wee-sa-kay-jac was Napi, or Old Man, who created the world and its animals and humans. However, on his first attempt he made a slip, producing buffalo who could kill people with their long horns and eat them. The results of a second effort were more to Napi's liking: this time the people had bows and arrows, knew how to make buffalo jumps, and were able to live off the buffalo in their land.

What all these aboriginal accounts share is an explanation of their origins that places them at creation in the lands they occupy. In that regard, as Joan A. Lovisek points out in relation to the Innu and Western Woodland Cree, most aboriginal accounts differ dramatically from the version favoured by western science. (Among the Tsimshians, in contrast, Susan Marsden, Margaret Seguin Anderson, and Deanna Nyce indicate that the Nisga'a have both a creation story about their *in situ* genesis and accounts that refer to migration from elsewhere.) According to the scientific story of creation, which is based primarily on archaeological and linguistic evidence, the ancestors of the aboriginal peoples of Canada came to North America from Asia, across what is now known as the Bering Strait. Sometime between 30,000 and 50,000 years ago, a prolonged ice age lowered the oceans by locking up vast quantities of water in frozen form. Migratory hunter-gatherers from Siberia began venturing eastward on what was a vast grassy plain, its width perhaps 1000 or even 2000 kilometres in places. Over many thousands of years these peoples made their way southward, most likely down a plateau between the ranges of mountains of the west or in the lee of the Rocky Mountain range as we know it today. Some of these peoples made their way far to the south, to central and even South America. Others, it is held, proceeded as far south as the modern-day southern plains states of the United States and then branched eastward in the direction of what are now the southern states of the eastern United States.

A variation on the theory of immigration from Asia emphasizes maritime approaches rather than a land bridge across what is now the Bering Strait. According to this alternative theory, Asian peoples travelled to North America on rafts, and some of them made their way southward along the narrow coastal area or again by boat. Of these, some would eventually make their way eastward. While this theory has a certain plausibility, material realities have limited its acceptance by social scientists. Since maritime travellers leave little physical evidence of their presence, archaeology has been unable to confirm the hypothesis. The same holds true of possible southward passages, either by immigrants across the Bering land bridge or by raft-borne arrivals, along a coastal area. The later rising of ocean levels would have erased the artifacts that could verify the presence of these travellers.

Economic Life
Whether they favour a lee-of-the-mountains or a coastal itinerary, scholars generally agree on the path of diffusion. Over thousands of years various groupings made their way eastward, and in some cases also northward and northeastward into portions of the northern United States and Canada. Many of the northeastern woodlands peoples in the United States and Canada are believed to have reached their locations approximately 12,000 years ago. In the western region, by contrast, the First Nations who would develop the Plains culture in the historic period probably reached and settled on the grasslands about 10,000 years ago. Whatever their eventual destination and whenever they reached it, all these communities developed ingenious adaptations to the lands in which they found themselves. In some cases, such as the nations that became known as Iroquoians, they acquired economic skills in horticulture to complement their abilities to hunt, gather natural foods, and fish.

Among the groups who eventually became established in various parts of modern-day Canada, there was a similarity in their adaptation to the climate and topography of the regions they inhabited. So, for example, with seaside-dwelling peoples such as the Beothuk of

Newfoundland and Mi'kmaq (Micmac) of Nova Scotia and other parts of the Maritimes, there was a heavy emphasis on harvesting the resources of the ocean as well as on hunting game in a seasonal round. For those who were located in good arable regions, such as the Iroquois Confederacy south of the lower Great Lakes or the Huron near Georgian Bay in what is now Ontario, the growing of crops emerged as a critically important activity. These eastern woodlands horticulturalists were famous for their dependence on what they called the Three Sisters: corn, beans, and squash. In some specialized localities, such as the lands along the northwestern shore of Lake Erie, the Iroquoian nation that would be known to Europeans as the Petun or Tobacco people also grew the item that provided their name. In more northerly regions, such as the lakes and forests of the Precambrian Shield, there was heavier reliance on hunting-gathering and on pursuit of an annual round of seasonal movements to take advantage of the availability of beaver, moose, fish, or other naturally occurring resources.

Vitally important, though insufficiently appreciated, aspects of the economies and lifeways that aboriginal peoples developed well before the coming of the Europeans were a common spiritual outlook and an interest in commerce. In spite of their many material and social differences, all these groups shared a view of humans and their place in the world that scholars call animism. Many of the chapters that follow point out, in Janet Chute's words, their "respectful treatment of animal bones" and other habits that reflect a particular attitude towards the non-human world. Aboriginal peoples believed, in short, that all creation was alive, or animate, and everything and everybody, including animals and fishes, were beings. Hence, a traveller might make an offering of tobacco at dangerous rapids to placate the spirit of the watery turbulence and secure his safe passage. Hunters would follow rigid rituals before setting out in pursuit of the beaver to ensure that their fellow being, the beaver, would allow itself to be taken by its human kin. After a successful hunt or fishing foray, prayers would be said to thank the beings who had given up their lives so that humans could live. This view of humankind's similarity to all other things in the natural world stood in sharp contrast to the attitudes towards creation held by European newcomers.

Like Europeans, however, natives shared a heavy involvement in trade. Because they lived in economically different zones that produced varied products, there was a strong incentive to travel to exchange goods they had in surplus but their neighbours wanted. Those who were well located geographically and produced a surplus of foodstuffs, such as the Iroquoians in the east or the Nuu-chah-nulth on the west coast of Vancouver Island, were able to establish themselves as intermediaries facilitating the transfer of products from one region to another. The chapters on the Wakashans and Tsimshians, for example, note the importance of an oily fish, oolican or eulachon, in inter-group trade on the northwest coast. Similarly, copper from the north shore of Lake Superior might end up, through intermediaries along the way, in the hands of the Mi'kmaq on the Atlantic. Or, from the western woodlands, furs and bone products might be traded to the agricultural Mandan south of the forty-ninth parallel by a people such as the Assiniboine who acted as commercial go-betweens. On the west coast, a number of groups played a similar facilitating role between northerly regions that had one type of product and other locations that specialized in different items.

Demographic Patterns
It is difficult to determine how many human beings lived in these various native communities before the Europeans came to the shores of North America. Part of the problem is the far-flung and diverse nature of the aboriginal populations involved. An additional factor is that, until recently, non-native scholars made a poor job of estimating what the figures might have been for aboriginal peoples before contact. Serious efforts at establishing these numbers were first made late in the nineteenth and early in the twentieth centuries, just as scholarly study of aboriginal peoples was beginning. However, this was also the era when the contemporary native population was at or approaching its nadir as a consequence of the drastic mortality rate that Alan McMillan cites in the case of the Wakashans. In all of Canada in the early decades of the twentieth century, government census figures for status Indians placed them at only slightly more than 100,000. To anthropologists and others trying to calculate pre-contact population, it seemed reasonable, knowing what they did about recent rates of population decline, to estimate that the numbers earlier had been two and one-half or three times what they were in their own day. Non-native scholars simply could not fathom that their presence in North America could have had any more deleterious effect than that.

In the latter decades of the twentieth century, scholarly estimates mounted steadily, driven in particular by a growing realization that the number of deaths due to European diseases, particularly in the southern hemisphere, was astronomical. Knowledge from French sources about the impact of disease on sedentary agriculturalists such as the Huron, of whom one-third to one-half died in the late 1630s and early 1640s, make it clear that similarly high figures for what is now Canada are also conceivable. Further evidence of initially high aboriginal populations has also come from the steady advance of archaeology, which indicates both that human habitation of northern North America occurred earlier than once thought and that pre-contact populations were higher than previously calculated. Scholars now assume with a fair amount of confidence that the mortality rate of aboriginal people between first contacts and the late twentieth century was as high as 90 or 95 percent. In other words, it is likely that the indigenous population of the western hemisphere when Europeans arrived was ten or twenty times what it is now. At the present time, estimates of total aboriginal population across Canada range up to one million, and there are even surmises that put the number at as much as two million. All such estimates must be used with caution, but what is clear is that there were large numbers of original occupants throughout the western hemisphere, including Canada. European and Euro-American concepts such as "the virgin land," or *terra nullius* in the favoured Australian formulation, are unsound and archaic.

In the pre-contact era, aboriginal peoples were distributed unevenly across the Canadian landscape, population densities varying according to the ability of the lands to support human life. Across the northern regions, in Arctic areas stretching from Labrador to the Beaufort Sea, were a succession of Inuit peoples. These peoples were the most recent immigrants from Asia, scholars believe, entering North America from Siberia just over 5,000 years ago and gradually spreading across the continent from Alaska to Greenland. Within Canada, the Labrador Inuit were found along the Labrador coast to Hudson Bay, with a few settlements on the southern part of Baffin Island. Later, some would establish themselves in the most northerly portions of what is now Quebec. The other major groupings were the Central Inuit, including groups on Baffin Island and the western shores of Hudson Bay; the Banks Island Inuit on Banks, Victoria, and other large islands off the central Arctic coast; and the Inuvialuit, or Western Inuit, who were located along the Arctic shore of the western part of the modern-day Northwest Territories and the easternmost portion of modern-day Yukon.

South of the Labrador Inuit were a number of Algonquian groups who depended primarily on hunting, fishing, gathering, and trading. On the island of Newfoundland, the Beothuk became known as "red Indians" because of the practice of decorating their bodies with reddish ochre. The most numerous of the eastern Algonquians were the Mi'kmaq, who, in terms of present-day geography, occupied most of Nova Scotia and Prince Edward Island and also stretched into northeastern portions of New Brunswick. Other Algonquian nations found in New Brunswick were the Maliseet, especially in the Saint John River valley, and the Abenaki to the south. To the northwest, in what is now Quebec, were many other hunter-gatherer groups. In the northeast, near and stretching into Labrador, were the Innu, whom the French termed Nascapi. To the west were the people the newcomers labelled Montagnais, and to the north a variety of Cree communities. The St Lawrence River, or the River of Canada as the indigenous people called it, was a main transportation route over which some interior Iroquoian groups travelled to the Maritime region, apparently to trade. French explorer Jacques Cartier encountered some of these farmer-merchants at present-day Gaspé in 1534.

The identity of the Iroquoians who used the St Lawrence River and inhabited large settlements at what are now Quebec City and Montreal is something of a mystery. Unravelling the identity of what anthropologists have come to term "the St Lawrence Iroquoians" is complicated by at least two factors. First, these people died out, moved out, or were driven out of the St Lawrence valley between the explorations of Cartier in the 1530s and the voyages of Samuel de Champlain in the first decade of the seventeenth century. Secondly, in the closing years of the twentieth century, both surviving Huron and Mohawk who are resident in Quebec contend that they are descendants of the St Lawrence Iroquoians, although Alexander von Gernet says in his chapter that such claims are contradicted by the linguistic evidence.

What is indisputable is that to the northwest and southwest of the confluence of the Ottawa and St Lawrence rivers were other major groupings of Iroquoians. To the southeast of Georgian Bay, accessible by a lengthy canoe route up the Ottawa, across Lake Nipissing and the French River, and down Georgian Bay, was the Huron or Wendat Confederacy. This large population of agriculturalists was divided into four nations, the Bear, Rock, Cord, and Deer; they were notable for their sedentary agriculture and their matrilineal and matrilocal practices. Like all Iroquoians, and unlike Algonquians, the Huron traced their individual identity through their mothers' lineage, and a newly married couple took residence in the longhouse of the bride's family. The Huron were also famous as traders, their ability to harvest a surplus of corn and their strategic location providing them with the opportunity to trade with the hunter-gatherers to the north and other farmers south of them.

The more southerly Iroquoians, some of whom were located in what is now the United States, were principally three. The Neutral, as their name suggests, were a group located between two larger forces of Iroquoians who found it sensible to try to maintain peaceful relations with both. The Petun, or Tobacco, nation was long considered to have been the principal provider of tobacco, an extremely important role given the prominence of tobacco in aboriginal spiritual practices, but Alexander von Gernet maintains that they did not specialize in this essential crop. The use of and trade in tobacco were extremely widespread. Southeast of the Neutral and Petun, in fact south of Lake Ontario and stretching eastward towards the Hudson River, was the League of the Five Nations, or the Iroquois Confederacy. This federation, which appears to have begun forming only a century or so prior to the coming of the Europeans, was fashioned for both military and commercial reasons. It brought together in a political association Iroquoian nations known (from west to east) as Seneca, Cayuga, Onondaga, Oneida, and Mohawk. (Later, in the second decade of the eighteenth century, the league would be expanded to six with the addition of the Tuscarora, who had moved northward to escape military pressures.) Iroquoians were sedentary and lived in large bark-covered dwellings known as longhouses; the Five Nations were particularly known as the Hodenosaunee, or People of the Longhouse.

Sedentary habits and longhouses were not typical, however, of First Nations in those parts of Canada between southern Ontario and the Pacific coast. These peoples were Algonquians, Siouans, or Athapaskans, the last of whom are dealt with in the chapter on the Na-Dene. All these groups were hunter-gatherers who followed a seasonal round of migration in pursuit of foodstuffs, raw materials to manufacture objects of various kinds, and opportunities to trade and participate in communal social and spiritual activities. In present-day northern Ontario and northeastern Manitoba were the Ojibwa, or Anishinabe as they called themselves, and Cree. Prior to European penetration of the continent, a number of Siouan peoples such as the Assiniboine in the southeast of what is now the prairies were found to the west of the Ojibwa and Cree, as well as Na-Dene groups in the woodlands to the north. In the most westerly region of the western interior was another confederacy, the Blackfoot, which illustrated how mobile and heterogeneous aboriginal populations could be. The Blackfoot Confederacy consisted of the Stoney, a Siouan group; the Sarcee, originally an Athapaskan or Na-Dene group that had migrated from the far north; and three Algonquian nations known as the Kainai (Blood), Siksika (Blackfoot proper), and Tsuu Tsina (Piegan). The Blackfoot in southwestern Alberta were only the northern portion of a larger Blackfoot community that stretched down into Montana in the United States.

What is now the province of British Columbia had the greatest ethnic complexity and heaviest population density. In the interior alone there was a bewildering variety of hunter-gatherers, stretching from the Ktunaxa in the southeast to the Carrier in the central Interior. In the northern interior were found other hunter-gatherers of the Na-Dene linguistic family such as the Chilcotin and Tutchone. However, the greatest complexity of all was found along the Pacific coast and on offshore islands. Some of these coastal peoples are classified as Na-Dene, as in the instances of the Haida and the Tlingit of the northern coast. Two prominent trading peoples, the Nuu-chah-nulth (Nootka) and the Kwagiulth, belonged to the Wakashan linguistic family, while the Salish grouping embraced a number of nations such as the Coast Salish and Bella Coola to the north. Around 1800 the Salishan included twenty-three interlinked languages. The Tsimshian similarly included Gitksan, Nisga'a, and Tsimshian, with each of them in turn comprising a number of smaller units. All in all, British Columbia before contact was as it is now: the region of the country with the greatest diversity and linguistic complexity among its aboriginal population.

The other northerly linguistic grouping is classified by scholars as Na-Dene. Besides the groups that were found in what is now British Columbia, this family encompassed nations that are often referred to as Athapaskans or Dene. They included, among many others, Slavey (North and South), Gwich'in (Loucheux), Tagish, and Chipewyan in the subarctic region. Living as they did in a harsh land, these communities tended to be relatively small and highly dependent on the vagaries of the lands and waters for survival. Those who dwelt and foraged in the most northerly fringe of the subarctic also had to worry about rivalry and war with the Inuit. Athapaskans and Inuit were inveterate enemies, both struggling for survival in a challenging and sometimes inhospitable landscape.

Migration Patterns

Prior to contact, aboriginal mobility must be understood in two senses: seasonal and long term. Virtually all aboriginal communities moved, in whole or partially, at various seasons of the year in search of economic opportunities and social interactions. This was most obviously true in the case of hunter-gatherer-fishers; for example, some eastern Algonquians, after hunting in small, family-based parties in northern Quebec during the winter, would migrate to fishing locations at particular points on rivers in the spring and then to summer locations for trade and socialization. However, seasonal movement was also the case for minority portions of sedentary peoples such as the Iroquoians and many of the coastal peoples on the Pacific. From their villages, parties would set out to trade or to war with other groups. Usually these expeditions were composed of males, but on the Pacific it was by no means unusual for women to be part, and in some cases leaders, of trading expeditions. Many chapters of this book provide examples of the seasonal rounds pursued by a variety of aboriginal peoples.

The other form of mobility was not seasonal, and it resulted in long-term if not permanent relocations. This movement was the shift, usually over many years, of a group from one region to another, most likely in search of economic opportunities but sometimes also as a consequence of military setbacks. Thus, while it is not clear precisely why the St Lawrence Iroquoians moved out of the river valley in the latter part of the sixteenth century, their doing so would not have been a rarity. In the west, as Patrick Moore notes, the presence of the Sarcee in the shadows of the Rockies was merely one instance of an Athapaskan people migrating far to the south in search of game and trade. Their movement paled beside that of another northern Athapaskan group, the Apache, who ended up in the American southwest. Mary C. Marino's chapter on the Siouans provides several examples of migrations into Canada well into the historic period, and Janet E. Chute explains the Ojibwa's westward movement and adaptation to Plains ways. Another variation on the migration theme emerged in northwestern Ontario, Joan A. Lovisek observes, where the mingling of Cree and Ojibwa over many decades led in the twentieth century to the emergence of the ethnic subgroup and language dialect now known as Oji-Cree. It is hardly surprising that human populations that reached their pre-contact locations in North America by vast migrations over thousands of years continued to move and adapt to new terrain once they were rooted in North America. As one eminent scholar, Bruce Trigger, has put it, Europeans did not introduce change to the aboriginal peoples of what is now Canada. They were merely the latest form of change for them.

Aboriginal-European Contacts

A useful way of understanding the general impact of the European presence on aboriginal peoples in Canada is to focus upon the reasons that the two groups, native and newcomer, had for coming into contact and, in most cases, establishing a continuing relationship. It tended to be the case everywhere but Yukon that the principal factor that first brought the two together, trade, encouraged cooperation. Other motives behind native-newcomer contact were Christian evangelization and military alliance. Commercially motivated relations forced the European to seek at least a minimal level of acquiescence from the indigenous peoples, but interactions established for religious and strategic reasons tended to have negative consequences for natives. What should also be borne in mind is that contact – for whatever reason and in every region – inevitably introduced diseases to which aboriginal peoples had limited or no resistance, resulting in horrendous loss of life. Also highly destructive was the process of settlement and resource exploitation by Euro-Canadians that was well under way across the country by the nineteenth century. The onset of the settlement and mining frontiers everywhere led to the dispossession, economic marginalization, and attempted assimilation of aboriginal peoples at the hands of the Canadian state and Christian churches. In the long sweep of native-newcomer relations, this era – a harrowing epoch from which aboriginal people have been emerging over the past half-century – was the most destructive. That was when their numbers declined drastically, their community cohesion withered, and their sense of themselves as vibrant individuals and collectivities suffered the greatest damage.

It seems strange to reflect that such a concatenation of effects should have been set off by the prosaic codfish. The first European contact, by the Norse about the year 1000, was apparently motivated by a desire to colonize and establish permanent settlements, but hostility from the indigenous population on the northern peninsula of Newfoundland drove the Vikings out. Although trading developments and climatic conditions deterred European settlement for close to five hundred years after the abortive Norse effort, knowledge of the northern sea routes to North America was not lost. The protein-rich fish stocks of the Grand Banks off Newfoundland remained an annual magnet to fleets from a variety of western European ports, as the fact that the Portuguese called Newfoundland the "land of the baccalos," or codfish, clearly indicates. The fishery was soon supplemented by whaling, particularly in the Strait of Belle Isle and at the mouth of the Saguenay, where Basque whalers – with the benefit of harpooning techniques learned from the Labrador Inuit – established a dominant position.

From the Atlantic fishery, with its seasonal visits and occasional (though unrecorded) encounters between aboriginal coastal peoples and Europeans, emerged the second great commerce of Canadian history, the fur trade. Many fishing captains probably shared the experience that Jacques Cartier recorded in his 1534 narrative of coasting the Baie des Chaleurs, where he met some Algonquians, probably Mi'kmaq, who by holding furs up on sticks towards the sailors indicated that they wanted to engage in barter. The principal object of these and later aboriginal traders was the Europeans' iron, which was a great improvement over the limited copper and the bone and wood from which they traditionally fashioned utensils and weapons. In the seventeenth century, the European market for furs, especially beaver pelts, expanded dramatically owing to the simultaneous development of fashion-enhanced demand for broad-brimmed men's hats made from compressed beaver fur and the near-exhaustion of European sources of supply such as the Baltic. Other furs were valuable, too, but beaver was the most important through the seventeenth century. Also in that century France in particular would be stimulated to maintain contacts with aboriginal people because of a desire to convert them to Christianity. This motive was not unique to the French; both non-Catholics in England and Catholics in Spain and Portugal similarly sent missionaries to the native peoples of North America from the seventeenth century onwards.

Whether drawn to the northeastern shores of North America by fish, furs, or faith, the Europeans found it necessary to establish harmonious relations with at least some of the aboriginal peoples with whom they came into contact. Even seasonal fishing visits would be dangerous in the lightly crewed, small craft should the Mi'kmaq, for example, try to repel the strangers. For those, like the English in particular, whose lack of salt forced them to land to dry their catch on shore, a hostile aboriginal populace was an even greater menace. For the fur merchants, aboriginal toleration of their presence and cooperation in their activities were vital. Not only did the Montagnais and Huron know how to locate and take pelts, but in some cases they also processed the pelts and in almost all instances they transported the furs to market, usually at Montreal from the mid-1600s onwards. In the case of beaver, natives turned the raw pelts into a highly desirable trade item by wearing the furs against their bodies as a cloak for a season. The combination of heat, abrasion, and body oils removed the coarse longer hairs, leaving the soft downy fur that hatters needed, and made the skin supple. Finally, if the Huron or Montagnais would not put up with the stranger in their midst, there would be no opportunity to spread the Christian message. In native society the exchange of personnel was a favourite way of facilitating trade and guaranteeing non-belligerence. The Huron accepted Jesuits at missions in Huronia because the priests' presence eased the commercial relationship and guaranteed the strangers' good treatment of Huron vendors who took their furs to market in the summer. Whether the missionaries realized it or not – and the sources suggest that usually they did not – they were hostages to the very trade that they often decried.

That the French had to accommodate aboriginal practice by exchanging personnel was only one of several indicators that the trade in animal furs that developed, first in New France and later in the western interior and on the Pacific coast, was an exchange that compelled cooperation between newcomers and natives. Another sign was the necessity for early French traders to learn aboriginal languages, in particular Huron, in order to barter. In the western fur trade, especially after the English Hudson's Bay Company began to travel inland in the late eighteenth century to compete with Montreal-based traders, similar evidence of cooperation and aboriginal influence is found both in the way in which native women were married to whites and in the manner in which consumer demands were heeded. For the many western traders, both French and English or Scottish, the wooing and wedding of an aboriginal partner had to be done according to the customs and requirements of her culture. (The fruit of these unions were the Metis, as Olive P. Dickason explains.) Would-be suppliers of western native traders also had to pay careful attention to the demanding standards concerning type, quality, and price that Dene and other traders had as to cloth, iron goods, and "luxury'" items such as alcohol. In the Pacific fur trade that developed after initial Spanish contacts with the Nuu-chah-nulth in the 1770s, the Europeans had to fit their activities into the well-established trading patterns that antedated their arrival. Newcomers who tried to maximize their profit by circumventing middlemen such as Chief Muquinna of the Nuu-chah-nulth found themselves under attack by the aggrieved natives.

Though the fur trade encouraged cooperation, it also had unfortunate aspects. By far the worst was epidemic disease, which killed tens of thousands over the centuries. The first recorded sufferers were the Huron, who lost between one-third and one-half of their numbers to diseases and aggression by the Five Nations Iroquois in the late 1630s and 1640s. The western interior also saw major epidemics in the 1730s, 1780s, and 1830s. The 1730 and 1781–82 outbreaks exterminated the Michele band of Upper Ktunaxa and reduced the Chipewyan by one-half. The outbreak of an epidemic in the 1830s severely shrunk the numbers of the Assiniboine and Mandan, thereby restructuring alliances in the Canadian fur trade because the agricultural Mandan disappeared as trade partners for northern groups. Similar patterns of epidemic disease, which was invariably introduced at fur trade posts, were to be found in British Columbia, especially after the maritime phase gave way to the land-based trade early in the nineteenth century.

Second only to disease was the commercially inspired violence that the fur trade sometimes stimulated. The dispersal of the Huron by the Five Nations in the late 1640s was only the most recent instalment in the continuing story of Iroquois attacks on rival nations that had begun in the 1620s with the Mohican and would continue into the 1650s. A different type of fur-trade violence occurred in the western interior during the so-called competitive trade era, in which the Hudson's Bay Company and the Montreal-based North West Company employed sharp trading practices, extensive use of alcohol, and violence directed against both native males and their spouses to gain an advantage. Finally, the most enduring consequence of the fur trade was over-trapping of animals, an abuse of the ecosystem that had ended the commercial usefulness of an area such as Nova Scotia by the eighteenth century and made some native groups dependent on Euro-Americans.

Also harmful to the long-term interests of the aboriginal peoples was the century of diplomacy and warfare that dominated in the eastern half of the continent from the dawn of the eighteenth century until the aftermath of the War of 1812. Although Europeans and their colonial allies often talked of "using" native peoples in their warfare, the reality was that aboriginal groups from the Atlantic littoral to the Michigan-Wisconsin territory decided whether to fight and with whom to ally according to calculations of their own interests. So, for example, the Mi'kmaq and Maliseet, as Janet Chute underlines, fought with the French in the struggle for the continent that lasted until 1763, not because the French "used" them or even because most Mi'kmaq had converted to Catholicism, but rather because they opposed the English; the latter were oriented towards settlement and agriculture, the former were still primarily a commercial people who cooperated with native peoples. Similarly, the resistance to British rule in the interior after 1763 that American historians term "the conspiracy of Pontiac" was in fact an alliance of inland groups who, by joining forces against the Thirteen Colonies, sought to keep the expanding agrarian frontier penned east of the Appalachian mountain chain. The same forces were at work during the American Revolutionary War, when a majority of nations fought with the British against the American rebels, not so much for love of King George III as in an attempt to defend their lands from expansive American agriculture. Finally, the Shawnee leaders Tecumseh and his brother the Prophet fashioned an alliance that fought with the British and British North Americans in the War of 1812 in an effort to regain control over interior lands and deter the further encroachment by frontiersmen of the young republic.

The motivation on both sides during the century of diplomacy and alliance was quite simple. European powers such as Britain and France sought native allies because the peoples of the eastern woodlands were exceptionally able warriors in battle and powerful deterrents before a clash. George Washington and a party of Virginia militiamen learned first-hand of native military prowess when they were thumped and sent packing out of the Ohio valley in 1755. A countryman of Washington, Brigadier-General William Hull, demonstrated in 1812 how effective the threat of aboriginal attack could be. Hull surrendered Detroit to British forces without firing a shot, so fearful was he of the large native companies that were rumoured to accompany his British attacker. The native groups that fought – and it is important to realize that not all nations were drawn into the European and colonial military tangles – did so primarily in defence of their lands. In the long struggle for the eastern half of North America, aboriginal peoples tended to favour the more northerly, less agricultural European group over the more southerly, more agrarian-oriented people. Tragically, in every case from the struggle for the Nova Scotia peninsula in the 1750s to the bloody confrontation in the Ohio country in the 1760s to efforts in both the Revolutionary War and the War of 1812, the more northerly power failed to win a lasting victory. The final result of the century of diplomacy, alliance, and warfare was the dispossession and marginalization of the aboriginal peoples in the face of the expanding agricultural frontier of the Europeans and their colonial offshoots.

Treaties and Agreements

Unlike the era of alliance, which affected only the southeastern part of the future Canada, the age of agricultural expansion and resource-extraction was one in which the aboriginal peoples of every region were affected. The onset of this new age varied from place to place: farmers began to take over Nova Scotia in the late eighteenth century, southern Upper Canada (Ontario) after the War of 1812, parts of British Columbia in the middle of the nineteenth century, and the prairies from the 1860s onward. Similarly, the extraction of naturally occurring resources, chiefly forest and mineral, was initiated at different times in various regions. Upper Canada experienced a clash in the late 1840s as the mining frontier expanded into Ojibwa country, and British Columbia went through more destructive confrontations over coal lands and gold-bearing rivers and lands in the 1850s and 1860s. Gold seekers initiated the first of a series of harrowing invasions of aboriginal lands in Yukon late in the 1890s, though the rush was short-lived and non-native transients mostly left within a decade. By the heyday of the Klondike gold rush, however, southern economic interests were beginning to invade the Shield country, then still dominated by aboriginal peoples, for hydroelectric energy (Quebec), base minerals (Ontario and the Northwest Territories), and coal and hydro (British Columbia). Wherever and whenever native peoples experienced the onset of settlement and resource-extraction, the results were the same: the relationship that was formed with Euro-Canadians was the worst aboriginals had experienced to date.

The reason for the trauma that aboriginal peoples suffered from early in the nineteenth century until at least the middle of the twentieth can be appreciated by focusing on the economic aims of the newcomers and the role native communities played in relation to those aims. In contrast to earlier periods when the Europeans' pursuit of furs or aboriginal souls or alliances led the outsiders to seek cooperative relations with at least some natives, the settlement era was marked by the strangers' wish to possess lands that aboriginal peoples held for sedentary agriculture, for silviculture that levelled the forests, or for the minerals and energy that lay beneath the lands or in the waterways on which First Nations depended for an extensive hunter-gatherer economy. From the standpoint of the European, the aboriginal peoples, who in the commercial and martial epochs had been essential as partners and allies, were now obstacles to the Europeans' pursuit of their own economic interests. Compatible motives were supplanted by competitive goals, and the result was the replacement of cooperative relations with hostility. Given the Europeans' new desires to till the lands and harvest their resources, the aboriginal peoples were, in the word of historian E. Palmer Patterson, "irrelevant."

Since aboriginal peoples were now, at best, incidental to Europeans' objectives and, at worst, an obstacle, the newcomers began through their colonial administrations (or after 1867 through their national government) to fashion policies that would displace First Nations from the lands the strangers coveted. In Canada the campaign to remove the aboriginal peoples was not military for two reasons, one positive and one negative. On the positive side, the experience in the eras of commercial partnership and military alliance had left a tradition of working with aboriginal peoples, an approach that took concrete form most notably in the Royal Proclamation of 1763. This imperial document acknowledged a minimal version of aboriginal land rights and enjoined colonial societies to negotiate through the representatives of the crown for access to native lands. Less noble were the demographic and military realities: colonial and Canadian governments until the twentieth century lacked the population numbers, financial resources, and military muscle to remove aboriginal opponents by force of arms. The absence of a tradition of hostility to aboriginal peoples as a whole, along with demographic and financial weakness, meant that the removal of aboriginal communities from the path of progress would be conducted peacefully, but nonetheless destructively and effectively. Negotiated dispossession and cultural assimilation were the chosen instruments. In concrete terms, this involved land-surrender treaties and policies designed to expunge aboriginal identity, aboriginal ways, aboriginal beliefs, and, perhaps most important of all, aboriginal techniques for relating to and interacting with the land. The approach was not conquest, but treaty; never actual genocide, but cultural genocide.

There had been treaties between natives and Europeans before the onset of the settlement frontier. Those treaties, however, had usually been concerned with the cessation of military hostilities. The 1701 Treaty of Montreal, by which the League of the Five Nations agreed to end six decades of warfare with the French and live in peace with them and their Canadien offspring, was an example of an early peace treaty. Similarly, the Halifax Treaty of 1752 between the Mi'kmaq and British was a vain attempt by the Europeans to ensure peaceful relations with a long-standing opponent, in return for which the Mi'kmaq were conceded control and rights of usage over their lands.

The treaties of the settlement frontier were different; they involved not the ending of war but the surrender of land. In the 1770s the British military began to negotiate with the Mississauga, an Anishinabe group of the eastern woodlands, for access to the lands in the Great Lakes basin that they had moved into and taken over after the dispersal of the Huron in 1649.

These pacts with the Mississauga and later with others ensured peaceful access for Britons and their allies to aboriginal lands in return for monetary compensation. The stimulus behind this innovation was to a minor degree the Royal Proclamation and, more practically, the pressing necessity to find lands quickly on which to relocate allies, both non-native Loyalists and defeated aboriginal allies such as the Mohawk. A similar pattern prevailed after the War of 1812 and even more so once the 1820s ushered in a period of heavy British immigration to southern Upper Canada. In the period down to the 1850s almost all of southern Upper Canada was covered by land-surrender treaties, and a start was made on some critically important lands in the mineral-bearing Precambrian Shield. One innovation in treaty-making was introduced after the War of 1812 when the British shifted from providing compensation in one-time payments to promising smaller annual payments, or annuities. Two other innovations were introduced in the first two treaties in Shield country, the Robinson-Huron, and Robinson-Superior, which were negotiated in 1850 after Chief Shingwauk and some Ojibwa threatened miners who were operating on their lands without native authorization. The Robinson treaties included a promise of reserves and a written guarantee that the natives could continue to hunt and fish throughout the territories surrendered until they were taken up by non-natives for uses that were incompatible with hunter-gatherer exploitation.

The Dominion of Canada inherited and applied the treaty precedents that had been developed in early Ontario when it turned to the task of integrating the western lands it acquired from the Hudson's Bay Company in 1869. If the leaders of the young country had any doubts that they should negotiate with the First Nations in the west for peaceful entry, such doubts were removed during the winter of 1869–70 by the actions of the Metis communities, both francophone and anglophone, at the Red River settlement (at the site of present-day Winnipeg). Canada's arrogant failure to talk to the Red River Metis, who numbered some 12,000 and formed most of the population of Red River, sparked great fear and insecurity among many of them that the coming of Canadian rule would dispossess them of the lands that they held only by a customary title, and, in the case of the French-speaking and Roman Catholic Metis, that their cultural institutions such as schools might be in jeopardy as well. The Red River resistance organized by Louis Riel forced the Dominion to negotiate the terms on which the territory that the Metis controlled would become part of Canada. In particular, Riel secured agreement in the 1870 Manitoba Act that the region would enter as a self-governing province rather than a territory administered by appointees of Ottawa, but the failure to get provincial jurisdiction over crown lands and natural resources greatly diminished the usefulness of provincehood. More relevant to the issue of treaty-making was the clause in the act that set aside 1.4 million acres (567,000 hectares) for future Metis families in recognition, as both the act and Prime Minister John A. Macdonald expressed it, that they shared in "Indian title."

The Metis resistance and the Manitoba Act merely underlined the fact that Canada would find it prudent to negotiate with the approximately 30,000 First Nations peoples in the west rather than attempting to barge into the region. The national government had a healthy respect for the Plains peoples such as the Blackfoot and Plains Cree, and it realized that it could not afford financially to force its way into the west. At the beginning of the 1870s, when the annual Canadian federal budget amounted to about nineteen million dollars, the Americans were spending twenty million dollars a year on Indian wars in their west. For their part, the Saulteaux, Assiniboine, Cree, and Blackfoot were open to negotiation because they recognized that they could not prevent an influx without bloody and probably self-defeating warfare, as well as because the main resource on which the Plains culture was built, the buffalo, was rapidly declining. The result of Canadian prudence and native concern was the negotiation of seven numbered treaties between 1871 and 1877 covering a vast territory from northwestern Ontario to the Rocky Mountains and from the international boundary to a point about halfway up the present-day prairie provinces. In return for unimpeded access to this enormous kingdom, Canada gave initial payments and annuities to each aboriginal person, promised reserves on which native peoples could learn alternative ways of supporting themselves if that became necessary, and provided a variety of other forms of help such as farming assistance, and, in Treaty 6 in the central region of the North-West Territories (present-day Saskatchewan and Alberta), aid in the event of "famine" or "pestilence."

The prairie treaties, which built upon the tradition established in colonial Ontario, would set the pattern for the next half-century. In the late decades of the nineteenth century and early years of the twentieth, Canada would move to conclude treaties with First Nations whenever non-native economic interest in aboriginal lands in a particular locality emerged. For example, Canada showed little interest in treating with Na-Dene peoples in northern British Columbia until the Klondike gold rush made clear the importance of access routes to Yukon. The result was Treaty 8, which covered the northeastern part of the province. A parallel case was Treaty 11, signed with the Dene of the western part of the Northwest Territories one year after oil was discovered at Norman Wells in 1920. By the interwar period of the twentieth century, large portions of Canada were covered by these land treaties, although some important areas were not. British Columbia, where prior to Treaty 8 only fourteen treaties covering tiny areas near European settlements on Vancouver Island had been concluded, was for the most part still aboriginal land. The same was true of some portions of the two northern territories and also of Quebec. In fact, most of Quebec remained untouched by land treaties until 1975, when a confrontation between the James Bay Cree and the provincial government over access to the James Bay drainage system for hydroelectric power development led to a court challenge by the Cree and then the negotiation of a tripartite agreement among the Cree, Quebec, and Canada that is known as the James Bay and Northern Quebec Agreement. In most other parts of northern Quebec, Labrador, and the Maritime provinces, anything resembling land-surrender treaties still does not exist. For sharply differing reasons, British Columbia and Quebec in the 1990s emerged as the potential flashpoints for aboriginal and Euro-Canadian differences over land.

Canada's Evolving Policy towards Aboriginal Peoples

The signing of the seven numbered treaties in the west ushered in a long period in which the aboriginal peoples were treated by the Canadian government as objects to be administered towards an assimilative conclusion. Although many of the policies developed by the new Department of Indian Affairs after 1880 were formulated principally to implement the terms of those treaties, especially following the final collapse of the buffalo economy, in many instances the same policies were applied to status Indian groups – and to a lesser extent to non-status and Metis groups as well, not to mention Inuit as circumstances entailed – throughout the country. Many of these policies were embodied in the omnibus legislation known as the Indian Act, first codified in 1876, frequently amended since, and still on the books in the late 1990s. In general, the array of policies developed in the 1880s and beyond for the administration and attempted assimilation of aboriginal peoples is often known collectively as "the policy of the Bible and the plough."

The heart of this policy thrust was the campaign to assimilate First Nations by a variety of mechanisms. Perhaps the most important was a perverse educational policy, but also significant were efforts to crush indigenous cultural practices, to reshape the economic foundations of western peoples especially, and to impose Euro-Canadian notions of governance on aboriginal communities across the country. West of Ontario, the locus for much of this campaign was the reserves that in due time were portioned out in compliance with the numbered treaties of the 1870s. Many of the aboriginal groups expected the reserves to operate as refuges in which they could adapt to Euro-Canadian economic ways while maintaining familiar hunting and gathering practices. Two unconnected developments rendered that hope illusory. In the first place, the collapse of the buffalo economy was rapid and total, the shaggy beasts almost completely disappearing by 1879 and leaving Plains peoples destitute and requiring rapid changeover, rather than gradual adjustment, to sedentary agriculture on the reserves. Unfortunately, the policies pursued by the Department of Indian Affairs made adjustment to sedentary agriculture difficult. The department insisted upon a centralized and paternalistic administration of reserve affairs, leaving native peoples little scope for initiative or risk-taking. In particular, a bizarre set of agricultural policies known as "peasant farming," which are treated below in Eldon Yellowhorn's chapter on the Plains Algonquians, actively discouraged self-reliance and advance towards commercial farming. These policies compelled reserve farmers to sow and harvest their crops by hand, attempted to control their access to markets, and prevented their availing themselves of working capital through a variety of clauses of the Indian Act. The result by the mid- and late 1890s was that western reserve farmers were abandoning the attempt to make the transition to large-scale, sedentary agriculture.

This abortive phase of attempted economic adjustment was followed by a systematic and prolonged effort to erode the land base of western reserves. Since the collapse of native farming efforts in the face of the peasant farming policy occurred just as heavy European immigration was beginning after 1896, a demand arose to acquire "unused" or "surplus"' reserve lands by securing surrenders from the bands and making these lands available for non-native development. During the first decade of the twentieth century a series of manoeuvres, many of them ethically dubious if not plainly illegal, were connived at by officers of the Department of Indian Affairs to alienate reserve lands. This campaign to take over reserve lands was continued in different form during World War I, when the Greater Production Scheme gave the department the power to control reserves in the interest of producing more foodstuffs for the war effort. The result of these assaults on western reserves was that, when native populations began to increase in the late 1920s or 1930s, the reserves were inadequate to support them. What ensued, beginning in the 1950s and 1960s and continuing during the remainder of the century, was a heavy migration to western cities.

Indian Affairs officials in the late nineteenth century could not imagine the difficulties their farming and land policies would create because they expected that the great Victorian solvent, education, would produce generations of Indians who would be independent. During the 1880s Indian Affairs educational policy veered increasingly towards reliance on residential schools, principally because these custodial institutions were believed to be more effective in assimilating children. This system of schools, which would persist until the late 1960s, grew by the 1920s to a total of eighty institutions, which were operated in uneasy partnership by Indian Affairs and a variety of Christian missionary bodies. Although residential schooling never reached more than a minority of status Indian children, and far tinier minorities of non-status and Metis ones, they did enormous damage to those who did experience them. (Joan A. Lovisek points out that few James Bay Cree received any form of schooling before 1950, but Patrick Moore stresses the adverse impact that residential schools had on the Dene.) Underfunding and excessive reliance on missionary staffs resulted in the schools' failure to provide rudimen- tary academic instruction effectively and problems such as excessive workloads for students, poor diet, and inadequate care by overworked staff. Physical punishment was common in most schools, and in some both sexual and physical abuse were frequent. The residential schools also hurt children psychologically because in institutional settings their inadequate staffs did not provide emotional nourishment for the young people. Indeed, the entire school system, which was predicated on the racist assumption that aboriginal identity should be replaced with Euro-Canadian, denigrated native culture and identity.

In that respect residential schooling ran parallel to other efforts to reshape native peoples' spiritual practices and political behaviour. Beginning in 1885, expanding in 1894, and continuing with varying intensity until 1951, the Indian Act discountenanced social and religious practices of both west coast and prairies First Nations. In the case of some of the northwest coast peoples, the prohibited practice was the potlatch, a ceremonial that was related, as Alan McMillan explains in the chapter on Wakashans, to almost every aspect of the social and political life of the community. The objection to the potlatch was the same as that directed towards summertime dance ceremonials on the prairies: by encouraging practices such as giving away property that were antithetical to the possessive, individualist ethos of Euro-Canadian society, these social and spiritual practices deterred the replacement of aboriginal values and identity with European ones. The campaigns against the potlatch, the sun dance, and the thirst dance were intermittent and of varying intensity and success, as Patrick Moore notes, but even though they did not succeed in eliminating these aboriginal ceremonials they did reinforce the notion that Euro-Canadian society considered native ways inferior.

Precisely the same message was conveyed by the lengthy effort that the Department of Indian Affairs made to refashion native political practices. Unlike the provisions against the potlatch and prairie dances, the assault on aboriginal governance was carried out across the country. Here the target was distinctive aboriginal political practices, such as leadership by hereditary chiefs, or even, in the case of Iroquoians such as the Mohawk, the powerful influence of clan mothers in selecting new male chiefs from particular lineages. Gradually from 1869, and more aggressively after the middle of the 1880s, Ottawa tried to encourage or force bands to adopt elective chieftains and councils. While hereditary leaders, or "life chiefs" as the Indian Act called them, were still ostensibly permitted, Indian Affairs assumed sweeping powers to depose them on vague grounds such as "immorality" or "incompetence." The reality that lay behind this assault on indigenous traditions of governance was an assumption that the destruction of old-style leadership would result in native communities that were more amenable to Indian Affairs policies in other areas such as education, spiritual practices, and economic development. It is not surprising that many aboriginal communities rejected attempts to impose Euro-Canadian elective institutions, and some of the resistance efforts, such as at Akwesasne around the turn of the century or on the Six Nations reserve along the Grand River in Ontario in the 1920s, reached impressive proportions. At Akwesasne, the Mohawk resisted to the point of using firearms, and their Mohawk kin on the Grand River took their efforts to repel Ottawa's attempts to interfere with them politically to the League of Nations. Although the campaign at Geneva failed, the Mohawk would persist throughout the rest of the century with their position that they were not subject to Canada.

The Political Response of Aboriginal Peoples

In fact, in the twentieth century aboriginal resistance to the various crusades by Indian Affairs and its missionary allies to remake native communities increasingly took a political form. Efforts to organize politically began before World War I in British Columbia, where a long-festering dispute over land drove the diverse First Nations to combine politically. The next phase occurred after the war, when an army veteran, Lieutenant F.O. Loft, attempted to organize the League of Indians of Canada. Loft's initiative did not endure, but during the 1920s the organizational torch passed to the prairies, where the League of Western Indians kept it lit. Also during the interwar period, fledgling provincial associations began to emerge, as in the establishment of the Indian Association of Alberta in 1939. Slowly after World War II these tendencies would coalesce in the formation of national bodies to speak on behalf of aboriginal peoples. The first enduring effort was the National Indian Council (NIC), which took shape in 1961. In 1968 the NIC subdivided amicably into the National Indian Brotherhood (NIB), a body of status Indians, and the Canadian Metis Society, a vehicle for the political aspirations of Metis and non-status groups. Eventually the NIB would refashion itself in the 1980s as the Assembly of First Nations (AFN), and, as Olive P. Dickason explains, the Canadian Metis Society would evolve into the Native Council of Canada in 1970, the Metis National Council after the constitutional scrum of the early 1980s, and the Metis Nation of Canada in the 1990s. Among the Inuit, the Inuit Tapirisat of Canada had been founded in 1971. For aboriginal peoples throughout the country, the twentieth century was a time of political organization.

These political bodies, though they differed on specific issues, were motivated by a common desire to throw off the paternalistic policies of the federal government and assert native control over their own affairs. For status Indians in particular, the principal obstacles to their successful development were the Indian Act and the Department of Indian Affairs that administered it. The act treated First Nations people legally as wards, or minors, with the department occupying the role in law of adult trustee over their affairs. This legal doctrine of Indian infantilism was most starkly revealed in the Indian Act's provisions that reserve lands could not be pledged as collateral for loans and that an Indian's will was not legally valid unless and until approved by the department. However, the paternalism pervaded Indian Affairs administration. For Metis and non-status Indians, the principal complaint for most of the twentieth century was that the federal government refused to accept any responsibility for them. The result for these groups was that they were marginalized and forgotten, particularly in prairie Canada, where attitudes towards them were hardly charitable. For Inuit groups in Quebec and the Northwest Territories, the major problems were similarly related to Ottawa's neglect, although in their case the highest court in 1939 imposed jurisdiction for Inuit on the federal government against Ottawa's will. All aboriginal peoples had numerous complaints and valid reasons for organizing politically.

Since the 1960s two tendencies have dominated in the political relations between native peoples and the government. On the one hand, native peoples have been motivated by concern about everyday problems such as inadequate housing and health care or schooling for their children that did not give them a fighting chance of succeeding in the modern world. These grassroots concerns frequently resulted in political campaigns to gain control over policy in areas that mattered greatly to them. The best example of this process was Indian control of Indian education, which the National Indian Brotherhood demanded in the early 1970s and Ottawa conceded in 1973.

On the other hand, however, native peoples' practical concerns have frequently been forced to take a back seat to issues that non-natives put on the public agenda. A gross example of this tendency was a federal-government white paper in 1969, which proposed the elimination of "Indians" as a separate legal category, supposedly in the interests of eradicating the ghettoization that was holding them back. It took a strenuous campaign by a united front of national and provincial groups of status Indians to get the white paper shelved. However, from the late 1970s to the 1990s the concern among non-native political leaders about constitutional renewal forced aboriginal leaders to play the constitutional game, too. Beginning in 1977 with efforts to defuse the separatist threat of the first Parti Québécois government, and continuing through the 1980s and into the 1990s with the battles over repatriation of the British North America Act in 1981–82, the Meech Lake Accord from 1987 to 1990, and the Charlottetown Accord in 1992, the powerful current of Canadian politics has drawn aboriginal leaders to emphasize constitutional issues. In particular, the leadership since the early 1980s has stressed the desirability of getting a definition of the aboriginal right of self-government embedded in the constitution and implemented in practice. The pursuit of aboriginal self-government has absorbed enormous amounts of time and energy on the part of aboriginal political leaders while deflecting attention and resources away from more mundane needs such as reserve housing, clean water, better schools, and improved health care.

The other preoccupation of aboriginal political leaders since the early 1970s has been the land question. Beginning in 1974 the government of Canada created a two-stage land-claims resolution process. One part concerned what the government called "specific claims," which were allegations that some treaty or other lawful obligation had not been discharged by the Crown. The other category, comprehensive claims, concerned claims to land based on aboriginal title in regions where this form of customary proprietorship had not been eradicated by treaty. British Columbia, the two (now three) northern territories, and portions of northern Quebec and Labrador have been the major arenas for the contentions over comprehensive claims. Gradually in the 1990s some progress began to be visible in this area, but at the end of the decade there were still many comprehensive claims outstanding – as, indeed, was also true of specific claims – while non-native opposition to redressing these issues rose and fell and the ability of the public coffers to provide compensation for past wrongs and neglect shrank. The land question, like aboriginal self-government, contentious and potentially explosive remains.

Conclusion

Although aboriginal peoples in Canada have been on a harrowing journey since the coming of the Europeans at the end of the fifteenth century, there are signs of progress and self-confidence among them. The constitutional readjustment of 1982 gave explicit constitutional protection of "aboriginal and treaty rights," and the Royal Commission on Aboriginal Peoples, appointed by the federal government in 1992, emphatically endorsed the inherent right of aboriginal self-government in 1996. The courts have also provided substantial support, especially in a series of Supreme Court decisions between 1985 and 1990 that greatly strengthened the legal understanding of aboriginal rights in such matters as fishing on the west coast and spiritual practices by Huron in Quebec. In spite of ill-advised efforts by the Conservative government of Brian Mulroney to cap funding for post-secondary education for native students, the number of aboriginal graduates of universities and colleges continued to rise dramatically. Data reported in 1995 indicated that almost three-quarters of aboriginal students were reaching grade twelve, compared with less than one-fifth of status Indians only fifteen years earlier. In the corresponding period the number of status Indian young people enrolled in post-secondary education leaped from 4,500 to 27,000. Native artists and performers in the 1990s were a major presence in music, theatre, television, and art. In their respective chapters, Patrick Moore, Janet E. Chute, and Louis-Jacques Dorais all provide examples of Haida, Algonquian, and Inuit artists and musicians who have enjoyed success commercially and artistically.

Perhaps most revealing of all are the numerous signs of restored pride among most aboriginal groups. Eldon Yellowhorn, for example, notes the development among the Plains Algonquians of the pow-wow movement from the 1950s onward, and Alan McMillan testifies to the revival of the potlatch among the Wakashans after the legislated ban was deleted from the Indian Act in 1951. Another manifestation of this same proud sense of self and community was the increasing tendency in the 1990s of those of aboriginal ancestry, as Olive P. Dickason notes in relation to the Metis, to speak publicly about their heritage. In this respect, the decennial census of 1991 yielded a significant fact. The number of people reporting themselves as being of aboriginal heritage jumped in that survey by more than 41 percent compared to only five years earlier. While about 711,000 respondents in 1986 said they considered themselves of aboriginal ancestry, in 1991 just over one million gave themselves that identification. It might well be that this visible willingness to stand up and be counted as aboriginal peoples is the most convincing evidence of all that a spiritual, political, and cultural revival is under way in native communities across the country.

FURTHER READING

General works on aboriginal peoples fall into two major categories: ethnographic studies, and historical accounts of the indigenous peoples and their relationships with European newcomers. In the former group, the most useful survey is Alan D. McMillan, *Native Peoples and Cultures of Canada: An Anthropological Overview* (Vancouver, 1988), which superseded Diamond Jenness's *The Indians of Canada* (Ottawa, 1932). The more historically focused studies that are cited most often are Olive P. Dickason, *Canada's First Nations: A History of Founding Peoples from Earliest Times* (Toronto, 1992), and J.R Miller, *Skyscrapers Hide the Heavens: A History of Indian-White Relations in Canada* (Toronto, 1989; rev. ed., 1991). Dickason is most helpful for the period before the War of 1812, Miller for subsequent eras.

The earliest and most enduring post-contact phase was the commercial partnership in the fur trade. The seminal work here was H.A. Innis, *The Fur*

Trade in Canada: An Introduction to Canadian Economic History (Toronto, 1930; rev. ed., 1956), although Innis neglected the native side of the trade partnership. Innis's work has been updated and supplanted for western and northern Canada by A.J. Ray's *Indians in the Fur Trade: Their Role as Hunters, Trappers, and Middlemen in the Lands Southwest of Hudson Bay, 1660–1870* (Toronto, 1974) and *The Canadian Fur Trade in the Industrial Age* (Toronto, 1990). Important regional studies of the commercial partnership are D. Francis and T. Morantz, *Partners in Fur: A History of the Fur Trade in Eastern James Bay, 1600–1870* (Montreal, 1985); R.A. Fisher, *Contact and Conflict: Indian-European Relations in British Columbia, 1774–1890* (Vancouver, 1977); and James R. Gibson, *Otter Skins, Boston Ships, and China Goods: The Maritime Fur Trade of the Northwest Coast, 1785–1841* (Montreal, 1992).

For the successive phases following the commercial period, the best approach is via regional studies. These include G.A. Friesen, *The Canadian Prairies: A History* (Toronto, 1984); Jean Barman, *The West beyond the West: A History of British Columbia* (Toronto, 1991); Fisher's *Contact and Conflict*, cited above; Ken S. Coates, *Best Left as Indians: Native-White Relations in the Yukon Territory, 1840–1973* (Montreal, 1991); and Kerry Abel, *Drum Songs: Glimpses of Dene History* (Montreal, 1993).

Studies of particular themes in the period of settlement, treaties, and the Indian Act are far too numerous to list here. A useful place to begin is with analyses of policy such as Noel Dyck, *What Is the Indian "Problem"? Tutelage and Resistance in Canadian Indian Administration* (St John's, 1991), and E. Brian Titley, *A Narrow Vision: Duncan Campbell Scott and the Administration of Indian Affairs in Canada* (Vancouver, 1986). Citations for specific studies can be found in the bibliographies of the general works by Dickason and Miller, cited above, or in J.R. Miller's historiographical essay "Native History," in Doug Owram, ed., *Canadian History: A Reader's Guide, 2: Confederation to the Present* (Toronto, 1994).

1

ALGONQUIANS / EASTERN WOODLANDS

Janet E. Chute

Identification and History

Eastern Woodland Algonquian peoples belong to two broad linguistic subdivisions: Eastern Algonquian speakers and Central (eastern Great Lakes) Algonquian speakers. Eastern Algonquian-speaking communities in Canada lie south of the Gulf of St Lawrence and in the Atlantic provinces, with representatives of one group, the Delaware, living in southern Ontario. Central Algonquian speakers reside north of the Gulf of St Lawrence, throughout most of Ontario, and in the prairie-parklands of Manitoba, Saskatchewan, and Alberta. The Woodland Algonquian population is large, reaching in excess of 100,000 in 1985; in the Atlantic provinces alone, there are 22,330 status Indians, of whom the Mi'kmaq (Micmac) number more than three-quarters. While similar in many respects, particularly in the way they have adapted to their environment, Eastern Woodland Algonquians exhibit considerable internal linguistic and cultural diversity.

Eastern Algonquian Speakers
The Abenaki, Delaware, Malecite, and Mi'kmaq comprise the Eastern Algonquian-speaking peoples examined in this section. The Passama-quoddy, who are linguistically and culturally related to the Malecite, currently have no representation in Canada, although their population in times past may have extended northward into New Brunswick. Ethnohistorians occasionally place the Passamaquoddy, Malecite, and Mi'kmaq in the Eastern Abenaki category, since all four groups participated politically in what was known as the Wabanaki Confederacy during the eighteenth and nineteenth centuries. Yet lin-

guists hold that the Passamaquoddy and Malecite dialects together form a language apart from Eastern Abenaki proper and that the Mi'kmaq language also retains its own linguistic distinctiveness.

Abenaki is a self-ascribed term which means "dawn land people" and relates to a number of groups whose traditional homelands extended from Maine to northeastern Massachusetts. A linguistic and cultural division exists between the Eastern Abenaki, resident in Maine, and the Western Abenaki, who originally occupied New Hampshire and Vermont. The exact geographic location of this boundary remains ambiguous, however, since after 1724 all the Western Abenaki either migrated to Canada or swelled the ranks of the Penobscot of northeastern Maine. The few remaining fluent speakers of the Western Abenaki language today reside on 500 hectares at Odanak, near Sorel, Quebec. Descendants of Eastern Abenaki live at Becancour, on the south shore of the St Lawrence River opposite Trois-Rivières, Quebec.

The Eastern Abenaki linguistic category subsumes speakers of the Penobscot, Kennebec, Arosaguntacook, and Pigwacket dialects whose traditional homelands in Maine lay along the Penobscot, Kennebec, Androscoggin, Presumpscot, and upper Saco rivers. During the early seventeenth century these peoples formed a confederacy under a chief named Beshabes, but they suffered political disunity upon Beshabes's death in a war between the Abenaki and the Mi'kmaq. None practised intensive horticulture, although they grew some corn, beans, squash, and tobacco. In the early 1600s, when annual winter climatic conditions were colder than today, evidence of marginal horticulture was sighted only as far north as the upper Kennebec River. Most people came to the coast to hunt sea mammals, collect shellfish, and trade, and, in so doing, fell prey to European-introduced diseases and became embroiled in local wars with English colonists covetous of their lands.

During King Philip's War of 1675–76 in New England, thirty Kennebec-speaking Wawanock, unjustly charged with having conspired to injure English settlers near Pemaquid, migrated to the Jesuit mission at Sillery on the St Lawrence. Although religious and trade ties between these people and the French had been close since the 1640s, the Wawanock movement constituted the first of a series of permanent Eastern Abenaki removals to Canada. Owing to severe social disruption bred by repeated epidemics and native-settler conflict, none of the peoples originally united in the early seventeenth century under Beshabes's confederacy, except the Penobscot, retained a presence by 1750 in their traditional homelands. Increasingly involved in intercolonial warfare by 1690 on the side of the French, most left for Canada following a devastating English attack in 1724 on a Jesuit mission at Norridgewock.

By contrast to the coastal Eastern Abenaki, Western Abenaki, such as the Sokoki and Penacook, were interior peoples who inhabited the middle and upper reaches of the Connecticut and Merrimack rivers of New Hampshire and Vermont. Villages were formed of arrangements of multi-family long bark dwellings, each of which housed members of one patrilineage. Their hunting territories extended northwest, almost to the Canadian border. Encouraged by the French, the Sokoki and Penacook launched war expeditions after 1642 against the Iroquois, who harassed French trade, and Iroquois retaliations drove many northward during the 1660s. By 1670 Sokoki resided near Montreal and Trois-Rivières, and a substantial Penacook village arose at Missisquoi on the eastern side of Lake Champlain. When the Jesuits established the Saint-François mission at Odanak in 1700, they not only drew Western Abenaki from settlements already situated along the Saint-François River, but also attracted Sokoki, Penacook, and Eastern Abenaki from a Jesuit mission on the Chaudière River whose earliest residents had relocated from Sillery. These Abenaki retained close relations with their kin still remaining in New Hampshire and Vermont, and fought side by side with them until the close of the French and Indian Wars in 1760. The Saint-François community remained neutral during the American Revolution and after 1783 absorbed most of the remaining Western Abenaki into its settlement. When the Western Abenaki relinquished northern New Hampshire in 1798 for the purposes of white settlement, they did so in the name of the Saint-François chiefs.

In 1805 the British Crown granted these Abenaki a second site on the Saint-François River, at Durham. Following the close of the War of 1812, in which Abenaki fought on the British side, some families returned each year to their ancestral lands south of the border to hunt, fish, and guide, while others utilized grounds north of the St Lawrence River abandoned after 1830 by Algonkin near Trois-Rivières.

As a tribal name, *Delaware* refers to descendants of about forty culturally and linguistically related village bands which, until the early seventeenth century, occupied lands on either side of the Delaware River in northeastern Massachusetts, Delaware, New Jersey,

New York, and Pennsylvania. Prior to epidemics and piecemeal migrations, this population exceeded eight thousand. Villages were composed of hickory-sapling and chestnut-bark longhouses encircling a chief's dwelling, which doubled as a council forum and whose walls were hung with large wooden masks denotive of chiefly status. Delaware are scattered throughout the eastern and central United States, and representatives of their two principal linguistic and cultural subdivisions, Unami and Munsee, migrated to southern Ontario in the late eighteenth century. Unami Delaware today reside on 1,250 hectares at Moraviantown, east of Thamesville on the Thames River, while Munsee dwell on 1,040 hectares at Munceytown (Muncey), upriver from Moraviantown. Unami also live among the Six Nations Iroquois on the Grand River.

Hailing originally from the northern sector of the Delaware homeland, Munsee-speaking groups migrated northwest after conflicts with the Dutch, settling by the early eighteenth century on the north branch of the Susquahanna River. After 1765 most of these Munsees moved to Goschgoshing on the Albany River in northwestern Pennsylvania, where Moravians erected a mission in 1768. By this time a single-family, peaked-roof house type had replaced the traditional longhouse.

Unami speakers, forced from the Lehigh valley by the Pennsylvanian government in 1737, settled first on the north branch of the Susquahanna River and then spread into Ohio. Some joined the Six Nations Iroquois and, though retaining their distinct Algonquian identity, ended up after the American Revolution on Six Nations lands in southern Ontario. Most, however, formed the core of a new expanding tribe known as the Lenape, which means "the people." By 1750 this entity had emerged from under a burden of Iroquois domination which had loomed over the Delaware since the mid-seventeenth century. Moravians from Goschgoshing and their Munsee converts after 1770 set up missions among the Ohio Delaware. Around the same time an Ohio Muncee group, unconnected directly with a mission, moved northward and eventually settled at Munceytown on the Thames. Moravian Delaware, following a massacre in 1782 by American militiamen at the Ohio Moravian community of Gnadenhutten, fled to Michigan and from there to Canada, where in 1792 they established Fairfield (now Moraviantown, Ontario). Today, descendants of these Delaware live in settlements little different from other native communities in southern Ontario.

Malecite reside in New Brunswick and southern Quebec and speak a language which is intelligible to northern Maine's Passamaquoddy speakers and related only somewhat more distantly to eastern Abenaki. The name *Malecite*, which means "lazy or bad speakers," was ascribed to them by the Mi'kmaq. The Malecites' name for themselves is *Wolastokwiyok*, meaning "people of the beautiful river," which refers to the way they view their principal homeland along the drainage basin of the Saint John River in New Brunswick.

The Malecite currently possess six reserves along the Saint John River: at Edmundston (Madawaska or Saint-Basile), Kingsclear, Oromocto, St Mary's (Devon), Tobique, and Woodstock. These tracts, with a total land base of just over 3,600 hectares, vary considerably in size. Tobique, located near Perth and the largest New Brunswick reserve, contains 2,690 hectares, while that at Oromocto encompasses less than 20 hectares. Viger, 3,700 hectares in size, lies in Quebec south of the St Lawrence River near Rivière-du-Loup.

Malecite territory originally covered a far more extensive area, including parts of southeastern Quebec, the interior of New Brunswick, and northern Maine. This region's climate is continental, with hot humid summers and cold snowy winters. Mixed deciduous and conifer forests blanket the rolling landscape, cut across by interconnected rivers, streams, and lakes. Yet the local native population, identified in the early seventeenth century by Samuel de Champlain as belonging to a group he termed the "Etchemins," has remained small. Although it has been estimated that prior to 1590 their population may have reached 7,600, by 1612 their numbers had been reduced to 2,500 by epidemics, a tragic legacy of contacts with European fishermen bearing diseases against which the native inhabitants had little immunity. Today, the population stands at over 4,000.

Unlike their Mi'kmaq or Passamaquoddy neighbours, the Malecite were not a maritime-oriented people. Their prowess in trade and warfare lay in their expert canoe navigation of the upper river and lake systems drained by the St Croix and Saint John rivers by which they could reach the St Lawrence valley in eight days. With the coming of European trade, first with Basque, Breton, Norman, and Portuguese fishermen, and later with French, Dutch, and British colonists, semi-permanent Malecite settlements arose to reap the benefits of such exchange at the mouths of major rivers flowing into the Atlantic. The palisades around the village of Ouigoudi on the Saint John River enclosed large multi-family rectangular lodges as well as conical bark wigwams. A central council house, as big as a "market hall," accommodated assemblages of over one hundred persons.

By the late seventeenth century, relations between the Malecite and the Europeans traders had changed so substantially that the influence of the *grand sagamore*, a chief whose territorial jurisdiction encompassed an entire river system, began to wane. The insistence of French colonial administrators that missionaries live in Malecite communities undermined the reputations of chiefs and traditional men of knowledge, since the missionaries were equipped with medicines and healing techniques better able to combat European-introduced diseases. Recollect priests maintained a mission on the Saint John River from 1619 to 1624. Malecite also visited missionaries labouring among Abenaki peoples to the south of them and, after 1632, the Jesuits stationed at Rivière-du-Loup. In 1671 the Recollects returned to the Saint John. One early task of these missionaries was to encourage the Malecite to relinquish their coastal trading communities for strategically situated interior sites with riverine communication to the Penobscot to the south and the French to the north. From 1690 to 1700 the French commandant in Acadia, Joseph Robinau de Villebon, had his headquarters on the Saint John River, first at Jemseg, later at Nashwaak, and finally at the river's mouth. With local Recollect support and inducements in the form of annual gifts from the French Crown, Villebon directed his native allies during King William's War (1689–97) to conduct raids on New England. In time the missionaries successfully induced the Malecite, who formerly had depended on the hunt and riverine fishery, to raise corn, beans, pumpkins, potatoes, and grain. Since horticulture obviated the Malecite's former reliance on summer trade expeditions to their southern Abenaki neighbours for corn and other foodstuffs, the French discovered that they could call during the summer on Malecite villages for men to fight in their colonial wars and find most of the male population at home.

For the next sixty years the Malecite joined the French during intercolonial hostilities against the British, especially when roused to action by the incitements of their priest, Father Germain, who laboured among the Malecite from 1740 to 1763. Yet the Malecite were not pawns of the French. Missionaries such as Germain knew that the native population was fighting as much for its own interest in protecting its lands as it was for French presents. Like traditional *sagamores*, the priest might persuade but he could not coerce. Nor were the British the Malecite's most dreaded foe, for sporadic warfare continued with the Mi'kmaq until the mid-1750s. Wooden palisades about the major horticultural village of Meductic, located on the Saint John River below present-day Woodstock, and a smaller settlement located on the Nerepis River were erected as much against Mi'kmaq attacks as they were against the Iroquois and English.

Following the end of French rule in the northeast, the Malecite abandoned Meductic, and many of this village's former inhabitants moved to Aukpaque, on land granted them by the British in 1767 near present-day Fredericton. Each year Aukpaque's residents met in council to settle disputes and allocate winter hunting territories on a large island near their village. Although the Malecite participated in three treaties of peace and friendship with the British, in 1725, 1749, and 1760, the claims of American rebels in 1776 that British settlers eventually would take away native lands led a Malecite splinter group to join an abortive attack on Fort Cumberland. This incident split the Aukpaque council into pro-British and pro-American factions. Lieutenant Governor Michael Francklin, who as a young man himself had experienced a year of captivity among the Malecite during which time he learned their language, and his deputy, James White, successfully persuaded the Malecite to continue at peace with Britain. Yet the rebel warnings proved prescient, for Loyalist expansion after 1783 meant the end of the Malecite's traditional hunting and fishing way of life.

After the loss of Aukpaque to Loyalists in 1794, the Malecite population grew more dispersed. Most of the former Aukpaque population moved to nearby Kingsclear, close to a Roman Catholic mission station, where they obtained a reserve. They also received two small islands called "the Brothers" near the mouth of the Saint John in 1838. Other bands continued a hunting and trapping existence along the upper reaches of the Saint John River where they came into conflict periodically with Mi'kmaq hunters and trappers moving inland from the Gulf of St Lawrence coast. One camping ground located near the Roman Catholic mission of Saint-Basile in the vicinity of Edmundston became a reservation. Farther south along the Saint John River, a large tract at Tobique, originally embracing 6,400 acres, was set aside to encourage agriculture.

Meanwhile, opportunities to engage in commercial ventures and wage labour attracted Malecite both to the south shore of the St Lawrence and to the lower Saint John River. Several families from

Tobique migrated to Isle Verte and Cacouna townships in Quebec, where a reserve was eventually set aside for them at Viger. By the late nineteenth century, small reservations were established at Woodstock, Oromocto, and in the vicinity of Fredericton as Malecite progressively became involved in commercial handcraft ventures, boat loading, and river driving.

Until the early twentieth century, the Malecite also held a reserve near the mouth of the St Croix River. Gradually the Malecite abandoned uneconomic reserves like those on the St Croix and the Brothers. Small non-reserve settlements disappeared. By the mid 1800s rectangular houses with pitched roofs and lean-to outbuildings had replaced the conical wigwam almost entirely. After 1900 whole families migrated seasonally to participate in the commercial potato and blueberry harvest, while, starting during World War II, large numbers of men and women seeking permanent work began to move to industrial centres in Maine, Connecticut, and Massachusetts. Many who left returned after a time, however, drawn by loyalties to their extended families and strong cultural and community ties.

Another Eastern Algonquian people, the Mi'kmaq, speak a distinct language, of which three different dialectical variations are spoken in Nova Scotia, New Brunswick, and southern Quebec. While the name *Mi'kmaq* has been translated variously as "allies" and "ones of high ability," the Mi'kmaq refer to themselves as *elnu*, meaning "the people." Their territory included all of Nova Scotia, Prince Edward Island, lands in New Brunswick along the Northumberland Strait and the Gulf of St Lawrence, the Gaspé peninsula, and a sector of southwestern Newfoundland. It is also possible that they occupied southern coastal New Brunswick before Malecite expansion downstream to the mouths of the Saint John and St Croix rivers in the late sixteenth century. Mi'kmaq occupation of Newfoundland, prior to the early eighteenth century when French colonial administrators encouraged Mi'kmaq warriors to join French military expeditions to this island, remains controversial. Oral traditions recount that bands regarded southwestern Newfoundland as an alternative resource area whenever moose became scarce on Cape Breton Island. Archaeological evidence substantiates that, prior to their contact with Europeans, the Mi'kmaq hunted seals and walrus on the Magdalen Islands, and thus it is possible that a population so well equipped for marine travel may have ventured, by way of St Paul's Island in the Cabot Strait, to Newfoundland as well. Mi'kmaq birchbark canoes exhibit raised gunnels amidships which militate against the craft's swamping in rough water. These mariners also obtained shallops in trade by 1600 and sailed them as far as southern Maine.

Mi'kmaq currently occupy communities throughout their ancestral homelands. Because their reserves cut across a range of different ecological zones, resources and economic opportunities differ from place to place. On Nova Scotia's southwestern coast, community members have access to lobster, crab, and shellfish beds, while settlements on large rivers in New Brunswick and Quebec like the Miramichi and Restigouche focus on seasonal runs of salmon. Some villages still employ a distinctive identifying mark; for example, since the late seventeenth century a salmon has represented the Restigouche peoples. Major reserves include Maria and Restigouche in Quebec; Big Cove, Burnt Church, Eel Ground, and Red Bank in New Brunswick; Annapolis, Arcadia, Bear River, Cole Harbour, Gold River, Horton, Millbrook, Pictou Landing, Pomquet-Afton, and Shubenacadie in Nova Scotia; Escasoni, Membertou, Nyanza, and Whycocomaugh in Cape Breton; Lennox Island in Prince Edward Island; and Conne River in Newfoundland.

French clerics and colonists at Port Royal established positive enough ties with the Mi'kmaq that in 1610 the sagamore Membertou and twenty-one members of his band requested baptism. In following years Mi'kmaq-Acadian intermarriage occurred. Members of the Mius d'Entremont family in southwestern Nova Scotia retained close and lasting connections with the native women by whom they had children, although they never married any of their consorts. In one instance a Mi'kmaq chief, Jehan Claude (Glode), married Marie Salé, a French widow. Such unions gave rise to the surnames Mius, or Muise, and Glode in use in Mi'kmaq communities today.

The Mi'kmaq after 1690 proved such valuable military allies that, when the Treaty of Utrecht transferred mainland Nova Scotia to British control in 1713, the French tried to relocate bands on Cape Breton, which was still in French hands. When this plan failed, French colonial authorities after 1720 began to distribute annual presents, which they transported from the newly erected Fortress of Louisbourg on Cape Breton to bands who resided deep inside British territory. Such distributions most frequently took place on Cape Breton. Between 1716 and 1722 Abbé Antoine Gaulin settled bands in nascent horticultural communities at Antigonish and Shubenacadie. Gaulin was, along with Abbé Pierre-Antoine Maillard and Abbé Louis-Joseph Le

Loutre, one of three graduates of the Séminaire-des-Missions-Étrangères in Paris who laboured indefatigably among the Mi'kmaq most of their lives. In 1724 the main Antigonish mission moved to Mirligueche (Malagawatch) on the Bras d'Or Lakes in Cape Breton, where in 1735 it came under Maillard's auspices. At each site the Mi'kmaq planted some corn, beans, squash, European-introduced potatoes, and grain but produced no surplus for transport to Louisbourg as the French had hoped. Engaging in economic endeavours more suited to their culture, all-male groups set off annually for the seal hunt on the Magdalene Islands to satisfy Louisbourg's demands for seal oil, leaving their wives and children behind.

From the 1720s to the late 1750s, the French at Louisbourg divided the coastline of the Mi'kmaq's territory into "commands," which they viewed as being under the aegis of prominent men. Commissions, gifts, and medals were allocated to these chiefs, who were encouraged to attack British crews that came ashore for water or provisions. Whenever war erupted between France and Britain, Mi'kmaq ransomed the captured crews and sailed the ships to Louisbourg to obtain prize money. These practices continued until 1745–46, when a terrible plague accompanying an ill-fated French expedition ravaged native bands so extensively that their population fell to one-third its previous size.

Such a disaster evidently gave certain bands pause to reflect on their options, for after this date several began making overtures to the British. When Le Loutre left his Shubenacadie headquarters for a visit to France in 1752, a native delegation from his own mission signed a treaty of peace and friendship with the British at Halifax. Other bands soon followed suit. This seeming defection from the French cause often has been cited as evidence that the Mi'kmaq lacked even a nascent tribal organization. However, in 1754 a grand sagamore by the name of Argimault called for removal of both English and French forts in the Isthmus of Chignecto region on behalf of the entire Mi'kmaq people. His petitions and those of others demonstrated that the Mi'kmaq's most pressing concern lay with the native community's ability to retain a measure of political jurisdiction over its traditional territories in the face of warring colonial powers intent on dividing up the same lands for their own interests.

Owing to a treacherous attack made on a Mi'kmaq band at Jeddore by British sailors, the main body of Mi'kmaq rededicated itself to fighting the English until the fall of New France in 1760. Mi'kmaq also assisted certain Acadian families during the Acadian removals of 1755 and 1758 and in some instances adopted Acadians into their bands. Yet at least one chief, Penall Argomartin from Gold River in Nova Scotia, went to Quebec and fought alongside the British on the Plains of Abraham. To encourage the Mi'kmaq to sign peace treaties in 1760 and 1761, Lieutenant Governor Jonathan Belcher verbally promised to remove settlers from a vast tract of land extending from the Baie-des-Chaleurs southeast to Cape Breton and inland to Shubenacadie. On such assurances, representatives of all bands signed peace agreements in 1760 and 1761, only to have the British formally retract them later.

Finding British settlement after 1760 rapidly obstructing their use of former hunting and fishing grounds, the Mi'kmaq adopted a peripatetic existence, selling baskets and wooden implements to rural homesteads. Their numbers, hovering near 1,000, were too small to excite major concern in the expanding British villages and towns, although, during the American Revolution, bands along the Northumberland Strait were, with some reason, suspected of "nefarious" activities against Loyalist newcomers. A number of chiefs in 1783 received licences to occupy lands, and up to 1810 a few individuals and small groups had lands granted to them. A series of orders-in-council between 1820 and 1840 secured yet more tracts for occupation, and by the turn of the nineteenth century Mi'kmaq were living on more than sixty allotments. Several engaged in farming had purchased property in the Annapolis valley area, while chiefs along the Miramichi and other rivers in New Brunswick struggled to manage a burgeoning system of land and resource leases under their reserves' jurisdiction in the face of settlers who sought to wrest land from native control.

In 1940 and 1941 the Nova Scotian government undertook to settle all Mi'kmaq on two reserves at Shubenacadie and Escasoni. Encouraged to participate in this centralization program by offers of housing, jobs, and educational and community services, many Mi'kmaq relocated, only to find that neither of the communities' economic bases could support increased numbers. By the mid-1950s many had moved back to lands they once had vacated. On Prince Edward Island and in Pictou County in Nova Scotia, bands did not possess formal reserves until the late nineteenth century, when tracts were set aside for them. Though much former Mi'kmaq land has been expropriated or ceded over the years, additional lands occasionally have been purchased, and the community at Conne River in Newfoundland only recently has acquired reserve status.

Central Algonquian Speakers
The Algonkin, Ojibwa, Ottawa, and Potawatomi comprise the Central Algonquian-speaking peoples of Canada. They bear close linguistic and cultural resemblances to one another. Some diversity does exist, but cultural boundaries between peoples are often ambiguous. For instance, the *Nipissing*, or "[people] at the lake," are included with the Algonkins for the purposes of this chapter, even though they are linguistically, but not culturally, distinct from the Algonkin.

It has been argued that, prehistorically, the Nipissing, Ojibwa, Ottawa, and Potawatomi formed a uniform cultural and linguistic group extending from Lake Nipissing to lands southwest of Sault Ste Marie and westward to an undetermined boundary somewhere on Lake Superior. Ecological adaptations to differing environments within this vast area fostered variation in social organization, with flexible bilateral-band societies arising to the north and patrilineal clan structures emerging farther south. The Algonkin, Nipissing, many Ojibwa, and some Ottawa dwelt within a mixed coniferous-deciduous forest zone near the northern limit of corn cultivation. The Potawatomi, whose original homeland lay on the lower Michigan peninsula, engaged more extensively in horticultural pursuits. Iroquois incursions and mission activity compelled representatives of all these groups to relocate from time to time in American territory. Yet only the Potawatomi, who were invited by the British government in the 1830s to settle on Manitoulin Island in Lake Huron or in southern Ontario, may be considered an "American" group among Canada's present-day Central Algonquian speakers.

The name *Algonkin* derives from a Malecite term meaning "they are our allies." Peoples belonging to this group reside in northeastern Ontario and adjacent portions of Quebec. Communities in the upper Ottawa River-Lake Temiskaming region include Argonant, Temiskaming, Long Point, Kipawa, Hunter's Point, and Wolf Lake. North of and along the Gattineau River drainage basin lie the settlements of Lake Simon, Grand Lake Victoria, Barrier Lake, and Maniwaki (River Desert). Golden Lake is situated in Ontario west of Eganville near the headwaters of the Bonnechère River.

Most of these communities are located north of the Algonkin's traditional homeland, which extended over the Ottawa valley. Population displacements, caused first by Iroquois incursions, later by settlement, and finally by lumbering enterprises, led the Algonkin progressively northward onto tracts used previously by them as winter hunting territories. Algonkin were located at Point-du-Lac near Trois-Rivières until 1830. Others joined the early French mission settlements of Sillery and, later, Sainte-Anne-du-bout-de-l'-île. In 1721 Algonkin, Nipissing, and Mohawk came together to establish three separate villages at Lac des Deux Montagnes near the Sulpician mission at Oka, north of Montreal. Remaining principally hunters, trappers, and fishers, with corn horticulture as a secondary occupation, Algonkin families departed each winter for their trapping territories, leaving their village almost deserted until spring. When a dispute arose at Oka in the 1840s between Mohawk and the Sulpicians regarding land tenure, heads of several Algonkin and Nipissing families petitioned the House of Commons for grants to lands they already occupied seasonally at Temiscaming and Maniwaki. In 1870 they acquired 620 hectares at Golden Lake. Algonkins also resided on lands around and within the boundaries of Algonquin Park, to which the Algonkin today argue they still retain rights.

During the early fur-trade era the Algonkin were a powerful people, well aware of their strategic importance in the Ottawa River trade. Around 1600, in addition to 700 or so Nipissing dwelling near Lake Nipissing to the west, at least six distinct Algonkin bands existed, the most noted being the Kichesipirini of the upper Ottawa valley. Other nations were the Weskarini (Petite Nation), Matouweskarini, Keinouche, Otaguottouemins, and Onontchataronon (People of Iroquet). These peoples exchanged hides, peltry, and dried fish with the Huron for corn, nets, and wampum during elaborate negotiations which often included a Feast of the Dead, adapted from a Huron ceremony. Not only did they play a major role as middlemen between the French and the Huron, they sought out the Dutch and, later, the English as well. They structured their exchanges around their own goals and proved defiant and proud. One Kichesipirini leader, Tessouat, charged tolls on Huron traders passing through his band's territory. In defence of his own interests, this chief in 1613 deflected the French from trading directly with the Cree by persuading Samuel de Champlain that an account, given by a young Frenchman of a visit to James Bay with the Nipissing, was false.

Traditional tensions between the Algonkin and the Iroquois acquired new impetus from fur-trade rivalries, and during the 1650s and 1660s many Nipissing and Algonkin temporarily fled west under pressure of Iroquois attacks or sought permanent refuge at French settlements and missions along the St Lawrence. While those who became attached to the Sulpician mission at Lac des Deux Montagnes spoke the Nipissing dialect by 1830, progeny of mixed Nipissing-Algonkin parentage who later moved to Maniwaki and Golden Lake came to be referred to solely as "Algonkin." Movement of peoples also required a shifting of territorial boundaries. When Eastern Abenaki settled at Bécancour in 1704, local Algonkin bands willingly not only vacated a large tract south of the St Lawrence River for their use but permitted the newcomers to place these hunting grounds under their own territorial jurisdiction.

Another Central Algonquian group, the Ojibwa, form the largest native community north of Mexico with a population of over 160,000 people, of which the Woodland Ojibwa are the most substantial part. In Canada, Ojibwa live in numerous reserve- and non-reserve communities from Ontario to Alberta, the largest population concentrations being in Ontario and Manitoba. Ojibwa also reside across the international border in Michigan, Wisconsin, Minnesota, North Dakota, Montana, and Oklahoma. Slight dialectical variations are discernible from east to west, although all Woodland Ojibwa speakers are able to comprehend each other.

The Woodland Ojibwa arose historically from the inclusion of a number of bands north of Lakes Huron and Superior into one entity termed *Ojibwa*. Two competing translations have been given for this word: "puckered up," which denotes a style of moccasin, and "voice of the Crane," which refers either to a noted chief named Crane or to a totemic unit. The Ojibwa call themselves *Anishinabeg*, meaning "human beings." Band names derived from animals and included Marameg ("Catfish [people]"), Amika ("Beaver [people]"), and Noquet ("Bear [people]"). During the early seventeenth century these bands, composed of several hundred persons and possessing patrilineal clans and high-profile leadership, interacted with the Ottawa and Algonkin in trading with the Huron. The Ojibwa were involved in the French fur trade as trappers and middlemen west of Lake Superior. Drawn by commercial opportunities, they spread west, although their principal location for festivities until 1670 remained at the rapids at Sault Ste Marie, from which place they derived the name *Saulteurs*, "people of the falls." After 1670 a second centre emerged at the French trading station of Chequamegon near Lapointe in Wisconsin. Both

Sault Ste Marie and Chequamegon lay near abundant whitefish fisheries and drew bands from around Lake Superior in the spring and fall of each year.

Woodland Ojibwa showed close similarities to the Ottawa and Potawatomi, with whom they had an alliance in the eighteenth century known as the Council of the Three Fires. All three had clans, each designated by a symbol called a *dodem*, or totem. One's totem determined whom one could or could not marry, since all who held the same totem were regarded as kin. Many Ojibwa, but not all, engaged in corn and squash horticulture and grew some tobacco, an important component of Ojibwa ritual. By the late eighteenth century the Lake Superior Ojibwa had twenty-three totemic clans within five kinship groups. In pursuit of new trapping territories for furs, and in wars against the Dakota and other groups southwest of Lake Superior, the Ojibwa occupied lands in Minnesota and Wisconsin where today, known as the Southwestern Ojibwa, they have large reservations.

In the interval between the Huron dispersal in 1649 and final peace with the Iroquois in 1701, Ojibwa-speaking peoples began to move into lower Michigan and adjacent lands in southern Ontario to become what is known as the Southeastern Ojibwa. In 1781 the British government induced the Mississauga to cede lands in southern Ontario for the use of the incoming Loyalist Six Nations Iroquois. A series of other land surrenders followed, the last in 1930.

Woodland Ojibwa settled in numerous communities between the western end of Lake Superior and the Red River, having started their westward migration after a smallpox epidemic in 1781 drastically reduced Cree populations formerly living in the area. These lands contained rich fur reserves, deer, abundant whitefish and sturgeon fisheries, and wild rice, of importance for ceremonial as well as subsistence purposes. Overhunting during fur-company competition prior to 1821 reduced fur-bearing animals, yet Ojibwa numbers continued to grow. In the late nineteenth century many were engaged in small-scale farming, although lack of external assistance and white covetousness caused such activity to wane by the turn of the twentieth century. Commercial pursuits in this region included the production for sale of sturgeon isinglass, sturgeon caviar, and wild rice. Unfortunately, overfishing by white commercial interests and the consequences of damming projects damaged the commercial viability of many fishing locations.

The westernmost bands of Ojibwa reached Edmonton House to

trade. Many kept to their Woodland way of life, using birchbark utensils, living in bark dwellings, and spending summers fishing in streams in the foothills of the Rockies and raising small gardens. By contrast, other Ojibwa bands that became known as the Bungee adopted the Plains way of life, particularly the horse, the buffalo hunt, and ceremonials such as the Sun Dance.

As early as the 1820s those Ojibwa south of Lake Superior suffered the incursion of logging enterprises and mineral exploration. Yet the native population north of Lakes Huron and Superior did not encounter such ventures on their lands until the mid-1840s. In 1849 a small Ojibwa and Metis group from the Sault area, in protest over its rights to land, timber, and minerals being ignored, confiscated a copper mine at Momainse on the north shore of Lake Superior. In response the government in 1850 made two treaties, the Robinson-Huron and the Robinson-Superior, with the claimant bands. Both treaties involved a cession of a vast territorial tract, promised hunting and fishing rights on unoccupied Crown land, and became the model for similar agreements known as the numbered treaties made after 1871 with native groups west of Lake Superior. During later treaty negotiations, the western Ojibwa proved especially persistent in demanding that their rights to resources as well as land be respected. In Treaty 3 negotiations in 1873 a claim to timber and subsurface rights in northwestern Ontario was argued so strongly that it contributes to the legal basis for conceptions of native title in this region today. Yet other Woodland Ojibwa located outside the Robinson treaty or numbered treaty areas met with obstructions and frustrations. One group, the Teme-Augama Anishnabai First Nation, located on Lake Temagami in northeastern Ontario, argues that it was misrepresented during the Robinson-Huron Treaty negotiations and for over one hundred years has been asserting rights to land and resources within a tract hunted over by its ancestors for thousands of years.

The name *Ottawa* derives from *Odwaw*, which means "traders." Ottawa in Canada reside east of Georgian Bay in Ontario, in southern Ontario, and on Manitoulin Island in northern Lake Huron. They, along with Ojibwa and Potawatomi, form the population of Walpole Island in Lake St Clair. Over 4,000 individuals in Canada ascribe themselves to the Ottawa category, although no community is exclusively Ottawa, because extensive intermarriage has occurred between this group and the Ojibwa. The largest single settlement, Wikwemikong, arose as the consequence of a migration of Ottawa in the 1830s from l'Arbre Croche, north of Grand Traverse Bay in Michigan, to Manitoulin Island under the auspices of Roman Catholic missionaries. Between 1838 and 1858 Roman Catholic religious leaders at Wikwemikong competed for native converts with energetic Anglican missionaries at a government-sponsored Anglican mission nearby at Manitowaning, populated principally by Ojibwa. The Wikwemikong Ottawa became strong defenders of their land and resource rights, and, when approached in 1862 to surrender title to their lands, rejected the offer. Their tract east of Manitowaning Bay still remains unceded territory.

The Wikwemikong Ottawa resided on lands that their ancestors had inhabited in the early 1600s but that had been abandoned for over two hundred years. Samuel de Champlain's expedition of 1615 encountered Ottawa at the French River, on Manitoulin Island, and on the Bruce peninsula, where they were operating as middlemen between Lake Superior peoples and the Huron. Champlain called the Ottawa *cheveux relevez*, owing to their practice of wearing their hair in a roached style. Throughout most of the later historic era they assumed a riverine mode of living in lower Michigan, where fish were abundant and good soils and an annual growing season of 180 days easily permitted horticulture. The French at Montreal, with whom they annually traded, recognized several subdivisions among them. These may have been local groups or patrilineal totemic units (or a mixture of both) and included the Kiskakon, "cut tail" or "bear"; Sinago, or "black squirrel"; Sable, or "sand"; and Nassauakuton, the "[people of] the fork." Their population, which in the 1640s exceeded five thousand, fled under pressure of Iroquois attacks west to the Straits of Mackinac, Green Bay, and southwestern Lake Superior. Wherever they went they maintained a more sedentary existence than their Ojibwa neighbours. Their villages of rectangular, barrel-roofed multi-family dwellings, covered with fir bark, cedar bark, or matting, were often palisaded. The most strategically placed of these villages became fur-trade centres which supplied corn, bark canoes, and guides for westward-bound fur brigades. From such centres they seasonally carried out communal drives for deer and fowl. The loss of their middleman position, however, compelled them to devote more of their energies to trapping, and after 1780 they pushed into Minnesota and towards the Red River, from where they extended their trapping activities as far northwest as Lake Athabaska.

The Mackinac bands remain the most important to an understanding of the history of the present-day Manitoulin Island Ottawa. After 1700, some Mackinac bands migrated south to join large multi-ethnic communities near Detroit. Those that lingered in the Straits of Mackinac area demonstrated continued attachment to their northern homeland by briefly retiring to Manitoulin Island in 1712 after defeating the Fox and Mascoutin. In 1742 the remaining Mackinac bands moved to l'Arbre Croche. After eschewing Pontiac's anti-British stance in 1763 and fighting on the British side in the War of 1812, they strengthened their British connections still further by removing to Manitoulin Island in 1837, following the Ojibwa's relinquishment of all claims to it. The Roman Catholic missionaries had introduced new crops such as potatoes, turnips, and wheat to their community, while in l'Abre Croche the Wikwemikong Ottawa proved to be one of the first groups to be able to subsist principally on the produce of their fields. Fishing and maple-sugar manufacture nevertheless remained important both for subsistence and commercial purposes. Perhaps because of its high degree of self-sufficiency, Wikwemikong remains a distinctive linguistic and cultural community, where about two-thirds of the population still speak their native tongue.

Those Ottawa who migrated into southern Ontario shared a historical background different from the Wikwemikong group, since they were not directly associated with any mission. After 1795, when most Ohio groups lost their lands, the Ottawa migrated to Walpole Island and adjacent areas. By the 1840s substantial numbers of Ottawa had also joined the predominantly Ojibwa communities of Parry Island and Shawanaga on Parry Sound and Christian Island in the eastern sector of Georgian Bay. Although merged with Ojibwa and Potawatomi, these persons never fully lost their Ottawa identity.

The last group to be discussed under the category of Central Algonquians is the Potawatomi, whose name has been translated as "people of the fire." Originally hailing from the lower Michigan peninsula, they later established, following warfare with the Miamis, Fox, Mascoutin, and Illinois, a vast "tribal estate" which by 1720 extended south of Lake Michigan and westward through Illinois and southern Wisconsin to the Mississippi. In this area they hunted, raised corn, beans, melons, squash, and tobacco, and fished. Until the mid-eighteenth century, palisades surrounded their villages of rectangular barrel-roofed lodges. Close allies of the French as well as followers of Pontiac in 1763, they gradually switched their allegiance to the British between 1763 and 1810. Most fought on the British side during the

War of 1812 and afterward travelled annually to military stations at Amherstburg, Drummond Island, and Manitoulin Island to receive distributions of goods and provisions for past services rendered the British Crown.

The Potawatomi lacked an overarching tribal organization until the 1640s, and even afterwards they never formed a centralized political entity. While a strong chief might be responsible for a number of villages, the primary functioning organization continued to remain the corporate exogamous patrilineal clan system. In the early nineteenth century there appear to have been around thirty of these clans, organized into six kinship groups. Each clan had an origin myth, a medicine bundle, and special rituals and obligations. Owing to population shifts over time, clan members became distributed among numerous villages, yet clan membership provided important cross-cutting social linkages among the widely dispersed population until the 1830s.

After the mid-1830s the American government set out to remove the Potawatomi living in southern Wisconsin and Illinois westward to Iowa. In response, about 2,000 of this tribe chose to emigrate to Canada either by way of Detroit and Port Huron or across Lake Huron to Manitoulin Island. Strangers in the settlements to which they came, these people had neither treaty rights nor government annuities. Eventually, however, they became assimilated into the Walpole Island, Sarnia, Kettle Point, Cape Crocker, Saugeen, Parry Island, and Manitoulin Island communities, where, while retaining memories of their historic migration in the late 1830s, they adopted the language and practices of their Ojibwa and Ottawa neighbours.

Economic Life

While Woodland Algonquians today rarely engage in traditional occupations, they still evince pride in their heritage as hardy and ingenious inhabitants of an environment characterized by alternating seasonal abundance and scarcity. Groups historically maintained a portable settlement pattern, fashioning their belongings from materials which were light in weight and extremely resilient. Their modes of transportation, dwellings, clothing, tools, and utensils all testified to their adeptness in barkworking, woodworking, hideworking, stoneworking, clayworking, and weaving reed and fibre materials derived from their mixed-forest surroundings. Equipped with a birchbark canoe, bark lodge coverings and bark storage containers, families could travel easily in the spring and fall. Sometimes moosehide, sprucebark, or elmbark canoes also were used. Snowshoes and toboggans facilitated transportation over winter hunting grounds. Women transported infants comfortably and safely on their backs using wooden cradle boards.

Canadian Algonquians tended to be hunters, fishers, and gatherers rather than intensive horticulturalists. North of the upper Great Lakes, horticulture, where it existed at all, remained marginal, and settlement patterns changed seasonally. Bands dispersed into small extended family groups during the winter. A few closely related men, with their wives and children, departed to hunt under the jurisdiction of the eldest male or best hunter. These groups congregated during the warmer months into larger assemblages at well-known camping grounds near riverine and lacustrine fishing sites. The composition of these summer bands nevertheless changed from year to year, as families spalled off and migrated throughout a region at will, visiting for trade, social reasons, or because of natural vicissitudes such as game scarcity or forest fires.

In the present-day Maritime provinces, crops other than tobacco were not grown prior to the arrival of Europeans, although furs, hides, copper, chert, and shell were traded for corn with horticultural groups south of the Kennebec River in Maine. As was the case around the upper Great Lakes, group size fluctuated seasonally. Hunters sought woodland caribou, moose, bear, and beaver for food and clothing, while smaller fur-bearing species such as fisher, fox, lynx, and muskrat provided pelts for domestic use and trade. Farther south, deer and the now-extinct woodland bison provided meat and hides. During the early twentieth century, deer ranges moved northward to replace caribou in the Maritimes, southern Quebec, and lands bordering the upper Great Lakes.

Along the Atlantic seaboard, Algonquian groups hunted sea mammals and collected shellfish and crustaceans. Anadromous and catadromous fish such as alewives, salmon, smelt, sturgeon, bass, and eels were taken seasonally during runs by spears, hooks and lines, shallowseine nets, and riverine weirs. In the Great Lakes region, similar fishing techniques were used to harvest seasonal runs of whitefish, lake trout, pickerel, and sturgeon. Gathered foods included ground nuts, wild grapes, and fiddlehead ferns in the east and wild rice in Ontario and Manitoba. Medicinal plants were also sought after.

Migratory birds, especially waterfowl, offered an important resource in both eastern and central areas. Bands living in regions with an annual growing season of well over one hundred frost-free days raised corn, beans, squash, and tobacco and traded crop surpluses with their neighbours for furs and other goods. Since stored horticultural produce constituted a significant proportion of these peoples' winter diet, their settlements had a more permanent character than those farther north.

Women cared for children, tanned hides, and made hide and fur garments, bark bowls, boxes, other bark utensils, and, prior to European contact, pottery containers. They sewed bark with split spruce root and used *babiche*, or rawhide thong, to web snowshoes. They also employed earthen pigments, shell beads, porcupine quills, and moosehair to decorate their garments and belongings with symmetrical double-curve motifs in the east, and floral and geometric designs farther to the west. Men fashioned items of stone and wood; among these were stone and wooden pipes, stone and wooden weapons, shields, traps, tools, snowshoe frames, and wooden ribs for birchbark canoes. Men's and women's economic roles were complementary and remained so well into the twentieth century.

Major changes occurred in these traditional economies after 1600. While exchanges of staples such as corn, dried fish, and peltry always had been important among indigenous populations, the fur trade led to the formation of trade and supply centres at new locations, accessible to Europeans. Bands eagerly sought iron and copper implements – kettles, axes, knives, needles, and guns – and developed a taste for glass beads, broadcloth, and introduced foodstuffs. By 1626 colonists in present-day Massachusetts had begun to trade with the Eastern Abenaki, exchanging wampum obtained in southern New England for furs. The Abenaki, in turn, reintroduced this wampum into the Quebec trade.

As a degree of dependence on European trade items ensued, both French and English sought to manipulate the distribution of these goods to induce the aboriginal population to act in accordance with colonial policies foreign to the bands themselves. Emphasis on trapping sedentary fur-bearing animals gave rise to a system of family hunting territories, inheritable in the male line. Chiefs along the maritime coast who channelled the transport and exchange of furs to their own advantage initially gained influence. After 1680, however, when the French redirected their primary energies from trade to colonial warfare, the status of such leaders waned. Jesuit and Capuchin missionaries sent to live in the native villages usurped the role of intermediaries between native bands and French colonial administrators. Horticulture, encouraged by missionaries, provided both a source of winter emergency rations and provision for warriors engaged by the French in raids on the English. By the early eighteenth century, the political milieu exerted a major influence on native ceremonial clothing styles as well, with chiefs' broadcloth coats, obtained in gift exchanges with colonial authorities, sporting epaulets and trim reminiscent of European military uniforms.

When the French era ended, the settlement of New England "planters" and later of Loyalists on former hunting grounds in the Maritime region led Malecite and Mi'kmaq to seek alternative forms of employment based on traditional skills but developed in new and creative ways. Men's woodworking abilities found outlets in the making of commercially saleable utilitarian items: potato and apple baskets, hampers, butter tubs, churns, axe handles, toboggans, snowshoes, wood baskets, and barrels. Mi'kmaq women sold the finely crafted quillwork bark baskets that they had made since the mid-1700s. "Fancy baskets" appeared on the eastern market as early as 1815. Men and women worked together in their production: men prepared the black ash, white ash, or maple splints, and women undertook the intricate basket weaving. While some products such as eel pots were indigenous, the fact that native splint basketry shows parallels with Swedish and German prototypes suggests that Europeans introduced this form of industry to southern coastal Algonquians and, over time, knowledge of the skill diffused northward. In the Maritime provinces around 1850, native craftspeople received free passage on steamboats and trains as an incentive for them to get their products to market and so remain self-supporting. Some enterprising individuals opened craft shops. For instance, in 1860 one shop on the St Mary's reserve near Fredericton offered Malecite, Mi'kmaq, and Huron merchandise for sale. The fancy basket industry continued to grow, with newer forms of braided sweet grass, or splint and sweetgrass together, taking their place beside older basket styles.

During the nineteenth century, men obtained income from guiding, river driving, lumbering, assisting on surveys, prospecting, and stevedoring. Guiding earned a man prestige, although, since it was gauged for an outside market, it precluded the use of traditional hunting strategies. Trapping for peltry and hunting to obtain moose hides continued, but competition with white settlers resulted every-where in scarities in fur-bearer and game animals by 1870. As well, damming of rivers in the Maritimes and Ontario after the 1840s severely damaged fish stocks in many rivers upon which bands had formerly depended. At locations with more than the one hundred frost-free days needed to bring crops to maturation, families farmed until the first decades of the twentieth century, although they some-times had difficulty acquiring the equipment and funds needed to sustain such enterprises. Uncultivated reserve lands quickly fell un-der the eye of covetous whites, and many hectares were alienated as the result of settler lobbying.

Early in the twentieth century, Abenaki, Algonkin, Ojibwa, and Ottawa joined lumbering camps both in Canada and the United States, and Mi'kmaq men from Restigouche, Quebec, worked on high-steel construction projects in Boston. On-reserve industries that were governed less by the seasons included stores, garages, and small construction enterprises. Since 1900 Malecite and Mi'kmaq families have gone seasonally to northern Maine for blueberry raking in late summer and potato harvesting in September and October. Fiddlehead fronds gathered by the Malecite in the spring find a ready market.

During the 1970s there was an emphasis on economic specialization as reserves sought to establish marinas, parks, tourist cabins, restau-rants, craft shops, and small art galleries. In some regions industrial pollution created serious obstacles to development: for instance, in the Kenora district of Ontario and at the Pictou Landing community on Boat Harbour, Nova Scotia. Yet increased knowledge of economic issues and problems also has led to more careful monitoring of eco-nomic development. The handcraft industry has diversified, with the Mi'kmaq leading the way in creating delicately coloured wood-splint flowers. The market for "dream catchers," based on an indigenous variant of the "cat's cradle" found among many northeastern Algonquian cultures, has grown phenomenally. At the same time, native youth have entered professional careers in art, medicine and other health professions, journalism, business and resource manage-ment, the justice system, education, law, and social work.

Unemployment levels remain high on Algonquian reserves. At Golden Lake, east of Ottawa, the unemployment rate is 30 percent, and it exceeds 70 percent in some Maritime communities. Attendant social problems are various, depending on area. Where residents depend on limited funding for housing from the Department of Indian Affairs, dwellings are often small and overcrowded. Plans are being made, however, to rectify these problems and provide affordable, attractive housing suitable to families with school-age children. Problems such as drug and alcohol abuse are being addressed at government-funded rehabilitation and health centres. Many communities have an educational counsellor, native police officers, an alcohol and drug abuse counsellor, nursing staff, and sometimes a social worker, all of whom may be native. But the challenges remain formidable. Local counsellors, medical personnel, and social workers often remain too overburdened to cope more than on a caseload basis with the mental and physical consequences, on both individuals and families, of systemic racism, unemployment, inadequate on-reserve housing, and lack of a good economic base for local development.

Some creative local solutions have been forthcoming. Dedicated individuals are involved in devising and managing sports and recreation programs. The native justice system in the Maritimes is experimenting with a locally controlled diversionary program which enables minor offenders to make reparations through community service. Architects are looking at the impact of housing on social issues and designing units, sometimes using local materials, with native cultural values in mind. All reserves have a central band office and several have attractive multipurpose cultural and recreational centres. Both modern and traditional elements have been blended at Wikwemikong on Manitoulin Island in the construction of a distinctive healing lodge modelled on the shape of an eagle, whose "wings" house the occupational therapy and counselling services and whose "breast" contains a central fire pit for traditional healing ceremonies.

Family, Kinship, and Social Organization

Kinship systems among Eastern Woodland Algonquians vary widely. The Algonkin, Eastern Abenaki, Malecite, Mi'kmaq, Ojibwa, and Ottawa have the extended family group as a basic unit. Persons in the past were attached either through consanguinity or marriage to a core unit composed of a prominent older man, his wife or wives, and his children. Brothers often hunted together, and post-marital residence was frequently bilocal. The Ojibwa and Ottawa, among others, permitted cross-cousin marriage. To members of these groups, parallel cousins, which are the offspring of one's mother's or father's same-sex siblings, are classified as kin and remain unmarriageable. Cross-cousin marriage refers to the practice of taking as one's spouse an offspring of one's mother's or father's *opposite*-sex siblings, or, in short, a female cousin (if one is a man) who is the daughter either of the brother of one's mother or the sister of one's father.

The greatest diversity in kinship reckoning lies along the Atlantic coast, although in common parlance today Algonquian speakers prefer to adopt English (or French) kinship terminology. The Malecite system exhibits a bifurcate collateral pattern, in that distinct terms exist for mother, mother's sister, and father's sister. Cousin terms follow an "Iroquois pattern" which distinguishes parallel cousins from cross cousins and may indicate the existence of cross-cousin marriage in the past. Knowledge of cousin marriage occurring at any time is denied by the Malecite, however, likely in conformity with the prohibition on first- and second-cousin marriage by the Roman Catholic Church. Malecite families have nicknames, such as "the people of the crow," and often a myth accounts for a name's origin. Age is also an important criterion, both terminologically and behaviourally. There are separate terms for older sister, older brother, and younger sibling, without reference to the younger sibling's sex. Elders are esteemed, and respect terms for grandmother and grandfather are applied to anyone much older than the speaker, even where no genealogical connection is apparent.

A similar emphasis on age permeates the Mi'kmaq system, which nonetheless differs because it is generational. Only in one's own generation are fine distinctions made for sets of male siblings, sets of female siblings, married siblings (regardless of sex), and younger and older siblings of each sex. In the third and fourth ascending generations, merely sex and generation of the relative are distinguished, and in all descending generations, except for one's own children, even the sexes are merged under one term. Cousins are terminologically and behaviourally equated with cousins. In this, the Mi'kmaq kinship organization shows parallels with the "Hawaiian cousin system" of the matrilineal Delaware in which siblings and cousins of the same sex are terminologically indistinguishable. One explanation equates the existence of generational cousin systems with the need for solidarity among large kin groups engaged in substantial economic endeavours, such as building fishweirs among the Mi'kmaq or communal deer drives among the Delaware.

The Western Abenaki at Saint-François traditionally possessed exogamous patrilineal, patrilocal totemic groups whose members regarded themselves as descendants of a remote male ancestor. In 1736 totems included the turtle, bear, beaver, otter, and partridge. The Abenaki probably engaged in cross-cousin marriage prior to sanctions imposed on the practice by the Roman Catholic Church. Bear and turtle moieties divided the population into two halves – the term "moiety" means "half" – for certain activities. Western Abenaki also exhibited a distinctive trait in that two male partners, as children, formed a special bond between themselves which lasted for life.

The Algonkin, Ojibwa, and Ottawa, like the Malecite on the east coast, have an "Iroquois cousin pattern" which classes parallel cousins and siblings together as kin and cross cousins as non-kin. A joking relationship exists between male cross cousins, or a male and female cross-cousin pair, which provides amusement for other persons present, since jokes are often ingenious and ribald. Parallel aunts and uncles are merged terminologically, in a bifurcate pattern by sex, with mother and father, and cross aunts and uncles are classified separately. Cross-cousin marriage occurred until the mid-nineteenth century, although it was restricted to the third descending generation among the Southwestern Ojibwa.

The Potawatomi historically had a strongly corporate "Omaha system" of exogamous patrilineal clans, dispersed among many villages. Children received one of their names from their clan's members, to whom they were bound by social and ceremonial obligations. A secondary, but still vital, emphasis was placed on matrilineal linkages. Kin groups were dynamic: during the eighteenth and early nineteenth centuries, segmentary lineages and clan segments pressed into new areas and set up villages, which maintained ties with their parent clans.

In all Woodland Algonquian societies, a special rite of passage usually followed a young boy's killing of his first big game. A girl's first menses often met with some sort of ceremonial rite. Women sought seclusion at this time and for each succeeding menses thereafter. Among many Woodland Algonquians, sexual continence was practised not only during menstruation but also during pregnancy and lactation. A Delaware girl, following her first menstrual seclusion, donned a special headdress that partially covered her face and indicated her readiness to receive suitors.

Marriage conferred adult status on men and women. Before marriage a Mi'kmaq man had to turn over most of each hunt to his chief; after marriage he gave only a small tribute. Marriage occurred after a couple remained betrothed for at least a year. Among most groups the man was required to perform one year's bride service for the parents of his intended, although chastity during this time was not so strictly observed among Central Algonquian speakers as it was in the east. Malecite and Mi'kmaq of both sexes observed strict sexual abstinence during this period of waiting. The man proved his prowess as a provider to his father-in-law, while the woman demonstrated her domestic skills by fashioning all her future husband's garments and footwear. Elders of a girl's family played a strong advisory role concerning partners, but she usually also exercised considerable choice in the matter. Presents of wampum often were made by a suitor to a girl or members of her family, but other indications of interest were purely symbolic. A Malecite youth tossed a wood chip into the lap of a girl he admired and, if she liked him, she returned the chip to him with a smile.

Among the Eastern Woodland Algonquians, marriages were often concluded with feasting and dancing in the presence of chiefs and family. Less ceremony attended marriages in the upper Great Lakes region. While many marriages were monogamous, chiefs often had more than one wife. Among the Delaware and Potawatomi, polygamy was fairly common and divorce almost as much so. By contrast, divorce rarely occurred among traditional Malecite and Mi'kmaq, owing to a strict moral code on the matter. By the mid-nineteenth century, pressure from missionaries had led to the disappearance from all areas both of polygamy and of the requirement that a man perform one year's bride service to his father-in-law.

Woodland Algonquians respected their elders. When an elder fell ill among the Malecite and Mi'kmaq, shamans attended the sick person, but, if the patient worsened, procedures such as dousing the invalid in cold water might take place to hasten death. This was not viewed as disrespectful. During funeral ceremonies, mourners traditionally placed grave offerings with a body, which was taken out through the side of a dwelling rather than a door. Traditionally, there was a great fear of ghosts; a light kept burning near a gravesite was believed to keep malicious spirits at bay. A band, clan, or medicine society held a funeral ceremony and feast, often over a period of four days in the upper Great Lakes region. The corpse was interred in either a seated or a prone position, although the Mi'kmaq were also known to have practised scaffold burial and to have cremated their dead. The Ojibwa, Ottawa, and Potawatomi placed a low rectangular, gabled "gravehouse" over a gravesite. The gravehouse had an opening in the front for the spirit to come and go and a marker post in front which stated the occupant's totemic designation and gave some indication of achievements, especially if the occupant had been a warrior. Until quite recently, food offerings were also left near the grave. Today, funerals, which last several days, usually take place in the home of the deceased. In the Maritime provinces, respect for the dead often is accompanied by prayers, singing, a feast, and an auction or distribution of goods on behalf of the person's family. Funeral ceremonies may follow either a Christian order of service or a ceremony favoured by contemporary traditionalists.

Social organization and leadership differed from group to group. Among the Eastern Abenaki, Algonkin, Malecite, and Mi'kmaq, the bilateral extended family comprised the fundamental group-building block, although patrilineal principles usually governed leadership succession within the village or local summer band. The Western Abenaki, Ojibwa, Ottawa, and Potawatomi historically had patrilineal clans. At Saint-François, the turtle mark and bear mark acted as the symbolic identifiers for two important organizational moieties within the Abenaki group and represented the Sokoki and the Penacook, respectively. These moieties functioned both in the council forum and during team sports. By contrast, the Delaware were matrilineal. Munsee and Unami sectors of the Delaware tribe had three kinship groups, or ubiquitous tribal subdivisions – Turtle, Turkey, and Wolf – each of which until the mid-nineteenth century contained a civil chief, a war chief, a speaker, and a messenger. The Delaware of the Six Nations also included one woman in the chiefly lineage as a "chiefmaker," a trait borrowed from the Iroquois. Among the Potawatomi, strong all-male village councils influenced chiefly appointments and activities, and there was a specialized warrior class, or sodality, which exercised policing functions. Only the Delaware, Mi'kmaq, and Potawatomi historically exhibited tribal structures, and, of the three, only the Mi'kmaq organization still remains in existence. The Mi'kmaq may have retained their tribal system owing to their villages' dispersed character, which rendered them less accessible to colonial scrutiny and manipulation. Yet it is highly improbable that any of these groups evidenced a tribal level of integration before 1650.

Among Central Algonquian speakers, leadership tended to be based mainly on the maintenance of reciprocity of interest between leader and led, whereas Eastern Algonquian leadership revealed more of an authoritarian nature, with tribute often required of a subservient retinue or class. Western Abenaki, Malecite, and Mi'kmaq societies displayed stratification in that chieftainships emerged within a limited number of high-ranking families. Succession to leadership usually followed patrilineal principles, although this rule was not inviolate, since a brother or nephew might gain precedence over a son if the band council deemed the former contender more worthy of the honour. A chief, or sagamore, supplied retinues of persons willing to hunt, go to war, or form trading parties under his aegis, and he also provided necessities such as canoes, dogs, and provisions for long journeys. Young men, not yet married, ate in his company and shared a portion of their hunt with his household.

During the early fur trade, these sagamores wielded considerable influence in their communities, although they could not coerce their followers to obey their wishes. The Malecite village of Ouigoudi at the mouth of the Saint John River had one head chief, Chkoudun, who represented the interests of the Malecite nation as a whole. Yet, as the Malecite dispersed to inland riverine sites under local headmen in the late seventeenth century, French missionaries came to assume many roles formerly ascribed to indigenous leaders. In later years, whenever strong Malecite leaders arose, factionalism ensued, though chiefs might be unobstructed in forwarding policies on behalf of individual bands. During the late 1930s through the 1960s, Chief "Billy" Saulis of Tobique, who championed the integrity of the native community against land grabbers, government negligence, and bureaucratic incompetence, was regarded as a leader after the old tradition in representing interests broader than those of a single reserve. Nevertheless, an attempt in the 1950s to establish a pan-reserve Malecite entity with a superchief and supercouncil under the name *Wolastok* was unsuccessful.

It was noted in the late nineteenth century that the Mi'kmaq divided their lands into seven subdistricts. Today, the Mi'kmaq still have a system of district chiefs who operate under the auspices of a grand chief and council, with headquarters in Cape Breton. Appointments to offices follow traditional principles, although their functions are primarily symbolic rather than actively political. The districts are: Onamag (Cape Breton), Esgigeoag (eastern Nova Scotia), Segepenegatig (the Shubenacadie district), Gespogoitnag (southwestern Nova Scotia), Epegoitnag and Pigtogeog (most of the Northumberland Strait region including Prince Edward Island), Sigenigteoag (the Memramcook district), and Gespegeoag (the Gaspé).

Until the early twentieth century, installations of life chiefs at Saint-François proceeded with considerable ceremony, which included giving the incumbent a new name. A civil chief, a war chief, and a council of elders of leading families comprised the Saint-François Grand Council. In 1771 wampum records for this community were entrusted to a special body formed of seven women and six men.

Among all eastern Woodland Algonquian peoples, men traditionally achieved status through their prowess in the hunt, in medicinal powers, and in warfare and trade. A young man gained manhood once he killed his first big game. Women traditionally acquired prestige through their skills as herbalists and midwives. At the other extreme, war captives and slaves constituted the lowest social echelon. Delaware adopted captive native, white, Mexican, and black children, and occasionally purchased slaves.

Modern reserve life is primarily egalitarian, although stratification exists where certain families are accorded prominence. Educational attainments also confer status. While the family constitutes the most important unit, other organizations cross-cut reserves and so sponsor a wider sphere of social interaction. Visiting among extended kin members has always been a popular pastime. Those who gain higher education often foster interest in their particular field among youths with whom they come in contact. The same may be said of those who excel in sports. Church-related events and festivities, educational workshops and displays relating to native culture and aboriginal rights, boy scouts, cubs, girl guides, baseball, hockey, lacrosse, and societies such as Alcoholics Anonymous bring people together from different communities. Young people occasionally gain band or federal-government sponsorship to attend conferences on indigenous issues in other provinces or countries. The modern powwow, which had its birth in the rejuvenation of native traditions and values, draws not only Canadian Algonquian individuals but also native persons from many other parts of Canada and the United States to participate in musical, artistic, recreational, and social events.

Culture and Religion

All Eastern Woodland Algonquian peoples subscribed to a cycle of legend and myth regarding tricksters and "transformers" (powerful beings who created the earthly landscape), which could be recounted only during the winter months, when formidable spiritual agencies

were considered to be underground or asleep. Differences in this respect were slight: Central Algonquian speakers merged the roles of
trickster and transformer into a single personage called Menabosho,
Nanabush, or Wiske, whereas the Eastern Abenaki, Malecite, and
Mi'kmaq endowed their hero Gluscap primarily with transformer
traits, leaving trickster attributes to lesser characters, such as Snowshoe Hare and Racoon. Gluscap, a lone and clever leader, used his
powers to benefit his people in times of crisis. He contended with evil
beings who prevented his people from obtaining resources which
were rightfully theirs, pitching his wiles against Half-stone Man, his
perennial adversary. Odziozo, the Western Abenaki transformer, exhibited many of the same traits as Gluscap.

Origin myths, along with other folk beliefs, endowed the natural
landscape with mythical figures and symbolic appeal. Even potentially threatening spirits bestowed benefits if approached in a respectful manner. Rites of divination using bones, also known as
scapulimancy, were practised, and taboos existed regarding wastage
of resources and the respectful treatment of animal bones. Storytelling, whether of a mythic character or based on events recounted from
memory, often focused on the acquisition and control of power. Power
might be obtained in several ways: by birth, through visionary experience, or by some vicissitude of nature. For instance, a child born with a
cowl was considered to exhibit special aptitudes. Certain objects, because of their strange appearance, were viewed as capable of conferring good luck in specific pursuits. Among many groups, stone or clay
concretions were considered the manufacture of little wild people
who lived near water or on hilltops and could be used to divine the future. Not all powers were viewed as helpful, however. A possessor of
dangerous, unpredictable power was termed a *buoin* among the
Ojibwa or a *buoin* or *puwowin* in the Maritimes. European folk myths
regarding witches influenced Mi'kmaq and Malecite stories about
buoin.

The Potawatomi are the only Algonquian people in Canada who
assigned children to a "senior" or "junior" side of a moiety, which
divided their society into halves depending on each persons's birth
order and in keeping with certain dualistic cosmological beliefs. Even
team membership in a gambling game which uses a wooden bowl,
round-bone counters as dice, and sticks to keep score, known among
the Potawatomi as *kwesekenek* (*waltes* or *altestaken* in the Maritimes),
followed that division. In this the Potawatomi were closer to the

Fox and Kickapoo than to Central Canadian Algonquian-speaking groups. Variants of this gambling game are played universally throughout the Eastern Woodland region, and owners of bowls and counters are almost always women.

Modern Woodland Algonquian artists have produced various and exceptionally beautiful works by drawing on traditional themes and using traditional media in novel and unique ways. Artists and sculptors exhibit widely and their works hang in major galleries. The familiar school of Woodland art, which derives from the pathbreaking endeavours of Norval Morriseau of Lake Nipigon, Ontario, demonstrates but one ingenious facet of the wealth of creativity shown in recent years by the Woodland Algonquian community. This people has produced a number of writers and also excellent film-makers, among them Cathy Martin and Alanis Obomsawin, whose works, sponsored by the National Film Board, document native issues and culture.

Traditional Woodland Algonquian religious beliefs centred around the attainment and use of spiritual power. The Mi'kmaq or Malecite *ginap* displayed a kind of power which enabled a person to perform major feats, whereas the power of a shaman focused more on healing, divination, and, at times, shamanic retribution. The shaman's art was shrouded in secrecy. Often ritual paraphernalia were kept in a medicine pouch and revealed only in ceremonial contexts. A shaman treating a patient would blow, or suck through a bone tube over the affected part, to extract what was believed to be the source of the malady.

All Woodland Algonquian believed in a host of supernatural entities which governed every facet of the natural world. Many groups required a pubescent youth to fast in order to obtain a vision of a spiritual guardian who would accompany him for the rest of his life. The Mi'kmaq regarded the sun as the supreme being, a belief they may have inherited from Ohio valley natives who established satellite communities in New Brunswick and Nova Scotia about 1,500 years ago. Most societies revered the bear and performed specific rituals when this animal was killed or captured. Supernatural beings included the sun, moon, stars, thunder, animal "bosses," a horned water snake, a water panther, powerful birdlike entities, a trunkless being who was all head and limbs, the little people mentioned above who resided near water or on hilltops, and cannibal giants such as Chenoo among the Mi'kmaq and Windigo among the Algonkin and Ojibwa. Certain islands and mountaintops were viewed as dwelling places of fearsome supernaturals such as the Abenaki *bmola*, a dreaded flying creature.

From the early seventeenth century onwards, the native populations of the Maritimes and southern Quebec were introduced to Roman Catholicism. The majority still remain attached to a special form of Catholicism which shows a degree of syncretism with the indigenous belief system. Membertou, a prominent Mi'kmaq sagamore, accepted baptism at Port Royal in 1610, and numerous Mi'kmaq and Malecite have followed his lead. After the conquest of New France by Britain in 1760, an event that made the position of the Catholic Church difficult for more than a decade, the Mi'kmaq in particular chose to hold attenuated ceremonies on their own or to visit the islands of Saint-Pierre and Miquelon to receive the sacraments from French priests. For over two hundred years, moreover, the Mi'kmaq have regarded the Roman Catholic festival of Sainte-Anne, held around 26 July, as a national holiday. Yet Mi'kmaq communities such as Shubenacadie have not been reluctant to accept assistance proffered by other denominational agencies, such as the several educational and settlement projects sponsored by the Methodist Walter Bromley in 1813–14.

Early missionary endeavours in the Great Lakes area during the French regime, by contrast, had little long-term influence on the resident native population. Apart from the Moravian Delaware, the Algonquians of southern Ontario remained unattached to any denomination until a remarkable camp meeting at Ancaster in 1823 recruited Peter Jones of the Mississauga nation as an advocate of the Methodist cause. During the next ten years, Jones's preaching kindled interest among other southeastern Ojibwa, several of whom became energetic native exhorters. The Methodists established a number of Ojibwa model agricultural communities, of which the best known lay on the Credit River, near the present-day city of Mississauga. In the late 1830s and 1840s Roman Catholic and Anglican missionaries actively began proselytizing in the Lake Simcoe and northern Lake Huron areas, while Chief Peguis became the first Western Ojibwa chief to espouse Anglicanism at Red River, in what is now Manitoba. Yet, in most Woodland Algonquian communities, particularly in the west, elements of the traditional belief system remained intact.

Shamanic practices may also be traced in the Maritime region. In 1778, despite the presence of a Roman Catholic priest, Malecite chief Pierre Thomas summoned shamanic powers to his aid in determining which side to ally with during the American Revolution. After lying motionless for almost an hour, Thomas rose and stated his preference for the British cause. In the mid-nineteenth century, Mi'kmaq held that performance of a certain dance called the *neskouwadijik* rendered the dancer invincible against bullets. These practices tended to be more individualistic than those in the Great Lakes region.

Among Eastern Canadian Algonquian speakers, only the Mi'kmaq and Delaware have been recorded as holding major annual village ceremonies. In the Mi'kmaq springtime ritual, a woman tended a sacred fire for a specified length of time, after which she and the village chief participated in a revitalization ceremony. In one Delaware ceremony called the Big House Ceremony, or *gamwing*, performed during planting and after corn harvest, men who had dreamed of a guardian spirit danced in a circle around two central fires to the beat of drums. At intervals a man would stop, recite a story about his spirit guardian, and then sing a song he had acquired during his vision experience. This ceremony survived into the early nineteenth century.

Ojibwa, Ottawa, and Potawatomi religious practitioners often belonged to the Grand Medicine Society, or Midéwiwin, or the lesser-known Wabano society, whose members manipulated natural phenomena in order to demonstrate power sufficient to attain specific ends. Wabano ritual involved the handling of fiery substances, such as red-hot stones or coals. By contrast, the Midéwiwin, a ranked organization, required its adherents to pass through a number of stages en route to acquiring powers deemed capable not only of protecting and healing but also of reviving the world system. A third class of shamans, known as shaking-tent conjurors, consulted with spirits for curing, divining the future, locating lost persons or objects, and sometimes for shamanic retaliation against enemies. The conjuror's ritual necessitated the construction of a small pole framework, covered except for the top. The shaman inside this structure acted as an intermediary with spirits who shook the tent as they entered. Shaking-tent conjurors and members of the Midewiwin and Wabano societies always worked for a fee.

All Woodland Algonquians used the sweat lodge for purification purposes and hunting rituals, as well as to obtain and demonstrate religious power. Since the 1960s this sweat lodge ceremony has been reintroduced and combined with practices from Plains or Iroquoian sources. The talking circle, burning of sweet grass incense, chanting, and drumming have become important elements of these contemporary ceremonies. Some reserves are split into factions between those who prefer to follow Christian practices and those who espouse the neo-traditionalist perspective. For instance, in the homes of devout Roman Catholics, funeral rites may last for two or three nights, during which guests sing and recite rosaries. Among traditionalists, drumming, songs, and chanting occur in honour of the deceased.

Education, Language, and Communication

Children traditionally learned by emulating members of their parental generation. Parents accorded them considerable freedom in which to learn roles and skills considered appropriate to their age and sex, and bestowed rewards on those who achieved socially approved goals. Children who failed to conform encountered informal sanctions, such as teasing or withdrawal of attention. Fear of bogey-men, wild supernatural beings, or past traditional enemies such as the Iroquois was inculcated in young children to make them heed the limits of their social world. Some communities later extended the range of threatening personages to include white teachers, agents, and priests.

Formal schooling was extended at different times and places to Eastern Woodland Algonquians in Canada under the auspices of Anglican, Baptist, Congregationalist, Moravian, Presbyterian, Roman Catholic, and Wesleyan Methodist missionaries. Eleazar Wheelock, an American Congregationalist preacher, established a school for Indian children around 1750 at Lebannon, Connecticut, which in 1769 moved to Hanover, New Hampshire, on the Western Abenaki's traditional hunting grounds. In 1769 as well, this institution became Dartmouth College, and for the next eighty years it continued to draw some of its native students from the Saint-François community at Odanak, Quebec.

One early experiment that involved the removal of native students from their parental surroundings occurred in New Brunswick at Sussex Vale, where, for a span of seven years after 1797, Malecite children were apprenticed to rural families at the same time as they attended classes. Boys were expected to become farmers or rural labourers, girls to enter domestic service. To some degree, the idea at Sussex Vale was to teach Malecite youth British values, which would militate against their siding as adults with the Americans should hostilities arise between the British colonies and the United States. Although under the aegis of the London-based Society for the Propagation of the Gospel in New England, the Sussex Vale experiment was subject to the sorts of abuse which later haunted many Indian residential schools. A belief that native youth should be made to forgo all attachment to their indigenous culture permeated the ideology underlying the manual-labour and residential school systems, along with a presumptuous faith in the superiority of British culture and an emphasis on institutional self-sufficiency.

Methodists in Ontario during the 1840s established a manual-labour school at Alderville and a residential school at Muncey. An Anglican residential institution, known as Shingwauk School, was built at Sault Ste Marie in 1875 under the auspices of the Anglican missionary E.F. Wilson, who opened yet another school in 1888 at Elkhorn, near Brandon, Manitoba. Similar Roman Catholic institutions later opened at Spanish on the north shore of Lake Huron and at Shubenacadie in Nova Scotia. Presbyterians ran residential schools at Kenora and Birtle, Manitoba.

Residential schools survived into the early 1970s, when the federal government created a system of day schools; however, the emphasis remained on cultural integration into the Canadian mainstream rather than building on strengths inherent in native culture. Dropout rates remained high, and few students attended community colleges or universities. It was not until Woodland native organizations from the late 1960s onwards spearheaded a major campaign to compel provincial school boards to include constructive native content in their elementary and high school curriculum that things began to change. Workshops and conferences were organized to discuss modes of combatting systemic racism. Regional efforts included the activities in the late 1960s and 1970s of the non-profit corporation TRIBE (Teaching and Research in Bicultural Education), which involved the Malecite, Passamaquoddy, and Mi'kmaq in improving the status of native education in the Maritime provinces and Maine. By the late 1970s, moreover, native-studies programs were being offered by Native Friendship Centres, community colleges, and universities. Several universities have since then initiated specialized native access into their professional law, nursing, medicine, dentistry, and social-work programs; as a result, a new generation of highly educated natives has arisen. Finally, in 1995 the Mi'kmaq Education Authority gained control over aboriginal education in Nova Scotia, a feat that others, most prominently Treaty 3 First Nations in Ontario and Manitoba, intended to emulate before 1997.

In the area of language, Eastern Woodland Algonquians had sophisticated systems of ideogramatic representations by which they could communicate messages and keep records on wood, bark, or stone. Henry Rowe Schoolcraft, an American Indian agent at Sault Ste Marie from 1822 to 1841, first noted the use of such ideograms inscribed on bark scrolls or wooden boards in the context of the Ojibwa Midewiwin and Wabano societies. In addition, Algonquians adopted the Iroquois practice of mnemonically encoding, in transportable wampum belts, valuable data regarding major political decisions and transactions.

During the late seventeenth century, a Recollect missionary, Chrestien LeClercq, employed Mi'kmaq ideograms in producing a hieroglyphic writing system which was later "reinvented" by the Abbé Pierre-Antoine Maillard in the mid-eighteenth century. Maillard popularized the ideographic system for instructing his Mi'kmaq followers in brief catechistic responses, but the Mi'kmaq adapted it to convey other kinds of information. Some nineteenth-century hieroglyphic texts, mostly of a religious nature, are still extant.

After a Methodist missionary, James Evans, devised a syllabic writing system in the 1830s, recognition of the utility of the script spread rapidly southward to the Ojibwa living north and northwest of Lake Superior (Norval Morriseau, the Ojibwa Woodland artist, employs syllabic script in signing his native name "Copper Thunderbird"). In modern newspapers and journals, however, various Latin orthographies have gained precedence over hieroglyphics or syllabic modes of presenting information. By the nineteenth century the Mi'kmaq community had developed a phonemic script for representing its own language using the Latin alphabet, a script that a Capuchin missionary, Father J. Pacifique, modified in publishing the Mi'kmaq-language monthly, *Le Messager Micmac* (The Micmac Messenger; Restigouche, Que., 1906–42). More recently, in March 1974, a systematic version of the same script was introduced in *Agenutemagan*, a newspaper of the Union of New Brunswick Indians. In keeping with a renewed emphasis on preserving indigenous culture, native linguists are devising new and improved Latin orthographies not only to communicate ideas among adults but also to teach native languages effectively to the rising generation. Those interested in learning to speak Mi'kmaq and Ojibwa also may purchase language tapes and instruction booklets.

Woodland Algonquian regional organizations almost all publish newspapers or newsletters, in either the English or French language, depending on the province and the nature of their readership. Publications are of four types: local, ethnic, regional, and popular. Contemporary newsletters such as the *Nindawaabjig News* of the Walpole Island First Nation Heritage Centre convey information of local import. Serving a distinct ethnic community, the *Micmac Nations News* (Sydney, N.S., 1965–) remains the main voice of the Union of Nova Scotia Indians. The *Micmac-Maliseet Nations News*, published by the Mainland Confederacy of Mi'kmaq since 1990, addresses a yet wider native constituency, while *Native Life*, a glossy new magazine published in Ontario at the Georgina Island First Nation and devoted to native arts, health, culture, and political issues, appeals to general and native audiences alike.

Politics

On 1 October 1993 the Mi'kmaq and the province of Nova Scotia signed a historic agreement designed to recognize past agreements made between the two peoples. This commitment is renewed at a ceremony held the first day of October each year. Recognition of aboriginal rights is especially important to Woodland Algonquians living in the Maritime provinces and parts of southern Quebec and northeastern Ontario because no negotiations regarding land cessions have ever taken place in these areas. The legal arguments on which these peoples must base their claims to land and resources must stem from still developing, international conceptions of what constitutes aboriginal rights, as well as clauses from pre-Confederation treaties of peace and friendship, where they exist, signed with the British in the eighteenth century. Another recent addition to the mix – and one that holds great promise for Algonquian peoples – is the Supreme Court's 1997 decision in *Delgamuukw* that aboriginal title to land not covered by treaty remains unextinguished.

Land and resource issues constituted an important theme of discussion during the nineteenth and early twentieth centuries in Grand Council forums among the Mi'kmaq, southeastern Ojibwa, Ojibwa of the Treaty 3 area, and Saint-François Abenaki. Many of these councils' historical roots extended back as far as the mid-eighteenth century, if not earlier, and almost all lent their traditions of leadership and achievement to the modern regional political organizations which arose in the late 1960s. A White Paper introduced by the federal Liberal government in 1969, which advocated disbanding the Department of Indian Affairs, transferring Indian lands to the provinces, and giving native reserves municipal status, aroused universal condemnation in the native community. Across Canada, native regional organizations, where they did not already exist, came into being to protest the bill incorporating the White Paper's recommendations, and in 1971 the bill was withdrawn. Over the years several of these organizations, including those in Nova Scotia and Ontario, have undergone major changes. In 1984 the Mainland Confederacy split away from the Union of Nova Scotia Indians originally founded in response to the 1969 White Paper, to form a separate political jurisdiction, while the Union of Ontario Indians (with political roots in the 1920s) recently underwent restructuring to meet the modern demands of its mostly Woodland Algonquian constituents, who represent over one-third of that province's native communities.

Other regional organizations have had to overcome difficulties associated with the composite nature of their membership. Malecite and Mi'kmaq communities represented by the Union of New Brunswick Indians, founded in 1967, had not acted as close political allies since the late 1800s. For over a hundred years prior to this date, the positions of Malecite chief and subchief were held for life and ratified by neighbouring Abenaki, Mi'kmaq, Passamaquoddy, and Penobscot chiefs. Eastern Algonquian chiefs, with their subchiefs, assistants, and principal men known as captains, met periodically as members of the Wabanaki Confederacy. Devised to reach common positions on policies set forth by colonial powers, this alliance, with its great council fire at Caughnawaga (Kahnawake), Quebec, also preserved a corporate memory of past treaties and transactions recorded mnemonically in wampum records kept by each member group. With the disappearance of the Wabanaki Confederacy, political cooperation among the eastern Algonquians declined for many years. As noted above, an unsuccessful attempt was made during the 1950s to establish a pantribal Malecite political entity known as Wulastock. Yet, in recent times, the desire for greater unity has reasserted itself, owing to the political legacies left by several unique individuals, such as "Billy" Saulis at Tobique.

At the local level, in 1896 the Indian Act mandated three-year terms for elected chiefs, although the practice of selecting life chiefs did not end on many reserves until well into the twentieth century. In 1951 a revised Indian Act granted councils enlarged responsibilities but endowed the Department of Indian Affairs with veto power over all decisions. Today, an elected chief-and-councillor system continues in force, with band administrators and their staff assisting in the administration of community affairs.

When band councils and regional associations fail to address pressing problems effectively, grass-roots activist groups or protest movements arise. Woodland Algonquians were instrumental in setting up the pan-Indian Boston Indian Council in the early 1970s, they participated in protest demonstrations held by the American Indian Movement in the 1960s and 1970s, and they established "warrior societies" in defence of a wide range of causes. Native lobbying groups supported a campaign for reinstatement under the Indian Act of native women who had lost Indian status through marriage to non-natives, or persons of both sexes who had been involuntarily enfranchised, owing to their educational attainments or war service. This campaign achieved its goal in 1985 with Parliament's passage of Bill C-31, which amended the objectionable features of the Indian Act. Algonquian leaders also have operated forcefully within the Canadian political system. Ovide Mercredi, former leader of the Assembly of First Nations, is of Central Algonquian parentage. Elijah Harper, the member of the Manitoba legislature who played a leading role in destroying the Meech Lake constitutional accord, speaks a variant of Ojibwa and is of mixed Ojibwa and Cree ancestry, known as Oji-Cree. While their means and methods may differ, Algonquian leaders have done their share to elevate aboriginal concerns to a prominent place on Canada's national political agenda.

Intergroup Relations and Group Maintenance

In the past each Algonquian-speaking group maintained its ethnic boundaries by upholding and preserving cultural markers distinct to its own people. Seasonal rituals and various religious rites enabled such markers to retain a high profile over time within the native community.

Traditionally, stable relations obtained among neighbouring native entities as long as alliances and common interests bound groups together. While most general history texts present the Iroquois as the enemies of the Algonquian speakers, the picture is actually much more complex. The Ojibwa and Ottawa fought as frequently with the

Dakota Sioux to the west of them and with the Iroquois to the east. Over time, wars occurred in the northeast among many different linguistic groups; even as late as the mid-eighteenth century, conflicts among neighbouring Algonquian-speaking groups were fairly common. And entities that regarded each other as enemies one year might, through a new series of alliances, become comrades the next, regardless of either group's relations with external European interests. In the Saco War of 1607 the Mi'kmaq and Malecite fought together against Algonquian-speaking groups along the northern New England coast. Around 1755, however, the Mi'kmaq and Malecite were at war with one another, even though both nations were allies of France.

Two things are clear: similar dealings with the same European power did not necessarily foster a strong community of interest among native groups so engaged, and disagreements within groups concerning which European power to support at any given time did not cause irreparable damage to long-term group cohesiveness. Most of the Algonquian speakers remained attached to the French during the era of the colonial wars, although this was not true for the Penobscot of Maine, who wavered in their loyalty to France. By the 1750s Penobscot vacillation, as well as reversals in French fortunes in general, had also undermined Mi'kmaq confidence in their French allies. In consequence, several Mi'kmaq groups along the southwestern shore of Nova Scotia came to favour the British, and one Mi'kmaq chief in particular, Penall Argomartin of Gold River, is even said to have guided British troops to Quebec.

Events during the American Revolution and the War of 1812 indicated a much changed state of affairs, however, as many Ojibwa, Ottawa, and Potawatomi sided with the British against the Americans, while many Mi'kmaq and Malecite, still distrustful of the British, chose to remain neutral. In instances where the Mi'kmaq favoured active support over neutrality, as occurred around Pictou and Chignecto in Nova Scotia, bands upheld the American cause.

Before the mid-nineteenth century, certain members of native and non-native communities might interact together in the fur trade, in warfare, and in matters especially involving guiding and other related bush skills. Afterwards, however, racism became a potent force guiding both public and private relationships between natives and non-natives. It was not until the 1960s that native organizations grew strong enough to raise the awareness of all sectors of mainstream society to the insidious consequences of systemic racism on interracial relations. And, despite such efforts, a legacy of racism and paternalism still lingers.

To eradicate what were viewed as the worst abuses of paternalism, the criteria governing band membership, as noted above, were amended by Bill C-31 to include large numbers of women who formerly had lost their Indian status through marriage to non-natives. Yet such a decision has not been without its consequences. In the wake of Bill C-31, the population of many reserve communities has expanded rapidly; moreover, the native population as a whole is quite young and expected to grow as families have children. In response, band governments and regional organizations have redoubled efforts to prepare for the future by settling land-claims issues and matters regarding resource rights and management, as well as by encouraging economic development. Yet band councils also retain principal control over band enrolment and have been known to obstruct participation of a "Bill-C-31 person" in a community, even if the individual concerned has kin living on the reserve.

Where powerful families become self-sustaining politically over time, by gaining votes from their numerous kin in band council elections, they become essentially "family compacts." Even where councils work hard for programs to benefit their people, when caught between pressing community demands and what often seems a lethargic government bureaucracy, temptation arises for leadership to settle for what benefits they can get for their relatives. Concerns over the evils of nepotism has raised fears in some communities that devolution of too much power too quickly to band councils in the name of native self-determination may raise more problems on reserves than it solves. Alternative arguments hold that the federal government must wait until indigenous political leaders make substantial changes at the regional and national levels before burdening local governments with responsibilities they may not be able to handle either effectively or fairly. As these broader reforms occur, communities may not be so faction-ridden as many are at present.

Aside from personal commitment through kin ties and cultural roots, Eastern Woodland Algonquian youth evince a greater common awareness than in years past of treaty and aboriginal rights, as well as of losses incurred through mainstream society's negligence in recognizing and protecting such rights. Resentment, however, is tempered by hope for the rectification of these wrongs. Ambivalence towards Indian identity is beginning to fade as communities display pride in their cultural past and come to the realization that their social, economic, and political problems, while still extremely serious, are being addressed by their own people. Individuals of all ages and both sexes are acting together to present mainstream society with a range of diverse images to counter romantic, outmoded, or negative stereotypes. In response, broader Canadian society is beginning to learn that all natives, whatever their differences, not only have much in common culturally but share the same goals and aspirations for the future.

FURTHER READING

One of the best introductions to the Eastern Woodland Algonquians may be found in volume 15 of the *Handbook of North American Indians*, edited by Bruce Trigger and published by the Smithsonian Institution, Washington, D.C., in 1978. In addition, ethnographic monographs exist for individual groups. Those interested are encouraged to consult works by Edward S. Rogers on the Ojibwa, Frank G. Speck on the Mi'kmaq, W.H. Mechling on the Malecite, and Wilson D. and Ruth Sawtell Wilson on both the Mi'kmaq and the Malecite. An interesting recent study of an Ojibwa community appears in Edward J. Hedican, *Applied Anthropology in Canada: Understanding Aboriginal Issues* (Toronto, 1995).

There are several general works in which Eastern Woodland Algonquians are featured at length. These include John Webster Grant, *Moon of Wintertime: Missionaries and the Indians in Encounter since 1534* (Toronto, 1984); Laura Peers, *The Ojibwa of Western Canada* (Winnipeg, 1994); Boyce Richardson, ed., *Drumbeat: Anger and Renewal in Indian Country* (Toronto, 1989), sponsored by the Assembly of First Nations; Edward S. Rogers and Donald B. Smith, eds., *Aboriginal Ontario: Historical Perspectives on the First Nations* (Toronto, 1994); Bruce Trigger, *Natives and Newcomers: Canada's Heroic Age Reconsidered* (Montreal, 1985); L.F.S. Upton, *Micmacs and Colonists: Indian-White Relations in the Maritimes, 1713–1867* (Vancouver, 1979); and Ruth Holmes Whitehead, *The Old Man Told Us: Excerpts from Micmac History, 1500–1950* (Halifax, 1991).

Information on residential schools is provided in J.R. Miller, *Shingwauk's Vision: A History of Native Residential Schools* (Toronto, 1996). Population declines along the eastern seaboard are dealt with in two articles by Virginia Miller: "Aboriginal Micmac Population: A Review of the Evidence," *Ethnohistory*, vol. 23, no. 3 (1982), 117–27; and "The Decline of the Nova Scotia Micmac Population, A.D. 1600-1850," *Culture*, vol. 2, 107–20. A third source is Dean R. Snow and Kim M. Lanphear, "European Contact and Indian Depopulation in the Northeast: The Timing of the First Epidemics," *Ethnohistory*, vol. 35, no. 1 (1988), 14–33.

ALGONQUIANS / PLAINS

Eldon Yellowhorn

Identification and History

"Plains Algonquian" is a generic term that describes the linguistically related groups identified as Blackfoot, Cree, and Ojibwa. The Blackfoot Confederacy, as it is commonly known, includes the Blood, Peigan, and Blackfoot, and its traditional lands were in southern Alberta and southwestern Saskatchewan. The Plains Cree comprise the western branch of the Cree people, and their traditional lands lay adjacent to the parklands of central Alberta and southern Saskatchewan. The Plains Ojibwa, who inhabited parts of central Saskatchewan and southern Manitoba, also constitute one branch of a larger Ojibwa cultural group. The size of the pre-contact population of all northern plains Indians is unknown, but what is clear is that the number later fell precipitously, partly because of epidemic diseases that devastated the region in 1781, 1819, 1837, 1845, 1864, and 1869. In the mid-1980s the population was about 65,000, with 16,000 in southern Alberta, 20,000 in southern Saskatchewan, and 28,000 in southern Manitoba. Though the lifestyles and material culture of all three groups have much in common, their similiarities should not be construed as homogeneity; variety was also a characteristic of the Plains Algonquians.

Plains Cree speakers call themselves *Iyinow*, which translates as "the real people." The term "Cree" has an obscure and complex origin; however, it has become the accepted term to describe a large group spread out over an expansive geographic region. The name Blackfoot is a translation of the word *Siksika*, the Blackfoot's name for themselves; *Kainai*, the Blood's name for themselves, is a corrupt form of *a-kainaw*, meaning "many chiefs"; and the Peigan's self-designation, *Pikuni*, is a corruption of *apik'uni*, "badly tanned robe." Blackfoot, Cree, and Ojibwa speakers speak mutually unintelligible languages, though the relatedness of these languages is readily observable in the similarity of individual words, which not only sound the same but also carry the same meaning, and more particularly in the syntax.

The geological record offers an explanation of Plains Algonquian origins. Many thousands of years ago, episodic global cooling caused a succession of ice ages during which continental glaciers advanced out of the mountains and from the north and covered much of Canada. River systems could not drain into the ocean and the impounded water formed large inland lakes in front of ice dams. These glacial lakes flooded vast areas, easily exceeding the present Great Lakes system in size, and the altered landscape was dominated by water. The present landscape, scarred by the ebb and flow of continental glaciation, emerged approximately 12,000 years ago with the collapse of the continental glaciers. Glacial lakes, like Lake Agassiz, disappeared when drainage to the ocean was restored. Remnant lakes, like Lake Winnipeg, survive to the present, but traces of the glacial lakes remain visible in the form of stranded shorelines. By 6,000 years ago all of northern North America was free of glacial ice. Plants and animals followed the retreating glaciers right to the shores of Hudson Bay, and in turn they were followed by the first people, who, by about 200 c.e., had occupied all the suitable habitats along the shores of the glacial lakes, intensively exploiting the local floral, faunal, and lithic resources.

Algonquian cultures at this time probably would not have been recognizable as Cree, Blackfoot, or Ojibwa; instead, they were represented by an undifferentiated proto-Algonquian ancestral culture. Their languages were related more closely, perhaps existing as mutually intelligible dialects. Likewise, their customs and technology were similar. However, new modes of travel, technological innovations in food gathering, and adaptation to local resources built up the momentum of culture change. Geographic isolation placed each group on a unique trajectory, the cumulative effects of which resulted in distinct cultures and languages.

The arrival of the written word, in the journals of fur traders, surveyors, and missionaries, marks the beginning of history on the northern plains. Many of the names associated with contemporary native people in the west first appeared in print during this time, and a number of them fell short of accuracy. For example, David Thompson, the first European to visit the Peigan in 1787, identified them as "Peeagan," a misnomer that has endured to this day in the modified form of "Peigan." The ethnographic record also designated different tribes by geography and assigned each a homeland based on the impressions of the various authors who travelled among them. The Plains Cree were said to have originated in the region between Hudson Bay and Lake Superior, while the Plains Ojibwa were thought to have migrated to the plains from the Lake Superior area. Even the Blackfoot, the archetypal plains Indians, have been assigned a Woodland origin in the vicinity of the Eagle Hills in central Saskatchewan, from where they expanded westward just prior to European contact. Recently, historians have begun to reassess the accuracy of these accounts. It may be more than coincidence that these tribes appeared to be migrating westward at the same time and in the same direction that explorers, fur traders, and missionaries were travelling. In short, the supposed locations of tribal homelands and subsequent westerly migrations may reflect more the journeys of whites than actual tribal movements.

Today, the Plains Algonquian peoples live in communities known as reserves, the genesis of which is deeply rooted in the process of nineteenth-century nation-building. Post-Confederation Canada was determined to solidify its claim to the former Hudson's Bay Company (HBC) territory of Rupert's Land, which it had annexed in 1870. The sparse population of Canadians in this region, the desire to incorporate the colony of British Columbia into the federation, and the search for new agricultural land prompted the young country to embark on the ambitious project of building a transcontinental railway. Accomplishing this objective would mean crossing unceded territory occupied by the various tribes of Indians.

Following the policy established in the Royal Proclamation of 1763, the Canadian government established a treaty commission which was given the mandate of negotiating the acquisition of Indian lands, to which, under the proclamation, the Indians themselves held title. Thus, between 1870 and 1877, commissioners traversed the plains negotiating treaties with the Plains Algonquian peoples. Provisions in each treaty varied, but in essence they all contained clauses for exchanging aboriginal title to the land for treaty lands and annuities as well as certain rights such as hunting and fishing. Treaties 1, 2, 4, 6, and

7 became the legal instruments which allowed Canada to claim the northern plains up to the Rocky Mountains.

Far from being passive observers of these developments, the Plains Algonquians were well aware of the events unfolding to the east and south of them. Some sought accommodation to the new regime and placed their faith in the treaty process. The Plains Ojibwa bands signed Treaties 1 and 2 in 1871, primarily because their traditional lands were already the core of white settlement in western Canada. Treaty 4 was signed by leaders of Cree and Saulteaux bands in 1874, and two years later Cree leaders signed Treaty 6. The Blackfoot Confederacy, as the westernmost tribal entity, did not meet with the Treaty Commission until 1877, at which time it signed Treaty 7. In all these cases, the reserved lands belonged to the Crown, which set them aside for the use and benefit of the Indians. The Indians did not own the reserved lands; ownership rested with the Crown.

The treaties created twenty-three reserves in southern Manitoba and southeastern Saskatchewan for the Plains Ojibwa. The Plains Cree settled on twenty-four reserves in southern Saskatchewan and southern Alberta. The Blackfoot Confederacy occupied three reserves in southern Alberta. Years later, in 1912 and 1918, the government sold half the Blackfoot reserve, located just east of present-day Calgary.

Each reserve was located within the traditional territory of the signatory tribes; however, the reserves varied in size, depending on the land-granting formula of the specific treaty. For example, Treaty 1 stipulated that each family of five would receive 160 acres of land, but Treaty 7 provided 640 acres for each family of five. The Plains Cree and Plains Ojibwa received land based on band units, but the Blackfoot Confederacy got land as tribal units, so that the Peigan, Blood, and Blackfoot each received their own reserve.

In the pre-treaty era, native bands were loosely organized, autonomous entities led by individuals whose leadership attracted followers. However, bands as defined in the Indian Act are a body of Indians who can live on a reserve for the purposes of administration. At present, each band is a legal entity which can choose its leaders for the office of chief and council according to procedures established in the Indian Act. Customary rules apply in some instances and provide an alternative to the format described in the act. The mechanics of choosing the chief and council operate on democratic principles – one person, one vote – in a secret ballot. There can be only one chief, with a minimum of two councillors and a maximum of twelve; however, a set formula (1 per 100 band members) determines the number of councillors. Typically, the term of office is two years, although by-elections can be called to fill vacant seats.

Outside the individual band, a common grouping consists of bands in a given treaty area; one such body is the Treaty 7 Tribal Council. Other organizations span provincial boundaries and treaty areas; these include the Indian Association of Alberta, the Federation of Saskatchewan Indians, and the Assembly of Manitoba chiefs. At the national level, Plains Algonquian bands are members of the Assembly of First Nations.

Economic Life

Northern plains economic practices emerged from the pragmatic act of making a living. Plains Algonquians participated in a resource-based economy, hunting, fishing, harvesting plants, and practising techniques of food storage designed to preserve surpluses for later consumption. This indigenous economy was self-sustaining, but it did not survive the shifting patterns of trade and resource harvesting that accompanied the historic era. Still, in the midst of all sorts of changes, the Plains Algonquians have demonstrated a remarkable capacity to reinvent themselves economically.

In the pre-historic period, several types of mammals had disappeared as their habitat was transformed into a warmer realm. Horses as well as giant species of mammoth, bison, ground sloth, and beaver – all staple food sources for early aboriginal peoples on the plains – became extinct. At the same time, one species, bison, came to dominate the grasslands. Although the plains supported many species of hoofed animals, such as antelope, elk, and deer, the bison was especially successful in adapting to the plains environment.

Throughout the pre-historic era, the bison was integral to the subsistence economy of aboriginal hunting cultures. Bands of hunters would ambush small herds of giant bison and other prey; they would store what they could, and, once the food was consumed, they would repeat the process. This method, while successful, was later replaced by the larger, more complex communal hunts associated with pounds and jumps. Scattered across the northern plains are locales where ancient Indian hunters drove herds over cliffs or lured them into corrals for slaughter. There is no clear reason for this change, but a rising population may have increased the demand on the food supply. The change also required an intimate knowledge of bison ecology and behaviour.

The availability of bison promoted self-reliance among the many bands, just as seasonally available resources, like berries and tubers, influenced settlement decisions. Simultaneously, the need for specific stone materials fostered interregional and intertribal trade. Tools made from flint and other such material have been found hundreds of kilometres from their parent quarry, a fact suggesting extensive aboriginal trade routes. As early as 11,000 years ago, silicified wood was traded into southern Saskatchewan, where no local quarry existed.

Indian groups living in proximity to known quarries would be expected to profit by controlling the traffic in stone materials and limiting foreign access. Some groups may even have specialized in processing tools rather than exporting stone, particularly since trading the finished product rather than the raw material would increase its value. Considerations like quality of workmanship, transportation distance, competition, production costs, and even negotiating skills would be factors in setting prices. Early historical accounts indicate that meetings for the purpose of trade occurred at regular intervals and followed standard protocols; representatives were selected, prices set, and disputes resolved. Bison hunters would visit the agricultural communities located along rivers and exchange meat and dressed hides for corn and other garden produce. It is probable that, during their visits to these communities, plains Indians acquired knowledge of how to cultivate small plots of tobacco.

Pre-historic trade networks were more likely to run along a north/ south axis than an east/west one, likely because major river-drainage systems were used as transport corridors for hauling goods by canoes. The presence of exotic items like conch-shell masks and ornamental shells on the northern plains, thousands of kilometres north of their origin in the Gulf of Mexico, is evidence of this movement. Overland trade routes brought obsidian and flint from the central plains and copper from the Great Lakes. Knowledge was also transported along this trade corridor, as the diffusion of ceramic technology from agricultural peoples in the south to hunting cultures in the north indicates.

One last modification in the plains economy occurred in the decades preceding the arrival of Europeans. After a 10,000-year absence from the North American plains, horses reappeared out of the southwest by the 1730s, moving from Mexico on existing intertribal trade networks along the familiar south/north axis. Their presence transformed the prairie economy in a manner analogous to the effect that automobiles have had on twentieth-century society. New concepts like animal husbandry and pastoralism accompanied the rapid spread of equestrian culture. As well, once incorporated into native commerce, the horse became an important form of currency. Mobility, personal property, and wealth all increased for some groups and individuals with the introduction of horses. Native manufacturing was the immediate beneficiary because of the constant demand for utilitarian items like saddles, bridles, and blankets. The aesthetic trades also benefited as artisans created decorative products to complement an owner's pride in his horse. Finally, horses became the cause of intertribal animosity, with warriors of one tribe raiding another tribe in search of the precious animal.

The arrival of the horse was only a harbinger of greater change. As early as 1750 an entirely new economic system – the fur trade – began to realign the indigenous economy, replacing the north/south axis with an east/west one and reorienting the traditional pursuit of game for subsistence towards an economic model characterized by exploitation. Because of geographical isolation, the Plains Algonquians were among the last aboriginal peoples to be brought into fur trade's sphere of influence. Like so much change that later proves to have radical consequences, it began innocuously enough with the arrival of products like metal pots, guns, cloth, and tobacco, and, initially at least, the quality of life for natives even improved, because natives themselves often controlled the terms and rates of exchange. Their pre-existing traditions of intertribal trade worked to their benefit, for it was often noted that they were shrewd traders who knew how to strike a bargain. They even adapted some of their traditional pursuits to take advantage of new opportunites. For example, the Ojibwa custom of harvesting wild rice was only partly for domestic use; bushels of grains also found their way into the fur-trade network. Similarly, communal buffalo hunts were modified to supply the trading posts with pemmican – meat that was dried, pulverized, and mixed with berries and grease.

By the time the fur trade finally declined in the 1870s, the cultures of the Plains Algonquians had been transformed beyond recognition. The enduring legacy of the fur trade was to leave the Indians in a state of chronic dependence that persists to the present day. Ultimately, by destroying the animal resources of their environment, it eroded not only their traditional economy but also their very way of life, forcing them to leave hunting behind for a sedentary existence on reserves.

The purpose of the treaty process was to encourage Indians to settle on reserves and adopt a farming lifestyle. Treaty 7, for example, stipulated that band members who were ready to start a farm would be given cattle, seed, and farm implements. The government also agreed to provide the natives with farm instructors. The Plains Algonquians experienced many obstacles as they embarked on this new enterprise, the greatest being government policy. The policy of "the Bible and the plow" – implemented by missionaries and Indian agents – was thought to be the key to a successful termination of "savage" ways of life. Furthermore, as agriculture became increasingly mechanized in the twentieth century, farming on native reserves remained tied to hand-tools and horse power. By explicit government direction – stemming from a desire to protect white farmers from Indian competition – reserve farmers languished in pre-industrial modes of agriculture. Indian farmers were not even at liberty to sell their crops, since strict controls were placed on the marketing of their produce. With Indian agents in charge of all trading between natives and non-natives, reserve farm produce often never arrived at market. As a result of these policies, and of the ban on homesteading off reserves and the surrender of reserve lands, Indian farming stagnated while communities surrounding the reserves succeeded.

In spite of these obstacles, some did well as farmers; indeed, the Blood became successful large-scale farmers after 1900. On some reserves, ranching became equal in importance to farming; here, again, the Blood led the way, starting a hugely successful ranching operation in the 1890s. Whether it was because of their pastoral experience with horses or the resemblance of cattle to bison, some Indian ranchers amassed large herds of cattle, and rodeos, cattle drives, and round-ups became integrated into local cultural practices. Owning a large herd of horses remained an essential display of wealth.

From the 1870s until the present, agriculture remained the mainstay of reserve economies. However, by the middle of the twentieth century, agriculture had reached its limits as a viable occupation. Increasingly, welfare replaced work and dependence supplanted self-reliance. Indian reserves became pockets of rural poverty amid the wealth created by prairie farming. Today, efforts to spur economic development and to improve the quality of life on reserves utilize sectors of commerce as diverse as service industries and entertainment. Small businesses like gas stations, convenience stores, restaurants, and laundromats are visible signs of a new entrepreneurial culture. As in the larger society, occupations tend to divide along gender lines, with men comprising the blue-collar workforce while women dominate white-collar jobs, including those in local band administration.

Language and Religion

Before the mid-nineteenth century, speakers of Blackfoot, Cree, and Ojibwa practised an oral tradition and had no formal writing system to record their words. This fact did not present an obstacle to non-verbal communication, since graphic symbols were used to augment spoken language. Various methods were available, including the petroglyphs and pictographs that are described as "rock art" and the application (by the Blackfoot and Cree) of mineral and vegetal paints on animal hides. Visions and narratives were etched on birchbark scrolls.

The diversity of languages on the plains required the use of interpreters, who often would live among the people whose language they wished to learn. Another method of communication was sign language, which was so standardized across the plains that two groups speaking different languages could communicate with each other. At times, when distance made speech impractical, signs were a logical alternative, especially if stealth was required.

In the nineteenth century, missionaries working with Cree and Ojibwa speakers, such as the Methodist James Evans, developed a syllabic orthography based on a phonetic construct of vowel/consonant pairs. Their initial motivation was to translate religious texts into the native languages. Later, this goal expanded to the more general objective of literacy. Blackfoot, Cree, and Ojibwa can be, and have been, written using standard Roman orthography.

As the number of native speakers declines with each new generation, owing to assimilationist pressures and to external influences like mass communications and media, aboriginal peoples are faced with the real prospect that their languages – including Plains Algonquian languages – may become extinct. In response to this threat, schools, which once had actively suppressed native languages, offer native-language courses as part of the regular curriculum, with Indian linguists bringing their expertise to the classroom. It is common to see instruction in Ojibwa, and post-secondary institutions, like the University of Calgary, offer courses in Cree and Blackfoot.

Native peoples have adopted other methods in the cause of preserving their culture. Even media such as television and radio, which have been the cause of so much cultural erosion, have surfaced as instruments for language retention; for example, Bullhorn Productions, on the Blood reserve in Alberta, produces videos in Blackfoot. Along the same lines, community newspapers have been launched to disseminate information and provide a forum for local concerns. Journals like *Kainai News* on the Blood reserve or the magazine *Tawow* (1970–), published in Saskatchewan, appeal directly to an Indian constituency. They also employ English as the lingua franca so that their audience is not limited to natives. Attempts have been made to include syllabics in print form; however, they have not been able to rival the popularity of roman orthography.

In terms of religious beliefs, narratives describing the origin of the world and its people are contained in the oral traditions of the Plains Ojibwa, Blackfoot, and Plains Cree. These stories were committed to the memories of individuals and recited only during the winter when long periods of inactivity were common. As entertainment they provided distraction, but as history they answered the more compelling desire to understand the mystery and reason of existence. Although the origin myths vary among the cultures, their remarkable similarity carries another echo of relatedness.

The primordial world of legend was inhabited by fantastic creatures that had miraculous powers. Humans were not yet a part of creation, although the cultural heroes of each of the three Plains Algonquian peoples, Naapii, Nanabush, and Wisahkecahk, certainly were active. For a variety of reasons, the original world was flooded with water. The only creatures capable of surviving were those whose natural habitat was aquatic. Thus, along with the cultural heroes mentioned, the beaver, otter, and muskrat appeared as central characters in the quest for dry land. As the stories of each of the peoples go, the mammals were persuaded to dive into the water, convinced that the hero could make a continent from a handful of mud. First, the beaver made several attempts, returning each time, exhausted, with only water in his webbed paws. Next, the otter tried and, after several failed attempts, admitted that he, too, was stymied. Finally, the muskrat was given his turn, but his small size and limited strength forecasted his failure. Undaunted, the muskrat made his attempt. Initially unsuccessful, he made one last try and was gone for so long that the others feared his demise. Indeed, the last dive nearly cost him his life, but, as his exhausted body was pulled from the water, he unfurled his paw, revealing precious dirt.

The hero needed no more than this tiny sample. With his magical powers he blew across the grains and instantly they began growing. At first a small patch of land floated on the surface, but when the hero blew again the island grew more. Repeating this action, he caused the land to grow until it reached the dimensions of a continent. Elated with their success, the tiny band of heroes proceeded across the new land. It was at this time that the landscape was sculpted into mountains, plains, and valleys. Rivers were etched into the land and ponds grew into lakes. Forests were created from the driftwood of the previous world and grasslands were made anew.

Since the flood had destroyed everything, new animals had to be created. With alacrity the hero set to work shaping figures from the newly formed earth. He breathed into the mouth of each animal to let it share the spirit of breath. In this way, mammals, reptiles, and birds came into being. The hero marvelled at the variety inhabiting this new world, but creation still felt incomplete. While meditating, he discovered the source of his discontent and proceeded with his final act of creation, forming some clay in his own image and breathing into it. The inert mud stirred to life and the first man gained awareness. Likewise, the first woman was made from clay and only then did creation feel complete.

While no formal form of religious practice existed among the Plains Algonquians, both the community and the individual participated in numerous rituals. The main communal ceremony was the annual Sun Dance, which was held to coincide with midsummer. Personal ritualism centred on the stages experienced in the progression through life. In all aspects of ritual, prayer was crucial to spiritual fulfilment. Holy people, or shamans, conducted ceremonies and guided the participants through the intricacies of ritual.

Spirituality among the Plains Algonquians could accommodate outside elements. Its flexibility was illustrated by its response to the appearance of horses on the plains during the pre-contact period. The Blackfoot regarded the presence of horses as a gift from the Water spirit or the Thunder beings, while the Peigan described horses as the last creation of Naapii, the Blackfoot culture hero, before he left the people. Horse societies, along with their accoutrements of songs and rituals, appeared as these animals entered the sacred realm of dreams and visions. The Blackfoot expressed their reverence for horses by making room for them in their spiritual lives, independent of the Europeans who introduced them.

The world of the Plains Algonquians was saturated with spirits; they were the agents that held the universe together, existing on a gradient from the omnipotent Great Spirit to the ordinary ghosts of deceased people. A range of entities, with varying degrees of power, were the cause of change on a minor or grand scale, or they could intervene in the personal lives of individuals. All people strived to have encounters with spirits, and shamans specialized in mediating contact between them. Spiritual life within the community was not gender-exclusive, although certain rituals, like the vision quest, were more commonly practised by men than by women.

Individual spirituality was preoccupied with dreams and visions. Dreams presented the opportunity for direct contact with spirits by creating an avenue into the spirit world; encountering a deceased relative while awake was a dreaded possibility that inspired fear, but in the dreamtime the dreamer's spirit met these disembodied souls as equals, thus negating any haunting experience. The spirits would enter the dreams of their living kin either just to visit or to transmit vital information. There was a random quality associated with these dreams, since the dreamer could not anticipate or control the encounters.

Visions, on the other hand, were deliberate attempts to contact the realm of spirits, to gain their insights, or to seek their counsel. During stressful times individuals sought certainty through visions and, with single-minded intent, purposely welcomed visitations. Receiving spiritual wisdom was accomplished through deprivation and exposure to the elements. Isolation from physical comfort expanded the limits of awareness, and, in this lucid state of dreaming without sleep, the seeker became receptive to the influences of spirits. Spiritual entities, for their part, would take pity on these vulnerable people and approach them to relieve their pain and suffering.

Seeking visions in times of distress was only one facet of this dialogue with spirits. The coming of age of an individual had its own ritual significance, and here spirit helpers again played an integral role. Vision quests were a rite of passage for adolescent youths. The candidate was cleansed in a ritual sweatbath and smudged with sweetgrass. Then, he or she was sequestered until discovered by a sympathetic spirit. Again, fasting and deprivation intensified the perceptions and allowed the individual to see past the limits of everyday reality. Spirit helpers, in this instance, dispensed guidance through visual representations and gifts of songs, prayers, personal adornments, and objects of power. Interpretation of the vision by an elder was necessary, since the meaning contained therein was often disguised in allegory. Intense, life-long relationships developed between dreamer and guide that were the source of personal strength during moments of crisis.

The Sun Dance, as it is referred to by anthropologists, was a uniquely plains ceremony and was practised in one form or another by all resident cultures. Common traits included a ceremonial lodge made of cottonwoods and with a sacred centre pole; thirst and abstinence from food and water; a sponsor fulfilling a vow; offerings to the sun; and ritual torture. The appearance of the ceremonial lodge is reminiscent of the buffalo pounds: traps constructed as circular enclosures with a centre pole, but without the rafters. Indeed, buffalo were a recurring theme in the Sun Dances, their presence marked by items such as a painted buffalo skull used as an altar and songs and dances dedicated to buffalo spirits.

Cree and Ojibwa Sun Dances were more similar to each other than they were to the Blackfoot celebration. In the Blackfoot tradition, a woman was the main sponsor, while a man performed the same function among the Cree and Ojibwa. An additional element, for the Cree and Ojibwa, was the invitation to thunderbird spirits to alight on a nest supported by the centre pole. Thirst was a necessary part of the ceremony and could be quenched by rainwater. The Blackfoot did not call on thunderbird spirits and, because drinking water during the day was thought to induce rain, it was prohibited. However, during the night the ban was relaxed. Active participants were also expected to refrain from eating, and a general feast, or exchange of food, officially brought the ceremony to its conclusion. The offering to the Sun was common to all three groups and generally took the form of bolts of coloured cloth tied to the centre pole.

Sacrifice was integral to the Sun Dance, and its manifestation took the form of abstinence from food or water, or of ritual torture. The latter involved individuals who had made a vow or were being initiated into a society. They would have their bodies pierced on the chest and upper back and thongs would be set into the cuts. The front thongs were fastened to the centre pole and the rear ones to a buffalo skull. In time to drumbeats and singing, the people would dance towards the pole and then away, repeating the movement four times. All the while they would blow on a whistle made from a hollow bird bone. At the conclusion of their dance they would pull until the thongs broke free from the centre pole.

This ceremony so outraged religious and government officials of Canada in the 1880s that it was officially proscribed. Indian agents at various plains reserves tried replacing it with sports days and other secular events. Through the period of its prohibition, which lasted until 1951, there were attempts by Indians to revive it, and in some instances it was practised in secret. When at last the restriction was lifted, the Sun Dance did not emerge in its original form, nor was it practised at all at its former locales. Many elements of the ceremony had changed; some were omitted, others forgotten, or the practition-ers simply died. Although the evolution of the Sun Dance continues, its central theme remains intact. It is a communal religious ceremony integral to cultural identity and a symbol of the vitality of Plains Algonquian culture.

During the mid- to late-nineteenth century, a new wave of religious belief – Christianity – spread across the northern plains. The region was a popular destination for missionaries of all faiths. The objective of missionary work was to bring Christian civilization to a people deemed to be heathen, but, once established on Indian reserves, the churches developed a collaborative relationship with government and had the coercive powers of the state at their disposal. Often they became the eyes and ears of government and implemented its policies.

Catholic, Methodist, and Anglican missionaries enjoyed a near-monopoly of the mission field until the mid-twentieth century, when competing groups sent another wave of missionaries onto the re-serves. Since the 1960s denominations like the Latter-Day Saints and evangelical and charismatic movements such as the Full Gospel Church and Baha'i have enjoyed some success in converting reserve residents. In some communities, numerous religious groups are active (seven in the case of the Peigan, Blood, and Blackfoot reserves). As in the larger society, Indians have also begun to embrace "New Age" sects and cults, and many have abandoned all religion. In 1991 Statistics Canada reported that 14 percent of Indians chose the "no religion" option on the census form.

Group Maintenance

The displacement of the Plains Algonquians' traditional lifestyle has not diminished their capacity to express their ancestral cultural traditions, nor has it limited their ability to adopt new customs. This is best represented by the "powwow," which became the symbol of Indian pride in the late twentieth century. Prior to 1955 there had never been such events on the Canadian plains, but the Peigan imported the festival from their relatives, the Blackfoot of Montana, hosting the first "Indian Days" at their village of Brocket, Alberta. Their only objective in holding this annual event was to invite other communities to pitch their tipis in a camp circle and to join in the dancing and singing. Since then, the powwow has grown beyond all expectations, celebrated in Plains Algonquian communities in the prairie provinces and beyond. As a cross-cultural experience, it is a common thread that binds disparate groups together.

There is no all-encompassing culture to which Plains Algonquians adhere; instead, there are elements that each group shares. Change and continuity are two themes present in the archaeological record, and they are present today as well. The Plains Algonquians observe the traditions of their ancestors, but they are amenable to innovation. Some communities may cling to rituals and ceremonies that reverberate with ancient spirituality, but that does not mean they are static and incapable of change – rather, it testifies to the solid foundations of their sense of identity. The Plains Algonquians partake in an ancient culture while being full participants in a modern society.

FURTHER READING

The archaeological data that describe the physical environment and material culture of the plains appear in scholarly journals like *Plains Anthropologist*, the *Canadian Journal of Archaeology*, and *American Antiquity*. Occasional papers like *Dog Days in Southern Alberta* (Edmonton, 1986) examine specific regions in greater detail. The early natural environment of the Plains Indians is portrayed in R.C. Harris, ed., *Historical Atlas of Canada: From the Beginning to 1800* (Toronto, 1987), which brings together the expertise of researchers in history, ethnology, and archaeology.

The languages of the Plains Algonquians have been studied by several scholars. D.G. Franz analyses Blackfoot language in *Blackfoot Grammar* (Toronto, 1991), and, in collaboration with a native speaker, N.J. Russell, he has produced an English/Blackfoot dictionary, *Blackfoot Dictionary of Stems, Roots, and Affixes* (Toronto, 1989). G.L. Piggott and A. Grafstein's *An Ojibwa Lexicon* (Ottawa, 1983) is a technical examination of the Ojibwa language prepared for linguists. H.C. Wolfart and J.F. Carroll also have been active in Cree language studies; they are authors of an accessible guide, *Meet Cree: A Guide to the Cree Language* (Edmonton, 1973).

Ethnographic and historical material generated by people active in the fur trade is reproduced by the Champlain Society in two volumes: *Journals and Letters of Pierre Gaultier de Varennes de La Vérendrye and His Sons ...* (Toronto, 1927) and *David Thompson Narrative, 1784–1812*, edited by J.B. Tyrell (Toronto, 1916). Missionaries like J.D. McLean who lived among the Plains Algonquians also committed their reflections to print; see, for example, McLean's *The Indians: Their Manners and Customs* (Toronto, 1889). Literate natives published works as well, such as *The Traditional History and Character Sketches of the Ojibwa Nation* (London, 1850; repr. Toronto, 1972) by George Copway (Kahgegagahbowh). Some ethnographic work on the Blackfoot was published by the American Bureau of Ethnology, including J.C. Ewers, *The Horse in Blackfoot Indian Culture* (Washington, D.C., 1955).

The experience of the Plains Algonquians in the fur trade is studied in A.J. Ray, *Indians in the Fur Trade* (Toronto, 1974). Sarah Carter's *Lost Harvests* (Montreal, 1990) and H. Buckley's *From Wooden Ploughs to Welfare* (Montreal, 1992) examine the failure of government policy on prairie Indian reserves. An important thesis by D.G. Mandelbaum, "Plains Cree: An Ethnographic, Historical, and Comparative Study" (University of Regina, 1979), explores the customs of the Plains Cree. Recently, some native people have published their own intepretations of their traditional culture: for example, P. Bullchild in *The Sun Came Down* (San Francisco, 1985).

P. Brizinski has contributed an important volume on native studies in Canada, *Knots in a String* (Saskatoon, 1993), while A.D. McMillan, *Native Peoples and Cultures in Canada: An Anthropological Overview* (Vancouver, 1995), includes a section on the Plains Algonquians.

3

ALGONQUIANS / SUBARCTIC

Joan A. Lovisek

Identification and Historical Overview

The Algonquian-speaking peoples of the Subarctic occupy a region of almost three million square kilometres, extending from the coast of Labrador to the Peace River, in Alberta. The northern boundary corresponds with the coniferous treeline while the southern boundary is variable, spanning the lower St Lawrence River and the northern Great Lakes and extending west to include Rainy River, Lake of the Woods, Lake Winnipeg, and the northern prairies to the North Saskatchewan River. The pre-contact population was sparse and has been estimated at between 30,000 and 35,000.

The Subarctic Algonquians were known historically by several names but generally have been identified as the Cree, Ojibwa, Montagnais, and Nascapi. Innu is now used to describe both Montagnais- and Nascapi-speaking peoples. Based upon environmental adaptations, historical experience, and linguistic affinity, the Subarctic Algonquians can be divided into several groups known as the Innu, James Bay Cree, Moose Cree, Western Woodland Cree, Northern Ojibwa, and Saulteaux. Though these divisions are somewhat arbitrary, each group views itself as distinct.

Linguistically, the Subarctic Algonquian speakers (Innu, James Bay Cree, Moose Cree, and Western Woodland Cree) are bounded in the north by the Inuit, in the northwest by the Na-Dene, in the southwest by the Blackfoot (Plains Algonquian) and Siouans, in the southeast by Eastern Algonquians, and in the south by the Ojibwa (Central Algonquians). The Ojibwa (Northern Ojibwa and Saulteaux) are bounded to the south by other Central Algonquian peoples and to the southwest by Siouans.

Archaeological and biological evidence supports the theory that the Subarctic Algonquians made successive migrations from Siberia via the Bering Strait, across a now submerged land. For their part, Subarctic Algonquians have their own beliefs and traditions concerning how they came to be in the subarctic; these beliefs and traditions are founded in rich oral creation stories and translate into a spiritual and economic attachment to their lands.

Before contact with Europeans, the Subarctic Algonquians occupied enormous areas of the boreal forest, characterized by little diversity in animal species and extreme fluctuations in their populations. Exhibiting a basic uniformity in technical and social culture, and similarities in languages, they relied for their livelihood on fishing and hunting large game animals such as moose and caribou and small game such as beaver, muskrat, hare, squirrel, and porcupine. These provided not only food and clothing but raw materials (bones, antlers) used in the manufacture of tools such as needles, awls, spears, fishhooks, and bowstrings, as well as skins for housing. Since game and fish were subject to random and irregular population cycles and spawning periods, many Subarctic Algonquians were transient. Population varied depending upon how plentiful resources were at a given time and how easily they could be taken. Fishing sites not only provided food but were locations of social and ceremonial importance, permitting large concentrations of peoples. Cross-cousin marriage – the marriage of children of siblings of opposite sex – was practised to maintain social connections between dispersed groups and over generations. The Saulteaux, located in the southern rim of the Subarctic, established a more diversified economy which included agriculture, wild rice harvesting, fishing, hunting, and trapping.

The Subarctic Algonquians developed an economic pattern that was typically subarctic in nature: fluid seasonal coalescence and dispersion which served social, ceremonial, and economic requirements. Social relations were dominated by ties of kinship, which revolved around the nuclear and the extended family. The division of labour between men and women was not rigid, since each could do the work of the other. A dependence upon migratory food sources limited the development of territorial ownership and political organization. The latter was characterized by informal leadership by individuals who were able to demonstrate hunting ability and wisdom. A skilled and generous hunter made critical decisions concerning locations to find game and to camp. Personal autonomy, however, was paramount for all groups, and was expressed in a strong ethic of self-sufficiency and independence. Religious practices were embedded in hunting activity and included the shaking-tent rite, in which a shaman conversed with the spirit world in a specially constructed lodge, careful respect for the disposal of bones, and ceremonial drumming. The Saulteaux and some Cree groups participated in a healing and religious organization called the Midewiwin, in which members acquired healing skills through personal initiation and instruction.

There is no evidence that the Subarctic Algonquians lost their traditional methods of tool technology or their economic effectiveness after contact with Europeans in the seventeenth century, although the introduction of trade goods had a significant impact on settlement and warfare. Large-game hunting was initially aided by fur-trade goods such as muskets, knives, axes, and ice chisels. In the boreal forest, however, early muskets were less efficient than native bows and arrows. Reloading was slow, firing mechanisms failed in cold weather, ammunition was expensive and restricted to posts, the muskets frequently required repair, and malfunctioning often resulted in deadly accidental shootings. European technology, particularly guns and steel traps, contributed to the over-trapping of fur-bearing animals and the depletion of other natural resources.

By the nineteenth century, the influx of trade goods and ecological pressures had contributed to a large reduction in the size of caribou populations, which in turn resulted in an economic shift to increased trapping and dependence on small game animals and fish. Many Subarctic Algonquian groups responded to diminished caribou populations by alternating between hunting large game and trapping more sedentary species. Simultaneously, and indeed throughout their encounter with Europeans, the Subarctic peoples were exposed to diseases, especially smallpox, measles, and alcoholism, that also contributed to significant population decline.

The trade monopoly held by the Hudson's Bay Company (HBC) beginning in the mid-seventeenth century encouraged a sedentary settlement pattern in which the location of trading posts became central to Subarctic Algonquian settlement and social organization. This facilitated the work of Christian missionaries, who began religious instruction among some Subarctic Algonquians such as the

Innu in the seventeenth century. Not all groups accepted Christianity: among the Saulteaux of Rainy River, Christianity was proscribed until the late nineteenth century. Increasingly, the Subarctic Algonquians were confined to settlements and reserves through various treaties and, at the same time, the adoption of European practices and ideas together with large-scale economic development (mining, logging, and hydroelectric projects) in their former territories eroded their egalitarian social system and traditional economic activities.

In the twentieth century, there were fewer opportunities for economic independence in the welfare system than there had been in the fur trade; prolonged dependence on welfare and temporary employment forced many out of their communities for long periods to seek wages. Welfare dependence, along with the residential school system, seriously undermined the social fabric of aboriginal society, and, in the midst of these conditions, the task of holding communities together often became the responsibility solely of women.

Informal native leadership had been replaced in the nineteenth century by elected chiefs and councillors under the regime of the Indian Act. During the 1970s and 1980s many groups were able to assume greater control over the management of their local affairs and the development of their economic resources. Today, band councils and tribal councils provide the political structure for community action.

Innu

The Innu speak two Cree dialects, Nascapi and Montagnais, and number approximately 15,000, of whom approximately 2,000 live in Labrador and the remainder in Quebec. The Innu of Quebec reside in ten settlements: Quiatchouan (Montagnais du Lac Saint-Jean); Les Escoumins (Montagnais de les Escoumins); Pessamiu (Betsiamites); Montagnais de Pakuat Shipu (Saint-Augustin); Uashat (Sept Îles; Uashat mak Maniutenam); Ekuanitshu (Mingan); Nutashkuan (Montagnais de Natashquan); Uanaman-shipu (Montagnais de La Romaine); Maimekush (Montagnais de Schefferville); and Kawawachekamach (about nine kilometres from Schefferville, also known as Fort Chimo Nascapi). The Labrador Innu live primarily in two communities, North West River (Sheshatshui) and Davis Inlet (Utshimassit). The largest communities are Montagnais du Lac Saint-Jean, which had a population of 3,979 in 1993, and Betsiamites, with 2,722. Montagnais de Pakuat Shipu (Saint-

Augustin) is one of the smallest Innu communities, whose population numbered only 213 in 1993.

The name "Innu" means "human being" and is used by Innu to distinguish themselves from Inuit and other non-Innu. They regard themselves as a distinct people who inhabit *Nitassinan*, "our land." Innu see themselves not as belonging to discrete bands but as part of a fluid population. Those who inhabit the heavily wooded southern parts of their territory closer to the St Lawrence River and Gulf drainage system have been called Montagnais or "Mountaineers" by the French. Nascapi is a derogatory term meaning "uncivilized" and was inappropriately applied to the northeastern Innu who inhabit the tundra of the North Atlantic and Ungava Bay drainage area. The words Nascapi and Montagnais, however, are still used to distinguish two of the three dialects of Eastern Cree. The Nascapi dialect is spoken by the Schefferville and Davis Inlet Innu; the remaining Innu communities speak the Montagnais dialect. For many Innu, French is an accepted second language.

Innu prehistory is poorly known and controversial. Their territory was occupied by a hunting people adapted to both marine and land animals. The Innu may have had a maritime culture before being forced inland by Thule/Inuit people and may have been linked to the now-extinct Beothuk; their socio-economic system focused on big-game hunting, sealing, fishing, and trapping. Some time before contact, the Innu may have moved into the Subarctic as a result of Iroquois expansion into the Gulf of St Lawrence. As a non-horticultural people they were mobile, and extensive territoriality was an important feature of their economic system. The Innu were likely one of the first Subarctic Northern Algonquians to come into contact with Europeans, perhaps meeting the Jacques Cartier expedition in 1534. It is also likely they had encountered and traded with earlier Europeans such as the Basques, if not the Norse. Groups of up to 1,500 were reported to have met European ships for trade. At this time, the Innu have been estimated to number 4,000 people. After contact in the sixteenth century, the Innu became dependent upon new technologies such as muskets, powder, and shot, which intensified their intertribal warfare with the Iroquois and the Inuit. Trading vessels from Europe gradually contributed to the redirection of the Innu's seasonal movements towards the Gulf of St Lawrence.

The Montagnais-speaking Innu had a diverse economy based upon eels caught in the fall from the St Lawrence River, porcupine, bear, beaver, waterfowl, and caribou. Their hunting territories extended south across the St Lawrence River, and they participated in a regional trade with agricultural peoples such as the Abenaki, from whom they had access to cornmeal and tobacco. They traded these goods to Nascapi-speaking Innu, following trade routes and protocols established before contact. The Nascapi-speaking Innu relied to a larger extent on the hunting of caribou on the barren lands in the Ungava Bay region.

Innu settlement was characterized by extensive movement coinciding with seasonal cycles and community membership. This pattern was inimical to efficient fur trapping and to later attempts by missionaries to foster sedentary settlement. As trade goods became important to the Innu, however, seasonal cycles were modified to include visits to the fur-trade posts. The trade monopoly held by the HBC encouraged a process whereby the location of trading posts became important to Innu settlement and social organization. As the posts diminished in number and relocated to the coast, the Innu reorganized into much larger groups near the posts, thereby decreasing the size and number of bands. By the mid-twentieth century, large centres of permanent populations had emerged at Betsiamites on the St Lawrence, Schefferville (Innu were relocated there from Fort Mackenzie in 1947), Sept-Îles, and Happy Valley, near the Goose Bay air base on Hamilton Inlet.

The seventeenth-century Innu were organized in multi-family lodges housing between ten and twenty people. Several lodges composed larger winter bands of between thirty-five and seventy-five people. Membership was flexible within the groups and exogamy was usually matrilocal in nature, the husband joining his wife's group. The hunting group was the central socio-economic unit. Women worked with leather to make clothes, snowshoes, containers, and coverings, while men were specialists in wood work, including the making of canoes, toboggans, wooden utensils, and frames for snowshoes.

Innu social organization was undermined by the fur trade, as sudden wealth inundated local bands. The effects of the fur trade were mixed: trade goods may have arbitrarily created a dependence of the women on male heads of households and may also have intensified polygamy as a means of securing additional labourers for the processing of furs. Within the fur trade economy, women trapped for furs and prepared hides but men controlled the exchange of goods. The gradual adoption of European ways increasingly displaced the equality that had formerly prevailed in the economic roles of men and women.

A skilled and generous hunter who could acquire influence and a following became a leader, a *wotshimao*, and made critical decisions concerning locations to find game and to camp. Good hunters tended to be polygamous, since having more than one spouse indicated a hunter's ability to provide surplus meat. Rites of passage for men were closely tied to hunting ability. Personal autonomy, however, was paramount for the Innu, and it was reflected in a strong ethic of self-sufficiency and independence. The Innu saw themselves as part of a seamless creation that included humans and non-humans alike. Caribou were the centre of a religious ceremony called the *mokoshan*, a communal sacred feast which involved the use of caribou marrow and long bones to honour the spirits of the slain animals, as well as to avert and cure sickness. The best hunters were recognized during the feast and awarded guardianship over the bones. Hunting was a sacred act which required the wearing of elaborate painted ceremonial robes of caribou skin.

Some Innu, whose participation in the early fur-trade economy had declined with the growing depletion of fur-bearing animals, became attracted to Catholic missions near the St Lawrence River. They subsequently joined colonies such as that established in 1638 at Sillery, Quebec, which is often described as the first reserve in Canada. Missionaries, however, did not have major success until the mid-1800s, when many Montagnais-speaking Innu began converting to Anglicism and Roman Catholicism.

Religious observances were often mixed, incorporating both traditional and Christian concepts. The Roman Catholic Church became influential among the Innu of the St Lawrence and the eastern part of Labrador. Although the church discouraged first-cousin marriage, which would have included cross-cousin marriage (the marriage of children of siblings of opposite sex), and promoted farming over hunting, the absence of regular priests permitted the Innu to merge Christian and Innu religious beliefs.

After the 1920s reduction in the Labrador caribou herd forced the Innu to move into clustered camps in Voisey's Bay, south of Nain, a change marked by disease, starvation, and an increasing dependence upon government. Later, with the Hudson's Bay Company's closing of its small interior posts in the 1940s, the Innu concentrated their trading at select coastal communities such as Sheshatshui. New-foundland's entry into Confederation in 1949 had a profound impact on its Innu population, who now came under the control of the province. Since Newfoundland's game laws are among the most re-strictive in Canada, the Innu risked arrest every time they hunted. As the Innu found their land arbitrarily severed by Newfoundland and Quebec boundaries, they were further subjugated to legislation by both provinces that overrode their hunting and trapping rights.

The Innu were forced onto reserves in the 1950s to make way for large-scale industrial development, and by 1971 most Innu had moved into inferior government-built houses in settlements with inadequate sanitation. At the same time, beginning in the 1960s and continuing to the present, Innu territory has been sought for logging, mining, and hydroelectric development. Many Innu have entered a cash economy in conjunction with neighbouring Inuit and non-Innu, though fur trapping, fishing, and hunting are still important. Income derived from commercial fishing on the coast for cod, salmon, and arctic char, trapping of mink, otter, and foxes, and the sale of mocca-sins and snowshoes is supplemented by wage labour and social as-sistance. The traditional ethic of sharing has been undermined in the context of a wage economy and social assistance, for wages and welfare payments, unlike caribou meat, are not shared. Increased access to medical aid and dependable food supplies, however, have contributed to an increase in Innu population.

Innu artistic achievements are closely associated with spirituality, and hunting plays an important role. Innu women excelled in arts, con-verting animal and plant materials into sacred objects, including spe-cial embroidered cloaks and game bags used for hunting. Handmade moccasins and mittens are still worn today or sold to non-Innu. Story-telling remains a valued aspect of Innu culture, and it helps to close what has become an enlarging generational gap between children and elders. The Innu still make sweat lodges and use ceremonial clothes to hunt.

By the 1970s most Innu children were in school, where they were taught by non-Innu who deprecated their culture and language. Innu parents were denied social assistance if their children did not attend school. Today, the situation is somewhat better. Some teacher's aids are Innu, and a restructuring of the school system is being encouraged to accommodate the spring and fall hunts. Increasingly, as well, Innu women are playing a major role in the education of their children and in literacy programs.

Still, enormous problems remain. The suicide rate in northern Labrador is seventeen times the national average. Many Innu also suffer from alcohol addiction. The Innu believe that this type of self-destructive behaviour was unknown until the mid-twentieth century, when they began to lose control over their lands. They have increasingly turned to native healing to resolve these problems and have sought assistance from native-healing organizations across Canada. At the same time, they have organized politically. The early 1970s witnessed the establishment of three Innu political entities: the Conseil Attikameg-Montagnais in Quebec, the Nascapi Montagnais Innu Association in Labrador (now known as the Innu Nation), and the Nascapi of Schefferville. The last group was excluded from the James Bay Agreement in 1975, but it negotiated a separate agreement in 1978, known as the Northeastern Quebec Agreement, which granted it a new village (Kawawachikamach) and the right to local government.

A later piece of legislation, the 1984 Cree-Mascepi Act, recognized the native right of self-government and established a system of land management. The Labrador Innu, through the Innu Nation, began land-claims negotiations with the federal and provincial governments in July 1991. A framework agreement was signed on 29 March 1996, whereby the parties agreed to link self-government and land-claims negotiations. Talks regarding self-government began in May 1996, and a framework agreement was signed that October. In 1998, negotiations over a final agreement were still under way.

The Innu received worldwide attention for their protests against the building in 1979 of a North Atlantic Treaty Organization (NATO) air base at Goose Bay, Labrador. A few years later, in 1988, the Innu invaded the air base to protest low-level flights which threatened to decimate animal populations and end their hunting culture. Hundreds of Innu were arrested. Further protests followed, but in February 1996, after an environmental-review process from which the Innu withdrew on the ground that it was biased, the federal government and NATO signed a new agreement that allowed low-level flight training. Innu Nation president Peter Penashue denounced the government for ignoring the "rights and interests of Aboriginal people by entering into arrangements that alienate our lands and make it hard for us to practice our traditional lifestyle on the land." Notwithstanding this defeat, the campaign against NATO flights – an effort led by elders and women – has given the Innu a new sense of direction as they reassert their ownership over their lands and their identity as a people.

.The Innu have also been active on another front. On 20 August 1997 more than 250 Innu and Inuit protestors blocked construction of a road and airstrip designed to service a proposed mining development at Voisey's Bay, Labrador. The Newfoundland Court of Appeal granted an injunction to the Labrador Inuit Association against the Voisey's Bay Nickel Company, halting construction until the court had an opportunity to hear an appeal of another court decision allowing the work to proceed. At this point, the company decided to suspend construction and to enter into negotiations with the Innu and Inuit. The Innu position is clear: as Innu Nation president Katie Rich has put it, "Any development on our land must be done on our terms, with our consent."

Still another political battle has been waged by the Nascapi-speaking Innu of Davis Inlet. Innu settled on the Labrador coast in the twentieth century. Although more removed from contact with Europeans than the Montagnais-speaking Innu, at the beginning of the twentieth century they moved south to the St Lawrence River or to the Atlantic coast to winter near white settlements. Nascapi-speaking Innu also regularly congregated in the warmer months with the James Bay Cree at large interior lakes draining into the St Lawrence River, Hudson Bay, or Davis Inlet. Many Nascapi-speaking Innu remained largely independent of the fur trade, concentrating instead on the hunting of large game.

The Nascapi-speaking Innu of Labrador were forced to relocate to a post on the coast near Davis Inlet after a failed caribou migration in 1916. These Davis Inlet Innu originally consisted of two separate communities, one at Davis Inlet and the other on the adjacent barren grounds, but the two groups merged in 1924 as a result of the ministrations of a Roman Catholic priest. Because of their split residence on the coast and the barren grounds, two forms of community life emerged. The Innu on the barren grounds continued to hunt and maintain traditional social values, while those in the coastal settlement experienced the social disruption associated with twentieth-century reserve life. Following the controversy triggered in 1993 by the attempted suicide of six children, the federal and provincial governments entered into negotiations with the Innu over a proposed relocation. The Innu themselves were anxious to end their isolation in

Davis Inlet, which is 300 kilometres distant by air from the closest Innu settlement and hospital. Negotiations proceeded slowly, however, concluding only in November 1996 with the signing of the Mushuau Innu Relocation Agreement. Under this agreement, the Davis Inlet Innu are to be moved to the community of Natuashish (Little Sango Pond) on the mainland, where they will have a land base of about 2,000 hectares and services equivalent to those of other aboriginal peoples in Canada. The relocation is to take about five years. According to Katie Rich, the agreement "is a great achievement for all our people, but especially for the Elders who have been struggling for thirty years to build a better future."

James Bay Cree

The territory of the James Bay Cree includes the coast and drainage systems of Hudson Bay and James Bay from Lac Guillaume-Delisle to Rupert's Bay. Today, they number approximately 12,000 people; their pre-contact population is unknown. Neighbours to the Innu, Central Algonquians, and Inuit, they reside in ten settlements in Quebec on the east side of James Bay, many of which were formerly trading posts, including Waskaganish (Rupert House), Wemindji (Paint Hills, Old Factory), Eastmain, Wahpmagoostui (Great Whale River), Chisasibi (Fort George), and inland communities at Nemaska, Mistassini, Waswanipi, and Oujé-Bougoumou.

Linguistically, there are significant dialectical differences between the James Bay Cree and the Moose and Swampy Cree located on the western side of James Bay in Ontario, and there is also little historical evidence of close kinship ties between the two groups. However, in the 1950s some James Bay Cree emigrated to the Moose Factory area, where they established a community on lands belonging to the Anglican Church and are now known as the Mocreebec First Nation. Competition over trapping and hunting areas with the Moose Cree has contributed to intense hostility between the groups. Today, the Mocreebec, with 400 people, comprise the majority of a community residing between Moose Factory and Moosonee. In 1993 James Bay Cree communities ranged in size from over 300 at Nemaska to more than 3,000 at Mistassini (which includes Oujé-Bougoumou). With the exception of some elders, most Cree are bilingual, speaking their own language and either English or French. Cree is the language spoken in the home and in important community discussions.

Parts of the James Bay region were inhabited 5,000 years ago, and archaeological evidence indicates that the proto-Cree maintained regular contact with southern peoples. Of the four groups or nations identified by the Jesuits in the 1640s, the Lake Nipigon Cree (or Alimibegouek), Nisibourounik, and Pitchibourenik resided in the East Main and Rupert River drainage basin. Since these Cree groups had trading relations with the Nipissing, they were part of a pre-contact native trade network that included the Huron and Ottawa of the Georgian Bay-French River area and that indirectly led to the introduction of European goods into Cree communities.

The James Bay region was occupied by two distinct regional groups linked by kinship and economics: the coasters, or Wiinibeyk Iiyuu ("salt water person"), and those who lived inland, or Nuuchcimiihc Iiyuu ("inland person"). Historically, there were marked differences in community organization between the two. Coasters depended to a larger degree on maritime sea mammals and later developed close relationships to fur traders; caribou was more important to the Inland Cree, who retained their independence from the fur trade until the establishment of inland fur-trade posts in the nineteenth century.

The HBC established posts at Eastmain House and Rupert House (Charles Fort) in 1668. Thereafter, many Cree became "home guards" by providing fur traders with food and supplies, especially geese, snowshoes, and canoes. They also became more dependent on fur-trade goods, and Cree women often intermarried with fur traders. The Inland Cree were traditionally organized in small-scale winter hunting groups that exploited diversified resources, including wood-land caribou, beaver, ptarmigan, fish, and hare. In contrast to the Home Guard Cree, the Inland Cree did not undergo dramatic changes in their economic or social organization as a result of the fur trade. For much of the eighteenth century, Inland Cree seldom visited the fur-trade posts located on James Bay, and, when they did, they traded for goods that could be easily transported.

Religious beliefs were spiritually connected to hunting, specifically to relations with animal spirits. Imbedded in Cree culture was respect for animal spirits and fear of the cannibalistic windigo, which was culturally expressed by conjuring and religious feasts. Although seventeenth-century Jesuit missions were influential among some Mistassini at the Chicoutimi mission, Anglican missionaries, who arrived at Fort George in 1852, were often successful in instilling the idea of a Christian God by linking it to the notion of a powerful spirit known as Manitou. Native catechists interpreted Manitou as a "master of all spirits," the conceptual equivalent of the Cree concept of a "master" of animal spirits.

Christianity was effective at Great Whale River in 1857 after missionaries introduced the syllabic system, which became an important vehicle in the transmission of Christian theology. Although the syllabic system was restricted principally to church-related reading materials, and rarely used in everyday communication, it has recently become a means of informal communication. Since the 1970s the Cree have joined Anglican, Pentecostal, Evangelical, and Roman Catholic churches, where they have been instructed mainly in English. Conversions to Christianity – and mostly to Anglicanism – are ongoing.

Missionaries and governments brought great changes to Cree communities. The last quarter of the nineteenth century was especially turbulent, since the Cree were then exposed to whooping-cough epidemics, government agents, and prospectors. The opening of Abitibi in the 1920s and the decline in fur trading in the 1940s forced the closing of posts, a development that compelled larger numbers of Cree hunting bands to assemble at the few remaining posts.

The post–World War II period saw a dramatic transformation in Cree socio-economic organization. Decreasing fur prices altered the function of the posts, which now became centres for schools, medical aid, family-allowance cheques, and subsidized housing. This further increased the number of Cree living near the posts. The villages, however, lacked a Cree identity and indeed until recently were either named after a post or operated under a federally administered band name.

Government intervention accelerated during the 1950s and 1960s through attempts to "open the north" by building railways, roads, mining operations, and pulp and paper mills. Although this economic activity created French-speaking frontier towns such as Chibougamau and Chapais, the Cree at first did not benefit to any significant degree. After the HBC post at Mistassini closed, the Cree sought wage labour but were handicapped by their lack of French. As wage labour gradually became more accessible, it replaced hunting and trapping as the economic basis of Cree communities.

Although educational instruction, primarily in English, was offered from the 1920s under Oblate missions at Fort George, it was not until the 1960s that significant numbers of Cree children attended school, usually outside the community. Some Cree kept their children out of school to educate them in bush skills; others sent their children to school only after being threatened by government with the loss of their social assistance. For decades, schooling was not adapted to Cree culture. Recently, however, a Cree school board has been established to administer Cree schools, and the curriculum has been adapted to incorporate Cree values.

A major turning-point in Cree history occurred in 1971, when the government of Quebec announced, without consultation with the Cree, that it planned to construct an enormous hydro-electric project on James Bay that would divert several major rivers in the Hudson Bay drainage area and require the construction of dams, hydro transmission-line corridors, roads, and airstrips. An ancillary benefit of the project, the government claimed, was that it would open larger areas to mining. The Cree, then numbering only about 6,000 people, reacted within a year by filing an application for a court injunction to halt work on the project. In November 1973 Judge Albert Malouf granted the injunction, noting that Cree and Inuit land rights in the area had not been extinguished. The Quebec Court of Appeal overturned this decision a week later, and the case reached the Supreme Court in December 1973. With the Supreme Court's decision to hear the appeal, pressure on the Quebec and Canadian governments to reach a settlement with the natives became intense, and on 15 November 1974 an agreement in principle was reached. The Cree – who by now had organized themselves politically with the creation of the Grand Council of the Crees (Eeyou Istchee) – ratified the agreement one month later; the Inuit followed suit in February 1976.

The James Bay and Northern Quebec Agreement, which has the status of a treaty, was the first modern land-claims agreement that recognized aboriginal rights. In exchange for opening almost all of northern Quebec to economic development, the federal and provincial governments agreed to upgrade local services to national standards and to pay monetary compensation of $150 million ($15,000 per capita). As well, the agreement recognized Cree and Inuit rights to maintain their traditional culture. About 3,500 square kilometres of land, located in and around their communities, was allocated to Cree for their exclusive use; over another category of land, amounting to 40,000 square kilometres, they were to have exclusive hunting, fishing, and trapping rights; and on a third category of land, the Cree could hunt according to a quota system in all areas except those already developed or in the course of development. Finally, the agreement extended a large degree of native self-government. Twenty-one municipalities were created (thirteen Inuit, eight Cree). The governments of these municipalities were to have control over health, education, and other local matters. To coordinate local administration, umbrella bodies such as the Cree Regional Authority, the Cree Board of Health and Social Services, the Cree School Board, and the Cree Construction Corporation were subsequently established. In addition, an Income Security Program, administered by the Cree Trappers Association, gave the Cree the power to manage wildlife and assured a guaranteed income to hunters and their families.

Over the last couple of decades, changing political relations with non-Cree have created new models of leadership which place a premium on bicultural education and which in some cases have led to new definitions of status and prestige. Economically, Cree hunters have been able to recover some of their former status in the community because of the Income Security Program. At the same time, the construction of permanent roads has improved access to hunting territories, enabling hunters to hunt from a central point rather than establishing several base camps. Hunting has also become mechanized through snowmobiles, which have made it possible for the Cree to maintain longer traplines. The Cree also outfit and train non-Cree sports hunters and are employed in large industrial companies and in small local services. Cree handicraft production has become a sizeable business: the Cree market local craft productions, including high-quality embroidered work, moccasins, snowshoes, and hunting decoys.

In the midst of the unprecedented changes introduced by technology, the Cree have been able to sustain a viable hunting economy based upon moose, beaver, fish, and geese while also managing their own language classes and cooperative stores. Since the James Bay Agreement of 1975, the Cree have moved from a society based on small villages to one that is more regional in scope and well organized politically. Today, as in the past, decisions are reached by consensus in a process coordinated by elders. The band council is the main body responsible for dealing with governments external to the Cree community.

Recently, the James Bay Cree have been active participants in the debate over Quebec secession. Concerned about their future in a sovereign Quebec, the Cree have repeatedly insisted that they have the inherent right to self-determination and accordingly that their status in Canada – specifically, their relationship to the two levels of government, federal and provincial – cannot be changed without their consent. On 24 October 1995, six days before a Quebec referendum on seccession organized by the Parti Québécois government, and following an intensive consultative process undertaken by a special commission established for the purpose, the Cree held a referendum which asked the question, "Do you consent as a people that the Government of Quebec separate the James Bay Crees and Cree traditional territory from Canada, in the event of a Yes vote in the Quebec referendum?" The results of the Cree referendum were unequivocal: 96.3 percent of those who voted answered No.

Moose Cree

Cree who speak the Moose Cree and Swampy Cree dialects number 35,000 people and live in approximately 42 mixed communities of Cree and Ojibwa in Ontario and Manitoba; in 1993 these communities ranged in size from 2,729 people at Fort Albany, Ontario, to 425 at Fort Severn, also in Ontario. Speakers of the Moose and Swampy dialects occupy principally the west coast of James Bay from the Moose River in northeastern Ontario to the Churchill River in northern Manitoba. In Ontario they reside in the following communities: Moose Factory, Kushechewan, Fort Albany, Attawapiskat, Weenusk, and Fort Severn. Communities in Manitoba include York Factory, Churchill (with Chipewyan), Fox Lake, and Shamattawa. The Cree at Moosonee and Kushechewan belong mainly to the Attawapiskat and Weenusk First Nations. The Mocreebek who reside near Moose Factory and Moosonee are originally from Quebec and speak the James Bay Cree dialect. The Cree who speak the Moose and Swampy dialects refer to themselves as *ininiw*, meaning "person."

Many Cree communities in the northern parts of Ontario are mixed communities of Ojibwa and Cree which include significant numbers of bilingual Ojibwa-Cree; some of these speak what is known as Oji-Cree, which denotes the Severn dialect of the Northern Ojibwa. Depending upon their degree of isolation, some speak English. English was not usually learned, however, until children went to school. Bilingual Cree and Ojibwa usually have English as a second language.

Until the 1720s the Cree may have derived political advantages from their middleman role between Europeans and other natives. Cree access to large quantities of trade goods, however, was restricted by the distance over which goods were transported and by the size of canoes. In any case, the establishment of HBC fur-trade posts prompted the French to move into the interior region north and west of Lake Superior from the early 1700s on, thereby undercutting the Cree's position as middlemen. The result was a gradual westward shift for some Cree (hence becoming Plains Cree), some joining the Western Woodland Cree and others joining Assiniboine and Ojibwa groups. Through pre-existing trading alliances, the Cree were able to exercise control over the economy of two regions: west of Lake Winnipeg the Cree allied with the Blackfoot beginning in the 1730s; south of Lake Winnipeg, alliances were established with the Assiniboine, Mandan Hidatsa, and Saulteaux. However, the proliferation of trade posts across the west continued, with significant consequences for the Cree. Though they still traded with whites, they modified their participation in the fur-trade economy by providing provisions to increasing numbers of fur traders, principally in the form of bison meat, grease, pemmican, wild rice, fresh game, vegetables, and fish. By 1850 the Cree's middleman monopoly was a thing of the past.

Similar to the James Bay Cree, some Cree called "Home Guards" elected to remain permanently on the Hudson Bay river mouths to service the posts. The Home Guard Cree provided food, primarily geese, as well as furs, supplies, and equipment to the fur traders, and in the process they became more dependent on traders for food and clothing, even though they provided more food to the traders than they received. The social composition of the Home Guard Cree population changed through intermarriage with traders, resulting in large mixed-blood populations. The development of trading specialists and the Home Guard created two distinct economic patterns and communities.

Though the Cree first encountered missionaries in the late seventeenth century in the form of Jesuits stationed at Fort Albany, sustained efforts to convert the Cree did not occur until the nineteenth century. One of the most active missionaries of that time was the Methodist James Evans. Travelling widely throughout the area, Evans not only spread the Christian message to traders and Cree alike, he also attempted to convert the Cree by instructing them in a system of phonetic syllabics. The system was transferred from community to community through copies on birchbark. These "talking birchbarks" that "spoke" of the Great Spirit were well received by the Cree. Although no uniform system existed across the Subarctic, and syllabics often competed with Roman orthography, syllabics has enabled the Cree to learn in their native language and to publish newspapers.

The response to Christianity by the Cree was mixed. Some adopted it and were even ordained as priests, and some were converted to Christianity without understanding it. Traditional beliefs did not disappear, for the Cree merged concepts of both belief systems. In 1842–43 a native religious movement led by the Cree prophet Abishabis spread through Cree communities between Churchill in present-day Manitoba and the Albany River in Ontario. Reflecting native distress in the face of Christian proselytization and declining economic resources, the short-lived crusade attempted to reclaim the old ways of life. By the 1930s, however, most Cree were nominal Christians. The most recent denomination to enter some Cree communities is the Pentecostal Church. At Moose Factory, Cree influences on Christianity are apparent in the establishment of the Cree Gospel Church and the Native New Life Church.

Christian missions also provided education to the Cree, initially through boarding-schools at Fort Albany (1902), at Fort Hope (1910), and in 1945 at McIntosh, Ontario, near Sioux Lookout. This form of accculturation forced Cree children from their homes and disrupted communities. Today, most Cree communities have their own elementary schools. Communications and long-distance learning are also available through the native communication service Wawatay.

The governments of Canada and Ontario entered into treaties with the Cree (and Northern Ojibwa) beginning in 1905 (Treaty 9) and ending in 1930, under which Cree ancestral lands were surrendered in exchange for reserves. Meanwhile, beginning in the 1890s, Cree communities began to have greater access to material goods from the newly constructed Canadian Pacific Railway via Wabigoon. Their isolation was further relieved in 1930 after the Ontario Northland Railway established a station at Moosonee. Since the late 1940s Cree located at York Factory (which closed in the 1950s), Winisk, and Attawapiskat have been attracted to wage labour in the larger centres of Churchill, Moosonee, Moose Factory, and Fort Albany. The construction of a radar base in 1955 at Winisk brought temporary employment but further disrupted the trapping economy. After this economic boom, the Cree returned to trapping and have developed local commercial industries in tourism, arts and crafts, and construction.

In 1973 the Cree (and Ojibwa) who signed Treaty 9 organized themselves politically into a Grand Council. Through this organization, now called the Nishnawbe-Aski Nation, the Cree maintain several community and economic programs, including treaty-rights and land-claims research, health and medical services (such as treatment for alcoholism and drug abuse), and native-leadership training. The Nishnawabe-Aski Treaty area is the largest in Ontario, covering about 650,000 square kilometres and containing 50 native communities with approximately 30,000 residents.

Western Woodland Cree

The Western Woodland Cree identify themselves as *iyiniwak*, "real or true people." Today, they reside in communities in Manitoba, Saskatchewan, and Alberta, with a population of approximately 40,000. Although their pre-contact population is not known, some research suggests a pre-contact population for the Moose, Swampy, and Woodland Cree of 20,000.

The Western Woodland Cree can be divided into separate peoples by geographical range and dialect: Swampy (Maskekowak) at Nelson River; Rocky or Missinippi Cree (Nihiawak) at Churchill River, in northwestern Manitoba; and Woods Cree (Sakaw-iyiniwak) in Saskatchewan, Alberta, and northwestern British Columbia. The Rocky or Stone Cree constitute a major branch occupying portions of northern Manitoba, Saskatchewan, and Alberta. To the north of the Western Woods Cree are the Athapaskan-speaking Chipewyan; to the east, the Swampy and Moose Cree; to the west, the Dene-Tha branch of the Beaver; and to the south, the Plains Cree.

The Western Woods Cree of Ontario live in the following communities: Brunswick House (includes Northern Ojibwa), Chapleau Cree, Constance Lake (includes Northern Ojibwa), Flying Post (includes Northern Ojibwa), Matachewan (includes Northern Ojibwa), Missanabie Cree (includes Northern Ojibwa), and New Post. In Manitoba, Western Woods Cree communities are Chemahawin, Cross Lake, Fisher River, Grand Rapids, God's Lake, Mathias Columb, Moose Lake, Nelson House, Norway House, Oxford House, Split Lake, and The Pas. The Western Woods Cree of Saskatchewan live in Canoe Lake, Cumberland House, Lac la Ronge, Peter Ballantyne, Red Earth, Shoal Lake, Sturgeon Lake, and Waterhen Lake. Alberta Western Woods Cree communities are Bigstone Cree, Driftpile, Duncans, Fort McMurray (includes Chipewyan), Grouard, Little Red River,

Lubicon Lake, Sawridge, Sturgeon Lake, Sucker Creek, Swan River, Wabasca, and Whitefish Lake.

The Western Woodland Cree of the Upper Churchill and Athabasca rivers have often been misidentified as Athapaskan. Although some Swampy Cree moved west to the Nelson River from south of Hudson Bay in the late 1700s, the Rock and Strongwoods Cree were long-time residents in the west. The Cree today are descendants of peoples who inhabited the boreal forest west of the Nelson River and Lake Winnipeg for centuries before the fur trade, and their history has been a complex one of amalgamation, migration, and relocation.

According to archaeological evidence, the Western Woodland Cree have occupied northern Manitoba since 1200 c.e. and were the original inhabitants of the Churchill drainage basin as far west as the Peace River, Alberta, since about 1400 c.e. Their western limits, however, are still debated by archaeologists. Although Cree territory was temporarily abandoned after the 1781 smallpox epidemic, by the mid-1800s the Cree had returned, as did other "Home Guards" Cree who had elected to remain near HBC posts to supply provisions to the fur traders.

Following the establishment of inland trading posts, the Cree settled along the Albany River in Manitoba and Saskatchewan with other Cree bands to become the Rock Cree, who speak the Woods Cree dialect. After 1715, they traded at the HBC's York Factory, where they were known as the Michinipi, and later, from 1717, at the Churchill post. The Cree continued to hunt throughout the period of fur-trade competition in the late eighteenth and early nineteenth centuries, focusing not only on beaver but on moose, caribou, lynx, and wolves. Women fished, collected plants, trapped small game, constructed lodges, prepared hides and pelts for clothing, cut wood, cared for children, and hauled toboggans. They also decorated clothing with elaborate floral bead and quill work.

Traditionally, Cree spiritual relationships to animals were viewed as the product of harmonious interactions between the hunter and the master spirit of each species. Some Cree believed that the spirit Kicimanitow created the earth and its inhabitants, while others believed that the earth and its inhabitants had always existed. The religious ceremonies of the Cree of the Saskatchewan River system included the Goose Dance, or Goose Feast, which symbolized the cultural importance of waterfowl to the Cree and was characterized by a sacred pipe ceremony, speeches, prayers, singing, and drumming. The purpose of Cree ceremonies was to maintain spiritual relationships of respect between Cree and the animals, which was expressed by the proper treatment of the bodies and bones of animals killed. During the early 1800s, for some groups such as the Red Earth Cree, the Goose Dance was incorporated into the Saulteaux-influenced Midewiwin ceremony. This followed an influx of Saulteaux from southern Manitoba, Ontario, and Minnesota.

The economic shift to fur trapping, particularly of non-migratory animals such as beaver, reduced the size of the hunting groups to nuclear or polygynous families during the fall and winter. Hunting groups were led informally by male leaders known as *okiamaw*, who were respected for their experience, and decisions were implemented through a process of group consensus. A hunter maintained a special place in the community, although status was also achieved as a shaman. The competitive fur-trading environment between 1760 and 1821 contributed to increased harvesting of fur-bearing animals, and the result was a gradual depletion of game and a growing dependence upon fur traders for tools and food. Compounding the Cree's difficulties was a smallpox epidemic in 1781, which forced a move southwards to the Saskatchewan River drainage basin. By the end of the century the Cree had returned north, to form new groups around trading posts.

The closing of HBC posts after the amalgamation of the HBC with the North West Company (NWC) in 1821 shifted trading west into the Saskatchewan River area and south into Cumberland House at The Pas. Posts located near fishing sites became principal gathering sites for the Cree. Encouraged by ready access to store supplies, the Cree grew increasingly sedentary. At the same time, Cree exposure to Christianity through missionaries increased after 1840. Although some groups such as the Red Earth Cree were reluctant to adopt Christianity, by 1878 many Cree had been converted. At Pelican Narrows, Saskatchewan, the majority of Cree were converted by an Oblate priest.

In the political arena, the Western Woodland Cree Elijah Harper, as a member of the Manitoba legislative assembly, generated national media coverage in 1990 by blocking ratification of the Meech Lake constitutional accord on the ground that it failed to recognize aboriginal rights. On another front, the cause of the Lubicon Cree of northern Alberta has attracted nation-wide attention over the last decade. Overlooked when Treaty 8 was drawn up, the Lubicon have been struggling for more than fifty years for recognition of their rights, an effort that intensified after oil and gas development began on their lands in 1979. In protest against such incursions, as well as against their lack of a reserve and the social problems (alcoholism, suicide, and the like) that accompanied their abysmal living conditions, the Lubicon organized a nationwide museum boycott of a native exhibit at the Calgary Winter Olympics in 1988, and that same year they set up blockades outside their community, preventing access to any company lacking a Lubicon-issued permit. The RCMP were sent in to dismantle the roadblocks, and twenty-seven people were arrested in the ensuing confrontation. Subsequently, the province of Alberta and the Lubicon signed an agreement concerning the size of a proposed reserve, but negotiations with the federal government then broke down. The federal government's next step was to arrange the creation of a new band with more compliant leadership, which accepted the offer previously turned down by the main body of the Lubicon. This did not solve anything, however, and in the early 1990s the Lubicon kept up their fight. Eventually, in 1995 the new federal Liberal government announced its intention to reopen negotiations with the Lubicon.

Northern Ojibwa

The Northern Ojibwa are a branch of the Ojibwa occupy northwestern Ontario and Island Lake, Manitoba (St Theresa Point First Nations), in the upper drainage areas of rivers that flow northeast into Hudson and James bays. They refer to themselves as Ojibway, or Anishinabe, meaning "the original people." Since the Northern Ojibwa's environment is similar to that of the Cree, they share more cultural traits with their Cree neighbours than with other Ojibwa. They do not exhibit Ojibwa features of clan organization or practise the Midewiwin (except at Sandy Lake).

The Northern Ojibwa can be divided into two groups corresponding to dialect. The Northern Ojibwa who speak the Severn dialect frequently refer to themselves as Cree and reside in the Ontario communities of Big Trout Lake, Caribou Lake, Sandy Lake, Bearskin Lake, Deer Lake, Trout Lake, Sachio Lake, Kingfisher Lake, and Wunnumin. Immediately south of the Severn speakers are Northern Ojibwa who speak the northwestern Ojibwa dialect. They live at Osnaburg, Lac Seul (mixed with Saulteaux), Cat Lake, and Martin

Falls, Ontario. The Northern Ojibwa living in the northern parts of
Ontario and Manitoba also reside in mixed communities with Cree
and are often designated Oji-Cree. Many Northern Ojibwa, especially
Severn speakers, speak Cree and English, although Cree is the choice
for liturgical purposes. At Lac Seul, for example, which is located on
the northern boundary between the Northern Ojibwa and the
Saulteaux, less than 50 percent speak English, while at Cat Lake less
than 10 percent speak English. Although no figures are available for
Severn speakers, the dialect continues to be used in the home, but,
for many, English has become the language of business.

Historically, the Northern Ojibwa were organized in units, called
bands by traders, that were larger than the nuclear family. Although
leaders had little formal authority, they were recognized for their
shamanic powers, hunting ability, and skills in bargaining with traders. During the summer the Northern Ojibwa congregated in large
groups along lake shores to fish. In the fall, they broke into small
hunting groups to move inland to their hunting ranges. Northern
Ojibwa bands were composed of hunting groups, which wintered
together and were closely related. Band sizes varied between 50 and
150, and larger regional groups came together when the weather was
good. Beginning in 1780, the Northern Ojibwa were intensively involved in a competitive regional fur trade.

The Northern Ojibwa shared common Algonquian Subarctic religious beliefs, including personal vision quests and proper respect for
animals. Shamans played an important intermediary role in the shaking tent and the *wahbeno*, which involved mystical communications
through fire. Although Methodist missionaries reached as far as the
Albany River basin in 1844, missionary efforts intensified between
1880 and 1920 when Anglican missionaries began work among the
Northern Ojibwa at Weagamow Lake (Round Lake, Ontario). As Anglican missions expanded to other locations, Cree and mixed bloods
were converted, and a number were ordained to serve the spiritual
needs of the Northern Ojibwa in the Severn River. Many were forced
by circumstance to mission stations to supplement their trapping, and
communities formed around fur-trade posts such as Lac Seul.

In the twentieth century, although the Northern Ojibwa economy
was based primarily on fish and big game, irregular game cycles and
aggressive fur-trade polices implemented by governments, including
punitive conservation measures and restrictions on steel traps, contributed to a shift to fish and hare; hunting groups were eventually

reduced in size to that of the nuclear family. Major land cessions by treaty were made among the Northern Ojibwa in 1905, and further cessions in 1929–30 (Treaty 9) forced many Northern Ojibwa to move closer to village sites to collect treaty payments and participate in Christian services. Today, the Northern Ojibwa are part of the Nishnawbe-Aski Nation, which represents Cree, Ojibwa, and Oji-Cree members of Treaty 9 and Ontario members of Treaty 5.

Saulteaux

To the south and west of the Northern Ojibwa are Ojibwa who speak what linguists have described as the Saulteaux dialect. The name Saulteaux was applied by Europeans as a political identification to denote related peoples whom French Jesuits in the 1640s described as "Saulteurs." "Saulteaux" appears in historical records, often interchangeably with "Ojibwa." The people who speak Saulteaux generally do not refer to themselves as such, preferring the names Ojibway or Anishinabe.

The Saulteaux are located on the southern rim of the Subarctic and display cultural features more representative of the Southwestern Ojibwa than of their northern neighbours, the Northern Ojibwa. They reside in the southern part of northwestern Ontario and northeastern Manitoba, from the boundary waters in the Rainy River and Lake of the Woods drainage areas west to the Red River valley and the height of land separating Lake Winnipeg from the Lake Superior drainage systems, and then on to Poplar River and across the prairies. In Manitoba, Saulteaux communities include Little Black River, Hole River, Brokenhead, Roseau River, Berens River, Fort Alexander, Peguis, Little Grand Rapids, Pauingassi, Sandy Bay, Jackhead, Fairford, Lake Saint Martin, and Poplar River; they also live with Cree speakers in God's Lake, Island Lake, and Bloodvein. In Saskatchewan, Saulteaux reside at Fishing Lake and Nut Lake, among other places. In Ontario, the Saulteaux communities include Pikangikum, Islington, Grassy Narrows, Eagle Lake, Lac des Mille Lacs, Iskutewisakaygun (Shoal Lake 39), Shoal Lake, Ochiichagwe'babigo'ining (Dalles), Wabasemoong, Washagamis, Whitefish Bay, Couchiching, Lac La Croix, Naicatchewenin, Nicickousemenecaning, Rainy River, Onegaming, Seine River, Stanjikoming, Rat Portage, Wabigoon, Wabauskang, Big Island, Big Grassy, and Lac Seul (mixed with Northern Ojibwa).

In contrast to the Northern Ojibwa, the Saulteaux are aligned historically and culturally less with Subartic Algonquians than with the Southwestern Ojibwa. In the past, the Saulteaux had access to reliable sturgeon fisheries, wild rice, large and small game, and plants, and they developed the technology to store surplus food. Kinship ties bound Saulteaux communities into a tribal organization, and marriage was arranged through a totemic clan system, in which persons having the same fish or animal totem (*dodem*) were considered related.

The animal species important to the Saulteaux were barren-ground and woodland caribou, moose, bear, fish, beaver, porcupine, hare, and waterfowl. The major fish were sturgeon, whitefish, and lake trout. Although vegetal foods were limited among the Northern Ojibwa to berries and lichens, they were more varied and abundant along the Rainy River/Lake of the Woods corridor, where wild rice and maple products were extensively harvested. Other plants were valued for medicines and for the manufacture of material items.

In the eighteenth century, large bands of peoples described as Saulteaux exercised control over their territory by establishing and enforcing a toll system. One such group, known to the French as the Monsoni (Monsounic), or Moose people, had increased their military strength through political alliances with the Cree and Assiniboine and were able to establish extensive trade connections in the Rainy River-Lake Winnipeg region with the agricultural Mandan Hidatsa. Saulteaux centres emerged near fishing sites, where large numbers gathered for religious ceremonies. So important was fish to the Saulteaux that they developed sophisticated fishing technology, which included hooks, spears, jack lights, weirs, scoop nets, ice chisels, various barbs, and specialized fishing medicines and ceremonials.

Protracted warfare with the Dakota in Minnesota contributed to dispersals and realignments of the Saulteaux, some permanent, some seasonal, which attracted migrations of families of Ottawa and Lake Superior Ojibwa, who established kinship ties with the resident Saulteaux. Saulteaux from the Rainy River and Lake Superior regions represented by the Bear and Catfish totems expanded south into Minnesota over former Dakota lands, while some Saulteaux and Cree moved to the northern plains in search of bison and furs. Although smallpox was reported for many areas in 1780–81, later followed by measles in 1820–21, the degree to which the Saulteaux were affected was uneven and depended upon several factors: the availability of food supplies in a given area, the seasonal concentration and location of the groups during the outbreak, the resistance that may have been provided by mixed-blood populations, and how efficiently groups communicated information about the epidemic and were able to retreat from potentially affected areas.

During this period of expansion and changing political alliances, military chiefs became important leaders among the Saulteaux, although local matters were the responsibility of hereditary village chiefs. Although widespread movements of Saulteaux contributed to variations in cultural and socio-economic practices, fishing and wild-rice harvesting were key elements of the Saulteaux economy and community. Both sexes contributed economically and shared responsibility for decision making. By this time, the Saulteaux had also begun to expand the commercial aspects of their economy to meet growing demands by fur traders. Saulteaux provided traders not only with furs but also wild rice, castoreum, sturgeon, big game, agricultural produce, and an extremely lucrative commodity which outlasted beaver-felt hats – isinglass, the swimming bladder of sturgeon, which was used to make paints, glues, and gelatin. Women traded *wattap*, (split roots from tamarack, jack pine, and spruce, used to repair canoes), wild rice, and maple sugar. The Saulteaux exercised considerable control over the fur trade by boycotting the sale of wild rice unless their demands for European goods were met.

An important focus for the Saulteaux was health and healing, likely a result of illness and epidemics, which was aided with an extensive pharmacopoeia and sacred songs, traditionally inscribed on birch bark. The Saulteaux elaborated the Great Lakes medicine society called the Midewiwin, or Grand Medicine Society, to meet their expanding cultural and political needs and in response to the influx of new trade wealth. The origin of this secret society has been traced archaeologically through birch-bark song scrolls to 1560 C.E. in the Rainy River region. This spiritual heartland also contains elaborate burial mounds attributed to the pre-contact Hopewell Culture, as well as the largest concentration of pictographs and birchbark scrolls depicting rites associated with Midewiwin healing. The Midewiwin was practised as far north as Sandy Lake, was common in the Lake Winnipeg area, and entered some Cree communities.

The Midewiwin became a focus for political power in the 1840s among the Saulteaux and was instrumental in their rejection of Christian missionaries. Although Saulteaux chiefs were interested in the educational opportunities offered by whites, they refused to accept schools run by missionaries. After the Midewiwin was banned in the late 1880s by the federal government, it was forced underground in the Rainy River areas but continued to be practised until the 1920s in the upper Berens River (today, it continues in a modern form in many communities). Some Saulteaux sought Christian sources of spirituality, which resulted in a blending of religious forms. The religious orientation for many Saulteaux today is a mixture of traditional and Christian, overseen by elders, both male and female. Some communities like Pikangekum have been inundated with an unprecedented number and variety of southern U.S. fundamentalist denominations, a development that has disrupted community ties and has been linked to an unparalleled number of youth suicides.

Saulteaux political organization varied depending on group size, the nature of the regional economy, and the degree of colonial interference. Many Saulteaux were led by hereditary chiefs who, with their councils, objected to and obstructed the fur traders' practice of arbitrarily conferring leadership on the basis of trapping skills. In ecologically richer areas such as the Boundary Waters of the Rainy River corridor of northwestern Ontario, political organization developed in the mid-eighteenth century into a complex system headed by a hereditary grand chief who represented collective concerns to external governments and commercial interests. Fur traders and missionaries were unable to penetrate or influence this system, especially among the Rainy River Saulteaux, who had developed non-hierarchical stratified layers of governance encompassing the roles of war chief, village chief, talking chief, pipe chief, and messengers – an arrangement that diffused political power while maintaining egalitarian principles. Chiefs who were also members of the Midewiwin represented Saulteaux political organization in the Boundary Waters and Lake of the Woods until the late 1880s and were prominent in treaty negotiations. Status was reflected in specific ranks and by kinship terminology.

The amalgamation of the HBC and the NWC in 1821 did not radically alter the competitive fur trade of the Rainy River/Lake of the Woods region, since the Saulteaux continued to have access to American fur traders and other free traders. Major land cessions by treaty began among the Saulteaux in Manitoba in 1871 (Treaty 1), in northwestern Ontario in 1873 (Treaty 3), and Lake Winnipeg in 1875 (Treaty 5). Although the Saulteaux entered into Treaty 3, they did not know at the time that the northern and western boundaries of Ontario had not been formally established. Escalating conflicts between the federal and provincial governments over Ontario's boundaries and resources developed during the 1880s, when Treaty 3 reserve lands and resources became a central component of the litigation in the *St. Catherine's Milling* case (1888). In this instance, a dispute over timber licensing between Canada and Ontario in the territory occupied by the Saulteaux led to a court case involving the division of legislative powers and the extent of aboriginal title. Ontario's challenge to the federal government's position that it was authorized to administer lands ceded by treaty succeeded in all the Canadian courts and then reached the Judicial Committee of the Privy Council in London. The Privy Council ruled that aboriginal title existed before the signing of treaties – in the sense that natives had the right to use land that was in fact owned by others – but that, once treaties were signed, this title could be abrogated unilaterally by the Crown (and hence by any legislative body of which was the Crown was a part). On this ground, the federal government's appeal was dismissed.

The limited recognition of aboriginal title in the *St. Catherine's Milling* case was later to form the basis of native claims to lands in areas not covered by treaties. For the Saulteaux in 1888, however, the results were not as positive. Throughout the protracted legal proceedings they were never advised, consulted, or represented, and, afterwards, Ontario refused to confirm the reserves negotiated by the Saulteaux without first acquiring valuable resources and lands and permitting economic projects which undermined the natives' traditional lifestyle. Some Saulteaux located at Sturgeon Lake (now Quetico Park) were forced at gun point to leave their reserve in the middle of winter. Since Saulteaux lands and fishing areas were adjacent to non-Indian settlement and commercial activities, their remaining lands were subjected to flooding through the construction of dams which destroyed lands, homes, and resources and degraded fishing. At the same time, Indian Act restrictions prevented agricultural development by prohibiting the removal of green timber despite treaty promises of farming assistance, while roads and hydro operations destroyed resources and cut communities in half. The loss of resources and access to ancestral lands forced many to depend on European food supplies, which has resulted in unprecedented alcoholism, tuberculosis, diabetes, and cancer. In addition, the dumping of methyl mercury from lumber operations, along with pesticides used to clear road and hydro rights-of-way, contaminated fish-spawning and game areas as well as religious sites and seriously affected Saulteaux health, resulting in many cases of Minamata disease.

With sedentary year-round residence on reserves and forced relocations of peoples, interpersonal conflicts – which had tradition-ally been defused by an individual's joining other bands – exacer-bated problems of social control. Witchcraft attacks and windigo scares, often sustained by alcoholism and drug abuse, afflicted many communities and resulted in high rates of suicide. The creation of reserves, often on marginalized lands without access to traditional resources of fish, game, or furs, combined with punitive provincial game laws, forced the Saulteaux into temporary low-wage labour and social assistance and into urban areas, often far away from their communities.

Residential schools were established by various religious orders to educate and indoctrinate the Saulteaux. Children were taken from homes and sent to often far-distant schools, where they were edu-cated in English and forbidden to speak their native language. Re-turning children were often strangers in their own communities. In the midst of all of this, women played a key social role, taking in parentless children and caring for elders. Since then, women have organized politically around issues concerning discrimination under the Indian Act, family violence, economic development, employment equity, and the Charter of Rights.

Some communities have developed their economic base through service-sector enterprises and government services, as well as trans-portation, marina, and other commercial projects. Local band admin-istrations on reserves have seen increased participation by women as men have been forced to seek off-reserve employment for long peri-ods. With increasing reserve populations, some communities, sup-ported by economic developments, have strengthened community ties, while others have become demoralized by increasing factionalism and social disruption.

Today, powwows – with their drumming, singing, praying, feasts, gift-giving, and speeches – sustain a corporate identity and link neighbouring native communities, while also educating non-Indians in matters concerning aboriginal culture and rights. Currently, the Saulteaux are represented politically by large organizations such as Grand Council Treaty No. 3, the Ontario Native Women's Association,

and numerous Friendship Centres, which together further their struggle for social and economic betterment and recognition of aboriginal
rights.

FURTHER READING

The Subarctic Algonquians are the subject of continuing scholarship, and so
current information on them is scattered through many publications, including *Ethnohistory*, *Papers of the Algonquian Conference*, *Native Studies Review*, and
Canadian Journal of Native Studies. The *Handbook of North American Indians*, vol.
6, *Subarctic*, edited by June Helm (Washington, D.C., 1981), is a comprehensive treatment of all Subarctic Algonquians. James B. Waldram, Ann Herring,
and T. Kue Young, *Aboriginal Health in Canada: Historical, Cultural, and Epidemio-
logical Perspectives* (Toronto, 1995), reports the results of intensive research
into the physiological, spiritual, historical, cultural, and environmental factors
affecting several aboriginal peoples, including the Subarctic Algonquians.

Frank Speck, *Nascapi: The Savage Hunters of the Labrador Peninsula* (1935;
repr. Norman, Okla., 1977), is a pioneering work on the Innu, while Georg
Henriksen, *Hunters in the Barrens: The Nascapi on the Edge of the White Man's
World* (St John's, 1973), explores the Innu from anthropological and historical
perspectives. A contemporary view of the Innu is provided in Cathy Kurelek's
article "Anthropological Participatory Research among the Innu of Labrador,"
Native Studies Review, vol. 8, no. 2 (1992), 75–97, which offers insight into the
role of Innu women and the problems in obtaining reliable research information on the Innu.

Daniel Francis and Toby Morantz, *Partners in Furs: A History of the Fur Trade
in Eastern James Bay, 1600–1870* (Montreal, 1989), explores the role of the James
Bay Cree in the early fur trade. Richard J. Preston, *Cree Narrative: Expressing
the Personal Meaning of Texts* (Ottawa, 1975), is a study of the basis of the Cree
world-view. Richard F. Salisbury, *A Homeland for the Cree: Regional Development
in James Bay* (Montreal, 1986), examines the impact of contemporary development on James Bay Cree communities.

Edward S. Rogers, *The Round Lake Ojibwa* (Toronto, 1962), is the classic
anthropological text on the Northern Ojibwa. Irving Hallowell, *The Ojibwa
of Berens River, Manitoba: Ethnography into History*, ed. Jennifer Brown (Fort
Worth, Tx., 1992), is a comprehensive anthropological study of the Saulteaux.
Laura Peers, *The Ojibwa of Western Canada, 1780 to 1870* (Winnipeg, 1994),
sketches the complex history of the western Saulteaux. John Tanner, *The
Falcon* (New York, 1994), interprets Saulteaux culture and history from the

point of view of a captive who was raised by the Saulteaux in the early nineteenth century, while William W. Warren, *History of the Ojibway People* (1885; repr. St Paul, Minn., 1984), provides a history of the Saulteaux based on interviews conducted in the 1850s. Tim E. Holzkamm, Victor P. Lytwyn, and Leo G. Waisberg, "Rainy River Sturgeon: An Ojibway Resource in the Fur Trade Economy," *Canadian Geographer*, vol. 32, no. 3 (1988), 194–205, documents the historical importance of the sturgeon fishery to the development of the Saulteaux in the Rainy River region.

James G.E. Smith, "The Western Woods Cree: Anthropological Myth and Historical Reality," *American Ethnologist*, vol. 14, no. 3 (1987), 434–48, investigates the historical dynamics concerning the identification of the Western Woodland Cree and their territorial movements. Robert A. Brightman, *Grateful Prey: Rock Cree Human-Animal Relationships* (Berkeley, Calif., 1993), examines the interconnections among Western Woodland Cree beliefs through a focus on the complexities of Cree-animal relationships.

4

INUIT

Louis-Jacques Dorais

Identification

Until the early 1970s, the Inuit were generally known as Eskimos. This deprecatory or, at least, slightly contemptuous term had entered the European languages – seemingly through French *Esquimaux* – during the sixteenth century. It had been borrowed from an Algonquian language, most probably Innu-Montagnais, where it meant either "raw meat eaters" or "those who speak a foreign tongue." The increasing use, among most Canadians, of the appellation "Inuit" stems directly from the growing political assertiveness of the natives of Canada's Arctic.

In the language of the "Eskimos," the plural word *inuit* (singular: *inuk*; dual: *inuuk*) means simply "human beings" or "people." This is the term the Inuit have used to distinguish themselves from other types of sentient beings: the *uumajut* (animals), *ijiqqat* (invisible beings), *allait, itgilgit,* or *unallit* (the Indians), *qablunaat, qallunaat,* or *tan'ngit* (the Europeans), and so on. Today, however, when it is necessary to distinguish between human beings in general and the ethnic Inuit in particular, the Arctic natives may refer to themselves, in their language, as *inutuinnait* ("the only genuine human beings": Arctic Quebec), *inuinnait* ("the genuine human beings": Arctic coast); or *inuvialuit* ("the human beings par excellence": Mackenzie coast and delta). The Mackenzie Inuit prefer to be known to English speakers as Inuvialuit.

The Canadian Inuit belong to a people who straddle the North American Arctic. In addition to the Inuit in Canada, Inuit can be found in the American state of Alaska (where they are known as Inupiat) as well as in Greenland, a self-governing territory within the kingdom of Denmark (where they call themselves Kalaallit). Proximate cultural and linguistic cousins of the Inuit, the Yupit (who, like the Inuit, are considered as belonging to the "Eskimos") inhabit southwestern Alaska and the eastern tip of the Chukotka peninsula in Russia, while the more distantly related Aleut live in the Aleutian islands (off southwest Alaska). In 1991 the worldwide Inuit population was about 101,500, out of a total of 130,500 Inuit and Yupit "Eskimos" (plus some 2,500 Aleut). Around 36,000 of them lived in Canada.

In the census of 1991, 30,090 Canadian residents declared a single Inuit ethnic identity. Another 19,165 declared a multiple Inuit ethnic identity (for example, Inuit/English, Inuit/French, and so on). Since this last figure seems highly improbable (in 1986 fewer than 10,000 persons had identified themselves as part-Inuit), we consider here as genuinely Inuit only those 36,215 Canadians who, in the 1991 census, claimed simultaneously both an Inuit and an aboriginal identity.

The vast majority (90.5 percent) of these people resided in the Northwest Territories and Nunavut (21,035), Quebec (7,030), and Newfoundland-Labrador (4,710), the balance (3,440) being dispersed troughout the other provinces. The bulk of the Canadian Inuit population was thus to be found within its original territory of settlement (*Inuit nunaat* or *Inuit nunangat*: "the land of the Inuit"): the coastal areas north (or at the fringe) of the tree line, along the shores of the Arctic Ocean, Hudson Bay, Davis Strait, and the Labrador Sea, between the Alaskan border and the Atlantic.

This territory was essentially the same as the one where the direct ancestors of the Inuit, the bearers of the Thule prehistoric culture, had settled some 1000 years ago. Like their predecessors in the Arctic, the so-called Dorset Eskimos (who became extinct one or two centuries after the arrival of the Thule), these proto-Inuit had migrated from northwestern Alaska, probably in pursuit of game. Both Dorset and Thule people belonged to the same ethnic stock: an Asian population particularly adept at reaping Arctic faunal resources, which had crossed the Bering Strait into North America some 8000 years ago.

All through the centuries, the descendants of these migrants preserved a remarkable cultural and linguistic homogeneity. Even now, for instance, the language of the Inuit remains practically the same from northern Alaska to Greenland. Called Inuktitut (or Inuttut) in the eastern Canadian Arctic, Inuinnaqtun on the Arctic coast, Inuvialuktun in the Mackenzie area, Iñupiaqtun in Alaska, and Kalaallisut in Greenland, it comprises several mutually intelligible dialects, ten of which are spoken in Canada.

Traditionally, the Canadian Inuit were subdivided into about ten different groupings or "tribes" (Mackenzie, Copper, Natsilik, Caribou, Aivilik, Southampton Island, Igloolik, South Baffin, Arctic Quebec, Labrador), which generally corresponded to dialectal subdivisions and relative genealogical discreteness (few marital unions occurred between members of different "tribes"). Currently, however, regional (for example, Arctic Quebec, Labrador, Baffin, Keewatin, and so on) and local identities are more relevant than the traditional ones.

Most of the present-day *Inuit nunaat* was already occupied by the Inuit at the time of their first sustained contacts with Europeans, over two hundred years ago. Only a few areas have since been added to this original territory. These include parts of the Mackenzie delta, as well as the southeastern coast of Hudson Bay, around Richmond Gulf and Great Whale River. Some Inuit also resettled near the trading posts of Churchill (Manitoba), Fort George/Chisasibi (Quebec), and Northwest River (Labrador), or – after World War II – at Happy Valley (Labrador), a few kilometres from the Goose Bay air force base. In the early 1950s, the Canadian government induced several Arctic Quebec and north Baffin families to move to Resolute Bay and Grise Fjord, two newly established communities on the high Arctic islands of Cornwallis and Ellesmere.

The traditional Inuit, whose culture was described by ethnographers such as Franz Boas, Émile Petitot, Lucien Turner, Knud Rasmussen, and Diamond Jenness, were nomadic. During spring, summer, and fall, they lived in small camps comprising between two and six families each. In winter, however, people gathered in larger camps which, at some periods, could consist of more than twenty-five families. Camps changed place according to the seasons, their members moving to locations where the different species of game or fish were known to be available. In Keewatin (west coast of Hudson Bay) and Arctic Quebec, many families went inland at the end of the summer to hunt caribou, returning to the coast when the snow cover was thick enough to enable sled travel. In both regions, several people stayed inland year-round, subsisting on a diet of fish and caribou meat.

Migrations did not occur at random. The same locations – or ones close by – were visited year after year, with the result that many families spent most of their life within a circumscribed area. Hunting territories had no fixed boundaries, and quite a few people occasionally moved to another district. Such moves, however, rarely transcended the limits of the dialect groups, which thus constituted the largest social and residential units.

With the founding of trading posts, Christian missions, and police detachments, a new type of settlement pattern rapidly emerged: semi-nomadic camps situated in the vicinity of Euro-Canadian installations. After World War II, with the establishment of federal schools, nursing stations, and administrative offices, the population was strongly encouraged to settle in a limited number of permanent villages. Some regions such as the northernmost part of Labrador, inland Keewatin, and the Arctic Quebec hinterland were then depopulated. At the end of the 1960s, a few camps were still to be found in Arctic Canada, but ten years later everybody was living in villages (with one exception, in the Bathurst Inlet area). The traditional snow igloo or semi-subterranean sod hut had definitively been replaced, as a permanent winter dwelling, by prefabricated wooden houses.

In 1991 *Inuit nunaat* comprised a total of forty-six communities with a majority native population, plus eight more settlements where a sizeable Inuit minority lived among a European and/or Indian majority. As a last vestige of nomadism, most of these towns and villages had outlying camps, where people resided for short periods at various times of the year. The regional distribution of these fifty-four settlements was as follows: Northwest Territories, thirty-three; Arctic Quebec, fifteen; Labrador, six.

By southern standards, Inuit communities are small. In 1991 only 15 of them had more than 1000 residents. The largest one, Iqaluit (Frobisher Bay), did not exceed 3,550 inhabitants (2,250 Inuit and 1,300 non-natives), while the smallest, Bathurst/Baychimo, held only some 80 people. A majority of villages were ethnically homogeneous, with the proportion of Inuit residents hovering between 90 and 95 percent of their total population.

Despite their small size and isolation (with a very few exceptions, no roads link them with the outside world or neighbouring communities), the Inuit settlements now possess most of the amenities found in southern Canada: schools, stores, telephone, television, and the like. This may partly explain why the vast majority of the Canadian Inuit still live and work in their original territory. No more than 10 percent of them reside outside *Inuit nunaat*, many of these emigrants being either students or individuals holding a temporary job at the Ottawa, Montreal, or Yellowknife headquarters of a northern organization.

History

The process by which Canadian Inuit became a sedentary people was closely related to the increasing economic, political, and social integration of the Arctic natives with the Western world. The first contacts between the Inuit and Europeans may have occurred in southern Labrador and northern Newfoundland, which were visited by the Greenlandic Norse colonists around 985 C.E. But it seems more likely that the native *skraellingar* ("pagans") encountered by these visitors were rather of Amerindian stock.

If such is the case, it was not before the sixteenth century that Inuit/European contacts really began. At first, these tended to be hostile. In 1566, for instance, an Inuk woman and her child, most probably kidnapped in Labrador the preceding year, were exhibited in several European fairs. A decade later, when the British explorer Martin Frobisher discovered the bay that now bears his name, the local Inuit killed some of his crew, and in retaliation he captured three persons who were taken back to London.

Relations with the Inuit continued to be rather hostile till the early eighteenth century, when Dutch, Basque, and French whalers and fishermen – groups that had been regular visitors to the Strait of Belle-Isle and southern Labrador for two hundred years – succeeded in establishing a trade in blubber and furs with the northerners. Contacts became so frequent that, in order to improve communication, an Inuit-French-Basque pidgin language soon developed.

In 1771 the Moravian Brethren, a German Protestant church already present in Greenland, established a mission and trading post at Nain, in northern Labrador. A semi-settled community soon developed there, as well as around a few other Moravian congregations. In what was to become Arctic Quebec and the Northwest Territories, permanent contacts started only around 1830, when the Hudson's Bay Company (HBC) began establishing trading posts at the fringe of *Inuit nunaat*. It was not until the 1900s that the HBC opened stores more to the north, in the very heart of Inuit country. Long before that, however, Scottish and American whalers had already entered into contact with the Arctic natives, conducting trade with them and hiring them on their ships, in the Hudson Bay, Baffin Island, and Mackenzie Coast waters. By the end of the nineteenth century, most Canadian Inuit already possessed guns and steel traps and knew about tea, sugar, flour, and tobacco.

The traders and whalers were followed by missionaries. In 1876 the Anglican Edmund J. Peck established a mission at Little Whale River, on the eastern shore of Hudson Bay. He later moved to Blacklead Island, in the southeast Baffin area. At about the same time, missionaries were beginning to contact the Mackenzie Inuit. From these various locations, Anglicanism spread rapidly. Peck had transcribed parts of the Moravian translation of the Bible into the syllabic script devised half a century earlier by a Wesleyan missionary among the Ojibwa, James Evans. This script was easy to learn, and, in many regions of the eastern Arctic, it enabled the Christian message to be disseminated among the Inuit without the physical presence of European priests. After 1910 the Roman Catholics followed in the Anglicans' footsteps, so that by 1940 almost all of Canadian Inuit had become Christians.

On the eve of World War II, the Inuit lived in semi-nomadic hunting-trapping camps, except in Labrador, where permanent settlements were to be found. Their economic activities were oriented principally towards the fur trade. They possessed guns and motor boats, wore store-bought clothes, and ate biscuits and bannock. Most adults were literate in their own language (often in syllabic characters), and in Labrador and the Mackenzie delta their children went to mission schools. In some areas, however, the population had greatly diminished because of epidemics and famine.

At this time, the federal government, whose sole representatives were a handful of policemen, was just starting to take some aid to the Inuit. Only in the late 1940s did Ottawa become fully involved in Inuit administration. The war had disclosed the strategic and economic importance of the Arctic regions, and consequently the governmental attitude of laissez-faire was not appropriate any more. Within a few years, a complete system of educational, social, administrative, and health services was established throughout the Canadian north. Since such services had to be centralized in a limited number of locations, the Inuit were strongly encouraged to become sedentary, and, as mentioned above, the hunting-trapping camps disappeared during the 1960s and 1970s.

The adoption of a sedentary lifestyle, along with schooling, entailed the emergence of a generation of young bilingual Inuit knowledgeable about Western ways. It was this generation who, during the 1970s and 1980s, worked at redefining the relationship between Canada and its Arctic natives. Territorial and administrative agreements (James Bay, Inuvialuit, Nunavut) were signed, and new Inuit-run organizations were established.

Economic Life

The Inuit of old had moved to different locations according to the seasons, in order to avail themselves of the presence of game. They spent the winter in snowhouses (known as igloos, from the Inuktitut word *iglu*, "inhabited dwelling"), except in the Mackenzie and Labrador regions, where they lived in semi-subterranean stone and sod huts. Some north Baffin people also occupied huts in early winter. When spring came, huts and igloos were replaced by seal- or caribou-skin tents. Both winter and spring/summer dwellings were heated and lighted by a soapstone lamp burning sea mammal blubber.

From one region to another, the hunting, fishing, and gathering activities showed a high degree of similarity, even if they varied in important details. A typical eastern Arctic seasonal cycle would be as follows. During winter, the men waited for seal, either at the floe edge or at the breathing holes this animal maintains in the sea ice. The hunters used harpoons and, from the mid-1800s, guns. Men and women also trapped a few fox and fished through freshwater lake ice. Transportation was by sled and dog-team. At springtime, the men hunted seal basking on the floe ice, cautiously approaching the animal till it was within harpoon reach or rifle shot. They also lay in wait on the seashore, at those locations where the floe had begun to break, for marine mammals (beluga, narwhal, walrus, and several species of seal). In the Mackenzie region, break-up signalled the opening of the whale hunting season.

Summertime was the occasion for several productive activities: hunting from kayaks for the men, gathering wild berries for the women and children, and catching fish at stone weirs for family groups. In many regions, people went inland at the end of August (often travelling upriver in large sealskin boats called *umiat*) to hunt caribou till September or October. During these hunts, the women and children's task was to shout at the animals in order to induce them to run towards the concealed men who were waiting with their bows and spears.

Back on the coast during fall, the families prepared for the coming winter. While the men cached seal, walrus, caribou, and bird (principally goose and duck) meat, women made and mended winter clothing: hooded parkas, breeches, boots, mitts, and so on, all made of seal and caribou skin. Adequate clothing was – and still is – essential to survival in the Arctic.

The raw materials and food extracted from the environment fulfilled the immediate needs of the families. What could not be eaten, used, or cached by the hunter's, fisher's, or gatherer's immediate relatives was shared with his or her companions, according to quite complicated distribution rules. The Inuit were not a communistic society, but those in need expected to be helped by their companions. The few non-perishable surplus goods (skins, ivory, flotsam wood) were sometimes kept aside, to be later traded with other Inuit groups. When famine struck, however, the sharing rules did not apply any more; everybody then tried to survive by any possible means.

Between 1830 and 1930 trading posts were established in various parts of *Inuit nunaat* (for example, Fort Chimo, 1830; Great Whale River, 1855; Cape Wolstenholme, 1909; Aklavik, 1912; Chesterfield Inlet, 1912; Pond Inlet, 1912; Frobisher Bay, 1914; Pangnirtung, 1921; Cambridge Bay, 1923; Coppermine, 1927). As a consequence, commercial seal and beluga hunting, as well as the trapping of Arctic fox, became increasingly important, while subsistence hunting and fishing diminished accordingly. Store-bought food and clothing materials partly replaced the meat and skins that the Inuit no longer had time to procure by themselves, although people never became completely dependent on the traders. At the end of World War II, they could still be considered largely autarchic hunter-gatherers, except, perhaps, in the Mackenzie delta, where muskrat and fox trapping was so lucrative that subsistence hunting had almost become a thing of the past.

While trading posts, weather stations, police detachments, and military installations (since 1942) had provided a few salaried jobs before the end of World War II, post-war development provoked a tremendous increase in the need for local construction workers, janitors, general labourers, and interpreters. From 1959 on, the cooperative movement opened new opportunities in commercial fishing, arts, and handicrafts. Northern Labrador and Quebec's Ungava Bay area started exporting salmon and Arctic char to southern Canadian markets, and communities such as Povungnituk, Cape Dorset, Baker Lake, and Holman Island became known for their carvings and stone-cut prints. As an effect of these developments, the kayaks and dog-teams were rapidly replaced by outboard canoes and snowmobiles. Up to the early 1970s, however, only a small part of the Inuit population was involved in full-time wage work. Most individuals still devoted their time to hunting, fishing, and trapping, making ends meet with occasional odd jobs and/or transfer payments from the government.

During the 1970s, the establishment of a new administrative order, one increasingly under Inuit control, led to the sudden appearance of hundreds of new jobs in the fields of education, health and social services, management, public administration, transport and communications, trade, and so on. The percentage of full-time hunters and trappers decreased drastically within a few years, even if the new native administrations tried to provide aid to those interested in traditional economic pursuits.

Today, wage work within public services constitutes the mainstay of the Inuit economy. Yet this is not to say that everybody holds a job. On the contrary, widespread unemployment plagues the northern communities, and plans for sustainable development are badly needed. Hunting, fishing, gathering, and trapping cannot any longer provide a viable economic basis for modern villages whose standard of living approximates that of southern Canada. Even if traditional activities still provide the Inuit with an appreciable quantity and variety of fresh food, the symbolic value of these activities now appears as more important than their actual economic impact.

Kinship, Family, and Social Organization

For most contemporary Inuit, family relations, childbirth, and the transmission of names retain the significance they had in traditional times.

Inuit kinship is bilateral, that is, relatives on both the father's and mother's side are equally recognized as belonging to one's own kin group. Terminological details may vary from one dialect to another, but, on the whole, the kinship system is similar throughout *Inuit nunaat*. In Arctic Quebec, for instance, the individual makes a distinction between his or her father (*ataata*) and mother (*anaana*); grandfather (*ataatatsiaq*, "good father") and grandmother (*anaanatsiaq*); father's brother (*akka*) and sister (*atsa*); mother's brother (*angak*) and sister (*ajak*); and so on. He or she also distinguishes various categories of siblings: *angajuk* (elder sibling of the same sex as oneself), *nukaq* (younger sibling of the same sex), *ani* (brother, for a woman), and *naja* (sister, for a man). One's spouse is called *aippaq* ("one of a pair"), while a child is termed *qiturngaq*, whether it be a son (*irniq*) or daughter (*panik*). Assorted terms also exist for grandchildren, cousins, nephews/nieces, and in-laws.

Social solidarities are embedded primarily within family and kinship groups. Most households consist of a nuclear family, whether it be complete (the two parents and their children) or not (one parent with his or, more frequently, her children). Some households include the widowed father or mother of one of the spouses or, more rarely, an unmarried adult sibling. This type of household has replaced the patrilocal extended family of father and married sons with their spouses, which was formerly normative through most of *Inuit nunaat*.

Generally speaking, each household is related by kinship to a certain number of other households established in the same village. It is principally within these groups of related families that game is shared, visiting occurs, and various domestic services are rendered. Many people prefer to associate with relatives, and indeed it is common for some to describe members of their own kin group as their best friends.

Such groups are not completely inward-looking, however. People mix readily with non-relatives, and one major institution, marriage, entails the establishment of broader relations, since spouses must normally be chosen from outside one's own kin group. Most Inuit still marry other Inuit, although interethnic unions, especially those involving an Inuk woman and a non-Inuk man, are increasing rapidly. Also on the increase are separations and divorces, almost unknown two decades ago.

The position of women in traditional Inuit society has given rise to much debate among anthropologists. Some contend that both genders were practically equal, while others point out that myths and stories reveal the dominance of men (some of whom practised polygyny and female infanticide, though in a limited way). Whatever the case, women play a major economic and political role in contemporary Inuit society. They dominate many salaried occupations (in the field of education, for instance), and several of them have headed – or are still heading – major aboriginal organizations (including the international Inuit Circumpolar Conference). Some men resent the fact that they no longer are the principal providers and decision makers, and violence against women, often triggered by alcohol abuse, constitutes a problem in many communities.

Such changes in the respective roles of men and women have not modified both genders' attitude towards children. Children are numerous (individuals under 15 years of age account for about 40 percent of all Canadian Inuit) and generally loved. Births out of wedlock, a common occurrence, are not frowned upon, although elderly people point out that they were not so frequent when they themselves were young. A first child is often adopted by its grandparents, and, generally speaking, adoption constitutes an efficient way for sharing surplus – or unwanted – children with prospective parents. It frequently occurs that such parents are older people, widowed or not, whose offspring are starting to marry and/or move into another household and who need young children to enliven the home and, later on, help them with domestic tasks. Adopted children possess the same status as biological offspring, and in most communities they account for about 30 percent of all children.

In addition to their biological or adoptive parents' family name (surnames are in use since the 1960s), newborns generally receive from two to ten personal appellations. Most of these, whether traditional (that is, pre-Christian) or Christian, are transmitted from persons (the eponyms), deceased or not, who bore the same names and had received them at birth from somebody else. In a way, the eponyms revive in the newborn child, who must be addressed as his or her eponyms were. For instance, a boy named after his paternal grandmother (names are genderless in Inuktitut) is called "mommy" by his father, whom he must address as "son." In locations such as Igloolik (Baffin region), children whose biological sex differs from that of their principal eponym are disguised and raised till puberty as if they belonged to this eponym's gender.

Although the Inuit communities are now formally organized in the same way as their southern Canadian counterparts, with municipal administrations, government agencies, public schools, and so on, their most fundamental structure remains based on kinship and the family. Groups of related households may be found in every village. They generally constitute informal networks of families among which the density of kinship relations and the level of social interaction (sharing, visiting, and so on) are particularly high.

These networks are often called "clans" by the northern Euro-Canadian residents, but the term is misleading. Clans are generally defined as closed unilateral corporate units, while the Inuit kin groups are flexible, bilateral (they include people related through both their father's and mother's sides), and open-ended (one may enter them by marriage or adoption). It is thus preferable to call such networks "kindreds," which is the closest approximation to their Inuit appellation of *ilagiit* ("group of relatives").

Present-day kindreds often stem from traditional bands, those nomadic or semi-nomadic groups of relatives and in-laws who lived in seasonal hunting camps until the 1960s. When the bands became sedentary, they preserved their social role, even if their residential and economic functions rapidly disappeared. Since each of the newly settled communities generally comprised two or more bands, the villages became quite naturally subdivided into social units – the kindreds – in direct continuation with these bands.

In traditional times, the bands were usually led by their oldest able-bodied male member, who often possessed an *umiaq* (sealskin boat) and might enlist the support of a shaman. After the traders and missionaries came, the typical band leader owned an inboard motor boat and acted as catechist (or lay reader) for his extended family. In modern communities, leadership takes many forms. The kindreds may compete between themselves to have one of their leading members elected as village mayor, or they may try to take control of the local school, cooperative, or other administrative organizations. Whatever their nature, however, the leadership positions are now shared between men and women.

The presence of kindreds may partly explain why social classes or castes have not yet developed within Inuit society. Despite the fact that major occupational and income differences may now be found in the north, every individual still belongs first and foremost to his or her family and kindred, where he/she stands on an equal footing with everybody else. Kinship relations thus act as equalizers that efficiently counterbalance incipient social stratification.

Culture

Inuit folk tradition consists mainly of myths, tales, and songs transmitted orally from generation to generation or – in the case of songs – composed by well-identified individuals. Inuit myths tell how the world came to be as it is now. In the central Arctic tradition, they explain that, at the beginning of time, people never died. When becoming too old, they just let themselves fall head over heels from the sleeping platform and were thus rejuvenated. Since, however, new children were often found in eggs lying on the ground, the population was on the increase. One day, people realized that the island where they dwelt was in danger of sinking because of the weight of its inhabitants. An old woman then yelled: *Tuqu, tuqu, unataa, unataa* ("Death, death, war, war"). Death and war thus appeared and life began to take place as we experience it now.

Other myths describe how the genders came to be (the first "mother" was a male whose genital parts split open when he was about to give birth); how the moon (an incestuous young man) and sun (his abused sister) appeared; how day became distinct from night (a raven croaked *qau, qau* – "light, light" – and daylight succeeded darkness); or how the Inuit, Indians, Europeans, and *Ijiqqat* (invisible beings) are all descended from a woman who wed her dog and later became Sedna, the mother of sea mammals. Myths also narrate the adventures of Kaujjaarjuk, the poor orphan boy who finally triumphed over his persecutors; Lumaajuq, the evil mother transformed into a narwhal; Atungat, who went round the world with his sled and dog-team; or Kiviuk, a hero to whom many wonderful deeds are attributed. Tales of a more historical nature describe encounters between the *Tuniit* (the prehistoric Dorset Eskimos) and the Thule ancestors of the present-day Inuit.

Most myths and tales are now remembered only by a small minority of elderly individuals, even if the symbols and beliefs they convey still make sense to many people. Long associated with the pagan religion, they were frowned upon by the missionaries. Fortunately, however, interest in folk traditions has been revived – owing in part to self-educated intellectuals such as Taamusi Qumaq, Emile Imaroittok, and David Owingajak – and oral literature is now taught in schools and disseminated on northern radio and television.

Inuit music has been revived, too. Traditionally, it consisted of chants and drum dancing. People sang on various occasions: to tell about their hunting exploits; to mock their enemies or opponents (in a sort of singing duel); to cast a spell over somebody else; to amuse themselves (throat singing or juggling songs); or, simply, to lull a baby to sleep. Drum dances were generally held in winter, when several families gathered together in a huge ceremonial igloo *qaggiq*. Today, traditional songs and drums are heard only on special occasions: cultural festivals, Christmas celebrations, or occasional radio broadcasts. They have been replaced, however, by a vibrant new tradition: folk, religious, country, or even rock music sung in Inuktitut or English. Inuit singers such as William Tagoona, Charlie Panigoniak, Willie Thrasher, Charlie Adams, and Susan Aglukark are popular in the north, where they are often heard on radio and television, and have followings in other parts of the country as well.

As for traditional handicrafts, essentially utilitarian in nature, they did not have much in common with Inuit art as we know it now. The modern tradition of soapstone, ivory, and whalebone carvings, stone-cut prints, and sealskin appliqués was developed during the 1950s under the direction of James Houston and a few other Euro-Canadian artists and promoters. Geared exclusively towards external markets, it has become a major source of income for the Inuit. It has also enabled many talented artists, including several women, to become famous in the world's art circles and, sometimes, to find a place in museum collections; such artists include Kenoyuak, Pitseolak, Davidialuk, Joanasialuk, Kalvak, and Mona Thrasher.

Religion

The traditional Inuit practised shamanistic animism. There were no gods, but a multitude of souls filled the cosmos: human souls, spirit souls, animal souls, inanimate souls. The shaman (*angakkuq*), because of his/ her disposition and training (generally under another shaman), was the only one who knew how to bridge the gap between the various categories of beings and communicate with all of them, thereby transcending the boundaries normally separating the visible from the invisible, the human from the animal, or the male from the female.

During public seances, the shaman entered into a trance, and his/her soul travelled to the moon (where the protector of hunters lived), to Sedna's submarine abode, or to meetings with various supranatural beings. He/she was helped in this task by one or several auxiliary spirits. When encountering invisible beings, the shaman tried to obtain from them information on why things were going wrong. Illness or bad weather was often due to the fact that some of the numerous taboos to which the Inuit were subjected had not been observed. In such a case, the shaman asked people to confess their wrongs in order to restore harmony. If sea mammals were scarce, he/she could cajole Sedna into sending them back to the surface of the sea by carefully combing her long entangled hair.

The shaman also presided over collective rituals – at the winter solstice, for instance – where masks were often worn. At a more basic level, he or she was frequently asked to chant over the sick in order to heal them, or to practise divination by tying a string around somebody's head and lifting it (if the answer was negative, the head became too heavy to be lifted).

Human beings possessed three souls. One of them, the breath (*anirniq*), died with the body. The second, the name (*atiq*), was transmitted to newborn babies. As for the third soul (*tarniq*), its fate depended on the kind of death of its owner. Those who died violently (this included dying in childbirth) went to a pleasant place where food was plentiful and where the dead spent most of their time playing football with walrus skulls. By contrast, those who died from illness or old age were thought to go to a rather cold abode, without much food or many distractions.

From 1771 on in Labrador and from the late nineteenth century on elsewhere, traditional beliefs and practices started being challenged by the Christian missionaries. Despite some resistance on the part of the shamans, the Inuit converted quite rapidly, perhaps partly because they perceived some degree of similarity between the two religions. Both creeds stressed mutual help and charity, the observance of taboos (the Christian taboo forbidding any activity on Sunday is still scrupulously observed by many Inuit), the power of prayer, and the omnipresence of spirits (the missionaries convinced people that the shaman's auxiliary spirits, the *tuurngait*, were actually devils). By the late 1930s, most Canadian Inuit had already been baptized, but, until the 1950s, several syncretic religious movements combining traditional and Christian beliefs sporadically appeared all over the Arctic.

The missionaries belonged to three different denominations: Moravian, Anglican, and Roman Catholic. The Moravians confined themselves to Labrador, while the Anglicans entered the Arctic both from the east and from the west, progressively converting a majority of the Inuit. As for the Catholics, the last to arrive, their principal field of apostolate was the central and western Arctic, where they converted a majority or a sizeable minority of the population in a dozen locations. The Inuit country was divided into dioceses, one Anglican (the Diocese of the Arctic, with Iqaluit and Aklavik as episcopal co-seats) and two Catholic (Churchill–Hudson Bay and Fort Smith–Mackenzie).

The former missions have now become regular parishes; among the Anglicans and Moravians, the majority of ministers are Inuit, while, in the case of the Catholics, non-Inuit priests are assisted by married Inuit couples acting as catechists. Since the 1970s, the original churches have been competing with several new religious movements, generally attached to the Pentecostal tradition. In the early 1990s, these movements accounted for almost half of the population of several Arctic communities. Their success is due to four factors: they are totally controlled by the Inuit; they propose a style of life (without alcohol, drugs, and gambling) that appeals to those who suffer from personal problems; they promote "modern" values such as cleanliness, hard work, and respect for money; and some of their practices (possession by the Holy Spirit, the public confession of sins) are similar to traditional rituals. Currently, however, all religions, including the Pentecostal tradition, are losing support among young people, who tend to become religiously indifferent or, in some cases, wish to learn more about their ancestors' shamanistic beliefs.

Education

The training of a would-be shaman under an experienced *angakkuq* was the only type of formal education that existed in traditional Inuit society. General knowledge was informally transmitted from father to son and mother to daughter by enlisting the children's participation in hunting, fishing, and domestic tasks.

The first schools in the Canadian Arctic were established by the Moravian missionaries in Nain, Okak, and Hopedale (Labrador) around 1790. They provided basic courses in reading, writing, arithmetic, and religion. Inuttut was the sole language in use. By 1840 all of the Labrador Inuit were literate and a few of them even acted as teachers.

In the rest of *Inuit nunaat*, however, it was not before the end of the nineteenth century and the beginning of the twentieth that literacy was introduced by the Anglicans under the form of syllabic characters in the east and of a non-standardized alphabetical rendering of the language in the west. Even in the absence of formal schools, reading and writing skills spread rapidly, most people acquiring them from their relatives and friends.

After 1920 mission schools were established with the support of federal subsidies. There were thirty of them in 1950, including two boarding institutions in the Mackenzie delta. In the eastern Arctic, the missionaries taught partly in Inuktitut, but the Mackenzie boarding schools, which catered to the entire western Inuit population, completely forbade the use of this language. English was also the unique teaching medium in the federal day schools that began to spread throughout the Northwest Territories and Arctic Quebec from the late 1940s on. When Newfoundland joined Canada in 1949 and as a province acquired responsibility for education, English became the language of instruction in Labrador schools as well.

During the 1950s and early 1960s the federal establishments progressively replaced the missionary schools. In most settlements, teaching was limited to the primary grades, but in larger communities some secondary classes were also offered. Those children wishing to complete high school, however, had to go to the newly created boarding institutions in Inuvik (Mackenzie), Chesterfield Inlet (Keewatin), Iqaluit (Baffin), and Churchill (Manitoba).

Between 1964 and 1968 the Quebec government established its own primary schools in the north of the province, where teaching was conducted in both Inuktitut and French. The federal schools continued to operate, but from 1969 on they had to introduce some Inuktitut in the early grades. However, it was not until the 1970s that northern education came under the control of local people. In 1973 the government of the Northwest Territories became responsible for its school system, the administration of which was entrusted to elected boards of education, one for each region. Five years later, all Arctic Quebec schools were transferred to the Kativik School Board, an Inuit-controlled organization established under the James Bay and Northern Quebec Agreement.

In most Quebec and eastern territorial schools, Inuktitut has now become the sole teaching medium from kindergarten to grade three. The second language (English in the Northwest Territories and Nunavut, English or French in Quebec) is then introduced, but some Inuktitut courses continue to be offered throughout the primary and secondary levels. The native language is also sporadically taught in several Labrador and western territorial Inuit communities.

In a majority of the Canadian Arctic settlements, education is now available up to grades eleven or twelve. Post-secondary technical training is provided by Aurora College and Nunavut Arctic College (with six campuses in the Northwest Territories and Nunavut), Kativik School Board's adult education services (in northern Quebec), and the Labrador Community College (in Happy Valley). These establishments also offer some university-level courses in the fields, notably, of teacher and interpreter/translator training. Grants are available to Inuit students who wish to enrol in a southern Canadian institution of higher learning.

Yet, despite these incentives, the level of formal education remains lower than the average. During the early 1990s those who had completed grade nine accounted for less than 60 percent of the Inuit population (compared with 80 percent for Canada in general), while individuals with some college or university education did not exceed 6 percent of all Inuit (as compared with a Canadian average of almost 20 percent). Nevertheless, progress had been made since the early 1980s, when the respective percentages had stood at 39 percent (grade nine) and 4 percent (college education).

Dropping out of school still constitutes a major problem in the north. Still, almost all Inuktitut speakers can read and write their language, and most individuals under forty or fifty are also literate in English, at least to some degree. Education appears appropriate to a majority of the Inuit, and new curricula, more respectful of aboriginal culture than the current ones, are now being devised in various areas of the Arctic.

The principal problem with formal education in the Arctic is that it generates among its graduates professional expectations that cannot be met by the current labour market. Many young, educated Inuit, confronted by the lack of job opportunities – and also by the gap that separates them from their more tradition-oriented parents – tend to feel useless. They then often turn to alcohol and drugs, which may open the door to violence and suicide.

Language and Communication

According to 1991 census data, 24,995 Canadian residents had an Inuit dialect (Inuktitut, Labrador Inuttut, Inuvialuktun, and so on) as their first language. They accounted for 69 percent of the 36,215 individuals who identified themselves as Inuit. Their language thus was in much better shape than many other Canadian aboriginal speech forms, although its relative importance varied from region to region. In Quebec and the Northwest Territories, 94 percent and 81 percent, respectively, of all local Inuit still spoke or understood an Inuit dialect, but this was the case with only 25 percent of the Newfoundland-Labrador Arctic natives and with 17 percent of those residing in the rest of Canada.

Within *Inuit nunaat* proper, the percentage of speakers again varied considerably. The native language was stronger in Arctic Quebec (where 99 percent of all Inuit had Inuktitut as their first language), the Baffin region (96 percent), and Keewatin (95 percent) than in the Kitikmeot (70 percent) and Inuvialuit (25 percent) regions of the Northwest Territories and Nunavut. It was rather weak in northern Labrador, where about 50 percent of the local Inuit still understood Inuttut. In short, the future of the Inuit language appeared relatively secure in Arctic Quebec and the eastern Territories but in jeopardy in Labrador and the western Territories.

The decline of Inuttut and Inuvialuktun in Labrador and the west is confirmed by statistics on home language. In 1991 only 7 percent of the Inuvialuktun speakers habitually used their mother tongue at home. In the Kitikmeot region, this was the case with some 40 percent of those speaking the Inuinnaqtun and Natsilingmiutut dialects, while in Labrador only about 30 percent of all Inuttut speakers used the language in daily life. By contrast, 77 percent of the Keewatin speakers and 91 percent of those living in Arctic Quebec and the Baffin region still claimed Inuktitut as their usual home language.

Everywhere in the Arctic, it is English that tends to replace the native speech form, either as mother tongue or home language. In 1991, 27.5 percent of all Canadian Inuit still spoke only Inuktitut, but this percentage had decreased markedly since 1981, when 47 percent of the Arctic natives were unilingual. English is the prefered second language of the Inuit, although in Arctic Quebec, 9 percent of the aboriginal population spoke French (and another 5 percent French and English) in 1991.

As mentioned above, most Inuit speakers can read and write their language in one of the orthographies introduced by the missionaries during the eighteenth and nineteenth centuries. In recent decades, the regional aboriginal associations have devised standard versions of these writing systems. They include the Labrador Inuit Standard Epellation System (based on the Moravian alphabetical orthography), the Inuit Cultural Institute Standard Syllabary (with Arctic Quebec, Baffin, and Keewatin variants), the Inuvialuit Orthography (in the roman alphabet), and a poorly standardized alphabetical rendering of the Inuinnaqtun dialect.

Literacy in Inuktitut is reflected in the emergence of an Arctic Canadian literature, which appears mostly in periodicals. Apart from a few novels in Inuktitut, such as Markoosie's *Harpoon of the Hunter* (1969) and Salome Mitiarjuk Nappaaluk's *Sanaaq* (the name of the leading character; written in 1953 but not published until 1984), this literature consists mainly of autobiographies, descriptions of the traditional culture, and books for children. Contemporary authors include Emile Imaroittok, Alootook Ipellie, Michael Kusugaq, and Taamusi Qumaq. Several Inuit writers, such as Minnie A. Freeman, also publish in English.

Between 1940 and 1984 seventy-four Inuktitut/English or, in Quebec, Inuktitut/English/French newspapers, magazines, and newsletters were published in Canada. About thirty of them – along with two or three new titles – were still in circulation in 1992. These periodicals include community papers, the most prominent of which is the bilingual *Nunatsiaq News* (News of the Northwest Territories; Iqaluit, 1972–), newsletters from various aboriginal and government organizations, and religious, social, or cultural magazines. Within this last category, a few titles stand out: *Inuktitut* (Like the Inuit; Ottawa, 1959–), originally published by the federal Department of Indian Affairs but now the responsibility of the Inuit Tapirisat of Canada (the national Inuit organization); *Isumasi* (Your Thoughts; Rankin Inlet, 1990–), the Inuit Cultural Institute's magazine; *Tumivut* (Our Footprints; Montreal, 1991–), published by Arctic Quebec's Avataq Cultural Institute; and *Kinatuinamut ilingajuk* (Intended for Everyone; Nain, 1972–), an information bulletin published out of Labrador.

Since 1960 the written media have felt the competition of radio, originally broadcast on short wave by the Canadian Broadcasting Corporation's northern service but now available from over forty Arctic community stations. These are fed from three sources: CBC national programming; regional stations in Iqaluit, Inuvik, or elsewhere; and local production. The two last sources make wide use of Inuktitut and put the emphasis on local information. The community stations thus play an important part in fostering Inuit identity.

By contrast, television speaks mainly English and its northern content is not as conspicuous as that of radio. TV has been available since 1972, but at first many communities – including all Arctic Quebec villages – refused to receive the satellite signal because of its alleged lack of relevance in the Inuit context. By 1984, however, television was in use everywhere in the Arctic, and in many locations up to a dozen channels were available. Only a small part of the programming (about an hour a day) was in Inuktitut and/or had northern content. Most of it was produced by the Inuit Broadcasting Corporation and Taqramiut Nipingat and was broadcast by CBC North.

In 1992 an educational network, Northern Canada Television (TVNC), started broadcasting in the north. It now offers between three and six hours daily of Inuktitut production. This, combined with CBC North's Inuit programs, makes some seven hours of aboriginal television available on most days. The menu includes interviews, reporting, talks on traditional culture, local sports, and a few productions for children. Television is widely watched by the Inuit – although not as much as during the first few years after its introduction – and, when asked about their preferences, most spectators cite southern (often American) productions rather than programs in Inuktitut.

The electronic media thus play an ambivalent role in the Canadian Arctic. While community radio clearly fosters native identity, television does not and indeed has the potential to destroy Inuit values, language, and culture.

Politics

Until the early 1970s no aboriginal organization existed in the north; the only body over which local people exercised some economic and administrative control was the cooperative movement. But after 1969 a new generation of young, educated Inuit was able to react effectively to the challenge posed by emerging megaprojects, such as the Mackenzie valley pipeline and the James Bay hydroelectric development.

With financial aid and logistical support from the federal government, aboriginal asssociations were established in order to uphold Inuit rights in Canada. They included the Committee for Original Peoples Entitlement (COPE) in the Mackenzie area (1970); Inuit Tapirisat of Canada, the national organization (1971); the Northern Quebec Inuit Association (1971); the Labrador Inuit Asssociation (1973); and several other regional and/or special-interest organizations (for example, the Inuit Cultural Institute, and Pauktuutiit, the national federation of Inuit women). In 1980 many Canadian Inuit played an active part in the establishment of the Inuit Circumpolar Conference, an international association formally recognized by the United Nations as the sole official representative of the Yupik and Inuit peoples. This body is busy elaborating and implementing an Arctic policy devised by Inuit in areas from Siberia to Greenland.

One of the first concrete results of these organizations' activities was the signing of the James Bay and Northern Quebec Agreement in 1975. It gave the local Inuit collective ownership over a good part of Arctic Quebec, as well as financial compensation for the extinction of their aboriginal title to this territory. The agreement also provided for the establishment of a locally controlled administrative apparatus in the fields of economic development (Makivik Corporation), municipal administration (the Kativik Regional Government and village-level municipal councils), education (Kativik School Board), language and culture (Avataq Cultural Institute), health and social services, and so on. In 1989 Quebec's Inuit organizations began evolving towards a more politically autonomous form of administration, thus fulfilling one of the wishes of the two communities (Povungnituk and Ivujivik) that do not recognize the legitimacy of the current agreement.

In the Northwest Territories, municipal governments and regional boards of health and education were also put into place during the mid-1970s, but it was not until 1985 that a land-claims settlement was signed with the Mackenzie Inuvialuit. Six years later, at the end of 1991, the Canadian government reached an agreement (signed in 1993) with the Inuit residents of the Kitikmeot, Keewatin, and Baffin regions. Besides providing for developmental funds and ownership rights over about 10 percent of these three regions, the document mandated establishment on 1 April 1999 of a new territory, Nunavut, carved out of the Northwest Territories, with its own government, elected by all its permanent residents, and most of the prerogatives of the Canadian provinces. With an Inuit population accounting for about 80 percent of the total, it was to become the only jurisdiction within Canada to have a native majority.

With the exception of those living in Labrador, Canada's Inuit now seem to have reached (or to be on the verge of reaching) satisfactory territorial and political agreements with the federal government. They also participate actively in national politics. In contrast to Indians, they were never denied voting rights. Over the years, a few Inuit have sat in the House of Commons or, in two cases (Peter Adams and Charlie Watt), in the Canadian Senate. Moreover, several Inuit belong to the legislative assembly of the Northwest Territories, either as deputies or as ministers. The ranks of aboriginal politicians in the Arctic include a large number of women, some of whom have reached the highest positions: premier of the Northwest Territories (Nellie Cournoyea), president of the Inuit Tapirisat of Canada (Rhoda Inukshuk; Rosemary Kuptana); chair of the Inuit Circumpolar Conference (Mary Simon, now Canadian ambassador for circumpolar affairs; Rosemary Kuptana).

Intergroup Relations and Group Maintenance

In the past, the Inuit were often hostile towards the neighbouring Dene, Cree, and Innu (Montagnais-Naskapi) Indians, but this is no longer the case. Today, the Inuit realize that they share the same aboriginal status as the Indians and that it is in their mutual interest to fashion political coalitions.

As for their relations with Euro-Canadians, except for early skirmishes in Labrador and other areas, the Inuit never fought full-fledged wars with the *Qallunaat* (Europeans). On the contrary, initial hostilities were rapidly followed (except, perhaps, in the Mackenzie region) by a period when the Inuit welcomed the explorers, traders, and missionaries and taught them the skills they needed to survive in the Arctic. Moreover, because southern Canadians never attempted large-scale settlement in the north, the Inuit still constitute a majority within *Inuit nunaat* and, unlike many Indian nations, they do not have a tradition of land spoliation. For these reasons, no general animosity is felt towards whites, although some may resent the fact that it is often the non-Inuit who hold the best jobs in Arctic communities.

Another grievance concerns the justice system, which has been imported into the Arctic from southern Canada. In Inuit villages, where everybody knows everybody else, no crime can remain hidden for long, and offenders are easily discovered and taken to court. This yields a rate of criminality apparently higher than that of Canada as a whole, but in fact most crimes are petty offences: drunkenness, public disorder, minor battery, and the like. Many voices are pleading for a reform of the judicial system that would increase the role of the community and focus on rehabilitating – rather than punishing – the offenders. Some improvements have been made, but they are far from sufficient. These efforts include Inuit policemen, recourse to traditional forms of punishment (such as the temporary removal of the offender to a neighbouring community), and native justices of the peace (there is one Inuit judge of the Provincial Court in Newfoundland-Labrador).

Some journalists and social scientists may describe contemporary Inuit society as fraught with insoluble problems and lacking an identity, but such a vision is inaccurate. In fact, the Inuit remain optimistic about their future and their sense of identity is still strong. Most native northerners have a fairly clear idea who an *inummarik* ("full Inuk") or *inutuinnaq* ("real Inuk") is: an individual able to draw part of his or her subsistence from the land without renouncing the better aspects of modern life. These people realize that modernity is here to stay, and that traditional culture must reach an accommodation with wage work, formal education, and the new political and social organizations. In some cases – among the young in particular – this may generate problems of identity, but, in the main, the Inuit are conscious of their distinctiveness and of a continuity between the past and the present. Despite tremendous changes in their material culture, the Inuit preserve values, social attitudes, a relation to the land, and a sense of their uniqueness that set them apart from other Canadians.

Most Arctic natives still live in close-knit communities. There may exist petty rivalries among family groups or between neighbouring villages, but, generally speaking, social life goes rather smoothly, despite occasional outbreaks of violence. The Inuit prefer to reach decisions through discussion and consensus, and there are no real cleavages betweeen the population and its leaders, the men and the women, or even the young and the old. This kind of informal *esprit de corps* seems to preserve Canada's Inuit against external assimilative pressures. For the moment, their sense of identity and their aboriginal organizations clearly define the boundaries of their community. It remains to be seen, however, if the Arctic natives will be able to maintain over time the fragile equilibrium between tradition and modernity, between what some Arctic Quebec Inuit call *maqainniq* ("going on the land") and *kiinaujaliurutiit* ("the means for making money").

FURTHER READING

The most complete description of Inuit prehistory, traditional culture, and contemporary history to 1980 is the *Handbook of North American Indians*, vol. 5, *Arctic*, edited by David Damas (Washington, D.C., 1984). Other general introductions to Canadian Inuit culture include Asen Balikci's *The Netsilik Eskimo* (Garden City, N.J., 1970), and Hugh Brody's *Living Arctic: Hunters of the Canadian North* (Vancouver, 1987). Brody has also published an insightful description of con-tacts between Inuit and Euro-Canadians: *The People's Land: Inuit, Whites and the Eastern Arctic* (Vancouver, 1991). Released much earlier but not outdated is Nelson Graburn's *Eskimos without Igloos: Social and Economic Development in Sugluk* (Boston, 1969), which describes cultural and social change in a small Arctic Quebec community. A more recent community study is Louis-Jacques Dorais, *Quaqtaq: Modernity and Identity in an Inuit Community* (Toronto, 1997).

Keith Crowe's *A History of the Original Peoples of Northern Canada* (Montreal, 1991) is probably the most popular introduction to northern aboriginal history, while Quentin Duffy's *The Road to Nunavut: The Progress of the Eastern Arctic Inuit since the Second World War* (Montreal, 1989) offers a more specialized overview of recent political developments in the Canadian Arctic.

In the fields of Inuit language and literature, Louis-Jacques Dorais presents a thorough description of the linguistic situation of the Canadian Inuit in "The Canadian Inuit and Their Language," in D.R.F. Collis, ed., *Arctic Languages: An Awakening* (Paris, 1990), 185–289. A few Inuit authors are cited in the text. An excellent autobiography is Minnie Aodla Freeman's *Life Among the Qallunaat* (Edmonton, 1978). The best anthology of Inuit literature is Robin (McGrath) Gedalof and Alootook Ipellie's *Paper Stays Put: A Collection of Inuit Writing* (Edmonton, 1979).

In addition to the Inuit periodicals listed in this chapter, the *Inuit Art Quarterly*, published in Nepean, Ont., by the Inuit Art Foundation since 1986, deals with all forms of Inuit art, while *Études/Inuit/Studies*, published at Université Laval, Quebec City, since 1977, is a scholarly (though generally readable) journal treating Inuit and Yupik anthropology, archaeology, history, art, language, and present-day conditions.

5

IROQUOIANS

Alexander von Gernet

Identification

The Iroquoian language family embraces a number of distinct peoples: the Huron, Petun, Mohawk, Oneida, Onondaga, Cayuga, Seneca, Tuscarora, Erie, Susquehannock, Nottoway, and Cherokee. The last four have little or no connection with Canada and are therefore not discussed in this entry; the remainder either lived in Canada at the time of first European contact or have moved there since. To this list of Iroquoian nations can be added two Iroquoian peoples that no longer exist, the St Lawrence Iroquoians and the Neutral.

The St Lawrence Iroquoians are also referred to as the Stadaconans and Hochelagans, after the names of their two communities (the present-day Quebec City and Montreal). They had vanished by the early seventeenth century and all that is known about their language derives from a vocabulary of two hundred words recorded in the sixteenth century. The other now-extinct Iroquoian people, the Neutral, obtained their European name from the French, who used the appellation Nation du Neutre to refer to any or all of the Iroquoian groups known as the Attiragenrega, Ahondihronon, Antouaronon, Onguiaronon, Kakouagoga, and Wenro. The term reflected the neutrality of these peoples in the seventeenth-century hostilities between the Huron and other Iroquoians.

The name Huron may derive from the Old French *hure*, a figurative term for rustic or hillbilly. Although the Huron are often considered a single people, they were actually a confederacy of four nations known as Attignawantan ("Bear People"), Attigneenongnahac ("Cord People"),

Arendahronon ("Rock People"), and Tahontaenrat ("Deer People"). Another group, Ataronchronon ("Swamp Dwellers"), while possibly constituting a fifth nation, was probably a component of the Attignawantan. Today, descendants of the Huron people live at Village-des-Hurons (Lorette) near Quebec City. They refer to themselves as Wendat, meaning "Islanders" or "Dwellers on a Peninsula."

It remains unclear why *petun*, an Old French term for tobacco, was used to designate a people known as the Khionontateronon, or Tiono-ntati. The common assumption that this nation specialized in tobacco production is unfounded. The Petun no longer live in Canada, although a people of mixed Petun-Huron ancestry called the Wyandot reside in Oklahoma.

The Mohawk, Oneida, Onondaga, Cayuga, Seneca, and Tuscarora comprise the Iroquois – a specific designation that should not be confused with the more inclusive Iroquoian language family. The name Iroquois first appeared in a Basque-Micmac pidgin language before being adopted by the French. Despite its disparaging connotation – it meant "killer people" – the term has persisted even in aboriginal parlance. Some traditionalists favour Haudenosaunee or "People of the Longhouse." The languages spoken by the Iroquois are more closely related to one another than they are to other Iroquoian languages such as Huron; Mohawk and Oneida have an especially close relationship. By the sixteenth century the Iroquois had formed an alliance known as the Iroquois Confederacy, or League of Five Nations. When the Tuscarora joined this confederacy in 1722–23, the Five Nations Iroquois became the Six Nations.

Contrary to popular opinion and frequent assertions by Iroquois traditionalists, at the time of first European contact there were no Mohawk, Oneida, Onondaga, Cayuga, or Seneca living anywhere in what is now known as Canada. Today, however, numerous Iroquois people are settled in Ontario and Quebec. Most live south of Brantford along the Grand River, Tyendinaga (east of Belleville), Akwesasne (near Cornwall), Kahnawake (near Montreal), Kanesatake (near Oka), Oneida of the Thames (southwest of London), and Gibson in the Muskoka district. While the federal government recognizes the residents of each of these communities as a "band" and their land as a "reserve," many of the inhabitants prefer the terms "First Nation" and "territory." It is estimated that forty to fifty thousand people in Canada belong to the Iroquoian language family.

History

Some Iroquoian oral traditions allude to long migrations from the west, while many others refer to acts of creation at specific localities in the northeast. Such stories are contradictory and cannot be reconciled with the archaeological record, a fact that is not surprising, since these traditions were and are guides to the Iroquoian social, political, and spiritual order rather than literal accounts of what actually happened in the past. Although there are many variants of the Iroquoian cosmological legend, they all refer to Sky Woman falling on earth piled on Turtle's back. This theme was recorded among the Hurons in the seventeenth century and among the Iroquois in the nineteenth century, attesting to its longevity and persistence even after European contact. To this day, many Iroquois refer to North America as Turtle Island.

The origins of those Iroquoian-speaking peoples who, at the time of first European contact, lived in parts of what are now southern Ontario, southern Quebec, and upstate New York has been the subject of lively scholarly debate for over a century. Since Iroquoians form an intrusive wedge between the eastern and central Algonquian peoples, it was originally thought that they had migrated into the area relatively recently. By the 1950s scientists were beginning to trace systematically the archaeological record of historically known Iroquoians. The new evidence pointed to a long development of Iroquoian cultures from ancestral hunting and gathering peoples living in the same region rather than to a migration into an area already occupied by proto-Algonquians. Much data have since accumulated to support what is now commonly referred to as the *in situ* theory of Iroquoian origins. In the 1990s, however, researchers found reasons to suspect that Iroquoians migrated into Ontario, Quebec, and New York State at approximately 900 C.E., bringing their languages and established culture with them. While debate continues, proponents of both the *in situ* theory and the more recent incursion model have reached a consensus that Iroquoians were definitely present in the region by one thousand years ago.

The Iroquoians of 1000 C.E. were not organized into the nations we know today but lived in evenly dispersed fishing villages and farming hamlets located throughout the area bordering the lower Great Lakes. Archaeologists refer to the undifferentiated Iroquoians of New York State as Owasco and recognize them as the ancestors of the Five Nations Iroquois. Similarly, the Glen Meyer and Pickering peoples are regarded by Ontario archaeologists as the ancestors of the Huron, Petun, and Neutral. Over time, the culturally uniform Owasco, Glen Meyer, and Pickering villages, which had been scattered along river flats, began to converge and move to defensible and palisaded settlements on hilltops. By 1000 C.E. the language family had already split into many of the modern Iroquoian languages, but it was only after 1350 that the settlement pattern began to resemble the clusters of large fortified communities which typify the nations known from the historical record. Most scholars are reluctant to use national terms such as "Mohawk" for the period prior to 1500, since it cannot be assumed that the nations encountered by Europeans bore a close resemblance to prehistoric peoples. Iroquoian nations were not immutable entities either before or after European contact.

When the St Lawrence Iroquoians encountered the French in the early sixteenth century, they lived along both sides of the St Lawrence River. Linguistic and archaeological evidence indicates that they were a distinct people or peoples and were not, as was previously thought, ancestors of the seventeenth-century Huron or Iroquois. They greeted Jacques Cartier in 1535–36 but had completely disappeared by the time Samuel de Champlain arrived in 1603. They seem to have vacated the St Lawrence valley sometime prior to 1580. Although the introduction of European diseases may have played a part in their disappearance, the weight of evidence suggests that hostilities with other aboriginal peoples led to a dispersal during which the survivors were assimilated by both friends and foes. The majority ended up among the Huron, while others may have been captured and adopted by the Mohawk.

The other Iroquoian nations were contacted during the first quarter of the seventeenth century. At that time, the Huron numbered about 21,000 people and occupied six large settlements as well many smaller, satellite communities. The settlements were concentrated in the area between Lake Simcoe and Georgian Bay. Archaeological evidence suggests that at least two of the Huron nations had originally lived along the north shore of Lake Ontario and in the Trent valley but had moved north to modern-day Simcoe County shortly before European contact. The Petun, who numbered 8,200, lived in eight or nine villages and hamlets located a day's walk southwest of the Huron in what are now Nottawasaga and Collingwood townships. Neutral villages were established near the western end of Lake Ontario, between the Grand and Niagara rivers, as well as in the Niagara area of northwestern New York. The total Neutral population was probably in the order of 25,000.

The Mohawk lived in three principal villages and several smaller hamlets situated along a section of the Mohawk River valley west of modern Schenectady, New York. The Oneida had only one community, located west of the Mohawk homeland and southeast of Oneida Lake. The Onondaga inhabited two villages west of the Oneida homeland and just south of present-day Syracuse. West of the Onondaga, near what is now the town of Auburn, New York, were the three principal Cayuga settlements. The Seneca lived in two large and several small communities situated west of the Cayuga and south of modern-day Rochester. In 1625 the total population of the Five Nations Iroquois was little more than 22,000. Little is known about the Tuscarora during this early period, except that their homeland was in what was to become the state of North Carolina.

Much of the uninhabited wilderness between the homelands was used for hunting. Hence, the actual territory of each nation was significantly larger than the area in which the villages were located. For reasons ranging from exhaustion of soil fertility to depletion of firewood, Iroquoian villages were moved every one to three decades. These relocations were confined to the homelands and usually involved a distance of only a few kilometres.

This traditional pattern of Iroquoian settlement was significantly transformed during the second half of the seventeenth century. In 1649, after many years of sustained belligerence, the Iroquois drove the Huron from their Ontario homelands. Although many Huron perished, some found refuge among neighbouring groups, while others ended up living with their conquerors. One group of Huron, who had converted to Christianity, settled under French protection at Île d'Orléans near Quebec City. The Mohawk attacked this settlement and carried off many Huron, and after a series of relocations the remaining Huron ended up at Lorette. Another group had sought refuge among the Petun. This mixed Petun-Huron population was also driven from what is now southern Ontario by the Iroquois. Over the next two centuries it lived in present-day Michigan, Wisconsin, Ohio, and Kansas before finally settling in Oklahoma. The Neutral were dispersed by the Iroquois during the 1650s and effectively ceased to exist as an identifiable nation.

Following the diaspora of the indigenous inhabitants of southern Ontario, the Iroquois were free to use the territory for hunting. By 1670 the Seneca, Cayuga, and Oneida had established a series of small settlements along the north shore of Lake Ontario: Quinaouatoua (west of Hamilton), Teyaiagon and Ganestiquiagon at the mouths of the Humber and Rouge rivers (both in Metropolitan Toronto), Ganaraské (Port Hope), Quintio (western end of Rice Lake), Quinté (near Trenton), and Ganneious (near Napanee). This first Iroquois effort to settle in southern Ontario was short-lived. By 1688 the communities were either abandoned or taken over by the Ojibwa, an Algonquian people that drove the Iroquois back to their homelands in New York State. A few Iroquois lingered under the protection of Fort Frontenac at present-day Kingston.

Meanwhile, Jesuit missionaries succeeded in attracting Iroquoian "Praying Indians" to reserves established along the St Lawrence. In 1667 Father Pierre Raffeix and several French families founded La Prairie de la Madeleine on lands near Montreal. The first native inhabitants were Oneida and adopted Huron. By 1672 the La Prairie mission had a mix of people of many different ethnic backgrounds. Four years later the missionaries made an application for new lands and the La Prairie mission was moved upriver to the Sault-Saint-Louis, or Lachine Rapids, where it came to be known as Caughnawaga. In 1677 the newly relocated settlement had twenty-two Huron and Iroquois longhouses and was governed by two Huron and two Iroquois headmen. Despite the multicultural nature of the community, a constant stream of immigrants from the Mohawk valley eventually gave the Mohawk hegemony and Mohawk became the primary language spoken. Today, the community is called Kahnawake ("at the rapids").

In 1676 the Sulpician missionaries established a mission at Mount Royal on the island of Montreal. The aboriginal peoples who settled there were known as the Iroquois of the Mountain. Eventually, the mission was relocated to Lac des Deux Montagnes near the mouth of the Ottawa River. Although this village originally included people of Nipissing and Algonkin ancestry, many of these individuals moved away during the nineteenth century and the settlement became predominantly Iroquoian. This is the modern community of Kanesatake ("place of reeds"), known to most Canadians by the Algonkin name Oka ("Walleyed pike").

Migration to the St Lawrence during the last quarter of the seventeenth century caused a significant demographic depletion in the Iroquois homelands, particularly in the Mohawk valley. Persistent efforts by both the Mohawk and the English to convince the "Praying Indians" to return were not met with success, and by the end of the century there were only two Mohawk communities left in New York State. In 1755 a factional dispute and the need for more land prompted several

Kahnawake families to move up the St Lawrence to the new Jesuit mission at Saint Regis, near modern Cornwall, Ontario. The French hoped that this settlement would serve as an additional buffer against the British. Today, the community is known as Akwesasne ("where the partridge drums"). During the eighteenth century Kahnawake, Kanesatake, and Akwesasne joined with the Huron of Lorette and several Algonquian-speaking groups to form the Seven Nations of Canada. This confederacy, also known as the Federation of Seven Fires, was composed of Catholic mission settlements and should not be confused with the Six Nations, or Iroquois Confederacy.

In the aftermath of the American Revolution, the British were confronted with the problem of what to do with those Iroquois allies who had fought against the Americans and deserved restitution for the loss of their lands in New York State. In 1783 Governor Frederick Haldimand secured a site on the Bay of Quinte in eastern Ontario from an Ojibwa people known as the Mississauga. One Mohawk faction led by John Deserontyon agreed to settle there the following year, and the community it established is now known as Tyendinaga. However, the majority of Mohawk, as well as many Cayuga, Onondaga, Oneida, Seneca, and Tuscarora, were reluctant to live at the Bay of Quinte. In 1784-85 these Loyalist Iroquois chose to follow the Mohawk war chief Thayendanegea (Joseph Brant) to a large tract of land along the Grand River, which Haldimand had acquired from the Mississauga. The original grant included the entire river valley from source to mouth, but numerous controversial land transactions reduced this to the relatively small parcel that constitutes the modern Grand River territory of the Six Nations. Other Iroquois opted to remain in the United States.

In 1839, 242 Oneida who had remained in the United States after the revolution sold their lands in New York State, pooled their money, and purchased a tract of land near London, Upper Canada (Ontario), where they founded a community that came to be known as Oneida of the Thames or Onyota'a:ka. Later in the century, conflicts between the Sulpicians and Protestant Iroquois at Kanesatake, as well as a dispute about whether the Iroquois had any claims to the seigneury of the Lac des Deux Montagnes, led to violence and a sensational trial. The outcome was that in 1881 thirty-two Mohawk families voluntarily abandoned Kanesatake to live on lands in Muskoka purchased from the government of Ontario with money given by the Sulpician seminary. This settlement became Wahta ("maple"), more commonly known as the Gibson Reserve.

Lorette, Kahnawake, Kanesatake, Akwesasne, Tyendinaga, Oneida of the Thames, Wahta, and the Six Nations territory on the Grand River were not established in the traditional, pre-contact homelands. This contrasts with other aboriginal peoples such as the Inuit, who, for the most part, continue to live in the territories they occupied for millennia. It should also be kept in mind that peoples of Iroquoian descent are by no means confined to these communities. In some cases as many as half of those registered on official rolls live "off-reserve" in nearby towns and in large urban centres such as Toronto. The proximity of the modern Iroquoian communities to Canada's most densely settled non-aboriginal population has had a significant impact on the lives of Iroquoian peoples.

The Iroquoian presence in the Canada of the 1990s was confined to central Canada. By the end of the eighteenth century the expansion of the western fur trade had enticed numerous Kahnawake, Kanesatake, and Akwesasne residents to make their way into the west, where they sought employment with the North-West Company. Some married Cree women and settled near present-day Edmonton. Although a few descendants of these families continue to live in Alberta, there are no Iroquois communities west of Ontario.

Economic Life

For ten thousand years, all humans living in what is now Ontario and Quebec were hunters and gatherers. During the period 500–900 C.E. the ancestors of modern Iroquoians adopted the practice of cultivating corn, an innovation that had originated in Mexico. Growing corn and other foods such as beans and squash had a profound effect on Iroquoians, leading to a type of food-producing economy anthropologists call swidden horticulture, which required the preparation of garden plots and fields by clearing forests using the slash-and-burn method. As the clearings became the focus of activity for much of the year, people no longer travelled in small nomadic bands and became more sedentary. This was one of the reasons why Iroquoians had much larger villages, longer houses, and higher population densities than many of their Algonquian-speaking neighbours.

The adoption of swidden horticulture did not mean that Iroquoians completely abandoned hunting, fishing, and gathering. Scientific evidence suggests that, while cultivated foods represented 50 to 60 percent of the Huron caloric intake, almost a quarter of the diet consisted of wild plant foods, particularly fleshy fruits such as strawberries, and 15 percent came from animal and fish food. Of the many animals hunted by Iroquoians, white-tailed deer had the greatest dietary significance and were valued for their large skins. Deer were taken either by individual hunters or in large cooperative expeditions involving hundreds of men. Differences in cultural preferences and local ecosystems led to variations in Iroquoian economies. The Mohawk, for instance, hunted more than did the Huron. Similarly, the St Lawrence Iroquoians at Stadacona relied mainly on fish, eels, and land mammals, while those at Hochelaga had extensive cornfields.

All Iroquoians manufactured pottery vessels used for food storage, cooking, and carrying water as well as elaborately decorated ceramic smoking pipes, many different stone and bone tools, reed baskets, bark canoes and eating bowls, snares and fishing nets made from twine, clothes and bags made from animal skins, and a variety of ornamental objects. These items circulated in an internal economy and were occasionally offered in foreign trade. For the most part, Iroquoian communities were self-sufficient. Some, like the Huron, traded corn surpluses to their Algonquian neighbours in return for warm winter clothing. The Huron also obtained large quantities of black squirrel skins from the Neutral and used them to manufacture cloaks. Such trade was not only an integral part of the traditional Iroquoian economy but also served to solidify political alliances between nations.

New alliances emerged with the coming of the Europeans. By 1615 the Huron were trading directly with the French on the St Lawrence River while the Iroquois were trading with the Dutch on the Hudson River. European traders were especially interested in procuring beaver pelts which had already been worn as clothing over the winter, since this use released the long guard hairs and rendered them suitable for the manufacture of fashionable felt hats. For Iroquoians, hunting beaver and selling used clothing was an economical means of obtaining European goods.

Initially, the introduction of copper kettles, iron axes, and glass beads did little to alter traditional lifeways. Iroquoians regarded such European goods much as they viewed native copper and quartz crystals – as sources of supernatural power – and integrated them into existing cultural institutions. Yet sustained contact with Europeans eventually did have an impact. From the 1640s, the Iroquois acquired guns from the Dutch and used them in internecine warfare. Traditional hostilities intensified as the fur trade brought beaver to the verge of extinction and the Iroquois began seeking new sources of peltry outside their national territories. By the late eighteenth century, Kahnawake and Akwesasne men were working for fur-trading companies and were also employed as raftsmen and lumberjacks in the timber industry. In the early nineteenth century, increasing numbers of non-aboriginal settlers and a reduction in the land base led to a decreased reliance on subsistence hunting. At the same time, the creation of reserves precluded the traditional pattern of moving Iroquoian villages whenever the soil was exhausted. Iroquoians turned to European farming methods, including the use of plough and oxen. At some communities, the earlier horticultural and hunting economy was replaced entirely with intensive agriculture.

One of the most remarkable transformations in the economic life of the Iroquois began in 1886 when the Dominion Bridge Company began construction of a railway bridge over the St Lawrence near Kahnawake. In return for granting the firm the right to use reserve land for the bridge abutment, Kahnawake men were promised construction jobs. It soon became apparent that the aboriginal workers had little fear of heights and were very agile. By 1907 there were over seventy Kahnawake working as skilled bridgemen on various projects across the country. It was not long before every new structure that went up in Canada had an Iroquois riveting gang precariously balanced on steel girders high above the ground. In the 1930s Kahnawake men joined the Brooklyn local of the high-steel union and began work on some of New York's most famous bridges and tallest buildings. Within a few generations the Iroquois had moved from building bark-covered longhouses to erecting steel skyscrapers.

Given this early transition to full-time wage work, it is not surprising that today most Iroquoian people participate in the cash-based economy familiar to most Canadians. While many work in businesses run by non-aboriginal people, others have established successful enterprises on the reserves. During the 1960s the Huron at Lorette became famous for their well-crafted snowshoes and canvas canoes, which they sold by the tens of thousands. Some Iroquoian communities now have full-time economic development officers and are producing strategies for community planning. In many respects, hamlets such as Ohsweken at the Six Nations territory are little different from any other small town in southern Ontario. The vitality of commerce is promoted with slogans such as "shop local, shop native." While poverty is still evident, it is much less prevalent than in aboriginal reserves in northern Ontario.

Since Akwesasne is situated athwart the Canada-United States border, some residents have engaged in a lucrative, albeit illicit, international commerce, thereby bringing significant revenues into the community. Other business initiatives are supported by the Canadian government. A good example of a creative and successful enterprise is the Iroquois Cranberry Growers of Gibson. In the late 1960s, with the assistance of a government grant, the people of Wahta established a modern, fully mechanized cranberry-growing industry, which has provided local jobs and now affords an opportunity for an annual event in the tradition of Iroquois berry festivals.

Kinship, Family, and Social Organization

The traditional Iroquoian kinship system was complex and has sometimes confused anthropologists and even Iroquoians. In this system, the names for parallel relatives were different from those for cross relatives. For example, the Huron term for mother was also applied to mother's sister and the term for father to father's brother; a different pair of terms was used to designate a mother's brother and father's sister. Similarly, mother's sisters' and father's brothers' children (parallel-cousins) were called sisters and brothers, while only mother's brothers' and father's sisters' children (cross-cousins) were called cousins. A man's sisters' children were nieces and nephews, while his brothers' children were sons and daughters. Conversely, a woman's sisters' children were called sons and daughters, while her brothers' children were nieces and nephews. Obviously, the increasing use of English or French has masked many of these original nuances.

Although the kinship terminology reflected a bilateral system, descent, inheritance, and succession passed in the female line, and the matrilineal extended family was the basic unit of Iroquoian social organization. Each Iroquoian longhouse contained a matrilineal group composed of mothers, sisters, and daughters as well as male spouses from other lineages. As the families grew, the longhouses were literally extended. The average Huron longhouse was 6.5 metres wide and 18 metres long, although some were close to 50 metres in length and a few prehistoric Iroquois longhouses were twice that.

By the nineteenth century the longhouses had been replaced by European-style dwellings. In 1847, when the Six Nations territory officially became a "reserve," the Crown allotted forty-hectare tracts of land to each male head of a nuclear family. Today, most families reside in individual housing that reflects differences in income and social mobility, and visitors encounter structures ranging from modest bungalows to large, middle-class homes. In 1995 there were 2,275 separate households in the community, the majority of which contained single nuclear families.

Traditionally, each individual belonged not only to a matrilineage but also to one of the many clans named after various animals. Clans were, for ritual purposes, also grouped into various combinations of phratries and moieties. An individual was a member of his or her mother's clan, and personal names were "owned" by clans. The clans were exogamous – that is, marriage could not occur with someone belonging to the same clan, even if the individual was from a different nation. When a man married, he usually moved to the longhouse of his wife's family, a practice known as matrilocality. This, of course, meant that the men living in the matrilineal longhouses were often considered outsiders. In modern times there has been a tendency for married couples to establish their own households. At the same time, a recent penchant for "authentic" clan-specific names has prompted a flurry of research and discussion about the appropriateness of certain marriage arrangements.

The traditional system made sense in the light of the gender-based division of labour. At the time of European contact, the forests were the domain of men, while the villages and their surrounding fields of corn, beans, and squash (the "three sisters") were the domain of women. The men hunted and engaged in warfare, foreign travel, trade missions, and diplomacy. The women planted and harvested the crops, gathered firewood, and prepared meals. These tasks required considerable cooperation among the women, who remained at or near the villages for most of the year. Female hegemony over village matters gave the ranking matrons or clan mothers control over the selection and removal ("dehorning") of chiefs, although they themselves did not hold public office. They also were free to express their opinions and defend their collective rights.

When swidden horticulture was replaced with intensive agriculture, men began working the fields. This, together with participation in the cash-based economy, changed the division of labour between men and women and brought more flexibility into the composition of kin groups. Nevertheless, there has been some retention of the clan system, and Iroquois traditionalists continue to have great respect for clan mothers.

Intermarriage between Iroquoians and non-aboriginal people began in the seventeenth century and has become increasingly common since.

By the 1970s such unions constituted nearly half the marriages each year at the Six Nations territory. The Indian Act created a number of peculiar legal categories which affected the rights of Iroquois women and introduced a paternal bias not found in traditional Iroquoian society. For example, while Iroquois women who married non-aboriginal men lost their status as "Indians" within the meaning of the act, non-aboriginal women, regardless of their racial or national origin, gained Indian status once they married Iroquois men. It was only after these discriminatory provisions were repealed with the passing of Bill C-31 in 1985 that many Iroquois women became eligible to apply for status. The official rolls of Iroquoian communities have been substantially augmented as women return with their children, although long-time residents have not always responded with enthusiasm to this readmittance.

Traditional Iroquoian societies were theoretically egalitarian, with no individual possessing more wealth than another. The accumulation of goods was usually for the purpose of giving them away. Chiefs did, however, enjoy certain privileges not shared by others. Today, class distinctions are more apparent and, to a large extent, mirror non-aboriginal society.

Culture

Until recently, Iroquoians had no written language and culture was transmitted orally from generation to generation. Wampum belts, woven with strings of white and purple cylindrical shells, served as mnemonic devices to assist recall. Numerous myths, epic tales, and stories comprised a rich folk tradition. Apart from the creation legends, one of the most important traditions – represented by many versions and known as the Deganawida epic – recalls the founding of the Five Nations Iroquois League. It also details the Great Law, which provides guidelines for the political organization of the confederacy and its standardized inventory of metaphors and rituals.

Singing, drumming, and dancing have always been important to the Iroquois. Each summer many Iroquois participate in the powwow circuit, which brings aboriginal peoples from different communities together to socialize and take part in standardized, competitive dances involving spectacular costumes and prize money. Since most First Nations communities host powwows, several weekends are spent with friends or relatives throughout southern Ontario. The powwow is a modern, pan-Indian event and is not indigenous to the Iroquois, while the Peacemaker's Drum, or Tyendinaga Mohawk Singing Society, has as its main objective the promotion of Iroquois culture through spiritual and social activities, including the performance of traditional songs and dances. The Six Nations Women Singers have similar goals. Some people of Iroquois ancestry have also become successful singers, musicians, and actors in Western popular culture.

As interest in aboriginal peoples has grown in the Western world, the demand for Iroquoian-related books, artwork, crafts (especially black-ash splint baskets, beadwork, and stone carvings) has increased. Iroqrafts at the Six Nations territory, the Woodland Cultural Centre near Brantford, and the Akwesasne Notes Bookstore have served a vital role in promoting Iroquoian culture and history. Iroquois organizations such as Indian Art-I-Crafts of Ontario have helped sponsor numerous events, including the Toronto International Powwow held at the Skydome. Such events have attracted thousands of aboriginal and non-aboriginal people and have brought revenues to many Iroquois vendors.

Iroquoian culture has been documented in a voluminous literature covering a period of nearly four centuries. This information has had a feedback effect, as anthropological and historical works have influenced the Iroquoian understanding of their own culture and history. At the same time, some traditionalists have rejected academic reconstructions whenever they conflict with their own oral traditions. In response to the social pathologies that have characterized twentieth-century life in aboriginal communities, some Iroquoian people have not only accelerated the process of revitalization but have also begun formulating a new past. Culture, history, and politics cannot be easily separated in recent Iroquoian representations of themselves.

Religion

Like other aboriginal peoples in Canada, Iroquoians traditionally did not have a "religion" in the European sense but practised a type of animism or shamanism that did not clearly distinguish between natural and supernatural worlds. This belief system was of great antiquity and probably accompanied the first humans who migrated from Asia to North America. Although shamanism is most frequently associated with hunting and gathering societies, the adoption of horticulture did not completely alter the Iroquoian worldview, and many of the original features survived into the historic period.

According to this tradition, animals, plants, and even some inanimate objects had souls, and spirit beings inhabited every region of the cosmos. To propitiate these spirits, offerings of tobacco and other gifts were left at various locations, such as awe-inspiring cliffs and waterfalls. Speeches were accompanied by tobacco invocations, during which the powdered leaf was sprinkled on fires, so that the words could "ride" the smoke to the upper world. The Huron believed that every human possessed as many as five "souls," each with a different name, different functions, and different destinies in the afterlife. Some souls could be reincarnated, others lingered about the villages as ghosts, while others were sent off to the Land of the Souls after an elaborate ceremony.

Among all Iroquoian peoples, contact with normally invisible spirit beings was achieved by entering trance states through ritual fasting, monotonous singing, vigorous dancing, smoking, and the ingestion of a variety of psychoactive substances. Although there were shamans who specialized in these activities, by the time of European contact a democratized shamanism offered all members of the community the power to have revelations, which provided important spiritual guidelines for individual and collective action. For the Huron, virtually every major decision was influenced by a dream or vision. The Iroquois had a calendric cycle of planting and harvest ceremonies as well as the great midwinter festival held to reveal and fulfil dream obligations. There were also occasions for curative and prophylactic rituals performed by various medicine societies, including one whose participants wore wooden masks commonly known as False Faces.

The Jesuit missionaries have long been accorded a heroic place in Canadian history, although this image has recently been replaced with the view that they did as much harm as good. From an Iroquoian perspective, the most serious consequence of the Jesuit presence was the emergence of internal factionalism between Christian converts and traditionalists. This factionalism seriously weakened the Huron confederacy in the 1640s and made it more vulnerable to Iroquois attacks; after 1667 it also had a negative effect on the Iroquois and especially the Mohawk nation. In denominational terms, since communities such as Lorette, Kahnawake, Kanesatake, and Akwesasne were established as French missions, Catholicism has dominated much of their history. Tyendinaga and the Six Nations territory, with their links to the British, were always predominantly Anglican. By the late nineteenth century, the Anglicans were joined by Baptists, Methodists, Brethren, Mormons, and the Salvation Army. Modern visitors to the Six Nations territory are struck by the plethora of churches representing various denominations.

Unlike world religions such as Christianity, aboriginal belief systems were not dogmatically bound by sacred texts, and oral traditions were marked by a constant injection of new revelations based on dreams and visions. In 1799 Handsome Lake, a Seneca prophet living at the Allegany reservation in New York State, had the first of a series of visions in which he was instructed on his people's religious obligations. These included the outlawing of drunkenness, witchcraft, sexual promiscuity, and gambling, the reviving of traditional calendric ceremonies, and the sanctioning of the Protestant ideal of the nuclear family farm. The Handsome Lake religion (or Longhouse religion, as it is also known) was an indigenous revitalization movement that endorsed some accommodation with non-aboriginal society. As such, it spread rapidly in the Six Nations territory in Canada, but it was not introduced to Kahnawake until the 1920s and to Akwesasne until the 1930s. Though Handsome Lake adherents outnumbered Christians in the early nineteenth century, their numbers have since declined. Nevertheless, the Longhouse continues as an alternative to the Christian churches. Elders such as Cayuga hereditary chief Jacob Thomas and other ritualists have managed to keep the Gaiwí:yo (the Good Message, or Code of Handsome Lake) alive at the Six Nations territory, where over 1,000 adherents, with remarkable persistence, are continuing the celebration of traditional ceremonies. Long regarded as "pagans" even by Christian Iroquois, they are now more often esteemed as "genuine Indians."

Education, Language, and Communication

By the 1840s a number of schools operated by the Church of England (the New England Company) offered formal education to Six Nations children. Attendance was apparently irregular, since some parents regarded the schools as a threat to Iroquois traditions. One of the first, the Mohawk Institute, became a residential school and remained so until 1970.

As early as the 1870s Iroquois chiefs had at least some say in local educational policy at the Six Nations territory, and a few Iroquois people were employed as teachers. Nevertheless, speaking in Iroquoian languages was forbidden, and going to school was often a humiliating experience. School attendance was made compulsory in 1920. In the 1990s there was a devolution of responsibility for education from the federal Department of Indian Affairs to the Six Nations community, although painful memories of the residential school system still linger.

The Huron language is now extinct, although ethnolinguists have laboriously reconstructed a rudimentary vocabulary and grammar from early French-Huron dictionaries. Today, the Huron at Lorette speak French. The Petun spoke the same dialect as the Attignawantan Huron. The Huron name for the Neutral, Attiouendaronk ("they who understand the language"), suggests that the now-extinct Neutral dialects were closely related to Huron.

While the five Iroquois languages are not extinct, they are certainly endangered, since fluency in them is restricted primarily to elders. Based on figures provided to the Royal Commission on Aboriginal Peoples in 1992, of the 16,443 people officially registered on the rolls of the Grand River territory of the Six Nations, only 285 (1.7 percent) spoke one of the Iroquois languages fluently. Of these, 246 (86.3 percent) were Cayuga, Mohawk, and Onondaga over the age of fifty.

There are signs of hope for Iroquoian languages. While English remains the language of instruction in many facilities, including the Kahnawake Survival School, native language instruction has been added to the curriculum of certain schools. In 1970 some Six Nations elementary schools taught fifteen minutes of Cayuga or Mohawk. Such initiatives evolved into immersion programs, and by 1990 enrolment represented 15 percent of the total elementary school population. Today, most schools at Six Nations offer instruction in at least one Iroquois language. Academic institutions such as the Centre for Research and Teaching of Canadian Native Languages at the University of Western Ontario have done much to rejuvenate Iroquois languages. A number of dictionaries and grammars on various dialects have also been published in recent decades.

Iroquois newspapers have come and gone, although *Akwesasne Notes* (Rooseveltown, New York, 1968–), "The Official Publication of the Mohawk Nation," has served as a forum for the promotion of an Iroquois consciousness for many decades and has had subscribers from all over North America. In 1995 it evolved from a newsprint format to a glossy quarterly magazine. Other papers, such as *Tekawennake* (Ohsweken, Ontario, 1970–) and the *Turtle Island News* (Ohsweken, 1994–), reach readers at Six Nations and provide an aboriginal perspective on local, regional, and national events, as well as lifestyles, food, sports, arts, and business. The *Eastern Door* (Kahnawake, Quebec, 1991–) does the same for Kahnawake. Iroquois intellectuals have also written books and pamphlets. One of the most popular is *A Basic Call to Consciousness* (1978), a traditionalist manifesto that has become an influential text in an emerging Iroquois cultural nationalism.

English is the language of Iroquois media, including local radio stations. It is also the language of most prose and poetry. The various versions of the "Iroquoian Cosmology," published by the Bureau of American Ethnology in 1903 and 1928, as well as the "Huron-Wyandot Traditional Narratives" published by the National Museum of Canada in 1960, are rare examples of texts recorded in the original languages. Yet the lack of widespread fluency has precluded the development of a significant corpus of published literature in any of the Iroquoian languages. Even Chief Jacob Thomas's recent "Teachings from the Longhouse," while based on an Onondaga script, is available only in English translation.

Politics and Intergroup Relations

Shortly before European contact, the Mohawk, Oneida, Onondaga, Cayuga, and Seneca had formed a non-aggression pact that came to be known as the League of the Iroquois. Throughout much of the seventeenth century, this league did not have a unified foreign policy but was intended to keep spiritual unity and peace among the Five Nations, each continuing to act independently of one another in their relations with Europeans. By the 1680s, however, there had emerged a political, diplomatic, and military confederacy intended to represent a unified pan-Iroquois politics. Theoretically, the confederacy, or confederate council, had fifty hereditary chiefs representing various clans, with each assuming the name of his predecessor. Decisions were reached only through unanimous agreement. In recent times, the league and the confederacy have often been regarded as one and the same.

The confederacy was not always in agreement over policy towards the French and English and, later, British and Americans. In fact, the council fire, which was located at Onondaga, where the confederacy chiefs usually met, was symbolically covered in 1777, thereby dissolving the confederacy. After the American Revolution, two council fires were rekindled, one on the American side and one at Six Nations in Canada. The Canadian version of the confederacy remained in power throughout the nineteenth century, although it was under constant pressure from the British and Canadian governments.

Kahnawake, Kanesatake, and Akwesasne were not part of the Iroquois Confederacy, although they maintained their own hereditary chiefs. In 1888 the Canadian government introduced a system of electing chiefs at Akwesasne. That same year Akwesasne became the Mohawk member of the American version of the confederacy. Today, Akwesasne has three governing bodies: the Mohawk Nation Council (nine hereditary chiefs appointed for life), the St Regis Tribal Council (recognized by the United States), and the Mohawk Council of Akwesasne (an elected body of twelve chiefs and one grand chief recognized by Canada). This situation, together with the fact that Akwesasne lies in five jurisdictions (Canada, the United States, Ontario, Quebec, and New York State), has made its relations with the external power structure among the most complicated in North America.

In 1924 the Canadian government also dissolved the confederate council at Six Nations and replaced it with an elected body. The hereditary chiefs continued to meet, and today there remains a division between the elected council and the confederate council. The latter rejects all Canadian Indian legislation since 1867, and there have been several attempts to overthrow the elected band councillors. The confederate chiefs uphold a version of the traditional Great Law and are generally followers of the Longhouse religion. Their ultimate aim is to have Canada recognize the confederacy as the government of the Six Nations. At the present time the majority of Six Nations people do not, however, wish to replace the modern elected council.

Relations with the federal government have most often been dominated by issues of local interest to each Iroquoian community. The construction of the St Lawrence Seaway in the 1950s generated difficulties at both Akwesasne and Kahnawake. In particular, owing to the terms of the Indian Act, an Akwesasne woman living on the Canadian side was no longer considered an Indian if she married an Akwesasne man living on the American side. The international boundary led to a host of problems with border crossings and duty-free passage, some of which are currently being resolved in the courts. In April 1990 nightly fire-fights with automatic weapons between pro- and anti-gambling factions at Akwesasne resulted in massive police intervention by both Canadian and U.S. governments. Cigarette smuggling has also contributed to tensions, both within the community and in relations with non-aboriginal society.

The unique historical circumstance that led to the establishment of various Iroquoian communities in Canada has meant that large-scale land claims do not play as important a part among the Iroquoian peoples as they do among many other aboriginal groups. Nevertheless, the Six Nations have been actively pursuing the possibility of reclaiming or obtaining compensation for land they lost along the Grand River. Claims by Iroquoian people have also led to landmark court decisions.

For example, in the 1990 case of *R. v. Sioui*, the Supreme Court of Canada decided that the Huron of Lorette could not be prosecuted for cutting trees, camping, and making fires in a nearby provincial park because "treaties and statutes relating to Indians should be liberally construed and uncertainties resolved in favour of the Indians."

The Oka crisis of 1990, with its violence, protracted armed stand-off, and bridge blockade, brought the Mohawk of Kanesatake and Kahnawake into the international limelight. Precipitated by a proposed expansion of a golf course onto disputed lands, the affair became a metaphor and rallying cry for various aboriginal grievances, not only in Quebec but across the country. Although members of the militant Warrior Society received most of the press coverage, they were opposed by more moderate Iroquois who worked behind the scenes to resolve the crisis.

As the tension between traditionalist and modernist forces continues in Iroquoian communities, the promise of self-government is met with considerable ambivalence. Who will ultimately wield power remains uncertain. Meanwhile, Iroquoian people are committed to rebuilding the social fabric of their lives and leading their nations into a prosperous future.

FURTHER READING

Article-length introductions to each of the Iroquoian peoples are found in the *Handbook of North American Indians*, vol.15, *Northeast*, edited by Bruce Trigger (Washington, D.C., 1978), *Aboriginal Ontario*, edited by Edward S. Rogers and Donald B. Smith (Toronto, 1994), and *The Archaeology of Southern Ontario to A.D. 1650*, edited by Chris J. Ellis and Neal Ferris (London, Ont., 1990).

Popular books on the Huron include Bruce Trigger's *The Huron: Farmers of the North*, 2nd. ed. (Toronto, 1990), Nancy Bonvillain's *The Huron* (New York, 1989), Elisabeth Tooker's *An Ethnography of the Huron Indians, 1615-1649* (Syracuse, N.Y., 1991), and Conrad Heidenreich's *Huronia* (Toronto, 1971). The definitive scholarly study is Bruce Trigger's multivolume *The Children of Aataentsic: A History of the Huron People to 1660* (Montreal, 1976). Georges Sioui's *For an Amerindian Autohistory* (Montreal, 1992) is a philosophical polemic on Huron history written by a Huron.

Lewis Henry Morgan's classic *League of the Ho-dé-no-sau-nee, Iroquois* (Rochester, N.Y., 1851) has been reprinted in many different editions and remains the best general book on the Five Nations Iroquois. More recent popular summaries include Frank Speck's *The Iroquois*, 2nd. ed. (Bloomfield Hills, Mich., 1955), Barbara Graymont's *The Iroquois* (New York, 1988), Dean R. Snow's *The Iroquois* (Oxford, U.K., 1996), and Nancy Bonvillain's *The Mohawk* (New York, 1992). There is a vast corpus of academic scholarship on the Iroquois. A sample of the most significant studies has been compiled and reprinted in the multivolume *An Iroquois Source Book*, edited by Elisabeth Tooker (New York, 1985). The "Iroquois Reprints" series by Iroqrafts at Six Nations has revived many other out-of-print classics. A good example of interdisciplinary approaches to Iroquoian studies is Michael K. Foster et al., *Extending the Rafters* (Albany, N.Y., 1984).

Informative books on the rich ceremonial life and belief systems of the Iroquois include Elisabeth Tooker's *The Iroquois Ceremonial of Midwinter* (Syracuse, N.Y., 1970), William Fenton's massive study, *The False Faces of the Iroquois* (Norman, Okla., 1987), and James W. Herrick's *Iroquois Medical Botany* (Syracuse, 1995). Chief Jacob Thomas's *Teachings from the Longhouse* (Toronto, 1994) is a recent outline of the Handsome Lake religion by the only surviving Iroquois capable of reciting the Great Law from memory.

Scholarly works on the complex history of relations between the Iroquois and the European newcomers include Richard Aquila's *The Iroquois Restoration* (Detroit, 1983); Francis Jennings's *The Ambiguous Iroquois Empire* (New York, 1984); *The History and Culture of Iroquois Diplomacy*, edited by Francis Jennings (Syracuse, 1985); *Beyond the Covenant Chain*, edited by Daniel K. Richter and James H. Merrell (Syracuse, 1987); Daniel Richter's *The Ordeal of the Longhouse* (Chapel Hill, N.C., 1992); Matthew Dennis's *Cultivating a Landscape of Peace* (Ithaca, N.Y., 1993); Barbara Graymont's *The Iroquois in the American Revolution* (Syracuse, 1972); and D. Peter MacLeod's *The Canadian Iroquois and the Seven Years' War* (Toronto, 1996).

Readers interested specifically in the Grand River Six Nations community should consult *The Valley of the Six Nations*, edited by Charles M. Johnston (Toronto, 1964), Isabel T. Kelsay's *Joseph Brant* (Syracuse, 1984), and Annemarie Shimony's *Conservatism among the Iroquois at the Six Nations Reserve* (Syracuse, 1994). Sylvia Du Vernet's *An Indian Odyssey* (Islington, Ont., 1986) is the only book on the Gibson Reserve. Rick Hornung's *One Nation under the Gun* (Toronto, 1991) and Gerald R. Alfred's *Heeding the Voices of Our Ancestors* (Toronto, 1995) chronicle the history and recent politics of Mohawk nationalism at Kahnawake, Kanesatake, and Akwesasne. For aboriginal perspectives on contemporary issues, see the quarterly magazine *Akwesasne Notes*.

6

KTUNAXA

In Collaboration

Identification

The name Ktunaxa, now used in Canada by the Ktunaxa themselves, and the name Kutenai, by which the group is most widely known in both Canada and the United States (and the one still used by the Ktunaxa in the United States), refer to a single ethnic group with a single language. The word Kutenai is derived from the Blackfoot word *Kotona*, based on a Blackfoot pronunciation of the original Kutenai word Ktunaxa. *Ktunaxa* (with the stress on the penultimate syllable) is one of two words in the Ktunaxa language which refer to the Kutenai as a whole; the other is Ksanka, which is a Montana Kutenai word, though some Montana Kutenai use Ktunaxa. The "x" in Ktunaxa is pronounced, as it is in the Greek and Cyrillic alphabets, like the "ch" in "loch" or "Bach."

Kutenai currently is spelled three different ways. Apart from *Kutenai*, which has gradually become the standard spelling among scholars and has the advantage of being an international spelling of the name, there is also the distinctively Canadian spelling *Kootenay* and the American *Kootenai*. The Kootenay River itself changes its spelling as it flows south from the East Kootenay District of British Columbia into the United States to become the Kootenai River. The river becomes the Kootenay again as it flows north into the West Kootenay District of British Columbia, where it empties into Kootenay Lake.

Left over from an earlier time is the name *Kitunahan*, applied to the Ktunaxa language in an early classification of North American Indian languages. The languages are classified there according to language families, and so the "n" suffix is added to what would otherwise be *Kitunaha*, referring to the Ktunaxa language. The name Kitunaha has some utility today, because it is closely enough based on *Ktunaxa* to serve as a guide for those who find the latter difficult to pronounce.

The Ktunaxa people in Canada are gradually teaching modern-day residents of the Kootenay districts how to pronounce the name Ktunaxa, having renamed the Kootenay Indian Area Council the Ktunaxa/Kinbasket Tribal Council, and, more generally, using the name Ktunaxa as a word in the English language.

The Ktunaxa live in eastern British Columbia, the most northerly part of the Idaho panhandle, and a substantial corner of northwestern Montana. There are six modern Ktunaxa communities corresponding to six out of a larger number of historic communities, or bands, which each occupied some segment of the Kootenay River valley (the Kootenai River valley in the United States) and large areas of the surrounding country, most of it mountainous and heavily forested.

The name *Kinbasket*, as in the Ktunaxa/Kinbasket Tribal Council, represents a Shuswap community located within the Kootenay area of British Columbia. The Shuswap are an Interior Salish group. Many of the Kinbasket Shuswaps are also Ktunaxa in ancestry, so that the Kinbaskets, or the Shuswap band, at Athalmer, British Columbia, near Invermere, is in part a seventh Ktunaxa community.

The other six Ktunaxa communities are as follows. Starting in the north by the headwaters of the Kootenay River, close also to the headwaters of the Columbia River, is the Columbia Lake band, residing adjacent to Windermere, British Columbia; the St Mary's band on the St Mary's River, near Cranbrook, British Columbia; the Tobacco Plains band at Grassmere, British Columbia; the Montana Kootenai of the Flathead Reservation; the Kootenai Tribe of Idaho at Bonners Ferry, Idaho; and the Lower Kootenay band at Creston, British Columbia. In philosophical terms there is one Ktunaxa nation, but there are three tribal governments: the Ktunaxa/Kinbasket Tribal Council in Canada, the Confederated Salish and Kootenai Tribes of the Flathead Reservation in Montana, and the Kootenai Tribe of Idaho.

There is a traditional and also ethnographic distinction between the Upper Kutenai and the Lower Kutenai. The Lower Kutenai include the Lower Kootenay band at Creston, British Columbia, along with the Idaho Kootenai; the other groups are collectively the Upper Kutenai. The distinction refers to the course of the river, the Upper Kutenai living along the upper course of the river, while the Lower Kutenai reside along its lower course. This ethnographic distinction is very much an east-west distinction, so that one can just as well speak of the Eastern Ktunaxa, in the East Kootenay District of British Columbia and in

Montana; and the Western Ktunaxa, in the West Kootenay District of British Columbia and in Idaho.

On the basis of a few differences in the language which go along geographical lines, one can distinguish Eastern Ktunaxa from Western Ktunaxa, but one can also make a more finely grained, three-way distinction into Down-River Ktunaxa (Western Ktunaxa), Mid-River Ktunaxa (Eastern Ktunaxa), and Up-River Ktunaxa (also Eastern Ktunaxa). Specifically, the Montana Kootenai and the Tobacco Plains Ktunaxa are both Mid-River Ktunaxa, while the St Mary's Ktunaxa and the Columbia Lake Ktunaxa are both Up-River Ktunaxa.

In terms of pronunciation, the differences between the varieties of the language are actually less than those between the Canadian English spoken in British Columbia and the English spoken across the border in adjacent parts of the United States. With regard to vocabulary, the differences between the geographical varieties of the Ktunaxa language are more like the differences between Canadian English and British English; people generally know exactly what the differences are and consequently have no trouble understanding each other.

Ktunaxa stands alone as a linguistic lineage which has been independent for so long that its origins are nearly lost in the mists of time. Yet it is clearly connected to certain other languages by resemblances which cannot be explained by mere chance. While suggestions have been made that might be related to the Algonquian language family, and also to a language stock consisting of the Wakashan, the Chimakuan, and the Salish language families, evidence falls far short of proof. There is, however, a substantial body of evidence, as yet unpublished, that Ktunaxa and Proto-Salish, the common ancestor of all the Salish languages, together had an ancestor language in common, which can be called Proto-Ktunaxa-Salish and must have been much older than Proto-Salish. There has also clearly been linguistic contact between the Ktunaxa and the Salish.

Archaeological evidence indicates that the Ktunaxa have lived in the Rocky Mountain trench and other parts of present-day Ktunaxa territory for thousands of years. An increasingly long and detailed archaeological record is now coming to light, one that complements the evidence for Ktunaxa prehistory provided by the Ktunaxa language. Much of the more recent archaeological work is being done under the auspices of the Ktunaxa/Kinbasket Tribal Council, while linguistic research has gone on independently.

The traditional settlement pattern varied seasonally, with each band dispersed or concentrated at different times of the year to facilitate hunting, berry picking, root digging, and other types of resource-extraction, activities conducted over large areas. Today, communities are located in the centre of the territory that each surviving band occupied at the time of contact with Europeans, except for some of the present-day Montana Kootenai who were forced to move from the centre of their traditional territory.

Modern settlement patterns on reserves are dispersed, although, in addition to houses located at a distance from one another, there are small, distinct villages at Shuswap, Tobacco Plains, and Lower Kootenay in association with the reserve's local Catholic church. For the St Mary's reserve, old photographs show a village near the St Eugene Mission and church, a location now occupied in part by the St Mary's band office and band hall and by Ktunaxa/Kinbasket tribal office buildings.

There is a Ktunaxa legend that ends with the moral there will never be very many Ktunaxa but they will never be extinct. The size of the Ktunaxa population before the arrival of Europeans is estimated at about 5,000; however, because epidemics preceded the actual arrival of whites, this figure is strictly a matter of guesswork. In 1835 fur traders reported that there were some 1,000 Ktunaxa people in British Columbia, a number that declined to 702 in 1891 and 517 in 1911 (the latter figure did not include 63 Kinbasket Shuswaps). By 1924, the Ktunaxa population had grown to 1,050, of whom 501 were living in Canada, and in 1973 the total of Ktunaxa and Kinbaskets together was 571. Since then, the decline in population has been reversed. South of the border, the census of 1890 gave the number of Kootenai in Idaho and Montana as 400 to 500; in 1974 the Kootenai of Idaho were said to number 67; and by 1982 the number of Idaho Kootenai was reported to be 115.

The population of Ktunaxa reserves and reservations does not represent the total number of Ktunaxa people. Many have moved to distant locations, such as Vancouver, Calgary, Spokane, and Seattle, while still maintaining ties to their home communities. There has also been a certain amount of internal migration, from reserves into neighbouring towns, to larger towns close to other reserves, and from one reserve to another, sometimes involving the transfer of band membership.

In British Columbia, there has been no formal treaty between the Ktunaxa and non-natives and therefore no settlement of land claims. Large areas are at issue. The traditional economic base of the Ktunaxa people involved the use of the entire region for hunting and for the gathering of other natural resources. Later, ranching required open ranges, but these were closed off. Thus, while Ktunaxa population is now very much on the rise, the Ktunaxa communities still lack a sufficient land base.

The same situation prevails in the United States and indeed was the cause of the declaration of war by the Kootenai of Idaho against the U.S. government in 1974. Without a shot being fired, but with Kootenai war bonds being offered for sale on the streets of Bonners Ferry, the federal government relented and provided the Idaho Kootenai with the economic base that they had previously lacked.

History

The earliest written records that refer to the Ktunaxa are by people who were travelling from the east and first encountered the Ktunaxa on the prairies, east of the Rocky Mountains. This has led many writers, one relying on the other, to suggest that the Ktunaxa in fact originated on the prairies. Some also refer to a supposed Ktunaxa legend that the Ktunaxa migrated around six hundred years ago from Lake Michigan, a thesis that does not agree with archaeological and linguistic evidence or with genuine Ktunaxa oral accounts.

There are Ktunaxa stories about lost populations of Ktunaxa people on the prairies, and such stories, told by elders in recent times, have been tape-recorded. The stories can be divided into two categories. One tells of a group encountered by Ktunaxa people when they were far out on the prairies to hunt buffalo, a group that, to the amazement of the Ktunaxa, was able to speak their language, or at least knew some Ktunaxa words. The other category of stories tells of an extinct band of Ktunaxa people who lived year-round on the prairies just to the east of the Rocky Mountains but were almost completely wiped out by an epidemic, with some survivors being absorbed by other tribes and others joining the Ktunaxa people in present-day Ktunaxa territory. These legendary plains Ktunaxa people evidently called themselves Ktunaxa rather than Ksanka; they have been referred to in some accounts as the Tonaxa, or Tunaxa, but this is a version of the name Ktunaxa and so possibly may just be a mishearing of it by ethnographers.

One interpretation of such stories maintains that the Ktunaxa people as a whole originated on the prairies, and it further claims that the Piegans (a Blackfoot group) are of plains Ktunaxa origin. This idea of Piegan origin at least suggests that some plains Ktunaxa people joined the Piegans. There is also information provided by the Montana Salish that one of their own groups was called "Tunaxa" and that there are people of this ancestry among them today.

Stories of the now-extinct plains Ktunaxa mention the town of Fort Macleod, Alberta, over 90 kilometres east of the British Columbia border. There are also reports of there having been a Ktunaxa band at Michel, British Columbia, in the Crowsnest Pass area, on the B.C.–Alberta border, as well as another centred around Fernie, B.C., on the Elk River, far upstream from where the Elk River empties into the Kootenay in the territory of the Tobacco Plains Band.

Whatever the truth of these stories, any area of Alberta prairie that had earlier belonged to the Ktunaxa was claimed and occupied in the early historical period by the Blackfoot. Today, all the extant Ktunaxa bands have names based on the name of a place central to a much larger area; none of the now-extinct Ktunaxa communities was named for a place at the edge of their own traditional territory. The distances between Tobacco Plains, Fernie, Michel, and Fort Macleod are comparable to the distances between the places along the Kootenay River which mark the centres of the territories of the six extant bands.

Perhaps the first written mention of the Ktunaxa found to date is by Alexander Mackenzie of the North West Company. In 1793 he travelled to the Pacific Ocean, evidently through Ktunaxa territory, and on a map he produced in 1801 is the name Cattanahowes, which, if we remove the "s," looks like an approximation of Ktunaxa. In 1807 David Thompson, also representing the North West Company, founded Kootenae House, a trading post north of Lake Windermere in present-day Ktunaxa territory. Thompson had to brave the objections of Blackfoot people to establish trade with the Ktunaxa, since such trade would supply the Ktunaxa with rifles. His very use of the name Kootenae House for his trading post, rather than a name more like Kitunaha, suggests that Thompson arrived with a Blackfoot perspective on the supposed previous location of the Ktunaxa, rather than one acquired from the Ktunaxa themselves.

The establishment of Kootenae House by David Thompson began the fur trade in the region, on both sides of what would later become the U.S.-Canadian border. In 1881 fur-trading operations at Lake Windermere were moved to Fort Kootenay, near Jennings, Montana. A traveller who was at Fort Kootenay in 1854 claimed to have given some Ktunaxa a demonstration in the firing of a revolver, a weapon that they had apparently never seen before. This was at a time when, according to historical accounts, the Ktunaxa, along with Kalispels and other Montana Salish as well as Nez Perce people from farther south, were still making buffalo-hunting trips to the plains, where they sometimes wintered. For the southern neighbours of the Ktunaxa, such hunting expeditions sometimes kept them on the plains up to three years. Some of the historical accounts of trips to the prairies by these Rocky Mountain tribes mention the names, not only of traditional hunting grounds close to the Rockies, but also of much more distant locations, even points as far east as Lake Superior.

Though the Ktunaxa were visited by a missionary in 1842, Jesuit missions among them were not built until 1845. In 1874 Oblates founded the St Eugene mission near Cranbrook, where the Sisters of Providence later staffed a school. In 1891, while ministering to the Montana Kootenai, Father Philip Canestrelli wrote a grammar of the Ktunaxa language in Latin, entitled *Grammaticae Ksanka*.

Wild Horse Creek in the Kootenay District was the focus of a gold rush in 1863, and tensions between land-hungry miners and settlers led in 1887, at the first sign of armed conflict between the two groups, to the establishment of Fort Steele by the Royal Canadian Mounted Police. While peace was maintained, settlers continued to expropriate Ktunaxa lands. Reserves were established in 1888, but they were subsequently reduced in size.

Economic Life

Traditionally, the survival and prosperity of the Ktunaxa depended on a certain amount of versatility in making use of the resources found in all parts of their territory, from the valley floors through higher elevations, and even to the tops of some mountains for the right kinds of stone to make arrowheads. There was a belief that these resources were to be used collectively by the people of the community, which continues to this day.

Ktunaxa territory has been described as one of the world's greatest game preserves, and the Ktunaxa people used the entire region for hunting and for the gathering of other natural resources. Deer – both whitetail and blacktail – were hunted throughout the territory. Elk were important particularly for the Eastern Ktunaxa. At high elevations, there were mountain goats and bighorn sheep, and, for the Western Ktunaxa, there were caribou. Water fowl were especially plentiful seasonally on Kootenay Lake and communal duck hunts were important for the western, Down-River Ktunaxa. Men did the hunting, but the catch was evenly distributed to everyone who was in the camp at the time, even casual visitors.

The Eastern Ktunaxa conducted a large summer buffalo hunt on the prairies, one that reportedly could involve as many as eighty households as well as other tribes. The Spokanes and Coeur d'Alene are prominently mentioned as accompanying the Ktunaxa on these hunting expeditions, but the Ktunaxa could also find themselves on the prairies with Kalispels, Montana Salish, and Nez Perce, all pitted against the Blackfoot. There were also smaller fall buffalo hunts and a short winter one, done entirely on foot with snowshoes. Fishing was good in rivers and lakes throughout Ktunaxa territory. Both men and women fished. For the Western Ktunaxa on Kootenay Lake, fishing was especially important; they used fish traps and fish weirs, as did the Eastern Ktunaxa. In addition to the kinds of fish found throughout the region, including the salmon that managed to come all the way upriver into Ktunaxa country, there were landlocked kokanee salmon and also sturgeon in Kootenay Lake.

The traditional Ktunaxa house was a canvas-covered tipi, which is still occasionally used, especially for tribal gatherings. This type of house was completely portable, consisting of lodge-poles forming a conical frame with a fitted covering. In an earlier era, for the Eastern Ktunaxa, the covering was made of buffalo hides, resulting in a plains-style tipi. There were both winter and summer configurations of the basic design. In the early historic period, the Ktunaxa built log houses which compared favourably in terms of warmth with winter-style buffalo-hide tipis.

For the Western Ktunaxa, the same frame of lodge poles as used to make the plains-style tipi had a fitted covering of reed mats. For both the Eastern and Western Ktunaxa, there are ethnographic descriptions of a larger, more permanent kind of winter longhouse, dug into the ground, about a foot deep, with a wooden frame and reed-mat coverings.

The portability of Ktunaxa houses meant that entire villages were also highly portable, at least seasonally. This made possible a pattern of seasonal movement from one resource to another. At winter village sites located at the valley floor, fishing was conducted between March and May. The Western Ktunaxa relocated to particularly advantageous fish-weir locations in the spring. At Tobacco Plains, tobacco was planted in the spring. About May, women dug camas roots and bitterroots, when they were ready and where they were to be found. Mid-June was a time for the Eastern Ktunaxa to mount the summer buffalo hunt. After returning, women picked berries, as they ripened at different locations, especially serviceberries, huckleberries, and chokecherries. For the Western Ktunaxa, a task leader was appointed to organize a communal deer hunt. At Tobacco Plains in the summer, tobacco plots were harvested. There is a report that each band made its own distinctive blend of tobacco for its council meetings and to trade with other bands. The Eastern Ktunaxa hunted elk. After all of the food accumulated in the summer was processed, caches of it were made in the forks of trees in time for the Eastern Ktunaxa to lead the fall bison hunt into the prairies. Just before the first snowfall, this expedition returned and set up winter quarters. In the winter, before the short winter bison hunt, men repaired snowshoes.

After the early fur-trading era, ranching – including the keeping of dairy herds – was a major occupation for the Ktunaxa until the open range beyond reserve lands was no longer open to them. In more recent times, farming and ranching declined to the point where non-Ktunaxa people actually leased reserve lands for their ranching operations, but that trend has been halted and today reserve lands are again managed by Ktunaxa people, although this creates employment only for a few individuals.

For the Lower Kootenay, fruit picking has been a source of employment locally, and, for the Ktunaxa in general, agricultural work farther from home was once a source of seasonal employment. The harvesting of Christmas trees is now a sizeable industry on some reserves, with Ktunaxa people from Canada taking truckloads of trees as far as Arizona to sell at locations rented from year to year for the purpose. There is a long tradition of Ktunaxa people fighting forest fires, and recently this has led to forest-management activities of a more general nature. For the Lower Kootenay band, at the southern end of Kootenay Lake, an arrangement with the conservation group Ducks Unlimited has been profitable.

Family, Kinship, and Social Organization

In the Ktunaxa language, there are reciprocal kin terms, the meaning of which differs depending on the generation of the speaker, and also kin terms that are used specifically by a male or a female. Kinship was traced from both sides of the family, bilaterally rather than matrilineally or patrilineally, although this later gave way to the European practice of patrilineal family names. Most Ktunaxa family names are literally patronymic, based on a man's individual name. When the man's name is a nickname, or a personal name of French origin given by the French-speaking nuns at the mission school, or a name made up by the nuns using English words, the result can be a distinctively native, or uniquely Ktunaxa, family name. There are also Ktunaxa family names inherited from non-Ktunaxa ancestors.

In the Ktunaxa language, there are no family names. When individuals are referred to by name, it is with a personal name, generally of French origin, but with a Ktunaxa pronunciation. These Christian names, along with a few religious terms, also from French, are the only words in the Ktunaxa language which reveal their foreign origin by having stress on the final syllable. There are also traditional Ktunaxa personal names. These are of a more private nature, although some Ktunaxa individuals of earlier generations were generally referred to using a shortened, nickname version of their traditional Ktunaxa name.

Traditionally, monogamy was the general rule, although wealthy men were reportedly expected to support several wives, usually sisters. There is a word in the Ktunaxa language which has the form of a kinship term and means either two women who are close friends or one woman who is another woman's rival for her husband. Behind the paradoxical modern meaning of this word lies the fact that in an earlier era it was the kin term for "co-wife." Between the time when Ktunaxa men could have co-wives and the present, there was an intervening era when the Catholic Church so dominated Ktunaxa cultural life in matters such as marriage that some elders born around 1900 did not believe that there ever was a custom of Ktunaxa men having more than one wife.

A young couple, it is said, would begin their married life living with the wife's parents. Related to this, there was a tradition of men not speaking directly to their mothers-in-law out of respect. One way to get past this taboo when a man and his mother-in-law were alone and needed to communicate was by speaking in the third person – for example, to a wall. There was also a tradition of brothers and sisters and male cousins and their female cousins not speaking directly to each other. There is a word in Ktunaxa to describe this brother-sister language, which again involved a special third-person way of speaking. Knowledge of these customs of indirect ways of speaking to opposite-gender relatives easily survived the influence of the Catholic Church on Ktunaxa family life.

The Ktunaxa are known for the respect they show the elderly, who are valued for their knowledge of traditions and of the language. As for the young, in the not-so-distant past, social workers from outside the communities could and did take children away from parents who were not thought to be taking proper care of them. This sort of intervention is now done within the communities, with the children being put in group-home settings when necessary.

Traditional Ktunaxa society was relatively egalitarian and lacked social classes. There are reports that some families were more prestigious than others, but such families won their superior status through their own abilities and hard work. Moreover, wealth carried with it the automatic obligation of generosity. Chiefs were elected, and, although some families are said to have provided more leaders than others, this was again the result of ability and diligence rather than inherited rights.

Not all authority in a Ktunaxa community was concentrated in one man. There was a distinction in the language (and still is) between a chief, who held office, and a guide chief, who was the leader of an expedition, such as a hunting party. Ethnographic accounts make further distinctions between war-party chiefs and specialized hunting chiefs. The Western Ktunaxa had a special chief for duck-hunting parties.

A century ago, under the regime of the missionaries and with the active participation of chiefs, people were publicly punished for gambling and drunkenness. In recent times, local communities have made an increasing effort to control the socially destructive behaviour of certain individuals. Alcoholism is seen as a fundamental problem which must be addressed in order for the communities to thrive. In contrast with a century ago, gambling is not generally seen in a negative light; indeed, gambling in the form of a traditional stick game is now seen as a valuable cultural tradition and one particularly to be encouraged for tribal gatherings. Bingo is also regarded as a healthy pastime.

Culture, Religion, and Education

The Eastern Ktunaxa were centred along the upper course of the Kootenay River, mostly in the Rocky Mountain trench, between the Rocky Mountains and the Purcell Mountains, putting them relatively close to the prairies and in close contact with plains tribes. Their material culture was characterized by equestrian trappings, buffalo-hide tipis, buckskin clothing, feathered war bonnets, pottery, and other elements that made them to all appearances a people of the prairies. They made pottery, but, for the most part, clay pots were replaced by iron kettles, obtained through trade, early in the historic period.

The Western Ktunaxa, west of the Purcell Mountains, were located deeper in the Plateau and thus were more like neighbouring Plateau tribes in their material culture. Their garments were fashioned with rush or reed materials, they made coiled baskets, and they used a distinctive bark canoe with bow and stern formed into a down-slanting sturgeon's nose pointing forward or back at the bottom along the keel line.

The general portability of villages militated strongly against large art objects, except decoration on clothing. Today, the Ktunaxa have a reputation as especially good tanners. Some still tan hides and make beaded buckskin clothing for sale and to wear at powwows. Drumming groups, including young people, maintain traditional songs, and the young actively participate in powwow dancing.

Among the Ktunaxa people, there is now a consensus that their religious beliefs and practices are a private matter that should not be discussed with outsiders. Earlier generations of Ktunaxa, especially in Canada, were the products of a conversion to Christianity that represented a veritable cultural revolution, a revolution that was antithetical to traditional Ktunaxa religion and that sought not only to replace this religion but to shape other aspects of Ktunaxa culture and society. Until quite recently, the Catholic Church was a central force in each community. At one time, every single Ktunaxa person in Canada enrolled as a band member was officially listed as Catholic, and today every Ktunaxa community in Canada has its own Catholic church building. Recently, the small size of congregations and low church attendance have led to the discontinuation of regular Sunday services on reserves, a development that has created a void in the communities. An exception is the participation of a priest at funerals, which still take place in each community's church building.

The active discouragement of traditional Ktunaxa religion by the Catholic priests and nuns at the St Eugene mission boarding school may well partly account for the intensely private nature of traditional Ktunaxa religion today. Ironically, those Ktunaxa people who remain Catholic sometimes find occasion to be almost as private about their religious faith as other Ktunaxa people are about their traditional beliefs and practices.

Before the arrival of missionaries, education was carried out close to home. Children learned largely by taking part in household and community activities. Grandparents told bedtime stories which revealed the difference between appropriate and inappropriate conduct. The character Coyote in traditional stories stands out as the perfect example of bad behaviour.

With the establishment of the St Eugene residential school, which served all the Ktunaxa communities in Canada, including the Shuswap Band, and even had students from the United States, things changed radically. The nuns would punish the children for speaking in either Ktunaxa or Shuswap, forcing them to speak English, although the nuns themselves, in the early years, would commonly speak to each other in French. With the closing of the residential mission school in recent times, students were sent to public schools in neighbouring towns, following others who had already taken the same route through the decision of their parents.

Around 1950, parents stopped trying to teach their children the Ktunaxa language; they were concerned about the children having the same difficulties in school that they had. The assumption was that the children would absorb Ktunaxa as they grew up, just as the parents had done. As it turned out, however, children generally did not learn the language, although some who were raised by their grandparents did better in this regard. Now, people look back on the decision not to teach the language as a mistake. Only recently have children again begun to learn Ktunaxa, but in a classroom setting or at language-immersion camps.

The Ktunaxa/Kinbasket Tribal Council has started its own school system, and the Lower Kootenay Band has its own school, independent of the council's system. Efforts have been made to incorporate traditional culture and language into the curriculum of the native-run schools, particularly at the pre-school level. The Montana Kootenai have had a local school in their community at Elmo, and they also participate in running a tribal college known as the Salish-Kootenai Community College. Language-immersion programs have been initiated. Ktunaxa communities also provide day-care programs. These are at least a potential vehicle for education in traditional culture and the Ktunaxa language.

Intergroup Relations and Group Maintenance

In Canada until recently, the Department of Indian Affairs granted native status to non-native women who married native men but took away native status for native women who married non-natives. The Ktunaxa opposed this rule and lobbied, successfully in the end, for greater control over tribal membership. In practice, local control has led to membership for those not on tribal roles, such as the offspring of native women who lost their status, while not cancelling the membership for those originally non-native women who were granted it under the old rules. In any event, the children of non-native women married to Ktunaxa are accepted as members.

In Montana, the issue has been whether the Confederated Salish and Kootenai tribal government, with its preponderance of Salish people, would decide membership regarding Kootenai people or whether it would be specifically Kootenai people on the reservation who would have this power.With newly instituted local control by Kootenai people, there has been some selectivity in the granting of membership. A panel given the responsibility of deciding the issue on a case-by-case basis takes into account not only an individual's ancestry but also his or her cultural identity.

To some extent, taking control of tribal membership is a matter of injecting a dose of reality into official community membership. Intermarriage has not been uncommon, and today, as it has been for generations, being a Ktunaxa person is not so much about percentage of ancestry as it is about identification with Ktunaxa ancestors, along with cultural identity and community participation.

FURTHER READING

General treatments of northwest coast natives include Robert H. Ruby and John A. Brown, *A Guide to the Indian Tribes of the Pacific Coast Northwest* (Norman, Okla., 1986), and Adolf and Beverly Hungry Wolf, *Indian Tribes of the Northern Rockies* (Skookumchuck, B.C., 1989).

Almost every book that makes any mention of the Ktunaxa (always using the spelling *Kutenai* or one of its variants) has serious limitations. H.H. Turney-High's ethnographic work (*Ethnography of the Kutenai*, American Anthropological Association, memoir 56, 1941) is laced with his own opinions and interpretations, but at least its point of view is transparent and thus can be compared to the unpublished field notes of another ethnographer, Claude Schaeffer, who did decades of ethnographic research with the Ktunaxa.

Transcriptions of Ktunaxa stories prepared by Franz Boas in 1914 – despite their idiosyncratic nature – provide direct access to the voices of Ktunaxa elders of an earlier generation. Alexander F. Chamberlain, the first person to receive a Ph.D. in anthropology in the United States, was a student of Franz Boas who studied the Ktunaxa and recorded some of their stories. He died young, and Boas included the Ktunaxa texts collected by Chamberlain, along with the texts that Boas himself had collected, in the book *Kutenai Tales* (Bureau of American Ethnology, bulletin 59, 1918). Chamberlain also wrote an article on the Ktunaxa in the *Handbook of Indians of Canada* (Ottawa, 1913; repr. Toronto, 1971), which was an extract from the *Handbook of American Indians North of Mexico* (Washington, D.C., 1907, 1910). He was responsible for the rumour that the Ktunaxa have legends and traditions indicating their origins east of the Rocky Mountains.

With regard to the Ktunaxa language, readers are referred to the following works among others: *Linguae Ksanka (Kootenai) Elementa Grammaticae* (Santa Clara, Calif., 1894); Mary R. Haas, "Is Kutenai Related to Algonquian?" *Canadian Journal of Linguistics*, vol. 10 (1965), 77–92; and Lawrence R. Morgan, "Kootenay-Salishan Linguistic Comparison: A Preliminary Study" (M.A. thesis, University of British Columbia, 1980). Kinship among the Ktunaxa is explored in Edward Sapir, "Kinship Terms of the Kootenay Indians," *American Anthropologist*, vol. 20 (1918), 414–18 and in Franz Boas, "Kinship Terms on the Kutenai Indians," *American Anthropologist*, vol. 21 (1919), 98–101. The life of a Christian missionary among the Ktunaxa is the subject of *They Call Me Father*, edited by Margaret Whitehead (Vancouver, 1988).

7

METIS

Olive P. Dickason

Identification

Canada's Metis were formally recognized as an aboriginal people in section 35 of the Constitution Act, 1982. No strings were attached, or definitions attempted. Louis Riel (1844–85), himself one-eighth Chipewyan, who died fighting for the recognition of his people, would have approved. Why, he asked in his last memoir, be concerned about the proportions of Amerindian/white mixture? "No matter how little we have of one or the other, does not filial acknowledgment and love create one law so that we can say 'We are Metis?'" Few Canadian Metis realize how rare it is for mixed-bloods to have legal recognition as a separate group, even though undefined; the Cape Coloureds of South Africa are among the few who have successfully asserted legal and political rights.

The term "metis" is derived from the Latin verb *miscere*, which means "to mix, mingle"; in Latin America, the Spanish derivative is *mestizo*. In Canada, the word "Metis" originally referred to persons of French and Amerindian ancestry; those whose white admixture was English were often called "country-born," a term that originated in India, as did "half-caste" (neither of which is in general use in Canada today). In India, "half-caste" referred to class, whereas in the Canadian context the reference was to racial origins; in either case, its implication of social inferiority was clear. "Half-breed" seems to have been first used in the Thirteen Colonies, spreading early in the nineteenth century to Canada, where it remained in general use until after World War II. A term that came to be used in the fur trade but is seldom heard now is *bois-brulé*. It is said by some to be a French version of the Ojibwa appellation *wisahkotewan niniwak*, "men partly burned"; an English version was "burnt (or scorched) wood people." Still another, *chicot*, has a similar connotation but is hazier as to its origins; it may have sprung from a family name. Today, "Metis," in both its English and French versions, has been generally accepted in Canada for all Amerindian/white admixtures.

There is no general agreement on criteria for an exact definition. For example, some western Canadians hold that the Metis are only those who can trace their ancestry to the Red River settlement, as recognized in the Manitoba Act of 1870 and in the Dominion Land Acts of 1879 and 1883. However, Treaty 3, the "Northwest Angle Treaty," signed in 1873, specifically included Metis and even designated land for them; the area the treaty covers is located largely in Ontario, with only a small portion spilling over into Manitoba. In Alberta, the Metis Population Betterment Act was amended in 1940 to require that the Amerindian admixture be not less than one-quarter for a person to claim to be Metis. This was rescinded because of opposition from Alberta's Metis Settlements General Council on the ground that it violated the fundamental right of the Metis to define themselves. The council accepts as Metis any person with any degree of aboriginal ancestry "who identifies with Metis history and culture." An earlier version had been "anyone with any degree of Indian ancestry who lives the life ordinarily associated with the Metis." Neither has been generally agreed upon; the Metis National Council, for example, is considering the following definition: "A person who has an ancestor who received a land grant or scrip under the Manitoba Act, 1870, or the Dominion Land Acts of 1879 and 1883, or who is recognized as Metis by other government agencies, or in church or community records." In popular usage, criteria can include physical traits, surname, occupation, and place of residence; some would add religion (Roman Catholicism). Others see community acceptance as a prime requirement, which can pose problems for Metis in urban settings, where communities tend not to be clearly defined.

A variety of factors have compounded the problem of Metis identification, the people whom the Cree refer to as *wemistikosheekan*, "not really a whiteman," or perhaps as *apet'ililew*, "half Indian." Amerindians who missed signing treaties (usually because they were away hunting) and who thus did not officially acquire Indian status are often referred to as Metis; indeed, one proposed definition would include persons with any degree of Amerindian blood who are not registered on a reserve. Amerindians who became enfranchised by such processes as earning a university degree or, in the case of women, marrying "out" automatically lost their status and frequently became known as Metis. In some areas, Metis and non-status Amerindians have added to the confusion by joining forces for recognition of their rights; in others, they keep separate. The 1985 amendment to the Indian Act, Bill C-31, allowing Amerindian women married to non-Amerindians to keep their status and pass it on to their children, added another twist, since it gave Amerindian status to persons who had been previously classified as Metis. Ovide Mercredi, former grand chief of the Assembly of First Nations, is one of these. In other words, as matters stand, not even racial mixing is universally recognized in Canada as essential to being Metis, at least in legal terms. The importance of these identification problems quickly becomes evident when it is remembered that constitutional recognition means that aboriginal rights relating to land and special political status are now involved.

A national Metis registry, to be jointly funded and operated by Ottawa, the provinces, and the Metis themselves, is under consideration; in the meantime, without agreed-upon and consistent criteria, there is no consensus about the numbers of people who can be legally classified as Metis in Canada. The Aboriginal Peoples Survey conducted in collaboration with the 1991 census listed 75,150 persons who reported Metis ancestry and 137,500 who reported descent from more than one aboriginal category (Indian, Metis, Inuit), as well as non-aboriginal ancestry, out of a total aboriginal population of 1,002,670. The Metis National Council disputes these figures on the grounds that the enumeration was incomplete. For one thing, there is no central data-collection system for Metis or non-status Amerindian births and deaths. Comparisons between one census and another are difficult, if they can be done at all, because of changes in concepts, questions, and procedures. On the question of population growth, two censuses that can be compared are those of 1941, when enumeration of the Metis was halted, and 1981, when it was resumed, because "both made an explicit attempt to individually enumerate persons of mixed Native ancestry." They indicate a Metis population growth of 177 percent, from 35,400 to 98,300. This was a period of growth for aboriginal peoples generally, a trend that has continued. For the Metis, there is also the likelihood that increased public awareness and changes in public attitude have made identification more socially acceptable. In the absence of a national registry, there can be only conjecture on the point.

In the meantime, the Metis National Council and its five provincial affiliates in Ontario, Manitoba, Saskatchewan, Alberta, and British Columbia consider that 350,000 would be a more realistic figure. As they break it down, Manitoba accounts for 103,000, Saskatchewan and Alberta for 110,000 each, British Columbia for 70,000, and Ontario for 40,000. These figures were obtained on the basis of membership in the provincial affiliates, along with extrapolations from other sources, particularly historical ones. Incidentally, the official projected growth rate for the Metis during the next 25 years is 43 percent. This is the lowest among aboriginal groups; the Inuit and non-status Amerindians are both projected at 59 percent, and status Amerindians at 52 percent. What is increasingly clear is that history has become more important than biology in defining the Metis, Canada's hidden people. Or, as writer Murray Dobbin observes, "it was not so much blood that was mixed ... but two dramatically different worlds."

Early History

Although today the Metis are particularly identified with the three prairie provinces, the mixing of the aboriginal peoples and Europeans has occurred from coast to coast. In the early days of New France, official policy encouraged this: Samuel de Champlain told the Huron that "our young men will marry your daughters, and we shall be one people." This was general French colonial policy at the time, a reflection of the fact that France's political dominance in Europe depended in part upon a large population at home, with a consequent reluctance to encourage emigration, even for purposes of empire. The alternative was to send out small groups of people, almost all men, who would intermarry with local inhabitants to produce new French populations overseas.

In Canada, difficulties with an unfamiliar and demanding climate as well as the requirements of the fur trade also encouraged intermarriage, placing as they did a premium on the survival skills and kinship networks of an Amerindian and, later, a Metis wife. According to a description by an eighteenth-century observer, Sieur de Diéreville, such unions were arranged with the father of the bride-to-be for a negotiated amount of trade goods. "The Girl, who is familiar with the Country, undertakes, on her part, to sell his Merchandise for a specified length of time; the bargain is faithfully carried out on both sides." That these arrangements worked to the collective advantage was generally acknowledged.

A closely related aspect was the dependence of early fur-trade posts for a large part of their food supplies upon Amerindian hunters, who were known as "homeguards" because they set up their base camps around the posts. Inevitably, there was intermixing with post personnel. The English had similar experiences when they established themselves on Hudson Bay in 1670, despite an official policy that was the opposite of that of the French: London's best efforts to prevent intermarriage were unavailing in the face of the exigencies of the trade, not to mention those of survival in the "Little Ice Age" (c. 1450–1850).

The policy of creating one nation discouraged the emergence of a separate Metis identity during the French regime. In the atmosphere that initially prevailed in Acadia and New France, cultural conformity was more important than racial origins; thus, mixed-blood children identified with one side or the other of their heritage. The fur trade, where the Amerindian connection was important, encouraged identification with the Amerindian side. When this led to the "French becoming Savage simply by living with the Savages," officials had second thoughts, and by the eighteenth century they were discouraging intermarriage, or at least trying to control it. A counterbalancing factor was involvement in colonial wars. French/Amerindian military alliances favoured identification with the French, who had both power and prestige. One of the best known products of this was Bernard-Anselme d'Abbadie de Saint-Castin (1689–1720), whose mother came from a line of Abenaki chiefs and whose father belonged to the minor French nobility; Bernard-Anselme became a French officer and commander in Acadia. Another factor favouring French identification was the comparatively close presence of colonial officialdom, as well as that of the common enemy, the English. As a result, the Metis communities that developed in Acadia generally considered themselves to be French, even as they recognized their blood ties with Amerindians. The choice was between being Amerindian-French or French-Amerindian; the concept of a nation in between, that was neither one nor the other, was latent but not yet developed.

A different situation emerged on the western frontier. In the Ohio valley (the "Old Northwest"), far from the centre of colonial administration, the fur trade was the dominant economic activity and the English were more successful than they had been in the Maritimes in competing for Amerindian alliances. This combination of factors favoured the qualifications of the Metis as trappers and traders, as interpreters and go-betweens in the continuing English-French confrontations, and as effective forest fighters in the colonial wars.

Amerindian influence in the way of life that developed in the Ohio valley was strong; marriages, for instance, were usually contracted *à la façon du pays*, "according to the custom of the country," which was, of course, Amerindian. In spite of missionary worries, such adaptations did not influence the French Metis to give up their Catholicism, which was retained to a remarkable extent even in the absence of clergy. Subsistence depended upon what was available locally, which meant hunting, gathering, and fishing, sometimes supplemented with small-scale farming. Wild rice and various roots were harvested where available, as was maple and birch sap for processing into syrup and (in the case of maple sap) into sugar. What social distinctions there were tended to be dictated by fur-trade connections; the Hudson's Bay Company (HBC) had a more formal hierarchical structure than the later-appearing North West Company (NWC). Many individuals were "freemen," in trade as well as employment, providing various services (as hunters, guides, voyageurs, and interpreters, among others).

Their sense of cultural identity found an expression in dress, which combined Amerindian and European elements; the Red River coat, made out of Hudson's Bay Company blankets, and the arrow (Assomption) sash, derived from Iroquois burden-strap designs, are well-known examples. The arrow sash has since become a badge of Metis national identification. Pipe smoking, an Amerindian inheritance, was universally popular, with tobacco often being mixed with chopped dogwood bark – *kinik-kinik*. The Metis of the Ohio valley were well on their way towards thinking of themselves as a "New Nation," but they were forestalled by the creation of the United States of America in 1783 and the consequent rush of European settlement, which overwhelmed their communities.

It was the "Far Northwest" (particularly today's Manitoba but also Saskatchewan and Alberta) that provided the setting which allowed for the crystallization of Metis national sentiment: isolation, the continuing importance of the fur trade, and the growing importance of the buffalo hunt. Far removed from centres of authority, Metis communities developed their own self-regulated, semi-nomadic way of life, mobile when necessary for hunting, trading, and trapping, semi-sedentary where supplementary subsistence farming was practical. An outstanding example was Red River at the forks of the Red and Assiniboine rivers (the site of today's Winnipeg), a strategic location, since it linked York Factory on Hudson Bay with St Paul, Minnesota, on the Mississippi River. It was situated within the huge but imprecisely delineated HBC land grant known as Rupert's Land, considered by many today to be the Metis homeland. As the Metis define the grant, it included the two Dakotas as well as Minnesota and Montana.

The Scottish settlers who arrived in Red River in 1812 under the auspices of Thomas Douglas, Earl of Selkirk, in collaboration with the HBC, were not only too few to challenge the dominance of the Metis, they were also dependent upon them for subsistence during the settlement's first difficult years; instead of overwhelming the Metis, the settlers acted as a catalyst that sharpened Metis awareness of their own distinctive culture and way of life. The economic basis for this phenomenon, the fur trade, by this time was dominated by two rivals: the British monopoly that was the HBC, with its quasi-governmental powers over Rupert's Land, and the freewheeling combination of partnerships that made up the NWC. The French-language Metis were for the most part connected with the NWC, which had emerged during the 1780s largely under Highland Scottish leadership. The "Nor'Westers," as NWC traders were known, encouraged the Metis as free traders and supported their claims to land by virtue of their Amerindian heritage. Although Metis of French descent were in the majority in the region, by this time others were represented in the national mix; some of those who would become the most active nationalists would be of English, Scottish, or other extractions. This complex of racial, cultural, commercial, and political diversities created a situation that was without counterpart elsewhere on the Canadian frontier.

Interaction of Europeans and Amerindians on the northwest coast followed a different pattern from that in the other parts of the country. For one thing, the climate was such that special survival skills did not have to be learned; for another, the coastal fur trade lasted for less than a century, soon giving way to agriculture, fishing, and lumbering, among other forms of economic activity such as gold mining. Nor did colonial rivalries have as direct an impact as in the east or the Ohio valley, so that military alliances with First Nations were not a political necessity; in fact, the very suggestion of such a move by ex-fur trader Governor Sir James Douglas aroused considerable unease on the part of the settlers. All this meant that, on the northwest coast, Amerindians and Europeans never developed the symbiotic relationships characteristic of other regions. There never was any question of support, official, economic, or otherwise, for the mixing of races. The Metis fact was not important, even though Douglas's wife, Lady Amelia, was a Metis from the North-West Territories.

The New Nation

France's colonial policy of "one nation" may not have succeeded, but what it did do was to set in motion a train of developments that culminated in the emergence in the Far Northwest of a "New Nation" which was destined to collide with the new country of Canada. The New Nation was built around a way of life that lasted until the fading of the fur trade and the disappearance of the buffalo herds, both of which occurred towards the end of the nineteenth century. It developed its own language (Michif, in several variations), music and dance, a flag, a bardic tradition, and a rich folklore. Michif, described in 1879 as "a French dialect ... unlike any of the *patois* of France," is today regarded by some linguists as a fully developed mixed language, a rare phenomenon. In its western range it correctly incorporates French nouns and noun phrases with a Plains Cree verbal system and syntax; in its more easterly range, it incorporates Ojibwa as well. English also creeps in, but in a French form. First noted by linguists in the Turtle Mountain region of Manitoba and North Dakota, it has since been reported in northern Alberta and as far east as Quebec. Commonly known as "Metis Cree," or less frequently as "French Cree," it is still spoken in scattered communities. Because it has been slow in gaining recognition as a developed language, rather than being "a bunch of jumble" varying from speaker to speaker, there is no consensus as to the exact nature of Michif. *The Michif Dictionary* (1983), gives only English to Michif equivalents, and even that is incomplete.

The Metis developed their own pattern for the buffalo hunt, based on that of Amerindian hunters while reflecting the military ethos of their French ancestors. Involving as it did the whole community, the hunt encouraged the *esprit de corps* that provided a foundation for Metis nationalism. Its best known symbol was the Red River cart, which in its classic form made its appearance around 1818–21, adapted from a European model via New France. With its large "dished" wheels (almost two metres high), rims wrapped in shaganappi (buffalo rawhide), it was well suited to prairie transportation. When in motion, the screeching of its ungreased axles could be heard from far away. The cart's body could be removed from the frame and placed on runners for use as a sleigh in winter.

In 1820, 540 carts went from Red River to the hunt on the western plains; by 1840 the number had reached 1,210. The average load of meat per cart was 360 kilograms, with 400 kilograms being a full load. In making pemmican, the meat was dried, pounded, and mixed with melted tallow; one buffalo could yield a 36-kilogram sack. Its manufacture has been called the west's first industry. By the 1840s the Metis had edged out their rivals, the Blackfoot, Cree, and Ojibwa, as the main providers of pemmican for the northern fur trade. At first, there were two principal hunts a year, summer and fall; later, from the second decade of the century, a winter hunt developed, a consequence of the American industrial market for buffalo robes. This came after railroads made practicable the transportation of the bulky, heavy hides.

Each hunt was preceded by a rendezvous for the selection of officers and the planning of hunt procedures. Discipline was strict, with offenders being tried before the council, very much in the manner of a court martial. The summer hunt could last for three months; later, the winter hunt was even more demanding. All hunts were marshalled behind a flag; it is not known if it was of the same design as the one adopted by the Metis when they set up their first provisional government towards the end of 1869.

Confrontation between the fur trade's blend of Amerindian and European ways and the European mores of incoming agricultural settlers exacerbated rivalry between the Nor'Westers and the HBC. The establishment of the United States–Canadian boundary in the Great Lakes area by Jay's Treaty in 1794 did not simplify the issues. The War of 1812 and the hard winters of 1812–13 and 1813–14 led to restrictions on the export of pemmican and on running buffalo, a practice seen as driving the herds out of the reach of the settlers. To the Metis, these were direct attacks on their way of life. Out of the ensuing events, which have been labelled the Pemmican War, emerged Cuthbert Grant, of Scots and Cree descent, who in 1816 was acclaimed "Captain General of all the Halfbreeds of the Country." The settlers were now seen as invaders taking lands that belonged to the Metis, who had been there first and who were bonded to the land through their aboriginal heritage. Asserting what he saw as Metis rights, Grant unfurled the Metis flag and led a group of buffalo hunters into confrontations that culminated in 1816 in the Battle of Seven Oaks. The Metis claimed a victory; the settlers saw only a massacre.

The concept of a "New Nation" that reached full form in that battle not only had come to stay, but would be reinforced by another victory against a much larger body of Sioux in 1851, in the Battle of Grand Coteau. These victories enriched an already rapidly growing national mythology, particularly in the songs of the Metis bard Pierre Falcon, son-in-law of Grant. Still remembered are his ballads "La Chanson de la Grenouillière" (in English "The Battle of Seven Oaks") and "Le Lord Selkirk au Fort William, ou La danse des Bois-Brulés," both of which were occasioned by Seven Oaks. Although Falcon's songs at one time were sung by voyageurs on fur-trade routes everywhere, only a few have survived, as most of them were not written down. Anges Laut's "The buffalo hunt" is believed to be a free translation of one of his lyrics.

That Cuthbert Grant played a central role in the emergence of the New Nation is beyond doubt; he has been called the "Father of the Metis Nation," a title he would share with Louis Riel. When the NWC and the HBC amalgamated in 1821 under the HBC banner, the new administration at first ignored Grant. That proved to be impolitic, and so in 1828 the company sought to harness his prestige in its favour by naming him warden of the plains, with the duty of preventing "illicit trade in Furs within the District." In other words, he was now protecting the company's interests rather than being concerned with those of the Metis or even with general justice. Other responsibilities followed, culminating with his appointment as a councillor for the District of Assiniboia, as Lord Selkirk's land grant was called. Meanwhile, the release of free trader Pierre-Guillaume Sayer in 1849, although he had been found guilty of illicit trading, effectively ended the HBC's monopoly, and as a result Grant's usefulness to the company.

At the peak of his career, in 1844, Grant had successfully negotiated a peace settlement with the Sioux, traditional enemies of the Cree and Saulteaux and consequently of the Metis. The peace lasted for seven years, until the battle of Grand Coteau. As leader of the Metis, Grant was eclipsed first by Louis Riel, Sr., and then even more dramatically by Riel's namesake son. Thus, in the end Grant lost out, both officially and with his own people. His career illustrates the complexity and ambivalence of the Metis position between two worlds, which continues today.

As for the fur trade, the Metis had become the principal source of manpower. In the mid-1840s they accounted for two-thirds of the HBC's rank and file and one-third of its officers. By the end of the century, Metis made up 72 percent of the company's workforce. This expansion, however, was mainly in the lower ranks; there were limits as to how high they were allowed to rise, limits that became steadily more restrictive as the century progressed. If the HBC monopoly was less and less capable of interfering with the activities of the Metis as free traders, especially after the release of Sayer, this was offset by diminishing prospects within the company's hierarchy. Similarly, with the NWC, the

Metis made up most of the rank and file, with limited prospects of advancement. Ironically, the fame of the plains buffalo hunters as mounted sharpshooters had reached the point where they were being used as a model for the training of military cavalry in some parts of Europe.

In other aspects as well, pressures on the Metis way of life were increasing. This was particularly evident in the buffalo hunt, which was expanding with the rising industrial demand for buffalo hides, encouraging overhunting as short-term prosperity overshadowed long-term considerations. The aboriginal belief that the free gifts of nature were to be shared by all was being challenged, not only because of over-exploitation, but also by an increasing number of immigrants, whose agricultural and industrial way of life was based on restricted access. Amerindian customs, once the key to survival, were becoming less acceptable socially. The Metis claim to special status by right of their aboriginal blood was dismissed on the ground that they had no more rights than those enjoyed by British subjects.

Nor were they having any luck politically. Their demand that Assiniboia be made a colony free of HBC control was also rejected, in spite of determined lobbying by Alexander Kennedy Isbister, a Metis lawyer and teacher living in London. As the British Parliament saw it, colonial status should not be granted until there was a sufficient number of white settlers in the region to ensure that they would have control. This was a period of population growth for Red River; the 1871 census counted 9,800 Metis, of whom 5,720 were French speaking, and about 4,000 whites; Amerindians had not been counted. In spite of this numerical dominance, Metis unease about their position in relation to Britain had been increasing ever since the troubles that had followed in the wake of the Selkirk settlement.

Resistance, Rebellion, and Aftermath

In the meantime, changing social mores were creating tensions in their own right as European standards, replacing those of the indigenous northwest, led to a series of scandals in which the Metis were targets for prejudice. These in turn exacerbated the political problems, leading to open defiance of the HBC's tattered authority. Voices were raised advocating "a temporary government formed by the people themselves for the time being until the British Government shall see fit to take the place in its own hands."

The period 1862–68 was marked by drought, grasshoppers, prairie fires, and crop failures. The buffalo hunt was receding in the distance, and the fisheries were at low ebb; even rabbits were at a point of cyclic scarcity. Already, before Confederation had been proclaimed on 1 July 1867, arrangements were under way for the transfer of Rupert's Land to Canada. Paragraph 146 of the British North America Act laid the basis for that eventuality.

An important issue was land survey, a requirement for the agricultural use of land. The square survey that was adopted by Canada threatened the Metis settlement pattern of river-frontage strip farms that had been brought from New France: long thin ribbons of land stretching back into woodlots, assuring each holder access to the river, the principal transportation route. When the Canadian government sent surveyors to Red River without consultation or even forewarning, the result was a confrontation in which Louis Riel informed them that they had no right to be doing such work without the permission of the people. Riel's position was that the HBC's trade monopoly did not include rights over the land and the people, and that before any transfer could be negotiated it would be necessary to deal with Amerindian and Metis rights. Recently returned from studying law in Montreal, Riel now took over the reins of Metis leadership.

As neither London nor the Metis would budge from their respective positions, the situation became a crisis when Rupert's Land was scheduled to be transferred from the HBC to Canada, 1 December 1869. In the political vacuum that resulted, Riel issued his "Declaration of the People of Rupert's Land and the Northwest" on 8 December. It stated that "a people, when it has no Government, is free to adopt one form of Government in preference to another, to give or refuse allegiance to that which is proposed." This position was in accord with international law, as Ottawa was only too well aware. Two days later, the Metis flag was hoisted, and on 27 December Louis Riel was elected president of Red River's first provisional government. To that point, it had been a bloodless coup.

The consequence of the Metis stand was the creation of the province of Manitoba in 1870, largely acceding to Metis demands. Among other provisions, the Manitoba Act set aside 1.4 million acres (500,000 hectares) for children of Metis heads of families. The distribution of the grants was so poorly handled, however, that by the time it was concluded only an estimated 15 to 20 percent of Metis beneficiaries had possession of their entitlements. In Metis eyes, this was a massive miscarriage of a promise to their people; it contributed to an ongoing exodus to the west and north as Metis sought locations where they could be themselves – *Otipemisiwak* (free people). It is estimated that as many as two-thirds of the 10,000 Manitoba Metis were involved. This pattern of behaviour owed much to Amerindian custom, in which dissenting groups were free to separate and form their own autonomous bands. There was also a movement towards the south, particularly to Montana, Minnesota, and North Dakota, where descendants of the Metis are known as "Canadian Cree" or, in North Dakota, as "Michif Indians." Economic considerations were also important factors in these dispersals, as they would be again in 1885. For example, the demands of the buffalo-robe trade, which peaked from about 1850 to the mid-1870s, were such that families which participated could not continue even part-time farming in the settlements but had to be close to the herds, where they established log-cabin camps. They were known as *hivernants*, "winterers." Besides that, rising prices during the 1880s made it profitable for Metis farmers to sell their lands and re-establish in less settled areas. In other words, the people were scattering for various reasons, both before and well after the confrontations. As for Riel, although he was elected twice to Parliament, in 1873 and again the following year, hostility against him, particularly in Ontario, was such that he was not able to take his seat. In 1875 he was offered amnesty for his role in the resistance of 1869–70, but only after a five-year banishment; by that time, he was already living in the United States.

The spirit of the New Nation survived even as the Metis adapted to the new economy that overtook them after the loss of the rich resources of the buffalo herds. Although assimilation into the dominant society proceeded apace, substantial numbers continued to retreat to the northern forests, where hunting and trapping still offered free common access. On the plains and in the parklands, the people turned to ranching and horse breeding as well as farming; freighting, logging, interpreting, and guiding also provided livelihoods. Some individuals, such as the perennial buffalo-hunt captain Gabriel Dumont, did well in the short term, participating in the "Wild West" shows that were so popular at the turn of the century on both sides of the Atlantic. In the longer term, Dumont and others followed their "freeman" tradition and established independent businesses. Dumont operated a ferry and had a small store, complete with billiard table. Another who prospered following a similar path was François-Xavier Letendre *dit* Batoche; his success is indicated by the fact that his sobriquet became the name of the settlement on the South Saskatchewan River, forty-four kilometres southwest of Prince Albert.

For most, however, the transition from frontier life meant a drop in living standards.To begin with, adaptation was not made easier by the disregard of incoming settlers for the rights of Metis or Amerindians, particularly in connection with land. A Metis proposal that reserves be set aside for them as was being done for Amerindians who signed treaties drew a cool official response: they were told to apply for land on the same basis as whites. Neither did the Metis elicit constructive suggestions when, in 1872, they asked the government for advice on "what steps they should adopt to secure to themselves the right to prohibit people of other nationalities from settling in the lands occupied by them, without the consent of the Community." Not surprisingly, land surveying continued to be problematic, since many Metis had not gone through the formalities of acquiring legal title to their properties.

The Metis were losing out on all counts: their claim to aboriginal right was not recognized, and even their claims to prior settlers' rights were being challenged. For instance, at Rat River, in the present-day Northwest Territories, eighty-four of ninety-three Metis claims were rejected out of hand because of insufficient cultivation. Five claimants who had houses considered to be adequate and who had cultivated at least two hectares received sixteen hectares; four who had cultivated four and one half hectares received thirty-two hectares. The Metis request that they be exempted from homestead requirements since they had defended the land against the Sioux drew no response. If the Metis often did not help themselves by being negligent about filing claims (they did not see the need for this, because in their eyes their aboriginal blood gave them the right to live wherever they chose), it could be pointed out that official survey maps were slow in appearing and, until they did, the Metis could not make legal claims. They certainly were not negligent about filing petitions for what they believed to be their rights; by 1885 they had sent fifteen.

In the meantime, in the mid-1870s the government moved to implement the Manitoba Act land grant by issuing scrip, an entitling certificate for land. Scrip (from the Latin *scriptum*, "written") was at first made out for varying amounts of cash for the purchase of land at a dollar an acre up to a maximum of 160 acres (64 hectares). This was soon increased to 240 acres (97 hectares). Instead of discouraging speculation, for which the program had been ostensibly designed, scrip, being transferable by means of a power of attorney, quickly became an instrument for encouraging it. Most Metis preferred to take cash for their scrip rather than land, and usually at a heavy discount.

On the other side of the coin, the capacity of the Metis to be effective in cross-cultural situations was demonstrated yet again during the negotiations for the early numbered treaties, in which they actively participated. The Metis James McKay, successful trader and politician, played a crucial role in the first six treaties. That this was appreciated by the Amerindians was evident during Treaty 3 negotiations when they told officials, "We wish that they [Metis] should be counted with us, and have their share of what is promised." The Ojibwa stressed the same point to Alexander Morris, lieutenant governor of the North-West Territories from 1873 to 1876: "We wish you to understand that you owe much to the half-breeds." Instead of recognizing their services, Ottawa amended the Indian Act in 1880 to exclude Metis both from the provisions of the act and from the treaties. In practice, however, Metis continued to influence negotiations, as well as to have the option of being included in the treaties if they qualified as Amerindians and so wished. Lord Dufferin, governor general of Canada from 1872 to 1878, remarked that the Metis were "the ambassadors between East and West." He attributed the rarity of frontier wars in Canada to the Metis, whom he saw as playing an essential role in maintaining the generally peaceful frontier. This made all the more ironic Canada's reluctance to recognize their aboriginal claims.

The stage was being set for the rebellion of 1885, in spite of the prosperity of the preceding two decades, which did not dim the Metis perception that their lands were being stolen, "and now they are laughing at us." A vague amendment to the Dominion Lands Act that appeared to recognize Metis rights had no consequences. In fact, the opposite seemed to be happening: in 1882 Dumont was one of those who signed a petition protesting being forced to pay for land they had occupied before the survey if it happened to fall into odd-numbered sections not being made available for homesteading.

During these years, the nearly completed Canadian Pacific Railway allowed more and more settlers to arrive in the west. Whereas in 1869–70 the Metis had held the balance of power in Red River, they were now outnumbered by whites. There seemed to be no way to get Ottawa's ear; even such a leader as Dumont was not able to get results. When Ottawa in 1882 named an investigator into the Metis complaints, he could not speak French and it was 1884 before he appeared on the scene. His report, sent to Ottawa at the end of that year, did not elicit action until early 1885. By that time, the Metis had already asked Riel for help. Riel, then a teacher in a Jesuit mission school in Montana, accepted the challenge.

Not only were the buffalo herds in full retreat, but two years of poor crops (1883, frost; 1884, wet harvest) had resulted in an extremely hard winter in 1884–85. In the midst of hunger and discontent, Riel struck a pacific note: over and over he repeated his peaceful intentions. He asked that Ottawa send adequate food rations to the west, and he even came to the defence of the white settlers, claiming that they were being charged too much for land. Ottawa was equally consistent in its apparent obliviousness to the western situation. It disarmed the North-West Territories militia, despite warnings that things were not as peaceful as they seemed. In 1884 Riel prepared to meet with Hector-Louis Langevin, minister of public works, in Prince Albert; Langevin cancelled the visit without warning. The Metis got nowhere when they asked that Riel replace Pascal Breland on the Territorial Council, on the ground that Breland was not effectively representing their interests. When Ottawa actually responded to Riel's 1884 petition requesting, among other items, that the Metis be treated with the full dignity of British subjects, jubilation was the order of the day. However, when the Metis examined the message more closely, they realized that all it promised was to set up a commission to enumerate those who were resident in the northwest in 1870, as well as their claims; it did not make provision for settling grievances. The disillusioned Metis agreed among themselves that, if necessary, they would take up arms "to save our country." On 19 March 1885 (the feastday of Saint Joseph, patron saint of the Metis) Riel proclaimed a provisional government, which he backed with a ten-point Bill of Rights, and the people armed themselves.

Riel's Bill of Rights reveals his concern for social justice for all, not just for the Metis. Besides the points already noted, it asked that patents be issued to all Metis and white settlers "who had fairly earned the right of possession on their farms," and that the districts of Saskatchewan and Alberta be created provinces "so that the people may no longer be subject to the despotism of Mr. Dewdney." (Edgar Dewdney was lieutenant governor of the North-West Territories, 1881–88). It asked for hospitals and schools, respect for "the lawful customs and usages which obtain among the Metis," that the region's administrative centre be moved to Winnipeg, and that the administration be for "the benefit of the actual settlers, not for the advantage of the alien speculator."

When fighting broke out, it did not last long; it was over for the Metis when they were defeated at Batoche on 12 May after a three-day battle;

on 15 May Riel surrendered. For the Amerindians, the end was formally signalled when Big Bear presented himself to a startled sentry on 2 July. The rebellion's toll was 53 whites killed, 118 wounded, and about 35 Amerindians and Metis killed. Of the 84 trials that resulted, 71 were for treason-felony, 12 for murder, and 1 (Riel's) for high treason. Of 81 Indians jailed, 44 were convicted and 8 hanged for murder. Of the 46 Metis who were taken into custody, 19 were convicted, 1 hanged (Riel), and 7 conditionally discharged; the rest were either unconditionally discharged or not brought to trial. Although Riel had become an American citizen during his sojourn in the United States, he was tried and convicted under the British doctrine that a person born a British subject could not lose that status through naturalization in another country. His lawyers' attempts to win his acquittal on grounds of insanity had been countered by Riel himself during his trial.

Although both Metis and Cree had been protagonists in the uprising, they had fought their own battles; there was mutual sympathy but no formal alliance. Riel, in taking the broad view when he included Amerindians and whites in his Bill of Rights, was implicitly acknowledging the dual heritage of the Metis.

One consequence of the "prairie fire," as the rebellion has been called, was the acceleration of the issuance of scrip, which now came in two forms, one for cash and one for land. Between 1885 and 1921, there were twelve commissions set up for scrip distribution. Eligibility varied as regulations changed over time; after 1899 it was tied to the date when a treaty was signed in a given region. Only Metis born after that date qualified. The vast majority chose money scrip; for instance, during the negotiations for Treaty 8 in 1899, there were 1,195 money scrips issued and only 48 land scrips. This reflected the fact that much of the land offered to the Metis was marginal for farming, besides being remote from land offices. Official attempts to control speculators, who encouraged the Metis to sell their scrip for a fraction of its value, met with resistance from the Metis themselves. In its final report on the scrip project in 1929, the year before control of Crown lands reverted to the provinces, Ottawa said that 24,000 claims had been recognized in the North-West Territories, involving 2.6 million acres (1,1052,183 hectares) in land scrip and 2.8 million acres (1,133,120 hectares) in money scrip. Later it would be claimed that over 90 percent of this scrip ended up in the control of banks and speculators.

Whereas Amerindians who signed a treaty had reserved land that could not be alienated, many Metis ended up as a landless minority –

"road allowance people," living on the fringes of both white and Amerindian communities – wandering from job to job, their traditional way of life being steadily restricted as agriculture and resource development became dominant. Even the Metis role as interpreters and mediators between Amerindians and whites became irrelevant as treaties settled issues. At the initiative of the Oblate priest Albert Lacombe, who had a trace of Amerindian blood but did not identify himself as Metis, Saint-Paul-des-Métis was established in 1896 in north-central Alberta as an experiment in helping the people to become full-time sedentary farmers. It was the first time since Treaty 3 that a tract of land was set aside for the exclusive use of the Metis. Each participating family was to receive 80 acres (32 hectares, one-half of the standard homestead allotment), as well as livestock and agricultural equipment to get started. Though the federal government of Wilfrid Laurier approved the project, it contributed only $2,000. Underfunded as it was, the project had difficulty providing the promised help to the fifty families who participated; most of them, discouraged, drifted away, usually to unsurveyed crown lands in the north where they could continue their accustomed hunting, trapping, and fishing. Their farm leases at Saint-Paul were terminated in 1908, and the following year the reserve was thrown open for French-Canadian settlement. In the meantime, the creation of Alberta and Saskatchewan as provinces in 1905 further complicated matters for the Metis, since they were now divided under different administrations, making it difficult for them to speak with one voice.

Metis Today

By the early twentieth century, most Metis were barely eking out a living even in good times; the difficult years of the Great Depression during the 1930s provoked disaster. In 1932 Joseph Dion, an enfranchised adopted nephew of Big Bear, formed L'Association des Métis de l'Alberta et des Territoires du Nord Ouest to help the people get established on their own lands. He was joined by activists Malcolm Norris and James Brady, both one-eighth Amerindian; together they reorganized the association into the Metis Association of Alberta in 1940 and launched an expanded land-settlement program in the northern part of the province. It had some success but could not keep pace with the widespread misery. Metis Maria Campbell vividly described her people's lot in her best-selling memoir, *Halfbreed* (1973). The province was finally moved to help, appointing a royal commission in 1934 under the chairmanship of Alberta Supreme Court Judge Albert Freeman Ewing. The commission's proposal that farm colonies be established in suitable locations, free from white interference, was implemented by the Metis Population Betterment Act of 1938. At the time, this was the most advanced legislation in Canada relating to Metis. Of twelve locations initially selected in north-central Alberta, ten were opened for settlement. Not all communities agreed to participate; Grande Cache, for one, held aloof. Today, eight participating settlements remain, comprising a total of 539,446 hectares and a combined population of nearly 6,000.

Administration is coordinated with the province through the Metis Settlements General Council (before 1990, known as the Alberta Federation of Metis Settlement Associations). The discovery of oil and gas triggered a series of confrontations between the province and the settlements over questions about land rights and royalties; in 1990 the Metis land base was entrenched in the Alberta constitution. With the establishment of an appeal tribunal and co-management agreement, the Metis settlements have won substantial control over their own affairs, and negotiations continue for further devolution.

Grand Cache entered into its own negotiations with the province when a coal mine began operation in the area. This resulted in 1,680 hectares, including a residential section, being set aside for the Metis. It proved to be insufficient for them to continue hunting and trapping, since the designated land did not have the necessary natural resources. Consequently, wage labour has become the mainstay for most of the resident Metis at Grand Cache.

The Metis of these settlements represent two principal traditions: those who trace their origins to Red River, and consequently to French, Algonquian (Cree, Ojibwa), Iroquoian, or Athapaskan ancestry and who are mostly Roman Catholic; and those from farther north, who are descended largely from Scots, Scandinavians, Athapaskans, Cree, and Inuit and who are predominantly Anglican. Farming, ranching, and intermittent wage labour are principal subsistence activities, supplemented with hunting, trapping, and fishing (where available). A study of the social structure of one of the settlements, Kikino (Beaver Metis Colony), has revealed that 75 percent of its population belongs to five extended families, each settled in its own neighbourhood. Unrelated families live in the more remote sections of the colony and are both physically and socially isolated. Today, although there is more inter-marriage between the families than in the past, social activities and organizations still tend to remain within particular extended families. This is also evident in religion, for each extended family usually identifies with a particular church. Prevailing languages are English and

Cree, with the latter for the most part being the second language. Baseball is the social activity that cuts across family lines and involves the community as a whole. In this social structure, and in politics as well, males are dominant. Factionalism reflects the primacy of family loyalty over that to the community. As with other fur-trading communities that were directly affected by the establishment of the settlements, living conditions improved somewhat in Kikino under the new regime.

Nearby is the larger mixed community of Lac La Biche, which also benefited from the Alberta settlement program even though it did not formally participate. Its location on fur-trade routes resulted in posts' being built there in the late 1790s. The French-speaking element, mostly from Red River, coalesced around the Oblate mission that was established in 1853. It forms a community that is still tightly knit, even though the influence of the church is lessening and the trend is towards marrying out and establishing nuclear families. Living is largely off the land; logging and road work provide intermittent wage labour. Many of the adults are trilingual, speaking English and Cree as well as French. Lac La Biche has the advantage of a commercial fishery cooperative in which both whites and Metis participate; tourism is also being encouraged. It is not known with any certainty how representative Kikino and Lac La Biche are of northern Metis communities today.

In 1940 Saskatchewan launched a program to train Metis to be farmers, which eventually led to the establishment of eleven government farm colonies. One of these, of about 1,200 hectares, was transferred in 1968 to Lebret Farm Land Foundations, owned and operated by Metis and non-status Amerindians. Negotiations to encourage farm colonies in other Metis communities, as well as to give the Metis greater control of certain provincial programs (like housing and welfare) and a share of resource revenues, ended in disagreement in 1987. In the meantime, Saskatchewan, with Manitoba and Quebec, has set up programs for the rehabilitation of fur production in over-exploited areas which, while not specifically for the benefit of the Metis, are obviously important for the maintenance of hunting and trapping. Registered traplines were introduced in 1940 in Manitoba; six years later they were adopted in Saskatchewan. At first these caused some difficulty since they interfered with traditional land use; however, they have proven useful for the control of trapping and so have been beneficial in those regions where agriculture is not practicable and industrial development not currently foreseen. In Saskatchewan, some programs combine fur production with farming.

The Canadian constitution of 1982 has not gone farther than the simple recognition of existing aboriginal and treaty rights. The defeat of the Charlottetown constitutional accord in the 1992 referendum took down with it a side deal, the Metis Nation Accord, by which Ottawa had agreed to be the primary agent in negotiating self-government with the Metis. For almost two centuries the Metis had been fighting to wrest this concession from Ottawa; the final irony was that many of them were among those who voted against the Charlottetown agreement, which they felt was being pushed through too fast. As matters stand now, Ottawa has reverted to its original position that the Metis, as ordinary citizens, are a provincial responsibility.

The Metis National Council's analysis of the Aboriginal Peoples Survey of 1991 presented a picture of the Metis as marginalized, a situation that the council blamed on the denial of Metis access to federal services and benefits which are available to other aboriginal peoples. The council reported that about 17 percent of Metis over the age of 15 had less than grade 9 education, compared with 13.9 percent of the total population. In at least one respect Metis were found to be worse off than Amerindians: only 3.7 percent of Metis had completed university education, compared with 5.1 percent of Amerindians and 11.4 percent of the general population. Metis women did somewhat better than men in this regard: 4.1 percent had university education, compared with 3.4 percent of the men. The only post-secondary institution controlled by the Metis, the Gabriel Dumont Institute, was established in Saskatoon by the Metis Society of Saskatchewan in 1980. The Manitoba Federation plans to establish a Louis Riel Institute.

Employment presented no brighter a picture: the unemployment rate for Metis more than 15 years old was 19 percent, almost double the national average of 10.3 percent. Of those who were employed, 60 percent earned $10,000 a year or less. On the positive side, Ontario had the highest Metis participation rate in its labour force, 73 percent, well above the national rate of 68 percent. Besides that, employed Metis of Ontario shared with the Northwest Territories the highest proportion of those earning $40,000 a year or over: in Ontario, 10 percent, and in the Northwest Territories 17.7 percent. This probably reflected the fact that 19.1 percent of employed Metis in Ontario, and 19.7 percent in the Northwest Territories, were in professional occupations, much higher than the national average of 6.2 percent for the Metis. The general population's national average for those earning over $40,000 was 12.7 percent.

The Metis of Manitoba and Saskatchewan had not only the highest unemployment rates but also the lowest employment income. In Manitoba the unemployment rate was 20.1 percent, and 64.2 percent of those employed earn less than $10,000 annually; in Saskatchewan, the figures were 20.9 percent for the unemployed and 67.8 percent for those earning $10,000 a year or less.

The fact that the constitutional recognition of the Metis as an aboriginal people has not been followed by the creation of federal programs commensurate with those in place for other aboriginal peoples is a continuing irritant. In the words of the Metis National Council, this inaction "is particularly discriminatory in view of the fact that the Metis already face serious disadvantages relative to other Aboriginal peoples due to their lack of a land and resource base and the application to them of federal and provincial personal income and corporate tax laws." An immediate goal is to secure a land and resource base, a "Metis Homeland."

Their sense of the importance of their own history, and of the need to keep it a living memory, has been a central theme in Metis cultural activities since the battle of Batoche. Within a few years of the battle, an annual commemoration became a major ongoing event that today attracts thousands. As well, in 1887 a group of former friends and associates of Riel, concerned that the Metis side of the story be presented, formed the Union Nationale Métisse Saint-Joseph de Manitoba for the purpose of collecting material about and researching the events of 1869–70 and 1885. A result was the publication of A.-H. de Trémaudan's *Histoire de la nation métisse dans l'Ouest canadien* in 1935. Promoting awareness of Metis history has been a principal activity of cultural groups ever since. In 1972 the Manitoba Métis Federation (MMF) Press was founded, later to evolve into the Pemmican Press, based in Winnipeg. This press was the publisher of the *Michif Dictionary*, mentioned above. The Louis Riel Historical Society, founded in Edmonton in 1986, aims to establish a museum and archives as part of a Metis cultural resource centre. Today, it functions within the Metis Nation of Alberta.

The resurgence of Metis nationalism has been signalled by the intensification of political activity which began in the mid-1960s. Spurred by such issues as the federal government's white paper of 1969 on Indian policy and the patriation of the Canadian constitution in 1982, the Metis have organized and reorganized in an astonishing array of groups, all dedicated to improving their lot one way or another.

Metis of the three prairie provinces joined forces in 1970 to form the Native Council of Canada. When the council assigned its two seats at the 1983 First Ministers Conference to non-status Amerindian delegates, breakaway Metis reorganized themselves into the Metis National Council. This body, as the voice for the five provincial organizations west of Quebec, does not speak for the Maritimes or for the Northwest Territories. The Native Council has reorganized itself as the Congress of Aboriginal Peoples.

Metis women have also been actively organizing. The Native Women's Association of Canada was formed in 1974, and the Women of the Metis Nation followed in 1986; in 1995 the latter merged with Alberta Metis Women, an offshoot of the Metis Nation of Alberta. Social problems, such as family violence, alcoholism, and substance abuse, are principal concerns. The growing awareness that these problems can best be solved within the communities themselves has given rise to the healing circle movement. As with the aboriginal people generally, most Metis politicians are men, whereas most of those involved in the healing circles are women.

Social and political activity has its counterpart in the arts. While there is no single art style that can be labelled Metis, still the blending of aboriginal and non-aboriginal themes was rapid and is widespread; beaded floral embroideries are a good example. Cross-fertilization has produced masterworks in architecture, sculpture, and painting, as well as through a whole range of crafts, including fashion design. Woodsplint basketry and Nascapi hunters' coats illustrate the last two categories. In architecture, the work of Douglas Cardinal, who designed the Canadian Museum of Civilization, is internationally acclaimed; in painting, works that immediately come to mind are those of Daphne Odjig, Jane Ash Poitras, Alex Janvier, and George Littlechild; in sculpture, Bill Reid is a pre-eminent figure

Film-making, literature, theatre, dance, and music – all have benefited from the Metis imprint. Film-making in particular has been flourishing since the advent of television and has brought figures such as Gil Cardinal to national prominence. Certain forms of country music and dance, derived from Celtic traditions as well as from other types of European folk dancing, have become closely associated with the Metis; the Red River jig, dating back to the beginning of the nineteenth century, has been called "one of few truly Canadian dance forms." The National Film Board's *The Fiddlers of James Bay* (1980) celebrated the fiddling tradition the Metis inherited from the Scots and made their own. In the realm of creative writing, Thomas King and Jordan Wheeler are among a growing number attracting national attention. Memoirs, such as Campbell's *Halfbreed* (1973), noted above, and more recently Brian Maracle's *Back on the Rez* (1996), remain a favourite genre for Metis and native writers generally. The same can be said for social commentaries, such as Emma LaRocque's *Defeathering the Indian* (1975) and Beatrice Culleton's partially fictionalized *In Search of April Raintree* (1983).

However, it is in the political arena that the greatest Metis activity is taking place, particularly since the 1982 Constitution Act. On the question of land, not only do the Metis disagree with the federal government on the issue of scrip, they have not forgotten their claim that the 1870 Manitoba grant of 1.4 million acres to "children of Metis" was mismanaged so that only a fraction of the grant remained with those for whom it was ostensibly intended. A suit launched in 1985 on behalf of all the Metis of Manitoba for the land in question, involving much of downtown Winnipeg, has since been allowed to lapse. The current lieutenant governor of Manitoba, Yvon Dumont, named in 1993, is a Metis.

Forming as they do such a small segment of Canadian society, the Metis have still played a unique role in Canada's history. As they see it, this reflects the fact that they were born of the meeting of two worlds, the first Canadians. Although their long official eclipse has ended, the work of rebuilding the Metis as a people has just begun, a people whom many would define on the basis more of their history than any other factor.

FURTHER READING

The widest-ranging study is still Marcel Giraud's *Le Métis canadien* (Paris, 1945), which remains useful despite some dated views. In English, it is *The Métis in the Canadian West* (Edmonton, 1986). A recent overview of the Red River Metis is Gerhard J. Ens, *Homeland to Hinterland: The Changing Worlds of the Red River Metis in the Nineteenth Century* (Toronto, 1996). A work of broader interest than its title indicates is Diane Payment, *"The Free People – Otipemisi-wak" Batoche, Saskatchewan, 1870–1930* (Ottawa, 1990). Her detailed description of Metis life applies to more of the western plains than just Saskatchewan.

Two useful collections of essays on various aspects of the Metis are Jacqueline Peterson and Jennifer S.H. Brown, eds., *The New Peoples: Being and Becoming Métis in North America* (Winnipeg, 1985); and F. Laurie Barron and James B. Waldram, eds., *1885 and After* (Regina, 1986).

Maggie Siggins, *Riel: A Life of Revolution* (Toronto, 1994), casts a sympathetic light on the controversial Metis leader. The most detailed study of the 1885 troubles, ranging through a wide variety of both contemporary and recent sources, is Bob Beal and Rod Macleod, *Prairie Fire* (Edmonton, 1984). Murray Dobbin takes a perceptive look at the Metis caught in the economic and political stresses of the 1930s and 1940s in *The One-and-a-Half Men* (Vancouver, 1981). On the literary front, an anthology that contains some examples of Metis writing is Agnes Grant, ed., *Our Bit of Truth* (Winnipeg, 1992). For current information, *The Métis Nation*, newsletter of the Métis National Council, Ottawa, is helpful.

8

NA-DENE

Patrick Moore

Identification

The linguist Edward Sapir first used the term Na-Dene to refer to a language family which he believed encompassed all Athabaskan languages as well as Tlingit and Haida. Scholars now use the term to refer both to this proposed language family and to those who speak the languages included within it. There is no common term used by native people to describe the entire group, although the term *dene* means "person" or "people" in many Athabaskan languages. There are at least forty Athabaskan or Dene languages within this family. Speakers of Athabaskan languages are located in the United States along the Pacific Coast, in the American southwest, and in western Canada and Alaska. The Navajo, who live in the American southwest, are numerically the largest single group of Na-Dene, with a population of approximately 200,000. Canadian Athabaskan groups together number about 35,000 and there are also approximately 7,000 Tlingit (1,000 in Canada) and 3,000 Haida (2,000 in Canada).

In recent years researchers have further outlined the relationships that Sapir originally proposed between the Tlingit, Haida, and Athabaskan languages. Tlingit, which is spoken in the Alaskan panhandle, northwestern British Columbia, and southwestern Yukon, is generally believed to be remotely related to Athabaskan languages. Another Alaskan language, Eyak, which was unknown to Sapir, has also been shown to be even more closely related to Athabaskan languages. Haida, which is spoken in the Queen Charlotte Islands of British Columbia and in southeast Alaska, is generally regarded as unrelated to Athabaskan languages and Tlingit. Substantial correspondences of vocabulary and of sounds have not been demonstrated between Haida and the other Na-Dene languages. Haida will be included in the discussion of Na-Dene peoples for the purposes of this chapter, however, since it was included in Sapir's original grouping.

In Canada there are many Athabaskan groups as well as Tlingit and Haida. The term that Athabaskans employ to designate themselves is *Dene*, and both terms, Dene and Athabaskan, have been used to refer to the entire language family and people speaking these languages. Tlingit is derived from the Tlingit word, ¬*ingât*, meaning "human beings." Similarly, Haida is derived from a Haida word, *hà.te* or *hà.de.*, meaning "the people."

It is difficult to divide the Athabaskan languages within Canada into discrete tongues with definite boundaries. Some, such as Tagish and Tahltan, which have traditionally been treated as separate languages, are mutually intelligible and might be regarded as dialects of a single language. Still others such as Slavey (North Slavey and South Slavey) have many dialects, only some of which are mutually intelligible. Gradual sound changes, patterns of migration, intermarriage, and trade have all conspired to change the distribution of languages and the territories occupied by their speakers. Finally, over the last century many of these languages have been replaced in daily use by English. Membership in any Athabaskan group must now be extended to include descendants who speak primarily English.

Of the approximately nineteen Canadian Athabaskan languages, all but one are still spoken by at least a few people. In some cases the names for these groups have changed over time, separate dialects have been grouped as a single language, or groups have lost their independent identity. The following is a list of language names in common usage as well as alternate designations found in some sources. Beaver (Tsattine); Babine (Witsiwoten, Northern Carrier); Carrier; Chilcotin (Tsilkotin); Chipewyan (Montagnais, Yellowknife); Dogrib; Gwich'in (Kutchin, Loucheux); Han (Han Kutchin); Kaska (Nahani, Pelly Indians); North Slavey (Hare, Bearlake, Mountain, Slavey); Northern Tutchone (Tutchone); Sarsi (Sarcee); Sekani; South Slavey (Slave, Slavey); Southern Tutchone (Tutchone); Tagish; Tahltan (Nahani); Tsetsaut; Upper Tanana (Tanana, Nabesna).

The origins of the Na-Dene remain a controversial subject. Linguistically, the diversity of languages present in the north argues in favour of a northern origin for the Athabaskan language family as well as for Eyak and Tlingit. There is little proof for any definite place of origin beyond this. Since Sapir, linguists have linked the Na-Dene languages to Asian languages, but their work is not conclusive.

The archaeological record has also been used to advance theories of an Asiatic origin for Na-Dene peoples. Archaeologists specifically point to similarities in the microblade technology which characterizes many archaeological sites in Siberia and in Alaska and Yukon from between 9,000 and 7,000 years ago. Microblades are small cutting edges which were used as fleshers, skinning knives, and arrow points. Microblades from this very early period show great similarity, both in the preparation of the "core," from which they were struck, and in the shape of the microblades themselves. Microblade technology cannot, however, be definitely linked to Na-Dene peoples or their direct ancestors. In subsequent periods there is little evidence of microblade manufacture in Alaska and Yukon for several thousand years until they reappeared in a different style around 5,000 years ago. The later style is distinct both from Asian technologies and from the earlier forms in Alaska and Yukon. Even if the early microblade users were direct ancestors of the Na-Dene, something that has not been demonstrated, any connection between these groups and Asia would stem from an early time period. The later diversification of Na-Dene languages and cultures undoubtedly occurred entirely within North America.

The Na-Dene peoples are widely distributed across western and northern North America. Within Canada, Athabaskan peoples are found across the subarctic between the coastal ranges of the Pacific and Hudson Bay, Tlingit along the Pacific coast of southeast Alaska and inland to adjacent parts of British Columbia and Yukon, and Haida on the Queen Charlotte Islands of British Columbia.

The location of the Na-Dene peoples has changed only slightly in the last three centuries in response to the arrival of Europeans in their territory. Following the establishment of York Factory on Hudson Bay in 1682, the Chipewyan, the first Na-Dene group to trade with Europeans, shifted their territory southward. On the northwest coast the Tlingit came into contact with Russian explorers in 1741, and during the nineteenth century Tlingit traders settled in the interior and eventually occupied a portion of Yukon and British Columbia.

Changes in the territories occupied by other Na-Dene groups are difficult to document. Terms such as Dogrib, Slavey, Beaver, and Kaska were not used consistently by early travellers in the region since most observers could not differentiate the languages accurately. However, it is known that the Sarsi occupied new territory after the introduction of horses to the northern plains, moving southward within Alberta and allying themselves with the Blackfoot.

European settlement has changed the distribution of the native population within Na-Dene territory. Fur trading posts became centres of economic activity, where furs and supplies of meat and fish were exchanged for trade goods, and eventually some natives resided at the posts. Tlingit and Haida were already settled in permanent villages before the arrival of European explorers, but some of these were decimated by disease while others came under military attack by Europeans. Many village sites were abandoned as Tlingit and Haida moved to larger towns such as Masset, Ketchikan, and Juneau.

There has been a rapid influx of non-natives to much of this region in the last century. Non-native farmers and ranchers moved into that part of the territory of the Sarsi, Beaver, and Chilcotin which was suitable for agriculture. Thousands of miners travelled to the Klondike in Yukon following the discovery of gold in 1896, and Dawson City was built on the traditional lands of the Han people. The development of mineral resources was a major factor in the growth of towns such as Dawson City and Whitehorse in Yukon and later Yellowknife in the Northwest Territories. Oil and natural gas developments contributed to the growth of other centres. During World War II thousands of U.S. army troops and construction workers built the Alaska Highway and Canol Road, and other roads soon followed across the north. In the period after the war, these new transportation links facilitated the exploitation of renewable resources, including furs, seafood, and forest resources.

In some areas the Canadian government negotiated treaties with Na-Dene groups. Treaty 7 was negotiated with the Sarsi in 1887; Treaty 8 in 1899 with the Chipewyan, Beaver, and some Slavey; Treaty 10 with some Chipewyan communities; and Treaty 11 in 1921 with other Dene groups along the Mackenzie River valley. Although reserves were set up in accord with treaty provisions in some areas (but not in Treaties 8 and 11) and other aspects of the treaties were implemented, some of the treaties' terms, especially respecting the cession of land, are still in dispute. As well, in the last two decades treaty making in the form of land-claims negotiations has taken place in those parts of Yukon and British Columbia not covered by existing treaties.

Prior to the fur trade the population of Athabaskan groups was quite dispersed. Camps consisted of only a few dwellings occupied by one or more extended families. The population density of this region was relatively low, as it is today. The Na-Dene groups of the northwest coast, the Tlingit and Haida, lived in larger settlements with as many as fifty houses, but the total population of these groups was still relatively small. Although the population was dispersed, the availability of game, fish, and other resources often brought together larger groups at specific times of the year for hunting, fishing, or religious gatherings.

Athabaskans moved within their home territory to locate game, productive fish lakes and streams, or other food resources. Hunters travelled widely in search of large game – be it caribou, moose, or bison – and their families also moved camp on a regular basis. Resources such as small game, fish, berries, roots, and medicinal plants which are most abundant in specific areas were targeted by family groups in their seasonal movements. Tlingit and Haida also dispersed at certain times of the year to take advantage of specific resources such as salmon, halibut, herring roe, oolichan, shellfish, and sea mammals.

Contemporary settlement patterns vary. The Sarsi reserve includes suburban housing developments adjacent to Calgary, and individuals from various groups have settled in other large cities such as Edmonton and Vancouver. Some of the Beaver reserves include agricultural lands with dispersed houses. In most of the smaller northern communities the houses are grouped quite closely together, much like villages in the rest of Canada. Native and non-native portions of the village may be partially separated because of historic settlement patterns. This may also be true when two distinct native groups live within one village, as in Fort Chipewyan where both Cree and Chipewyan are present.

History

The lucrative fur trade drove the expansion of European trading posts into Na-Dene territory for over two centuries, and the routes used by fur traders diversified as the volume of trade increased. Chipewyans, the first Athabaskans to come into direct contact with Europeans, met explorers on the coast of Hudson Bay in the early 1600s, but the Cree used newly acquired guns to dominate trade between York Factory, established in 1682, and the interior Athabaskans. When the post of Churchill was established in 1721, Chipewyan dealt with the Hudson's Bay Company (HBC) directly, and leaders such as Matonabee established their own trade routes to the interior. During this period, European diseases such as smallpox, measles, scarlet fever, diphtheria, and influenza plagued Chipewyan as well as other groups. One of the worst epidemics of smallpox killed more than half of the Chipewyan population in 1781–82 and most groups were unable to avoid periodic devastation.

In the 1770s a number of explorers established fur-trading posts in the interior as far as Lake Athabasca. These included Canadien traders working for the North West Company (NWC) as well as those employed by the HBC. The two companies set up numerous posts throughout the interior prior to their merger in 1821. These posts brought such groups as the Beaver, Slave, Dogrib, and Gwich'in into direct contact with white traders for the first time.

On the northwest coast, Russian explorers and traders found the Tlingit to be tough bargainers, defiant of Russian authority. The Tlingit took two Russian boats in their first encounter and they also captured the Russian fort at Sitka in 1804, two years after it was constructed. The Tlingit remained independent of Russian rule and established an extensive fur-trading network with the interior Athabaskan groups during the 1800s. The HBC also attempted to take command of the trade in this area by leasing part of Tlingit territory on the coast from the Russians in 1839 and by establishing posts in the interior to trade with the Kaska, Tahltan, and Tutchone directly. The Tlingit resisted this threat to their trade with the interior by maintaining tight control over the coastal passes and by destroying the HBC post at Fort Selkirk at the confluence of the Yukon and Pelly rivers in 1852.

Haida met and traded with many European expeditions, beginning with the Spanish explorer Juan Perez in 1774. They traded large numbers of sea otter pelts until these animals were virtually exterminated in the early 1800s. The Haida themselves were decimated by disease in the early nineteenth century and eventually abandoned many settlements. Commercial fishing, potato farming, work in the fish canneries, and later lumbering became important economic activities for Haida.

As a result of the fur trade, the Na-Dene became more familiar with the Christian beliefs of European traders. By 1820 Catholic and Anglican missions had been established at the Red River settlement in Manitoba, and in 1844 a Catholic missionary was sent to the Chipewyan. In the following two decades a number of Anglican and Catholic missions were established among the Chipewyan, Dogrib, Slave, Gwich'in, and Beaver. During this period native religious leaders, such as the Carrier prophet Bini, adopted elements of Christian belief which they combined with traditional practices. In the late nineteenth century and continuing into the twentieth century, several religious groups, including the Catholics, Anglicans, and Baptists, operated residential schools for native students. Students were often isolated from their families for long periods, and many recall being harshly treated.

On the west coast, Canadian Haida were evangelized by Methodists and Anglicans who discouraged some native customs such as potlatches. Potlatches are native ceremonies commemorating such events as the death of an individual, the anniversary of their death, the naming of a child, or the bestowal of a prestigious name on any person. The sponsoring clan often gave a large number of valuable presents to the invited guests, a practice that non-natives thought excessive and tried to discourage. A significant number of Tlingit became members of the Russian Orthodox Church while most in Canada became Anglicans or Catholics. More recently, other religious groups, including fundamentalist Protestant sects and Bahais, have attracted significant followings, particularly in Yukon and British Columbia.

Within the last century the fur trade in the north has been overshadowed by other economic activities. Large numbers of gold miners went to the Cassiar region of British Columbia in 1873, and many thousands descended on the Klondike goldfields of Yukon after 1896. Oil was discovered in large quantities at Norman Wells in the Northwest Territories in 1920, an event that triggered another influx of people. In many cases the development of these resources followed cycles of boom and bust. The construction of roads, airports, and modern communications networks has further facilitated the development of resources since World War II.

Economic Life

The traditional Na-Dene economy was largely devoted to subsistence activities, although there was also some long-distance trade for obsidian, copper, and sea shells. Iron may also have been traded along the west coast from sources in Asia before Europeans arrived.

The Na-Dene made use of a variety of plant and animal resources. For the Haida and Tlingit, resources derived from the sea and coastal rivers were of great importance. For Athabaskan groups in the interior, large game – including moose, caribou, and bison – was valuable for food and hides, but small game and fish often contributed an even larger portion of the diet. Prior to the development of trade with Europeans, the Na-Dene did not keep domestic animals. The Tlingit and Haida grew small amounts of tobacco, but potatoes and other crops were widely cultivated only after trade began with Europeans.

During the fur-trade period most Na-Dene maintained their traditional subsistence activities and also provided large quantities of food
for the consumption of the European fur traders. They traded fresh and
dried meat, fish, and in some cases crops such as potatoes. Some groups
resisted involvement in the fur trade, preferring to concentrate on their
traditional subsistence activities. Chipewyan bands known as "Caribou
Eaters," for example, continued to follow herds of caribou on the tundra
during most of the year. Similarly, many Beaver and Slave trapped so
few furs that Assiniboine, Objiwa, and Iroquois trappers were engaged
as trappers and sent by the NWC to Alberta. Game animals, such as
bison, were nearly exterminated in the Peace River region by these post
hunters.

The availability of iron tools, guns, fish nets, and sawn lumber for
boats may have strengthened local subsistence activities for many groups;
there is little evidence of a collapse of the traditional economies during
the fur-trade period. The periodic food shortages and incidents of
starvation which did occur reveal the inability of traders to transport
large quantities of food and the unpredictability of local food resources.
The Tlingit and Haida both devised institutions such as potlatches in
this period. The Tlingit became well armed and resisted Russian control
while expanding their own trade with the interior.

Major changes in the subsistence economy occurred with the exploitation of various resources and the expansion of government services
following World War II. Oil and mineral resources were developed on a
large scale, and, to support this kind of economic activity, roads, airports, and communication facilities were constructed. Some native people found employment in these projects, although in many cases the
workforce was dominated by non-native workers recruited from other
areas. In recent years First Nations have attempted to improve employment opportunities by negotiating agreements with firms planning
major developments in their regions. First Nations have had some
success in gaining employment opportunities for their peoples in the
Northwest Territories, Yukon, and British Columbia, where land claims
are being actively negotiated. Some First Nations also operate their own
corporations, which are involved in such fields as forestry, road construction, housing construction, air charter services, oilfield maintenance, agriculture, and fisheries.

In Yukon and Northwest Territories, the territorial and federal governments employ one-fourth of the labour force. The representation of
native people in government service is gradually increasing as a result

of employment policies and special training programs for native teachers, social workers, managers, renewable-resource officers, and police
officers. Students in these programs may receive support from their
First Nation or through the post-secondary and training programs of
the federal government.

In many cases Na-Dene employed in the wage economy continue to
follow traditional pursuits such as trapping, hunting, and fishing. Such
activities have continuing economic importance and represent a positive lifestyle that has deep cultural roots. There is ample land suitable
for traditional activities near most Na-Dene communities. Even in larger
centres such as Calgary and Yellowknife, the availability of vehicles
makes it possible for Na-Dene individuals to go into the bush to trap,
hunt, and fish as their ancestors did. The Na-Dene have adopted new
technology such as high-powered rifles, snow machines, and outboard
motors, but food resources are still used principally for personal consumption or shared through kin networks. In Canada, aboriginal people are subject to some game laws such as those protecting endangered
species and requiring registration of traplines. However, they have
successfully challenged laws that would have restricted their rights to
engage in subsistence activities.

The average Na-Dene income is relatively low by Canadian standards, and unemployment is several times the rate for non-natives in the
same region. Low employment persists even in communities located
near major resource developments such as mines and oilfields. The
creation of reserves facilitated resource development while isolating
natives from training and employment opportunities. In the past, Na-
Dene people, like most First Nations people across Canada, faced discrimination in education and employment. Today, however, increasing
numbers of Na-Dene people are successfully adapting to modern technology while maintaining a sense of identity and purpose through
traditional activities.

Kinship and Family

Kinship networks are extremely important for all Na-Dene groups,
since individuals require care as children, share a residence with other
members of their family, and may work and marry within the kin
network of their own or adjacent communities. Groups differ in the
extent to which they have maintained traditional kinship patterns and
apply these to contemporary life. The Tlingit and Haida maintain the

matrilineal clan system for purposes such as the giving of native names or the assignment of roles at a potlatch, but they now use their English names for most purposes. Inheritance of property, which was formerly in the female line, may now follow the male line as well. Marriage between two members of the same moiety is somewhat discouraged, but is more common than formerly, when it was considered a serious offence, punishable by death. Traditionally, for both the Haida and the Tlingit, the ideal marriage partner was someone from one's father's lineage. For this reason, lineages were often paired and the exchange of marriage partners over a number of generations was common. Marriages were formerly arranged by the respective families, but individuals now select their own mates.

Kinship also continues to structure the daily life of Athabaskans, although, as with the Tlingit and Haida, its role has changed over time. Western Athabaskan groups such as Southern Tutchone, Tagish, Tahltan, Kaska, and Carrier have matrilineal clans or moieties. Most individuals, including children, still know their native name and clan affiliation, but English names are more commonly used on a daily basis. While arranged marriages have been replaced by personal choice and dating, some western Athabaskans avoid dating members of the same clan. Marriages with non-natives, and with natives from neighbouring groups, are now common, and in some cases non-natives marrying into the group are adopted into the appropriate lineage. Formerly, distinctions were drawn between cross-cousins (mother's brother's children and father's sister's children) and parallel cousins (mother's sister's children and father's brother's children, who were called by the same term as siblings). Marriages within a clan were strongly discouraged and knowledge of clan affiliations helped individuals determine eligible marriage partners. Marriages between cousins are rare in these groups today and most younger people reckon kinship using English kin terms.

Athabaskan groups further from the Pacific, including Slave, Dogrib, Beaver, and Chipewyan, do not have formal clans. Some of these groups continue to name individuals in both native languages and in English since native languages are most strongly maintained in this region. In many cases English last names are based on native names which are then handed down in the male line. Among the Beaver and Gwich'in, parallel cousins are distinguished from cross cousins, but no such distinction is made among the Slave, Dogrib, and Chipewyan. Some anthropologists have proposed that the kinship system of these latter groups is bilateral rather than matrilineal. Others report that marriage patterns reveal differentiation between parallel and cross-cousins even where these relations are not currently distinguished in the language. It has also been observed that residence groups formerly were based on a core consisting of a group of brothers, or, alternatively, a group of sisters. As the Dene of the Mackenzie valley have settled in larger settlements, kinship relations have been recast. In some communities many younger people now use English kin terms and can no longer identify their more distant relations.

There are other aspects of kinship relations that have almost totally been abandoned in contemporary society. Traditionally, most Na-Dene were on familiar terms with certain relatives, while interaction with other relatives was restricted in various ways. Among the Haida, for instance, a man would treat his adult sister or his sister's daughter very formally and would not speak to his mother-in-law directly. Similar restrictions on touching or speaking to certain relatives existed for most groups at one time but are rarely observed today.

Young Na-Dene women are no longer secluded at the time of first menstruation. The Tlingit formerly isolated young women of high rank for up to two years so that they might receive instruction and prepare for adult roles. Young women among Athabaskan groups also stayed in a separate shelter at this period of their life, and western Athabaskan women wore a hood which completely covered the head for up to a year. These customs are not observed among young women at present.

Social Organization

The Tlingit and Haida traditionally had a greater degree of social stratification than did the Athabaskan groups, but in contemporary society much of the Tlingit and Haida class system has been abandoned. Traditionally, three hereditary classes were recognized: nobles, commoners, and slaves. The noble class included the children of prominent leaders who were given prestigious potlatch names. These wealthy individuals became the house owners and were also the only ones who might become the chiefs of the lineage to which they belonged. Commoners did not receive important potlatch names, had less access to resources, and did not own houses. Slaves were war captives and considered the property of wealthy nobles. The Tlingit in the interior still recognized prestigious names and the rights to use clan symbols, but slaves were uncommon there. Though contemporary Tlingit and Haida continue to pass down prestigious names of ancestors, great wealth is no longer a prerequisite to receiving this form of recognition.

Athabaskan groups situated nearer the west coast, such as the Carrier, Tahltan, Tagish, and Southern Tutchone, were also stratified into classes. Among the Carrier, for example, membership in crest groups, such as those of the Beaver, Grizzly Bear, and Raven, could be inherited from the mother or father. However, the right to use the symbols of the crest group, such as songs, titles, or depictions of the crest animal, was dependent on the ability of an individual to sponsor potlatches and thus served to stratify society on the basis of wealth. Currently, potlatches and the use of native names serve more to assert a native identity than to establish class status for these groups.

In Athabaskan groups further removed from the Pacific coast, individuals did not inherit membership in a class. Individuals might achieve recognition as hunters and secular or spiritual leaders, but this prominence was not hereditary. The right to use special symbols or names was not restricted to an upper class of noble families.

Institutions such as potlatches became fully elaborated during the early fur-trade period as the availability of trade goods allowed many individuals to raise their status by sponsoring spectacular potlatches. Trade with the interior also extended the cultural influence of coastal groups such as the Tlingit and Bella Coola into the interior. Potlatches were outlawed in Canada in 1884, but this ban was not enforced uniformly. Among the Haida, missionaries helped ensure that the ban was strictly implemented. The Carrier continued to hold modest potlatches although the practice was opposed by the Catholic Church. The largest potlatch in Yukon was held at Carcross early in the twentieth century and was partially funded by Skookum Jim, one of the discoverers of the Klondike goldfields. Contemporary Yukon potlatches are relatively modest undertakings by comparison.

In traditional Na-Dene societies the patterns of association were based on kinship networks. For the Haida and Tlingit, roles in potlatches were determined by membership and status within a particular lineage and moiety, a moiety representing one-half of the society. Among the Tlingit, for instance, all clans were grouped into either the Raven Moiety or the Wolf Moiety, terms that were also used by Athabaskan groups nearest the coast. For these Athabaskans, membership in a moiety determined such roles. Athabaskans farther from the coast did not have a system of moieties with reciprocal obligations, but extended kin groups under the leadership of one or more individuals often came together for dances, trade, or warfare. Following the period of intense missionary activity during the fur trade, church membership and activities became more important but never overshadowed kinship ties.

Traditionally, kinship also structured the location and composition of houses or camps, the membership of households, the formation of task groups, and visiting patterns between communities. In each of these areas the role of women was crucial. Again there is a division between the Tlingit, Haida, and Athabaskan groups near the Pacific coast, on the one hand, and those of the Mackenzie drainage basin, on the other. For the Tlingit and Haida, the owners of houses were also the leaders of a lineage. The members of a Tlingit or Haida household were all related through their mothers and grandmothers. Athabaskan groups near the Pacific coast had a matrilineal moiety system which similarly determined residence patterns. Some groups, such as the Kaska, had a moiety system but residence patterns more closely resembled those of the Mackenzie drainage basin. In this pattern, the core of a residence group was usually either a group of sisters or a group of brothers who, in the Kaska system, would all be of the same moiety. Living with them in each camp were their spouses of the opposite moiety, their children, and other relatives. Residence patterns are no longer structured strictly on the basis of kinship in larger modern settlements. Yet kinship remains an important factor in many communities in determining the location of houses and in structuring social interactions.

Leadership positions in the Tlingit and Haida communities were traditionally restricted to prestigious individuals who had inherited a high status and maintained that position by amassing wealth and prestige. In most cases these leaders were men, but, starting in the later fur-trade period, women often took more active leadership roles. The village chief was the most prominent leader in a particular community. Today's leaders may be in either a traditional or a modern mould or both. In Yukon, Sam Johnston, one of the traditional leaders of the Tlingit *Ishkitàn* or Frog Clan, became the first native speaker of the Yukon Legislative Assembly. David Keenan, a Tlingit who was well educated in public schools in British Columbia, returned to his home community of Teslin where he became chief, negotiated a land-claims settlement for his First Nation, and then became chairperson of the Council for Yukon First Nations in 1996.

Leadership among Athabaskan groups was not restricted to one class and depended more on the personal abilities of an individual. A person might show leadership by organizing hunting, trapping, or trading parties, or he might demonstrate spiritual powers by healing the sick or conducting religious ceremonies. Leadership positions were also accessible to women in some instances. Early explorers were themselves cast under the spell of influential native women such as Thanadelthur, "Jumping Marten," the Chipewyan woman who helped James Knight initiate trade with the Chipewyan, and the "Nahani Cheiftainess" who protected Robert Campbell from attack by Tlingit warriors during his visit to the Stikine region in 1838. There are numerous women leaders in contemporary Na-Dene communities, and they have been selected as mayors, chiefs, and members of the territorial governments. In the Northwest Territories, Ethel Blondin-Andrews, a North Slavey from Fort Franklin, is currently the Member of Parliament for the Mackenzie region. In Yukon, Judy Gingell, a Southern Tutchone from Whitehorse who was the chairperson of the Council for Yukon Indians for many years, has been appointed territorial commissioner. The role of traditional leaders is also respected by many communities which have created elder's councils to advise leaders on issues ranging from land claims to justice and social services.

Culture

Folk traditions survive in a variety of forms in all Na-Dene groups. All of these groups have active storytellers, some of whom, such as George Blondin – a Slavey from Fort Franklin, Northwest Territories – and the late Angela Sidney – a Tagish from Carcross, Yukon – have written books for the general public. Stories about a mythic time when animals spoke and took on human form are common to the groups, as are legends about monster animals from earlier ages which were destroyed or rendered harmless by various heroes. Historic events of the past often take on mythic qualities as they become part of the oral history of each group. Younger people find the tales fascinating and often visit elders at home or seek out stories in books. Traditions are also shared through the use of video and television. Many Na-Dene communities in the Territories and farther south receive the satellite signal of Television Northern Canada, which offers programming from Whitehorse, Yellowknife, and Iqualuit. Some of the programs from Whitehorse and Yellowknife are in native languages. There is also an international storytelling festival in Whitehorse each summer which features native performers from across the circumpolar north.

The Na-Dene practise many art forms. Skilled craftspeople make clothing with traditional materials such as moosehide, quills, beads, and furs. Haida carvers such as Robert Davidson and Bill Reid have become world-renowned. Reid and his apprentices have completed scores of major works including a depiction of the Haida creation story on display in Vancouver and a Haida war canoe currently exhibited in Paris. Tlingit carvers, including the Tahltan-Tlingit carver Dempsey Bob, have also produced many excellent masks and ceremonial objects. These artists are careful to preserve a link with past traditions, including the stories and beliefs of their ancestors. They often research older pieces in museums around the world but also emphasize the creative aspect of their work. As Dempsey Bob once remarked, "I like to tell people this tradition is not dead. We are still here and our best work, our most creative accomplishments, are still ahead of us."

Traditional dance groups and groups of singers and drummers perform at potlatches, drum dances, various community events, and for the general public at festivals and sports events. There are also fiddlers in many communities who perform music originally derived from European fur traders. Some Na-Dene perform with rock and roll or country and western bands. Gatherings in communities may feature a combination of traditional drum music, fiddle music, and contemporary popular music performed by different groups at the same event. Recreational activities such as hand games, also called stick gambling in some areas, are common.

Women are in many cases the organizers of community events. They have also been responsible for the revival of many art forms such as weaving and button-blanket design. Few women have realized the level of commercial success that some male artists have achieved, but this may change as theatre, television, and film-making become more important.

Religion

Traditionally, the Na-Dene recognized the existence of the souls or spirits of natural forces, animals, plants, land forms, and inanimate objects. They relied on religious leaders to ensure that adequate supplies of food would be secured and misfortune avoided, and the injured and sick were healed by individuals who used their own spiritual powers or directed the powers of other beings. Some Na-Dene believed in the possibility of reincarnation of human beings.

Today, the Na-Dene continue to have great reverence for the land and the natural world, even if they no longer pray or make offerings to spirits directly. In some areas native spiritual leaders, such as Slave and Dogrib "prophets," practise traditional forms of healing, but in others evangelical Christian healers direct the Holy Ghost or God to help those who require assistance. Often, Jesus receives thanks for the arrival of a hindquarter of moose or a package of cranberries. Some, but not all, Na-Dene accept the Christian doctrine of the immortality of the soul.

Missionary groups realized varying degrees of success in converting the Na-Dene in the nineteenth century. A Roman Catholic mission was established among the Chipewyan in 1844, and in the following two decades a number of Anglican and Catholic missions were established among the Chipewyan, Dogrib, Slave, Gwich'in, and Beaver. In general, the Roman Catholics were more successful in gaining converts in the Mackenzie region, a majority of the population is at least nominally Catholic today. Visits by the pope to Fort Simpson in 1984 and 1986 attracted thousands of Na-Dene from across the north.

The Gwich'in became strong adherents to the Anglican faith as a result of the missionary activities of Archdeacon McDonald and his successors, the Haida were evangelized by Methodists and Anglicans, and the Tlingit were exposed to the Russian Orthodox faith from an early date but few converted until the end of the nineteenth century. Presbyterians, the Salvation Army, and the Church of God recruited many Alaskan Tlingit, while the interior Tlingit were more likely to join the Anglican or Catholic churches. Catholics, Anglicans, and Baptists ran residential mission schools for native students, schools that were often intolerant of native traditions and languages and that, in some case, subjected students to the worst forms of abuse.

Over the last century, syncretic religious ceremonies have developed among the Carrier, Beaver, Slave, Dogrib, and other groups. Called in various regions "tea dance," "prophet dance," or "drum dance," these ceremonies combine traditional and Christian beliefs and are led by an individual termed, in a rough translation of the various words used in different Athabaskan languages, "dreamer" (Beaver: *na;tiè&*; Alberta Slavey: *nda;t*; Kaska: *ne;det&e*). These words emphasize the importance of dreams among the the Na-Dene as a source of understanding.

Younger people are less involved in church activities, although this too is not universally the case. Some are interested in traditional beliefs which offer a sense of native identity. Women are involved in all forms of religious activity. They often organize potlatches and are the most regular churchgoers. Some women, such as Ellen Bruce and Effie Linklater of Old Crow, Yukon, have been ordained as ministers in the Anglican Church. Others have become prophets of the syncretic tea dance or drum dance religion.

Education, Language, and Communication

Traditionally, children learned from their own parents and other relatives. For the matrilineal Tlingit, Haida, and western Athabaskans, the mother's brother might take a strong role in a boy's training, while girls looked to their mothers and grandmothers for instruction. Kinship networks and experiences in the community continue to be important, but these are now supplemented with formal education in schools.

In the nineteenth century, mission schools were initially intended for the children of traders and for orphans, but later Anglicans, Catholics, and other denominations operated residential schools for the native population. In many cases, students were taken long distances from their homes and confined for months or years without being able to speak their language or engage in traditional activities. The Canadian government supported the residential schools until the 1970s, when they were closed down and native students began attending public schools. Since then, there have been numerous court cases relating to sexual and other forms of physical abuse in the residential schools, and the negative experiences of many young natives in these schools have been linked to the various social problems that afflict Na-Dene society today.

The public schools in the North are directly administered by the territorial departments of education – with the exception of the Dogrib schools of the Territories, which operate under a separate school board – and serve both native and non-native students. In the provinces, some Na-Dene students attend schools operated by the local First Nation, while others attend provincial schools, often together with non-native students. In general, the level of academic achievement of Na-Dene students is below the national norms. A high percentage of students in most communities drop out of school in junior and senior high school. Some Na-Dene go on to university and successful careers, but on the whole native students experience difficulties with the present educational system. Native language and culture are increasingly represented in the school curriculum, particularly in the Territories; however, the bulk of the curriculum still reflects the culture of the dominant society.

Today there are speakers of every Canadian Na-Dene language except that of the Tsetsaut, a small group originally located south of the Tahltan in northern British Columbia. However, school programs in Na-Dene languages have not been effective in maintaining fluency despite the dedication of native-language teachers. English is used for instruction in these schools, with native languages' being taught only a few hours each week. Native-language instruction is most common at the elementary level, although in some areas there are classes at the secondary and college levels as well. The only communities where children are truly fluent are those in which native language is still the language of everyday life so that children learn it first. In 1996 these include the Dogrib communities of Fort Rae, Lac La Martre, Snare Lakes, and Rae Lakes, and some Slave, Beaver, and Chipewyan communities.

There are now written forms for all the Na-Dene languages in Canada, but there is a very low rate of literacy in them, and most materials written in native languages are designed for use with school language programs. In some areas, native language literacy was initiated by missionaries as early as the nineteenth century. Many missionary groups used them extensively in their church services at one time. Chipewyan was written in a syllabic orthography based on Cree and this system was also later used for Beaver and Slave. Hymns and Bible translations were written in syllabics and some individuals also used it to write letters. Archdeacon MacDonald wrote Gwich'in in an alphabetic system which was widely studied and used by those Gwich'in affiliated with the Anglican Church and which continues to be used in church services today. The Russians developed a Cyrillic alphabet for Tlingit, but this system was not widely used by the interior Tlingit. These early traditions of native language literacy are still maintained by a few older people, but most who can read and write now use the modern alphabetic systems which have come into use in the last thirty years.

The Northwest Territories has declared the five Athabaskan languages of the region to be official languages on an equal standing with English and French. This, along with other initiatives, has given native languages a higher profile, but the trend towards the exclusive use of English has not been reversed. The availability of television, the dominance of English in the educational system, and opportunities for employment in positions where English is used have all conspired to weaken the position of native languages.

The Na-Dene are represented both in the mainstream media and in separate media institutions operated by native organizations. The bulk of programming available on television and radio in most communities is in English and relates to non-native society. There is, however, some programming in native languages. As noted above, the programs of Television Northern Canada, which are available via satellite across the north, have considerable native content. There are also many local radio stations, such as CHON-FM in Yukon, which have a format of contemporary music combined with native-oriented news reports and commentary. In regions where the native languages are strongest, radio broadcasts are offered in them. There have also been several native-operated English language newspapers, such as the *Native Press* (Yellowknife, 1971–) and *Dan Zha* (Whitehorse, 1986–92). The development of native media has increased awareness of native issues and promoted self esteem among Na-Dene people generally. A large number of young people have also been trained as writers, producers, translators, and technicians with native media. Federal support has been vital to the development of native media, but some of these ventures are threatened by recent cutbacks.

Politics

Na-Dene have been increasingly active in politics, especially in the northern territories where they constitute a major part of the population. A number have been elected to the legislative assemblies of both Yukon and the Northwest Territories and other high posts in the government. Within national native politics Na-Dene have also played important roles. Georges Erasmus, a Dogrib from the Northwest Territories, was for several years the national chief of the Assembly of First Nations, which is based in Ottawa, and the late Harry Allen, a Southern Tutchone from Yukon, was national vice-chief for the northern region. Land-claims negotiations, particularly in the Northwest Territories, have also attracted national attention. The Yukon Native Brotherhood was established in Whitehorse in 1968 and the Indian Brotherhood of the Northwest Territories was organized in Yellowknife in 1970. Both groups were founded to press land claims, although they also dealt with wider concerns relating to social programs, housing, environmental issues, and native rights in general. In 1975–76 Justice Thomas Berger presided over a royal commission on the proposed Mackenzie Valley Pipeline, and his findings contributed to the rejection of the project by the National Energy Board two years later. Resistance to major development projects without accompanying land-claims settlements became strong in both territories in this period, and today land-claims negotiations are the focus of political activity for the Na-Dene in the Northwest Territories, Yukon, and British Columbia. In the Northwest Territories only groups in the northern portion of the Mackenzie valley have concluded agreements. Although a general agreement was ratified for Yukon in

1995, all groups have not completed their final negotiations. By far the most significant agreement concluded in Canada's north in recent years is that creating the new territory of Nunavut, in the eastern half of the Northwest Territories, which came into effect on 1 April 1999. Inuit constitute the majority in this new territory.

The nature of negotiations has changed from the era of the treaties, as modern agreements include provisions for comprehensive native self-government and for a continuing native role in the management of resources. Some individuals and native groups remain openly sceptical about any agreement which involves surrendering traditional lands or rights. Many more years of negotiation will undoubtedly be required, not only to achieve satisfactory settlements with non-native society, but to reconcile the opposing points of view within native communities themselves.

Intergroup Relations and Group Maintenance

Many social problems in contemporary Na-Dene communities – alcoholism, family breakdown, marital violence, teenage suicide, and so on – are due to the displacement of traditional ways of life by non-native culture. All levels of government have attempted to address these problems, with varying degrees of success, through counselling services, medical treatment, and law enforcement.

Social problems are worst in the poorest communities, particularly those situated on reserves. In many cases, traditional roles have been undermined by modern resource-development projects at the same time as the Na-Dene have not been allowed to share equally with non natives in the economic benefits of these projects. Most groups seek a more active role in economic development to help alleviate these problems and provide future opportunities for their communities.

The Na-Dene increasingly assert a separate identity within Canadian society while embracing many aspects of modern life. Most Na-Dene want to participate in contemporary society without sacrificing their unique identity and control over their traditional lands and resources. Conflicts have arisen with the federal government, the provincial and territorial governments, and private companies and developers when land is alienated without consent or when resource-development projects are proposed without local involvement. Resource development in the traditional territory of the Na-Dene has tended to pit native residents against non-native developers. Government policies concerning education, social services, medical services, and renewable resources are ongoing areas of concern as well. The threat posed by massive resource projects has brought native people closer together as they form organizations to represent their interests on provincial, territorial, and national levels.

Many Na-Dene are critical of the long history of economic domination by non-aboriginals in the areas of trapping, agriculture, oil and gas production, and mining. Some also have had personal experience of discrimination or abuse in non-aboriginal institutions, such as residential schools, or in dealing with the police or the Department of Indian Affairs. Most Na-Dene recognize both good and bad aspects of non-aboriginal society, however, and are not unduly embittered by their experiences. Non-aboriginals, for their part, tend to have a mixed view of natives, respecting (ironically enough, given their economic role in the north) traditional aspects of the native lifestyle such as self-sufficiency through hunting and fishing, while criticizing problems which result from the history of culture contact and economic domination, including alcoholism and crime. Conflicts are least strident in areas where native groups are able to negotiate for fuller participation in economic development.

The Na-Dene work closely with other native groups both locally and nationally. The Dene of the Northwest Territories have cooperated with the Metis in their land-claims negotiations, and the Council for Yukon First Nations (formerly the Council for Yukon Indians) has included non-status Indians since its inception. The Na-Dene participate fully in the national Assembly of First Nations and have been politically prominent within that organization. Members of other native groups have been welcomed into Na-Dene communities and there are many marriages between members of various native groups. In some communities such as Fort Nelson and Fort Chipewyan, there are separate bands representing Cree and Dene people, but elsewhere members of different groups are represented by a single band when they live in the same locality. The tendency of Athabaskan peoples to think in terms of inclusive social groups is reflected in the term *dene* itself, which has meanings encompassing progressively larger groupings of people. In its narrowest sense the term refers to the local group, speakers of an Athabaskan language; in a wider sense it is often used to refer to all native people; and in its broadest sense it includes all people around the world.

Inividuals who are adopted into a clan, who marry into the group, or who live in the same community are usually welcomed and accepted. Rights within the group are often determined by kinship, however, so that non-natives have a limited role unless they are integrated through adoption or marriage. In contrast, government policy has been openly and rigorously exclusive. Women who married non-natives were denied Indian status for many years, Metis were forced to relocate when reserves were established, and the reserves themselves served to separate native populations from adjacent communities and economic opportunities. In recent years native people have worked to overturn some of these exclusionary government policies. Native women and their children are now assured of native status.

The last two decades have seen a great awakening of cultural and political awareness among the Na-Dene. In many areas native names and kinship terms are being used once more, at least for ceremonial purposes, and women have been especially active in promoting cultural awareness as storytellers, language instructors, and directors of dance and theatre companies. This period has also witnessed the development of representative government in the Northwest Territories. Before 1975, the territories were governed by a council and commissioner appointed by the federal government and based in Ottawa. The initiation of an elected legislative assembly in 1975 led to greater native participation in governmental affairs. Native members were initially frustrated with the new assembly and resigned, precipitating a boycott of territorial politics by the Dene Nation. In 1979, however, natives won a majority of seats in the assembly, and two of them, James Wah-Shee and Richard Nerysoo, went on to become cabinet ministers. The process of land-claims negotiations in both the Northwest Territories and Yukon over the same period has also fortified native identity, while providing the impetus for the growth of native organizations, including bands, tribal councils, and organizations such as the Dene Nation and the Council for Yukon Indians.

The growing sense of political awareness and group identity also reflects the coming of age of a generation born into a traditional culture but educated in residential schools. The Na-Dene leaders of this period are able to speak from experience about what they treasure about the land and their way of life, and they also understand the implications of modern technology, government policies, and resource development. Commitment to future generations and to the maintenance of native identity remains high among the Na-Dene.

FURTHER READING

The best general introduction to the Na-Dene is the *Handbook of North American Indians*. Volume 6, edited by June Helm (Washington, D.C., 1981), covers the subarctic and includes most northern Athabaskans; volume 7, edited by Wayne Suttles (Washington, D.C., 1990), describes the groups of the northwest coast, including the Tlingit and Haida. The *Handbook* provides detailed information on the history and traditional culture of the Na-Dene, as well as extensive references for those who wish to pursue any topic in depth.

There are several more contemporary works in which the Na-Dene are featured. These include Michael Asch's *Kinship and the Drum Dance in a Northern Dene Community* (Edmonton, 1988); Hugh Brody's *Maps and Dreams: Indians and the British Columbia Frontier* (Vancouver, 1981); and Julie Cruikshank with Angela Sidney, Kitty Smith, and Annie Ned, *Life Lived Like a Story: Life Stories of Three Yukon Native Elders* (Vancouver, 1990). Kerry Abel's *Drum Songs: Glimpses of Dene History* (Montreal, 1993) provides a survey of the history of northern Athabaskans, particularly in the Northwest Territories. Frederica de Laguna's *Under Mount Saint Elias: The History and Culture of the Yakutat Tlingit* (Washington, 1972) gives a detailed description of the culture and history of the coastal Tlingit. Sergei Kan's *Symbolic Immortality: The Tlingit Potlatch of the Nineteenth Century* (Washington, 1989) also addresses the history and symbolism of Tlingit ceremonies. Mary Lee Stearns's *Haida Culture in Custody: The Masset Band* (Seattle, Wash., 1981) studies a Haida community in detail.

Other major works on the Na-Dene include Catherine McClellan et al., *Part of the Land, Part of the Water: A History of the Yukon Indians* (Vancouver, 1987), Richard Nelson's *Hunters of the Northern Forest: Designs for Survival among the Alaska Kutchin* (Chicago, 1973), and Robin Ridington's *Trail to Heaven: Knowledge and Narrative in a Northern Native Community* (Iowa City, Iowa, 1988).

9

SALISH

Bruce Granville Miller

Salish, or Salishan, is a language family composed of languages and dialects spoken by aboriginal peoples of British Columbia and the states of Washington and Idaho. The language family is commonly divided into Coast Salish and Interior Salish, and there are social and cultural differences between the constituent groups that largely overlap with this division. There are four major Canadian Interior Salish languages – Lillooet, Thompson, Okanagan-Colville, and Shuswap – whose speakers occupy the Plateau, the southern interior of British Columbia, a high, arid region between the Rocky Mountains on the east and the Coast Mountains on the west. The Upper Lillooet are located on the Fraser River near the present-day town of Lillooet. The Lower Lillooet (or Lil'wat), of the Pemberton valley, are closely connected to coastal peoples and were a major source for the introduction of new social practices and trade goods into the Plateau. The Nlaka'pamux (previously known as Thompson) live along the mid-Fraser and Thompson rivers. The Okanagan occupy the Okanagan valley along the international boundary. The Shuswap, the northernmost of the Interior Salish, reside in the territory from the Fraser River in the west to the Rockies on the east and the Thompson River on the south.

Coast Salish languages of British Columbia include Comox, Pentlatch, Sechelt, Squamish, Halkomelem, Bella Coola, and Nooksack. These languages, with the exception of Nooksack and Bella Coola, were formerly spoken, and some to a limited extent still are spoken, in the southern interior of Vancouver Island and the adjacent mainland along and near the Straits of Georgia. Nooksack was formerly spoken in one small area along the present-day international border on the mainland, and Bella Coola is spoken to the north of all other Coast-Salish-speaking communities, separated by Kwakwala. The Comox people (including the Homalco, Klahoose, and Sliammon) border the Kwakwala-speaking peoples on both Vancouver Island and the adjacent mainland. To their south, on Vancouver Island, were the Pentlatch, whose language became extinct in 1940. On the mainland, and to the south of the Comox, are the Sechelt and Squamish. The largest language group is the Halkomelem, which includes the Cowichan on Vancouver Island and the Musqueam and Sto:lo along the Fraser River.

Within the Coast Salish language grouping there are some fifty current bands. Most of the Canadian bands have small populations and are organized into tribal councils, umbrella organizations that provide an economy of scale in the provision of services. The membership of these councils varies as bands occasionally withdraw or join. There is a population of more than 21,000 band-enrolled Coast Salish peoples of Canada. Estimates for the era prior to the first smallpox epidemic of the late eighteenth century are unreliable, but the precontact population may have declined by half by 1820 and by two-thirds by the late nineteenth century. The low came in the early twentieth century, before the present period of rapid population growth.

Today, there are forty-five Interior Salish bands, with a population of more than 15,000. One source gives a figure of 13,000 Interior Salish as of 1835, long after the first epidemic, and a low of 5,348 in 1890. The precontact figure is not known. As with the Coast Salish peoples, there are affiliated Interior Salish communities in Washington State and Idaho. Several Coast and Interior Salish bands' traditional territories overlap the international border. Among these are the Arrow Lakes (Sinixt), a band no longer recognized in Canada and whose members are primarily enrolled members of the Colville Confederated Tribes in Washington, the Sumas, and the Semiahmoo.

Salish peoples tell creation stories of animals in human form, the ancestors of present-day human beings, and "transformers" (known as Coyote in the Interior), powerful beings who created the present landscape and modified the order of things, eventually making an environment hospitable for humans. The linguistic and archaeological records are different in emphasis, but both show great changes to the landscape and reveal Salish cultures created *in situ*. By 12,000 years ago, the retreat of the glaciers to the north and to nearby mountain tops left a new area to settle. In the Early Period, from 10,000 to 5,000 years ago, humans encountered a very different environment than exists at present. Glacial meltwater drove up sea levels, producing a saltwater flow up the Fraser River valley. Sea levels fluctuated wildly, so that today evidence of early occupation may be largely destroyed or underwater. Early peoples used lithic technology, as indicated by sites such as Glenrose Cannery near Vancouver. Nine-thousand-year-old pebble tools are found at the Milliken site in the Fraser Canyon and on the lower Fraser. Microblade tools were introduced from Eurasia to Alaska and to the northwest coast by 7000 B.C.E. In the Middle Period, from 5,500 to 1,500 years ago, sea levels stabilized, and increased stocks of salmon and new techniques for harvesting and preserving allowed for supluses, a more specialized economy, and the formation of large communities. In the Late Period, from 1,500 years ago to the time of contact with Europeans, Coast Salish cultures took their historic form.

Interior Salish prehistory was somewhat different. Linguistic evidence shows that a Salish expansion appears to have occurred via a gradual movement out of the homeland in the Georgia Strait into distant sites, perhaps to beyond the location of the Nuxalk, who were cut off from other Salish speakers early on. Following this, a group crossed the Cascade Mountains east and north into the Plateau and eventually diversified into the speakers of seven Interior Salish languages. Archaeological evidence indicates that the peoples of the Plateau were well established more than 9,000 years ago. The early populations may have had a way of life similar to Paleo-Indians on the Plains, harvesting post-glacial bison, deer, and elk, as indicated by Clovis points in the Okanagan. Microblades dating to about 6400 B.C.E. found on the Thompson River and skeletal material from 6200 B.C.E. (?) show reliance on land mammals. During the Middle Prehistoric Period, new tools were introduced and microblades disappeared sometime before 2000 B.C.E. The Late Prehistoric Period saw the emergence of large pit-house villages, varying in size from a few houses to large concentrations, a preferred housing style which survived into historic times. With surpluses of stored salmon, the western Plateau became a strategic trading area. In the Late Prehistoric Period, huge salmon runs supported complex settlements along the Fraser River. Near Lillooet, at Keatley Creek, for example, archaeological evidence indicates a population of 500 to 1,500 at its height, some 1,000 to 2,000 years ago.

History

A fur trader, Charles Barkley, reached the remote Coast Salish region in 1787, exploring the Straits of Juan de Fuca, and was quickly followed by others. Spanish ships under Dionisio Alcalá-Galiano and Cayetano Valdés y Flores Bazán, and the British under George Vancouver, arrived in 1792. Vancouver charted most of the region but missed the Fraser River. Simon Fraser, a North West Company fur trader, descended the Fraser River from the interior, through the difficult canyon, thereby being in 1808 the first European to establish the existence of the Fraser River. Land-based fur traders were at the mouth of the Columbia River in 1811 and in the Plateau region in the same period, creating a series of forts, among them Fort Shuswap in 1812–13. The Hudson's Bay Company (HBC) explored the Fraser in the 1820s, establishing Fort Langley in 1827. The Kwantlem, residents of the area, welcomed the traders and provided materials and labour. Some elite native women married men in the fort, furthering this connection. In 1843 Fort Victoria was established on Vancouver Island in Songhees territory, drawing native people from up and down the coast to trade and work for wages. The HBC began the process of establishing non-native authority in the region, a fact underscored by the appointment of the company's chief factor, James Douglas, as the first governor of the Vancouver Island colony in 1850.

In 1846 the Treaty of Washington divided the Coast Salish country into British and American territories, placing closely related peoples under differing political systems. In Canada, villages were treated as separate bands and small, local reserves were created, unlike the American pattern of large, consolidated reservations. In the 1850s Douglas purchased the lands of a few Vancouver Island bands, but these were the only lands to which native title was extinguished. All the same, land was taken by the Crown and reserves were established, leaving the unresolved issue of title to be worked out within a treaty process – still unfinished – begun in 1993.

After the delineation of the international border in 1846, the pace of settlement by non-natives increased. In 1858 gold was discovered along the Fraser River, leading to the arrival of tens of thousands of prospectors, many departing from the California goldfields. Organized into para-military groupings, miners killed and displaced an unknown number of Coastal and Interior Salish peoples. In addition, the miners began the process of imposing new names on the landscape. These names, including Boston Bar and American Bar, remain in use along the Fraser River. Canadian fear of American encroachment led to increased efforts to bring non-natives into Salish areas of Canada, especially along the border, and Sto:lo and other groups were quickly forced to move.

To make matters worse during this difficult period, the Salish peoples faced a series of devastating epidemics. Smallpox arrived by 1782, before the first white people themselves, killing perhaps two-thirds of the Sto:lo and other Salish people. More epidemics followed: smallpox or measles in 1824, measles in 1848, and smallpox in 1862. In addition, there may have been an 1801 smallpox outbreak. Influenza, venereal disease, and tuberculosis carried off huge numbers. Innoculation programs, initiated around missions and populated areas, reduced the death count in 1853 and in 1862. Disease disrupted seasonal economic activity, undermined native cultural practices by killing elders and curers, and may have opened Salish peoples to evangelization by Christian denominations.

The first missionary in the Coast Salish region was Modeste Demers, a Catholic, who arrived at Fort Langley in 1841. Oblates established a mission at St Mary's on the Fraser in 1863, and Bishop Durieu created a "theocratic state" among the Sechelt in the 1860s and 1870s, relying on a hierarchical system of authority. Methodists founded schools at Hope in 1859 and near Chilliwack in 1886.

Economic Life

In the period before contact both Coastal and Interior Salish peoples depended heavily on the huge salmon runs. However, the economy was not limited to this. The Interior winter villages were concentrated along the salmon-bearing Fraser and Thompson rivers and other waterways, but the economy was based on a pattern of seasonal movement. People moved in small groups from spring to fall and joined with others to form larger aggregations in the winter, conducting ceremonial activities from November through February. By March, stored foods were used up and resources near the winter home were sought, including trout and small game. Canyons provided good locations for net- and spear-salmon fishing, beginning in the spring. Fish were wind-dried, smoked, eaten fresh, and/or traded. Women processed the fish and also gathered various edible roots, green shoots, and berries, contributing over half of the total food energy consumed on the southern Plateau. In June, people carried reed mats to summer camps at progressively higher elevations to harvest roots for three months. Roots were dried or baked for ease of transport back to the winter village. In July and August, fish runs drew many to the rivers. In late summer, many moved again to the mountains for fruit harvests. Most groups exploited a large area, over-lapping with other Plateau peoples. Large-scale trading networks further helped reduce the risk of food shortages.

Coastal Salish peoples relied on salmon, roots, berries, birds, and small land mammals, but they also harvested sea mammals and shell-fish. There was less risk of starvation resulting from poor harvests, and economic activities on the coast differed from those in the interior. Most notably, the key resource areas were not open to use by non-kin, and surpluses were stored for status-enhancing distribution. During the winter, people congregated in villages located along waterways to carry out ceremonial activities; in the main, they relied on stored supplies, although shellfish were gathered. Large and small groups moved sea-sonally to the resource, and, in the spring, sea- and land-mammal hunting and fishing took precedence. In late summer and through the fall, plant foods were harvested and salmon fishing continued. Salmon were harvested with various technologies, including weirs, spears, nets, and artificial reefs. Members of Coast Salish communities located near the foothills hunted deer and elk. Great reliance was placed on cedar, which was used for house construction, canoes, tools, clothes, mats, boxes, and carvings. In order to take advantage of localized differences in foods and in production (only people in some locations could pro-duce canoes, for example), goods were exchanged via trade to non-kin, gifts to relations, and ceremonial potlatches.

There were dramatic changes to Salish economic practices following contact with whites. Initially, fur trading was the main interest of non-natives, and some natives benefited from their access to new trade goods. However, with colonization after the gold rush of 1858 came displacement. The Coast Salish peoples of the lower Fraser River were affected the earliest. Women lost their gathering grounds to settler farms, and families were displaced from prime fishing locations. In addition, fishing runs themselves were damaged through industrial harvesting, introduced by non-natives in the late nineteenth century, or through negligence. Accidents associated with the construction of a railroad line destroyed a massive fish run in the Fraser Canyon in 1913. Lake Sumas, a major site for giant sturgeon and other fish, was drained in the 1920s to provide farmland for non-natives.

Salish peoples began trading with non-natives early in the nineteenth century but shifted into wage labouring out of necessity as the era of fur trapping ended, seeking work as loggers, mill-hands, and, briefly, coal miners and sailors. Whole communities became engaged in seasonal fish harvesting and canning, the men working as fishers in small boats, the women in fish-processing plants. Starting in the late nineteenth century, families also worked as hop and berry pickers. There was a decline in economic opportunity in the first half of the twentieth century, as Salish peoples were displaced from the labour force by new immigrants in a largely racially segregated economy. Chinese, for example, were brought in for railroad construction, and Japanese and Scandinavians entered the fishery. As costs of doing business rose, native people found themselves unable to obtain investment capital to buy expensive fishing boats or to compete in emerging agribusiness, and they were also pushed out of the many entrepreneurial activities they had begun at the end of the nineteenth century. Henceforth, natives were concentrated in casual, unskilled, and seasonal jobs.

The continuation of subsistence activities may have reduced the impact of the Great Depression of the 1930s for some natives. However, underemployment, unemployment, and poverty remain economic realities. In the 1960s, federal funding provided for band employment for such positions as clerks, managers, and welfare administrators, positions held largely by women. Today, there are small-scale efforts at promoting tourism, and some bands have leased lands for residential and recreational uses. Some natives still practise salmon fishing in the Fraser and other rivers, and the Aboriginal Fisheries Strategy of the federal government has, since 1993, permitted a small native commercial salmon harvest. Some native fishers hold regular commercial licences, but by the 1990s salmon fisheries – and fishers' income – were in severe decline.

Kinship, Family, and Social Organization

The social structures of the Interior and Coast Salish peoples in the mid-nineteenth century differed somewhat, with more emphasis on hierarchy on the coast. In the Interior, society was held together by ties of kinship and friendship over a large area. These ties were cemented by regular gift-giving. Prohibitions on marriage between blood relatives linked villages by marriage and helped in the development of systems of alliance. Village chiefs exercised influence based on their reputations for spiritual qualities and pragmatic abilities, as did task group leaders, shamans, war leaders, and salmon chiefs. Interior Salish people practised gender equality, although there was a clear-cut division of labour by sex. Class differences did not emerge, and emphasis was placed on the autonomy of the individual. Slaves, often war captives, were held, but they were adopted into families without prejudice, except in those communities with strong ties to the more hierarchical coastal communities. Among all Salish, cousins were equated with siblings, and the levirate (the custom by which a male member of a deceased husband's family marries his widow) and sororate (the counterpart of the levirate for women) were practised, a system that contributed to the maintenance of relations between groups connected by marriage.

Among the Coast Salish, as with the Interior peoples, kinship was reckoned bilaterally, and marriage was prohibited with blood relatives, leading to the formation of broad networks of affinal relatives which sometimes cut across linguistic boundaries. Residential groups were the family, household, local group, and winter village. The family, consisting of a married couple, children, possibly wives and spouses of young adult children, dependants, and slaves, occupied one section of the winter house. The household included several related and cooperative families. Groups of blood relatives formed "houses" and shared putative common descent from a notable ancestor and rights to resources. Society was highly stratified, with communities divided into wealthy elite, common people, and slaves. Marriage was generally within one's class. Slavery was hereditary and slaves were the property of the master, but they lived within the longhouse and could obtain spirit powers. There were chiefs of local groups, generally men, and house chiefs of both sexes. Leadership was dependent on the acquisition of spirit power and on personal ability, and task group leadership was circumscribed. There was no formal, centralized political authority. Women were secluded at the time of menarche and stayed out of public life while unmarried; some assumed political influence after menopause.

Today, Salish people continue to rely on their network of relatives, and in many communities the extended families still serve as economic groupings. Families are no longer co-resident in winter houses, but the political life of communities continues to be carried out within the context of family solidarity.

Culture and Religion

Among the Coast Salish there has been a tremendous revival of ceremonial life, particularly the winter Spirit Dance, since the 1950s, with perhaps the greatest increases in participation coming in the 1990s. The resurgence coincided with the ending of the prohibition on potlatching in the Indian Act of 1951. In 1961 it was estimated that there were fewer than one hundred dancers in total, but by the late 1990s one could encounter five hundred or more dancers at a single gathering. Many new winter houses have been constructed for spirit dancing. Initiation into spirit dancing follows from a diagnosis of sickness or upon a decision by the individual or family to improve the initiate's life. Initiates are confined to winter houses for the winter, with the exception of time spent ritually bathing in the wilderness, are limited in their food and water, and receive spiritual advice and training. During this period of seclusion, initiates receive a song and spirit helper.

Potlatches, once held in other seasons, are now ordinarily held in the winter at spirit dances. Families wishing to give ancestral names to younger members, to bestow ritual prerogatives, or to hold memorials for the deceased invite guests from all over the Salish community to winter houses to witness the work. Funerals are another important occasion which draw large numbers of guests from throughout the region and often involve components from several religious traditions. Many families continue the practice of holding ritual burnings. A ritualist places plates of food into an outdoor fire to feed the dead and subsequently burns the personal possessions of the deceased. In some cases, all the items within the family house are removed and given away.

There has also been a revival of carving, weaving, and painting. Cedar carvings, baskets, and other objects are made by men and women and displayed in many homes. Among the many Salish artists, Susan Point, of Musqueam, is perhaps the best known. She works in the Salish idiom, producing carvings, prints, and glass works, and her massive carved pieces are prominently displayed inside the Vancouver airport. Summer festivals centring around canoe racing draw female and male racers, and thousands of others from all over the Coast Salish region, to socialize and to participate in team gambling (*slahal*) and other sporting events.

For both the Interior and Coast Salish, powwows – intertribal social and competitive dance gatherings – gained in popularity in the 1990s, with new events added to the calendar annually. Drumming is an important part of these events, and drumming groups also perform during ceremonial and public occasions. Many Salish songs are owned by families, and, owing to their connection to sacred winter ceremonies, cannot be sung at powwows. Powwows, like canoe races, bring together people from over a wide area.

A number of individuals play important cultural and intellectual roles in their communities and region. Some have arisen in response to the new interest in documenting community history and in preparing for treaty negotiations. Among these is Sonny McHalsie, a Sto:lo, who has spent many years researching Halkomelem place names and documenting Sto:lo connections to the landscape. He is employed by the Sto:lo Nation as a culture specialist. George Manual, 1921–89, a Shuswap, was a major figure in the World Council of Indigenous Peoples. His co-authored 1974 book, *The Fourth World*, was an important contribution to the study of contemporary indigenous peoples' circumstances.

Salish peoples continue to practise, as before contact, a ceremonial life focused on the maintenance of respectful relationships between humans and the spirits of animated, sometimes anthropomorphic, non-human beings, including animals, plants, rocks, water, and other immortals. Some of these spirits are thought to be beings organized into communities of their own, with will and intelligence. Humans are regarded as somewhat weaker than immortal spirits, who possess the power to change shape. Many immortal beings become guardian spirits for individual males and females, although this is ordinarily not explicitly revealed. Through a process of ritual purification starting in childhood, individuals can seek out guardians in areas of solitude where spirits live. Formerly, all successful, competent adults sought out such relationships; now, only some do. Canoe builders, warriors, and shamans, among others, were understood to have a particular spirit helper in order to do their work.

Important group rituals help to maintain relations with immortals, including the first salmon ceremony. Salmon are believed to live in the ocean in longhouses and to don their salmon clothes to swim upriver and make themselves available to humans. The first salmon to go upriver, the chief of the salmon, is treated ritually, cooked, and its bones returned to the water. The chief then resumes its form and informs the other salmon that it had been treated properly, thereby guaranteeing the return of the run. First-berry ceremonies are similar.

Since contact a prominent feature of religious life has been apocalyptic prophecy, inspired in part by devastating epidemics and social changes. Many prophets gained followers for a short time and disappeared with little trace, but others, such as Smohalla, on the Plateau, who rejected white influence, had greater and longer-lasting influence.

The Shaker Church, which combines Christianity and indigenous concepts of spirit power, is based on the death and rebirth experience of a Coast Salish man, John Slocum, in 1882. It was established in Puget Sound and adjacent portions of the lower mainland of British Columbia, and it is still active today. Christianity made inroads through the work of Catholic and Protestant missionaries in the mid- and late nineteenth century and, as noted above, through Salish people working independently and with their own interpretations of Christian "power." Many Salish are still nominally Christian, others are active Christians, and many participate in more than one religious tradition. Recently, Pentecostal ministers, often community members, have established followings among the Salish. Pentecostalism, however, has not developed an institutional infrastructure, and congregations disperse after the death or departure of the minister. A recent development has been interest in Plains or pan-Indian spiritual practices, including medicine wheel concepts. Some community members regard these practices as obstructing local spirituality.

Education, Language, and Communication

Before white contact, education was accomplished by the regular recitation of oral narratives (familiar stories, histories, genealogies, mythologies, and legends), through careful observation of the work of elders, by instruction of young women in menstruation huts, and sometimes by mentorship, as in the training of shamans. Of particular importance was the responsibility of grandparents to instruct grandchildren. Children were chosen to become family and tribal historians, and they regularly recited a repertoire of narratives to perfect their craft. The first schools were established by missionaries as day schools, but industrial, or residential, schools predominated in the late nineteenth century and through the first half of the twentieth. While the federal government became responsible for funding the schools, missionaries retained the management for many years.

By the late twentieth century, residential schools had been closed and bands began to develop their own schools. Communities such as the Sto:lo band on Seabird Island established their own culturally specific program, in their own facilities, and with some instruction in Halkomelem. Great emphasis is now placed on the retention of traditional languages. In the 1990s attention became focused on abuses in the residential schools, and many bands documented this history and sought redress. Admissions to colleges and universities increased dramatically in the 1990s, and the First Nations House of Learning, a resource centre for native students, was established at the University of British Columbia. More women than men have sought out post-secondary education, and many rely on federal funding provided to their bands for tuition money. A native law program at the University of British Columbia has produced a strong cohort of lawyers, and others have focused on education training to staff the new band-operated schools.

The decline in the number of speakers of Coast Salish languages reached a critical point by the 1990s. Some communities have only a few fluent speakers, despite efforts at training native-language teachers. Salish languages on Vancouver Island are in slightly better shape and not in danger of extinction, and Interior Salish languages are stronger still, with some viable school courses. However, English is the language of everyday use. Salish phrases are retained for ceremonial purposes in all communities.

There are several band and tribal newsletters and a regional journal, *Khatou* (Sechalt, B.C., 1982–), published by a Coast Salish band. There is evidence that coded radio transmissions were used to send information concerning potlatches during the period of their prohibition, and radio has long been a medium of communicating First Nations perspectives. Programs such as *The Native Voice* started in the 1940s. In the 1970s *Raven* became the "official Indian communications network of B.C." Several programs serve the native community today, although diminished by federal funding cuts. The media are now regularly used to publicize Salish political viewpoints. For example, in 1993, Sto:lo chiefs blocked a railway line into Vancouver, and media coverage prompted an immediate visit by the federal fisheries minister to address Sto:lo issues. Members of the Lil'wat Peoples Movement, an Interior Salish political group that has repudiated elected leadership, have also used the media to communicate their views.

Politics, Intergroup Relations, and Group Maintenance

Salish peoples have long been among the most influential among First Nations of Canada in their efforts at political action, although tactics have changed over the years. In 1906 a delegation of Coast Salish chiefs petitioned King Edward VII for recognition and settlement of land claims. Later, a delegation of Interior Salish chiefs of the Lillooet met Prime Minister Wilfrid Laurier concerning their land and resource rights in the absence of a treaty. Coast and Interior Salish joined the Allied Tribes of British Columbia to contest the efforts of a provincial commission, from 1912 to 1916, to reduce land holdings, and were able to delay implementation of the commission's recommendations. Later, Interior and Coast Salish joined the Native Brotherhood of British Columbia, a group interested in promoting the welfare of native people. New political groups arose in the 1960s, including the Indian Homemakers' Association and the Confederation of British Columbia Indians. Beginning in the 1970s, tribal councils were formed to press claims at the regional and local, rather than the pan-Indian, level. Salish leaders play an important role in national First Nations politics, and in 1997 Wendy Grant of Musqueam was narrowly defeated in the election for the grand chief of the Assembly of First Nations.

Political pressure and legal decisions led to the formation of the B.C. Treaty Commission in 1993. The commission requires that overlaps in land claims be resolved before entering the process, a circumstance that has caused tension between communities. The treaty process itself has prompted some bands to form more cohesive tribal organizations and to oversee treaty research and the delivery of social, economic, education, and health services. The number of Sto:lo Nation employees, for example, expanded tenfold between 1990 and 1997, from about 20 to about 200. As tribal governments have grown, leaders have struggled with the issue of honouring aboriginal practices while fulfilling the demands of funding agencies and federal policies. Some bands have instituted new procedures for the selection of band councillors, moving away from voting to the selection of family leaders.

There are serious differences among Salish peoples about what to do in the future. Some oppose the treaty process, believing that treaties will surrender too much of aboriginal rights and title. The Sechelt band went a separate direction in signing the Sechelt Indian Band Self-Government Act in 1986. The Sechelt assumed limited rights of self-government previously reserved under the Indian Act, with federal and provincial laws still in force. Critics argue that the Sechelt band has become the equivalent of a municipal government, rather than an autonomous First Nation.

With the build-up of the infrastructure of band and tribal government has come a greater participation of women as elected members of tribal councils. This is associated with the differential rate of women in tribal employment and in their development of expertise concerning governance and tribal services. Among the Coast Salish, the percentage of women councillors has risen from 11 percent in the 1960s to 28 percent in the 1990s.

FURTHER READING

There are a number of sources concerning the Salish peoples. Among these are Wayne Suttles's *Coast Salish Essays* (Vancouver, 1987). The *Handbook of North American Indians*, volume 7 (Washington, D.C., 1990), edited by Suttles, contains chapters on social organization, history, and religion. Joanne Drake-Terry has written an insider's account of Interior Salish history, *The Same as Yesterday: A Lillooet Chronicle of the Theft of Their Lands and Resources* (Lillooet, B.C., 1989). Similarly, the research staff of the Sto:lo Nation has produced *You Are Asked to Witness: The Sto:lo in Canada's Pacific Coast History* (Chilliwack, B.C., 1997), edited by Keith Carlson. Wilson Duff and Wayne Suttles authored the jointly published *Katzie Ethnographic Notes / The Faith of a Coast Salish Indian* (Victoria, 1955); the second part of this volume, a reissue of a work by Diamond Jenness, tells the story of a Salish "transformer" along the Fraser River. *Our Tellings: Interior Salish Stories of the Nlha'kapmx People* (Vancouver, 1995) is compiled by Darwin Hanna and Mamie Henry. Hilary Stewart's *Indian Fishing: Early Methods on the Northwest Coast* (Vancouver, 1977) contains excellent visuals. Paul Tennant's *Aboriginal Peoples and Politics: The Indian Land Question in British Columbia, 1849–1989* (Vancouver, 1990) describes the political activities of Coastal and Interior Salish. James Teit's 1900 classic, *The Thompson Indians of British Columbia*, originally published in 1900, was reprinted in New York in 1975, as was his 1909 *The Shuswap*. Wendy Wickwire and elder Harry Robinson produced *Write It on Your Heart: The Epic World of an Okanagan Storyteller* (Vancouver, 1989).

10

SIOUANS

Mary C. Marino

Identification

The Siouan First Nations in Canada – the Dakota, the Nakota, and the Lakota – belong to a large family of linguistically related tribal groups that occupied the central and northern plains region of North America. More distantly related tribes lived far to the south, near the lower reaches of the Mississippi River and in what is now the southeastern United States. The central and northern groups include the Mandan, Hidatsa, Crow, Chiwere, Dhegiha, Sioux (Dakota and Lakota) and Assiniboine (Nakota). The Nakota are known to have lived in what is now Canada since before the earliest European contacts; they are now resident in Saskatchewan and Alberta. Lakota, followers of Chief Sitting Bull, have lived in Canada since the battle of the Little Big Horn (Montana) in 1876. The Dakota have dwelled continuously in Canada since the mid-1860s, but they occupied the region intermittently long before that. Other Siouan-speaking groups, such as the Hidatsa, may have done so too, but we cannot be certain.

At the present time the Dakota reside on four reserves in Manitoba and three in Saskatchewan. The Manitoba reserves are Birdtail, Dakota Valley (formerly Oak River), Oak Lake, and Dakota Tipi (formerly Long Plain). The Saskatchewan reserves are Wahpeton, a few kilometres north of Prince Albert, Moose Woods, about twenty-five kilometres south of Saskatoon, and Standing Buffalo, near Fort Qu'Appelle. A fourth reserve in extreme southwestern Saskatchewan, Wood Mountain, is occupied by Lakota.

The Nakota have several reserves in Saskatchewan and Alberta. Carry the Kettle is located about one hundred kilometres east of Regina near

Sintaluta. Some Nakota live on White Bear reserve, near Carlyle, about two hundred kilometres southeast of Regina; this community also includes a few Dakota, as well as Cree and Saulteaux members. The Mosquito band, situated on a reserve south of Battleford, includes both Nakota and Cree. In Alberta the largest Nakota reserve is at Morley, east of Cochrane and just to the north of the Trans Canada Highway. There are also reserves at Eden Valley and Bighorn.

The traditional cultural and political divisions of the greater Siouan Nation were the *oceti šakowin*, the Seven Council Fires. The first four, Sisitonwan, Wahpetonwan, Mdewakantonwan, and Wahpekute are known collectively as the Santee, who spoke Dakota. The fifth and sixth, the Ihanktonwan and Ihanktonwanna, spoke Nakota. The seventh was the Titonwan, who spoke Lakota. This grouping, preserved through the oral traditions of the Siouan people, is highly suggestive of the chronology of the separation of its units. The Titonwan, who moved westward onto the plains, subsequently grew in numbers and subdivisions and are now the most numerous dialectal subgroup, yet they started as but one of the original seven. The Assiniboine, who also speak Nakota, but with substantial differences from the main group of dialects, may have separated before the *oceti šakowin* tradition crystallized. Descendants of all seven groups are numbered among the Canadian Siouans today, with the majority, apart from the Assiniboine, in the first four.

History

The ancestors of the Santee had their primary landbase in what is now Minnesota. The identification of Sandy Lake pottery at the Rum River (Mille Lacs) site to which the captured Père Louis Hennepin was taken by Wahpetonwan furnishes one means of defining the region occupied by the eastern Dakota. Sandy Lake ware has been found at a large number of sites in Wisconsin, Manitoba, western Ontario, and eastern Manitoba. Archival evidence reports Dakota occupation around Lake of the Woods in 1717–22 and Dakota war expeditions as far north as the head of the Churchill River. Cree place names in that locality (*puatsipi*) suggest some sort of Siouan presence. *Puat*, however, is not only used with reference to Dakota but can refer also to other Siouan groups, notably the Assiniboine or Stoney. A second consideration is the depopulation of the northern plains/western woodland region in the 1780s by a major smallpox epidemic. The earlier occupation of what is now Saskatchewan was massively disrupted, so that it is very difficult to trace named ethnic units (bands) from the eighteenth-century records into the nineteenth century. We are quite certain that the homeland of the eastern Dakota was Minnesota, and they likely occupied parts of western Ontario and eastern Manitoba during the seventeenth and eighteenth centuries and probably earlier, although whether other aboriginal occupants recognized the territories as theirs cannot now be established. Canadian Dakota claims to aboriginal occupation north of the 49th parallel have been central in their relations with both the Canadian and the U.S. governments.

The Assiniboine were mentioned by the French as early as 1640. Their presence in territories within modern Saskatchewan and Manitoba is clear in the 1693 journal of fur trader and explorer Henry Kelsey. According to Nakota oral traditions in Alberta, their traditional hunting territory lay along the eastern slopes and foothills of the Rocky Mountains.

The oral traditions preserve memories of warfare with Cree, Saulteaux, and Blackfoot, but the Nakota also maintained peaceful relations with the Cree during certain periods. Early explorers' accounts describe mixed encampments of Cree and Nakota, and such mixed communities are still in evidence today, as noted above. Some anthropologists have speculated that the Nakota were "cultural godfathers" of the Cree on the northern plains, as contact agents in the transmission of the economy and technology of bison hunting.

Archaeological materials dating from the immediate pre-contact period – about 1500–1700 c.e. – can tentatively be associated with the northern and southern branches of the Nakota. This is the so-called Mortlach phase, marked by a distinctive type of thin, compact pottery decorated with cord and check stamps in a variety of styles. The northern phase of this pottery and the other associated technologies may be northern Nakota, and the southern phase, southern Nakota. These two different populations – if such they were – appear to have been involved in different trade and exchange networks, judging from the kinds of "foreign" pots found in the two assemblages and the types of stone they used for their lithic artefacts.

The settlement of the Dakota in Canada began in the winter of 1863–64 with the influx of a party of refugees who, following the suppression of the Minnesota Uprising, were fleeing from the U.S. military. The Dakota claimed refuge in the North-West Territories (present-day Saskatchewan and Manitoba) and the protection of the Crown by virtue of the allegiance which they had demonstrated during the War of 1812. Within a few years they had established themselves in a territorial pattern which was later formalized in grants of reserve land by order-in-council.

Although there are oral traditions of conflict and raiding between Nakota and Cree, there were also intervals of peaceful coexistence in which they camped, hunted, and travelled together. Indeed, the multicultural First Nations communities that exist today, such as the White Bear community in Saskatchewan, are not that different in composition from ones that existed in early contact and pre-contact times.

Regarded as refugees from the Unites States, the Dakota were not admitted into treaty. Among the Nakota of Saskatchewan, the White Bear and Carry the Kettle bands signed Treaty 4 (1874), and the Mosquito band, Treaty 6 (1876). In Alberta, Treaty 6 also encompasses two Nakota reserves west of Edmonton.

Economic Life

The Siouan people in Minnesota in early contact times had a mixed economy, depending primarily upon hunting, fishing, and the harvesting of wild plants, with a very limited amount of horticulture. Staple foods included bison, deer, wild rice, wild fruits, and starchy tubers, such as the prairie turnip. Sugar was obtained from the maple and the box elder by drawing and boiling the sap. Methods of food preservation included drying both meat and plant foods and the preparation of pemmican.

The Nakota, after their early separation from the Dakota and northward and westward movement, adopted a plains-oriented economy, centred on the bison. They developed hunting techniques and equipment related to the new animal species but largely maintained techniques of food preservation and storage and those for the recovery and use of primary industrial materials, such as hide, bone, sinew, and plant fibres.

When the Dakota arrived in Canada they were close to starvation, having lost most of their possessions in the flight, and had to depend at first on supplies from the government and settlers at Fort Garry. Within a few years, however, they had made a range of economic adaptations that varied according to the locales in which they settled. The Manitoba groups at Birdtail, Dakota Valley, and Oak Lake began gardening and raising stock, supplemented by hunting, fishing, and wild plants. Bands situated near towns and villages supplemented successful farming and stock-raising livelihood with wages earned by hiring out their labour as domestic workers and farm hands. Their economic strategies were largely successful; they were good farmers and highly valued workers. Farming operations on the reserves declined, however, as agriculture became more mechanized and required ever larger capital inputs. The Dakota had no access to capital, and from the 1920s onward they fell behind neighbouring Euro-Canadian farmers. Dakota in Saskatchewan and Manitoba are now exploring ways of making their reserves economically viable in non-agricultural modes, such as recreational and gaming development.

Until the mid-1970s the majority of Siouans resided on their reserves and either worked there in farming and cattle-raising, or took seasonal short-term jobs off the reserves. In the last twenty years the quest for education and better employment, as well as the amenities of urban life, have drawn people off the reserves in growing numbers. At present, many live in the towns and major cities of the three provinces. Where the reserves are close to cities, many band members commute to school and work. Women who are heads of families commonly leave their children on the reserve with their grandparents or other kin while the mother pursues education or employment in the city, rejoining them during off-seasons and holidays.

Kinship, Family, and Social Organization

Both the Dakota and the Nakota lived in unstratified bands or villages based largely on kinship ties. Some families were more prosperous than others, and differences in material prosperity became more marked with the widespread introduction of horses after the mid-eighteenth century. The ownership of horses was a mark of prosperity in itself and also a means of acquiring and transporting other valued belongings. But material prosperity was esteemed only to the extent that it was accompanied by generosity. Liberality was required of the chief and his family and was the most important way for other families to demonstrate standing in the community. Thus material goods were constantly redistributed, and permanent distinctions of wealth were levelled out.

Generosity was, and is, the highest social virtue among the Dakota and Nakota, just as stinginess and meanness are the worst vices. A Dakota from Saskatchewan visiting a relative in Manitoba in 1972 described how he had spent half the morning at his kinsman's home without being offered so much as a cup of the coffee which the woman of the house was preparing in his presence. Where a Euro-Canadian might find such an episode laughable, the Dakota who heard (and richly enjoyed) the story were horrified by conduct they regarded as incomprehensible and shameful. It went beyond mere discourtesy or personal eccentricity to suggest a deep moral deficiency. This pairing of straight-faced comic narration with themes of deep moral significance is characteristic of traditional Siouan storytelling.

Marriage was forbidden between persons who were known to be closely related, and there was a strong tendency towards band and village exogamy. The newly married couple might camp near the bride's family for some time, especially if the couple was relatively young or the girl's parents needed their economic assistance. After the early years of marriage, the place of residence was at the couple's discretion.

Social behaviour within the residential group was dictated very largely by kinship norms. Tensions and potential conflict within the family were managed by patterns of compulsory avoidance and joking. Both men and women practised avoidance towards their parents-in-law; they were not supposed to talk to each other except in case of necessity. Brothers- and sisters-in-law, in contrast, observed a "joking" relationship, mostly verbal teasing – often rising to the level of an art form – which provided a sanctioned outlet for the tensions arising from the unremitting closeness of relationships among people who held often conflicting claims on one another's loyalties. Both avoidance and joking are still observed as norms of conduct, although the former is much less stringent and the latter is declining with loss of fluency in the language.

The status of women was relatively high. The commonly held view of Indian women as drudges, who toiled all day long while their men idled, reflects a Euro-Canadian bias. The native people did not view necessary work as drudgery. Men's hunting and raiding were high-intensity activities that took them away from the village or encampment for periods lasting from several days to several months. Women's work tended to be more evenly spaced. They and their older children provisioned the household with firewood and water and harvested vegetable foods during the appropriate seasons. They performed all the work involved in processing meat and fat and in preparing hides, as well as the manufacture of clothing and footgear and the construction of the tipi and its accessories. The economic contribution of the women was essential to the group's survival, especially in the northern areas, where the labour of every able-bodied adult was required for year-round survival. Women's skills and efficiency could make all the difference between a comfortable living and indigence or starvation.

A woman's life between puberty and menopause was strongly affected by her procreative powers. During menstruation women camped separately and avoided all contact with equipment associated with warfare and curing. It was believed that the powers associated with sexuality and procreation were incompatible with the those involved in warfare and medical practice, and both sexes governed themselves accordingly. Women separated themselves during menstruation and childbirth, and men observed sexual continence before embarking on war parties or major ceremonial undertakings. Both men and women who acquired training in curing techniques and the preparation of medicines would defer active medical practice until their procreative life was past its peak. This observance is still important to older Dakota, and the failure of Euro Canadians to be sensitive to this concern can be a source of anxiety. Younger women no longer separate themselves from the family during their periods, but at such times they will avoid visiting elders who keep traditional medicines in their homes.

Kinship ties among the Dakota and the Nakota are reckoned more widely than in Euro-Canadian society and are intensely important throughout life. Kinship tends to influence a variety of practical choices, including residence, occupation, allocation of time, allocation of duties within the family, and taking care of children. The traditional kinship vocabulary of the Dakota was extraordinarily complex and united large numbers of people into a network of responsibilities and rights which had ramifications beyond the local community or residential group. It enabled Dakota to relate themselves to most of the other Dakota they would encounter in their lifetime. The nuclear family was still primary, but the extension of terms widened the sense of respect, affection, and mutual obligation beyond the circle of the immediate family. Mother, mother's sisters, and father's brothers' wives were all addressed by one term (iná), and father, father's brothers, and mother's sisters' husbands, by até. Father's sisters and mother's brothers' wives were grouped as tuwíŋ; mother's brothers and father's sisters' husbands as dekší. One enjoyed a special relationship with each of these categories of relatives. Seven distinct terms were used for siblings, and sons and daughters of mother's sisters and father's brothers. These terms classified the relatives by their age relative to the speaker, their sex, and the sex of the speaker. Four more terms classified the sons and daughters of one's father's sisters and mother's brothers, according to their sex and the sex of the speaker. The fact that men and women used different kin terms for their siblings and cousins reflected the strong distinction between the sex roles. Women and men had very different, but mutually balanced, spheres of influence and responsibility.

Culture

Although Euro-Canadian material technology is used today in Siouan communities, many of the aboriginal craft traditions survive with considerable vigour. Excellent beadwork in both floral and geometric designs is produced, much of it for dance costumes, though many people wear and use beaded items as part of their everyday attire. The ancient Siouan decorative motifs were geometrical; older craftworkers still term the floral designs Cree or Chippewa. Some porcupine quill work is also done, often commissioned for costumes. One woman elder at Wood Mountain recalled the wild plants that her grandmother had used for colouring quills but stated that the plants no longer grew in her locality. She indicated an emphatic preference for one of the popular commercial fabric dyes. Siouan geometrical designs have been incorporated into hooked rugs at Standing Buffalo, just as they had been used decades ago on the U.S. reservations as motifs in embroidery designs on linen and cotton fabrics. Production of pottery seems to have been abandoned soon after introduction of metal utensils as a result of trading contacts. Craft cooperatives in Saskatchewan and Manitoba retail beadwork and items of worked hide. Items produced for sale are sometimes not the best specimens of Siouan technology.

Religion

The Dakota and Nakota share a certain mode of spiritual belief, though its details vary somewhat among groups and even among individuals. Traditional religious beliefs, still strong among Dakota, centre around the concept of *wakan*, a very difficult term to translate, which combines the meanings of spiritual force, power, and sacredness. *Wakan* resides in nature and is more concentrated and effectual in some places and beings than in others. The Siouan people believe in a supreme being, *wakan-tanka*, the Creator, and in a number of lesser supernatural beings which appear in the form of various animal species, such as eagles, hawks, and bison. There is a greater balance of good in some of these beings, and a greater balance of evil in others, but the benefit or harm of *wakan* depends as much upon how the individual approaches and uses it as on the power itself. Everything in nature – human beings, animals, plants, landforms, soils, bodies of water, rocks – was placed there by the Creator and may be a source of *wakan*. This being so, all nature is to be treated with respect. Human beings are not meant to dominate the natural world. They may take from nature what they can put to good use, asking permission and giving thanks through some return offering. The attitude is one of respect, arising from knowing one's place.

Christian missionary activity among the Dakota began in the 1820s in Minnesota and, as was common until very recently, strongly opposed Dakota spiritual belief and practice. Although many Dakota joined churches and adopted Christian beliefs, they sought to reconcile them with the traditional spiritual philosophy. The Old and New Testaments, hymnals, and catechisms were translated into Dakota, but even the elders find them problematic as sources of spiritual help. Many of the semantic constructs, and even word formations, fit poorly with the living structure of the language. Dakota dictionaries prepared by missionary teams reflect the religious agenda of the compilers rather than the authentic religious and spiritual discourse of the Dakota people

Belief and observance were, and are, deeply a part of everyday life. Communion with the spiritual world is sought through prayer and visions. Individual spiritual development requires one to seek blessings and knowledge through the vision quest, the *hambde ceya*, and also through participation in collective activities such as the sweat lodge, still of primary importance, and formerly, the *wakan-watcipi* (the Holy Dance Society). The truth of revelations gained through such spiritual exercises is judged by the worshipper and others by actual outcomes. Does the man or woman live according to the teachings they have received? Have the promised blessings actually come to pass?

Education and Behaviour

The education and upbringing of children in traditional society was widely shared within the kinship group, and this remains largely the case, especially on the reserves or in other contexts in which Dakota live near one another. Children were and still are encouraged to make their own decisions about matters affecting themselves, and they are allowed a degree of personal choice that may seem unusual by Euro-Canadian standards. For example, a seven year old might be asked if she wishes to have her teeth checked at the dental clinic. If she declines, that is her choice. At the same time, however, she is expected to look after herself and do her part in everyday life to the best of her ability; both her achievements and her mistakes are hers.

Most Dakota children attend schools off their reserves; a minority have access to schooling oriented to Siouan cultural standards and practices. Instruction in Dakota and Nakota has been available from time to time in some areas (notably, Morley, Standing Buffalo, Wahpeton, and Dakota Valley), but it does little to establish fluency if the language is not being acquired and used at home. Since, in the last two generations, many Dakota have married non-Dakota spouses, the home language increasingly is English. Where children live on the reserve but attend school in a nearby town there has often been a lack of continuity between home and school expectations.

The pursuit of education is complicated by a number of factors which are either absent or less pressing among Euro-Canadians. Many high school students experience strong peer pressure against academic achievement and towards early parenthood. The majority of women university students have children, living either with them or with relatives in the home community. The higher rate of illness and accidents among aboriginal children and youth affects these student parents severely.

Both the satisfactions and the frustrations of individual Siouan lives resemble those of Canadians generally. The unfavourable circumstances that affect community life – a limited resource base, relative poverty and isolation – also limit and frustrate individuals. The rates of suicide and substance abuse among aboriginal youth and young adults are matters of great concern but are not the defining characteristics of typical Dakota life experience. Many individuals go through some years of personal dislocation and stress during young adulthood and then find their sense of direction as Dakota and achieve personal satisfaction to at least as great an extent as the majority of Euro-Canadians.

Language and Communication

Although Dakota, Lakota, Assiniboine, and Stoney are considered by many speakers to be distinct languages, the first three are similar enough in their pronunciation, grammar, and vocabularies to be considered basically dialects of one language. Stoney is now a different, though closely related, language. In addition to the common consonants and vowels found in the majority of the world's languages, they have aspirated and glottalized consonants not found in the neighbouring

Algonquian languages or in English. The verb includes elements which indicate subject and object, whether an action is "realized" or "unrealized," location, instrumentality, number, and other shades of meaning. Where subject and object are independently expressed, the sentence structure follows a basic subject-object-verb word order. An unusual feature is the distinction between men's and women's speech in certain grammatical forms and in some of the vocabulary. Although the eastern Dakota have been in contact with Algonquian speakers for centuries, their vocabulary contains almost no traces of borrowing from Cree or Ojibwa.

Dakota has an orthography which was devised in the nineteenth century by a group of missionaries, led by Stephen R. Riggs, who began their work in Minnesota in the late 1830s. This writing system, with small local variations, is still in use, although literacy is confined almost entirely to people now in their sixties or older. Religious and educational materials have been published in the Dakota orthography for about 150 years, and a good deal of manuscript material – diaries and the like – is in existence, containing much valuable information on daily life and events in the late nineteenth and early twentieth centuries.

Dakota has a strong oral literary tradition, including sacred legends, stories, poetry, and songs. Oratory and story-telling have always been highly valued, and performance is judged by rigorous standards. Loss of the language has inhibited transmission of these traditional forms.

The language is in rapid decline in Saskatchewan and Manitoba. In the early 1970s many children on the reserves still learned Dakota as their first language; now this is exceedingly uncommon. Manitoba has the largest number of speakers, on the Dakota Valley Reserve. In Saskatchewan, the largest concentration of speakers lives at Standing Buffalo, and in Alberta, Morley has the majority of Assiniboine-Stoney speakers. There are probably fewer than a dozen speakers of Assiniboine left in Saskatchewan. A half-dozen or so of the Wood Mountain band, all older adults, still speak Lakota.

Attitudes towards language retention are somewhat ambivalent. Speakers strongly identify the language with the traditional culture, and loss of the language is perceived as a loss of Dakota, or even aboriginal, identity. However, there are very few contexts, even on the reserve, in which Dakota can be spoken daily. Imparting it to one's children as their first language is exceedingly difficult if one's spouse and the children's other caregivers do not speak it. Devising linguistically and culturally appropriate materials for teaching it presents formidable problems when the students' first and strongest language is English.

Politics and Intergroup Relations

The pre-contact Dakota lived in semi-sedentary villages or nomadic bands with chieftainship which tended to be hereditary. Political relations with neighbouring tribal groups varied cyclically between friendly alliance and intermittent warfare. The Dakota have a long-standing tradition of hostile relations with neighbouring Algonquians, especially the Ojibwa. This is still expressed in a somewhat deprecating attitude towards Algonquians.

The Canadian Dakota have been notably more conservative in the preservation of traditional beliefs and practices than their American relatives, because of their relative isolation on small, scattered reserves and their unique constitutional status as descendants of a group considered non-indigenous. Surrounded by large populations of Algonquian speakers, the Nakota in Saskatchewan have exhibited somewhat different patterns of group maintenance. Like the Stoney in Alberta who adhered to Treaty 7, many of their dealings with the federal government and with their neighbours have been influenced by efforts to obtain their treaty rights, especially as regards their landbase. The Dakota, as refugees, never adhered to any of the treaties, and, having received relatively little assistance from the Canadian government, they have enjoyed a larger degree of self-determination in consequence.

FURTHER READING

There is no one comprehensive introduction to the history and socio-cultural life of the Siouan First Nations in Canada. A historical overview of the settlement of the seven Dakota First Nations in Manitoba and Saskatchewan, focused on economic strategies, is presented by Peter Douglas Elias in *The Dakota of the Canadian Northwest: Lessons for Survival* (Winnipeg, 1987). A valuable account of the culture of the Stoneys of Alberta and the history of their relations with the Canadian government is provided by Chief John Snow in *These Mountains Are Our Sacred Places: The Story of the Stoney Indians* (Toronto, 1977). James H. Howard's *The Canadian Sioux* (Lincoln, Nebr., 1984) contains useful information relating to the period before 1972, but, as a source of narrative history, it is weakened by the lack of chronological framework and commentary on the accounts given by some of his Dakota consultants.

Alice Kehoe has published a short monograph, *The Ghost Dance: Ethnohistory and Revitalization* (New York, 1989), which provides a good account of the Ghost Dance religion in Saskatchewan and does much to link the recent histories of the Canadian and U.S. Dakota in the domains of values and cultural revitalization. Kehoe has also published an overview article on the Saskatchewan Dakota in *The Modern Sioux: social Systems and Reservation Culture* (Lincoln, Nebr., 1970), edited by Ethel Nurge. A standard source on traditional and modern religion is *Sioux Indian Religion: Tradition and Innovation* (Norman, Okla., 1987), edited by Raymond J. DeMallie and Douglas R. Parks. The articles in this book encompass far more than religion in the strict sense of the term: they address medicine and healing, psycho-social adjustment, and meaning of cultural symbols, within a perspective that includes both Canadian and American Dakota.

11

TSIMSHIAN

Susan Marsden
Margaret Seguin Anderson
Deanna Nyce

Identification

The people sometimes referred to as "the Tsimshian" actually belong to three related nations of northwest coast people. Since time immemorial the Gitksan, Nisga'a, and Tsimshian have lived as neighbours in what is now northwestern British Columbia just below the Alaska panhandle. The people in these nations identified themselves not only as Nisga'a, Gitskan, and Tsimshian but also according to the village in which they lived during the winter months, calling themselves Gitga'ata, Gitwangak, Gitwinksihlkw, or several dozen other local community names.

The territories of the Nisga'a, Gitksan, and Coast and Southern Tsimshian peoples comprise the watersheds of the Nass and Skeena rivers and the adjacent coast and islands from the Alaska panhandle in the north to as far south as Swindle Island.

These three nations share a common ancient heritage, their cultures display many similarities, and their closely related languages are the only surviving members of the Tsimshian language family. Linguists note that the languages of the Gitksan and Nisga'a are particularly closely related to each other and more distantly connected to the languages of the Coast and Southern Tsimshian. Yet, despite the close relationship among the languages and cultures of the groups in the Tsimshian language family, their recent histories and contemporary political aspirations are distinct.

The language of the Coast Tsimshian is called *Sm'algyax*, which means "real language." In that language Tsimshian means "entering the Skeena River [valley]" and properly refers to the groups that occupy the lower reaches of the river and the islands in the estuary of the Skeena. Prior to non-native settlement, there were ten groups occupying this area, with winter villages first dispersed in their territories in the valleys of tributaries of the Skeena and later in close proximity around Metlakatla in the area of present-day Prince Rupert. During the fur-trade period these groups amalgamated around Fort Simpson, and many of their descendants now comprise the populations of Metlakatla and Lax Kw'alaams (Port Simpson) as well as of Metlakatla, Alaska.

The term *Tsimshian* is also used for two communities located farther up the Skeena River near the Kitselas Canyon, Kitselas and Kitsumkalum, and also for three communities south of the Skeena mouth, Kitasoo/Klemtu, Hartley Bay/Gitga'ata, and Kitkatla. The two upriver communities are sometimes referred to as Canyon Tsimshian to distinguish them from the coast groups. The three communities south of the Skeena mouth were probably originally populated by speakers of the Southern Tsimshian language, Skuuxs, a fourth member of the Tsimshian family which is almost extinct, having been largely replaced by the language of the coastal Tsimshian during the last hundred years. The territories of the Tsimshian are located in mainland watersheds and on islands in Douglas Channel and on the mainland and coastal islands north to the mouth of the Nass River as well as in the Lower Skeena River watershed.

Gitksan means "People of the Skeena River." Many Gitksan commonly call their own language *Gitxsanemx* though older people refer to a more ancient form of the language called *Sm'algyax* and say that it began in their land, at the ancient settlement of Temlaxam, from where it spread to the coast among the Tsimshian people. A number of Athabaskan nations are neighbours of the Gitksan on the east, and frequent intermarriage with them has resulted in some exchange of features between their respective languages.

Gitksan territories are located in the watershed of the Skeena River above the Canyon Tsimshian and in the upper Nass watershed. Contemporary Gitksan communities are situated for the most part on or near village sites occupied for millennia. Three new villages were established in the late 1800s by early Christian converts from Kispiox, Gitsegyukla, and Kitwanga: Glen Vowell, Andimaul, and Cedarvale respectively. Of these, only Glen Vowell remains today as a Gitksan community. There are three regional groupings of Gitksan communities, with considerable social and economic integration within each region.

The Nisga'a call their language *Nisga'amx*. The meaning of *Nass* may derive from a Tlingit word for "food basket," which is how the Nisga'a regard the rich rain-forested river valley homeland which they have inhabited since time immemorial. Their territories are located in the Lisims watershed from Portland Canal to the upper Nass. There were many villages in the valley over the millennia; two were buried by a volcanic eruption around 1700. Several communities were established around missions at the end of the nineteenth century. The Nisga'a are currently situated in four main villages along the river: Kincolith at the mouth of the river; Laxgalt'sap (formerly known as Greenville) 30 kilometres from the coast; Gitwinksihlkw (formerly known as Canyon City); and New Aiyansh, the most inland of the four villages. After the mission village of Aiyansh was flooded in 1917, 1936, and 1960, the community was moved across the river to higher ground at New Aiyansh, and it is the only village not located right on the river, the only means of access before 1958. Until recently the four were connected to each other and to the outside exclusively by the river or by overland trails (later replaced by logging roads). Tidewater goes into the river as far as Greenville, and the two downriver communities of Kincolith and Greenville are sometimes referred to as the Lower Nass villages.

Estimating the number of Tsimsgian-speaking peoples is difficult. Population figures given by the Department of Indian Affairs include only "status" Indians and omit unregistered people, who may be as numerous and who are often as involved in community and cultural affairs as their status relatives. Further, because the Tsimshian, Gitksan, and Nisga'a peoples are matrilineal, whereas until the passage of Bill C-31 in 1985 Canadian law assigned official group membership only to males and their dependants, there are many people who are members of clans and communities who are not officially registered, and many registered people are members of bands outside the traditional territories of their own matrilineal clans.

With these caveats in mind, the on-reserve and off-reserve registered population of the three peoples in 1995 was 16,407. The Tsimshian numbered 6,221, the Gitksan 5,380, and the Nisga'a 4,806.

History

A fundamental fact of life for the Tsimshian-speaking peoples, as for all First Nations in British Columbia, is the non-recognition of their land rights by non-native society. The only treaties signed with the native people of the province were the Douglas treaties on Vancouver Island in the early 1850s and Treaty 8, which covers territory in the northeast.

Natives in other parts of the province have never entered into treaty, and the British Columbia government long claimed that aboriginal land title was extinguished in practice through successive pieces of provincial legislation. Obtaining formal recognition of their rights to land and self-government has been a constant concern of British Columbia First Nations, and in this struggle the Nisga'a and Gitksan peoples played a leading part.

Among all these nations there are ancient accounts of primordial origin within their territories. There are also oral histories for specific groups in each of the areas that point to at least two periods of migration into the northwest coast region, and these histories agree with the findings of archaeological and geological research. In the first period, peoples from the northeast, southwest, and southeast moved into an uninhabited land where the post-glacial climate and geography were very different from that of today. Over several centuries they spread over the entire region and established settlements inland and on the coast. This early period was followed, millennia later, by an age of extensive migration from the north, along the coast, and from the interior down the rivers. Again the people spread out through the entire region in a process that may have taken centuries.

According to Nisga'a tradition, all four Nisga'a clans were established by K'amligihahlhaahl in a primordial village on the upper Nass river. The Nisga'a believe that the land was given to them by the Creator and that they have inhabited their territory since "time immemorial." During the period of Christian evangelization in the late nineteenth century, a number of new settlements were established in which the resident missionary sought to create Christian enclaves. Often these were located in sites more accessible for the emerging transportation system of riverboats on the Skeena and coastal steamers.

Today there are a number of non-native people resident in many of the villages; some are married to community members while others work for the communities. These people often participate actively in cultural and ceremonial activities, and those who are long-time residents are frequently integrated through adoptions into one of the four clans so that they can participate with their neighbours in cultural activities. Numerous community members now reside in urban centres, where education and employment are more accessible, especially Terrace and Prince Rupert as well as Vancouver and Seattle, but even after generations they are considered to belong to the lineage of their mothers and grandmothers before them and to have a home in their villages.

Each matrilineal family or house among the Gitksan, Nisga'a, and Tsimshian peoples has a tradition, its *adawx* (history). The *adawx* links the family to its territories and establishes rightful ownership of the land and resources, which are managed by the chiefs (in Sm'algyax, *sm'oigyet*, plural: *sm'gigyet*; *sigidmn'anax*: chiefwomen). The *adawx* are distinct from the widely shared beliefs and stories told by elders. Some *adawx* tell of migrations of groups to their present territories from a homeland farther east known as Temlaxam. Other histories describe a migration from the north, and still others simply tell of the process by which people explored their territories and established covenants with the supernatural powers that govern them. In these accounts there is sometimes a description of the people already in the area and of how they welcomed the newcomers and let them settle and marry among them.

Human habitation in the area dates back at least thirteen millennia, developing by about 2,500 years ago into the cultural forms encountered at European contact. Though of course the archaeological record cannot identify such features as language or family line, there is no evident break in the record to show one group replacing another. Recent archaeological research suggests that it is likely that the original inhabitants were the ancestors of the Nisga'a, Gitksan, and Tsimshian peoples.

According to the archaeological record, the first several millennia after deglaciation were a time of small communities with self-sufficient economies based on large mammals and berries in the inland areas and on shellfish and sea mammals in coastal locations. When salmon became abundant it was the primary resource for both coastal and riverine groups. Wide dissemination of rare items such as obsidian for tools and weapons and dentalia shells for ceremonial purposes indicates extensive trade, though this may have been managed at the boundaries of each territory in accordance with strict laws of trespass described in oral narratives.

Around 3000 B.C.E. cedar forests became well established in the area and the technology for canoe-making began to develop. Trade became an integral part of the economy. By 1500 B.C.E. there are indications that the organization of society had become more hierarchical and that coastal and inland economies were interdependent. Dried salmon, mountain goat, caribou, berries, furs, and tanned hides were exchanged for dried seafoods and oolichan grease. Tools and storage containers were essential to this trade, and regional specializations developed in these technologies as well as in ceremonial items. By about 500 C.E. there is evidence for trade prerogatives in which some groups had privileged access to other groups. For instance, trade upriver on the Skeena River with the Gitksan became the prerogative of the leading Eagle clan group at Kitselas, and later another group shared this privilege; such lucrative rights had to be enforced and were sometimes a focus of conflict.

There is some evidence that goods from the Asian mainland were acquired centuries before direct contact, though these are rare and may be from shipwrecks rather than trading networks. It is certain, however, that European trade goods came to the Tsimshian, Nisga'a, and Gitksan before Spanish and British explorers entered the waters of the area in the 1770s. Some trade goods were obtained from Tlingit people trading with Russian settlements in Alaska after 1741, and early acquisitions may also have included goods that had been traded overland great distances from the east or south. The earliest recorded direct contact with Europeans was when the trading vessel *Princess Royal* visited the Kitkatla area in 1787. The Nisga'a also have accounts of trading directly with the Russians around this time.

The later presence of traders, missionaries, and Indian agents did not radically alter the ancient way of life, for trade goods along with new foods and ideas were added to the existing cultural repertoire without rending the fabric of society. Over time, however, as settlers entered the area to stay, efforts to impose white institutions were followed closely by legislation and regulations with the specific purpose of replacing native practices with Canadian ones. Systems of government, land tenure, justice, education, and resource management as well as religion and family structures were all attacked by laws enforced with escalating rigour. The period from the 1860s to the 1880s was a watershed marked by the influx of foreigners and their weapons; ultimately, a show of military force was used against several communities to quell their attempts to exercise their rights.

The Coast Tsimshian were most accessible, and in 1834 Fort Simpson was built in their territories at present-day Port Simpson. The trade centre became the site of the winter habitations of the coastal Tsimshian, and Nisga'a, Gitksan, other Tsimshian, Haida, and Tlingit came regularly to trade. The traders were not all genteel people by any means, and alcohol abuse and violence involving both company personnel and their Tsimshian neighbours were not uncommon. The first missionary to enter the area was William Duncan, who began his work at Fort

Simpson in 1857 and who by 1862 had established the mission village of Metlakatla at the site of an old winter village. By this time, traders and military and government personnel, who had become familiar in the area, had been joined by gold seekers en route to the Cariboo. Less than a century after Captain George Vancouver's voyage to the area, occasional tourists were already arriving on coastal steamers.

In 1873, shortly after British Columbia entered Confederation, the first salmon canneries on the Skeena and Nass rivers brought non-natives to the area in substantial numbers for the first time. While the people of Port Simpson and Metlakatla resisted the use of their territories by others, they came under great pressure as the pace of development escalated and particularly when land was being acquired for the northern terminus of the railroad. Though some missionaries in the area attempted to support the rights of the original inhabitants to their traditional territories, the combined forces of church hierarchies, provincial administrators, federal Indian administrators, and land speculators were arrayed against them. A turning-point for the Coast Tsimshian was the 1887 decision by the missionary William Duncan, as a result of strife with church hierarchy and provincial authorities, to move to Alaska with hundreds of Tsimshian. The turmoil of this period continues to echo in such communities as Lax Kwa'alaams, Metlakatla, and New Metlakatla, Alaska.

The home territories of the Southern Tsimshian were less visited by traders, and the people of Gitga'ata and Kitkatla frequently travelled to Fort Simpson to trade. Many converted to Christianity after Duncan established the mission community of Metlakatla, and indeed by 1873 Duncan claimed that all of the Gitga'ata had moved to the new village, which was probably accurate as far as winter residence goes. When Metlakatla was almost depopulated in 1887 by the move of Duncan's followers to Alaska, modern-day Hartley Bay was founded by a small group of Gitga'ata who did not wish to move so far from their territories. The Kitkatla people were reputedly more conservative, and fewer had become involved with Duncan, though eventually the community hosted a resident Anglican missionary. Kitasoo was closer to Fort McLoughlin, and for decades the people from this community tended to see their relatives most frequently when the latter were en route to Victoria or to coastal canneries. Klemtu, where the Kitasoo Tsimshian now reside, includes many people who speak the language of the Bella Bella people as well as the Tsimshian-speaking community residents.

The mouth of the Nass River is renowned for the rich oil of the oolican which return in great abundance each year. These small, smelt-like fish are valued primarily for their oil, which is traded to the inland and coastal peoples. The quality of the Nass River oolican is particularly rich, and this has traditionally forced the Nisga'a to defend their home-land and resources from invaders. The Nass mouth was visited by Vancouver when he entered the Portland Canal in 1793, and the Hud-son's Bay Company (HBC) first established Fort Simpson on the Nass River in 1831. However, the HBC moved to the present site of Port Simpson in 1834. While the territory abounds in wildlife and the tem-perate rainforest of the coast provided the Nisga'a with an abundance of shellfish and salmon, the climate and isolation of the valley were inhospitable to the sporadic attempts at agricultural settlement. Even-tually small reserves were laid out, but their inadequacy – comprising less than 1 percent of the traditional territory – has led the Nisga'a to engage in a lengthy struggle for their land rights. While settlers have attempted to establish themselves in the Nass valley, much of the area is unsuited to agriculture, and today the major non-native presence in near proximity to the four Nisga'a villages is the logging industry.

The territories of the Gitksan are less remote and also more hospitable to agricultural settlement. By the first quarter of the nineteenth century, the Gitksan were trading goods from Fort St James to their east, but there was no white settlement in their territories until the late 1860s, when the trading town of Skeena Forks or Hazelton was founded at Gitanmaax. In evidence presented in the recent court case *Delgamuukw* v. *The Queen*, Gitksan elders spoke of the efforts of their parents and grandparents to incorporate these early settlers, most of whom were traders and farmers. A century later the three small neighbouring com-munities called the Hazeltons are home to the largest body of non-native people who live in the territories of the Gitksan, along with the Gitanmaax band of Gitksan and the Wit'suwit'en community of Hagwilget. Many of the farms in the river valleys that were established by settlers are still occupied, though they cannot compete with large-scale agribusiness and operate mostly as producers of meat and pro-duce for the local region.

In their histories, the Gitksan remember the imposition of the British justice system. The event that first exposed the Gitksan to this system was the so-called Skeena Rebellion of 1872, when the people of Gitseg-yukla closed the Skeena River to travellers following the accidental burning of Gitsegyukla by two Euro-American traders. In response, two gunboats were dispatched to restore order. Two other incidents stand out: the 1888 shooting of a Gitksan for a crime for which he had already paid in the Gitksan legal system; and the unsuccessful thirteen-year pursuit of Simon Gunanoot for the alleged murder of a white man in 1906, for which he was finally acquitted after his voluntary surrender in 1919.

Once Euro-Canadian institutions became pervasive, the Tsimshian, Gitksan, and Nisga'a entered a period during which communities outwardly accommodated themselves to the new regime while developing strategies of resistance. After the federal government's passage of anti-potlatch legislation in 1885, legislation that was revised and enforced in the 1920s, communities with resident Indian agents hid their activities in various ways. When surveyors were working in the Gitksan area in the 1920s, the Gitanyow confiscated their equipment and sent the surveyors away; in the ensuing court case three Gitanyow men were convicted and two of them were sent to Oakalla prison for several months. Subsequent Gitanyow activity deterred settlers from establishing themselves in the region until a moratorium was finally placed on the sale of land in the region.

In the 1970s the Nisga'a, Tsimshian, and Gitksan peoples accelerated their ongoing political and legal struggles to secure control over their territories and their very existence as peoples. Several pivotal incidents have marked a shift in the relations between the First Nations and governments, notably the Supreme Court recognition in 1973 of aboriginal rights in the *Calder* case and the establishment of the B.C. Treaty Commission in 1993.

The British Columbia treaty process now involves most of the aboriginal communities in the province. However, entering negotiations does not guarantee territory or resource rights. In fact, since the onset of negotiations with the Nisga'a, the effect of the treaty process has been to unleash a wave of logging and other forms of primary-resource extraction in the northwest, the goal being to make as much profit as possible in the region before a settlement is reached. This has created particular difficulties for interior groups whose territories had been relatively untouched. Forestry harvests in some parts of the northwest have been estimated at three times the sustainable rate over the two decades since the Supreme Court's decision in *Calder*.

Economic Life

The ancient migrations by which this region was populated created a network of communities whose common heritage is commemorated in *adawx* and the related crests depicted on totem poles and housefronts. It was this network that facilitated the development of a complex system of commodity exchange, a trading system that became one of the most important factors in the sophisticated and thriving economy of the northwest coast. Although community size and location have varied since deglaciation, the present villages generally remain within a few kilometres of ancient settlements.

When Russian, European, and American fur traders visited the area, beginning in 1790, the coastal groups had direct access to the trade, while interior groups traded furs through coastal middlemen. When the sea otter were depleted, inland furs became the main product of exchange, and the Gitksan and Nisga'a communities played a key role in this trade by capitalizing on their direct access to the furs of the Tahltan and Tsetsaut to the north and the Wet'suwet'en in the east, as well as to the markets among the Tsimshian on the coast. This enriched all three groups and provided the wealth that supported a period of artistic productivity. The establishment of Fort St James in 1806, Fort Babine in 1822, Fort Simpson in 1831–34, and the Hagwilget post at Hazelton in 1866 did not undercut their control of the trade, since links of kinship and long-standing trading relationships drew trade to native partners resident near the posts and forced the trading companies to deal with Tsimshian, Nisga'a, and Gitskan middlemen.

The impact of the emphasis on land furs, as with the earlier sea-otter trade, was an escalation of resource extraction, increased wealth in foreign goods, and a fluorescence of ceremonial and artistic activity. However, as the European and Chinese markets for furs declined and the HBC consolidated its monopoly on the coastal trade at the mouth of the Nass and Skeena rivers and at the interior posts, the enormous profits from the trade in furs were replaced by modest returns, and a status quo developed in which trapping for furs to exchange for European goods, and later for cash, was integrated into the economies of the groups in the area.

The influx of gold prospectors in the 1860s was met in much the same way, by adding profits from prospecting, packing, and guiding to the pre-existing economy; the location on the Skeena River of the Coast Tsimshian and the Gitksan made this of particular benefit to them, though prospectors intruded on territories throughout the area without regard for native owners. From this period to the middle of the twentieth century, a steady flow of newcomers, who came to log, pack fish, mine, farm, or establish new communities, forced the Nisga'a, Gitksan, and Coast and Southern Tsimshian peoples to engage in political and legal battles to defend their territories, at great expense in terms of money, time, and economic opportunities lost as resources were extracted by outsiders.

An economic pattern developed in each community involving a mix of seasonal trapping and hunting, salmon harvest and preservation, spring and fall trade, and winter ceremonies. Many families combined this pattern with annual moves to the commercial canneries on the coast to work in the fishing industry, the women in the processing plants and the men as gillnetters and shoreworkers. By the 1950s multinational forestry companies and canneries were the key players in the economy of the northwest, and the way of life of all of the residents changed. As with the fur-trade period, there was a time of increased prosperity followed by consolidation of industries, depletion of resources, softening of foreign markets, and a marked decline, beginning in the early 1980s and nearing crisis proportions by the 1990s. Of the many thriving coastal canneries, only two now remain, and their workforces are shrinking. Many native people are still employed in the industry, but much of the labour force resides in Prince Rupert where the surviving canneries are located, and this circumstance weakens the economies of the native villages. Similarly, the smaller sawmills in the interior were shut down in the late 1980s to be replaced by one large, highly automated mill employing less than 10 percent of the original workforce. A major molybdenum mine at Kitsault on Alice Arm was closed during the 1970s because of protests, spearheaded by the Nisga'a, about the impact of dumping mine tailings into the sea, but mining has a foothold in the northern part of Nisga'a territory, and there is a small non-native community at Stewart.

In the 1990s the economies of the Tsimshian, Gitksan, and Nisga'a peoples continue to adapt. Forestry, fishing, harvesting of forest products such as pine mushrooms, sale of art, management of resources, government services and a growing tourism industry are the major sources of income. There is a high rate of unemployment in some communities, especially seasonally, related to the cycles of commercial fishing and logging. The cash economy is paralleled by a continuation of age-old patterns of fishing for salmon, halibut, and cod, harvesting shellfish and berries, and hunting and trapping, supplemented by some gardening, especially potatoes and berries.

Provision of educational, health, and social services to Nisga'a, Gitksan, and Tsimshian communities has been uneven and, on average, well below national norms. While there are increasing numbers of well-educated people from these communities working in the resource-industry, government, and professional sectors, there are also many people who have been marginalized by lack of access to critical services. The movement for self-government has been stimulated by acute awareness of these issues.

Federal and provincial initiatives have been underfunded and sporadic, and it has been difficult to establish long-term community-based responses to local needs. In some communities, the systems of social control that have been in place for many generations have held through the enormous stress of the past century; in others, these have been severely damaged, and nothing effective has been put in their place. The results – high levels of substance abuse and family violence, and large numbers of suicides and attempted suicides (in one village of fewer than 1,000 people, there were six suicides or attempted suicides in three months during 1994) – have been tragic and are issues of great concern among native people.

Kinship, Family, and Social Organization

Indigenous oral narratives and archaeological and linguistic research indicate that the earliest form of social organization among the Nisga'a, Gitksan, and Tsimshian peoples were paired single-clan villages composed of several housegroups, each led by a head chief and other lesser chiefs. From the earliest times the clans were interconnected through patterns of intermarriage, since marriage within one's clan is incestuous. Reciprocal exchanges of services and feasting to mark rites of passage and other ceremonial events also linked opposite clans. At some point the paired single-clan villages came to occupy one village site. While intermarriages eventually broadened the links among communities, the underlying system still holds. For example, there are no Gitksan villages with more than three clans, and where there are three, two of them tend to function ceremonially as one.

Housegroups, or houses, are extended matrilineal family groups which each belong to one of the four clans. The members of a housegroup share the same history of origin and the crests derived from that history. The housegroups are also the landowners in these societies, each owning discrete watersheds, mountains, and other contiguous geographical territories, both on the mainland and on the coastal islands. The four clans represented among the Coast and Southern Tsimshian, Nisga'a, and Gitksan are the eagle, wolf, raven, and killer whale; among the

Gitksan and some Nisga'a, the killer whale is replaced by the fireweed. All members of a clan consider each other brothers and sisters, and marriages must be with members of other clans. There are now elected band councils and chief councillors in all the communities, but these function largely in administering the affairs of the village.

Each housegroup has a series of names that are associated with territories, and these are ranked in importance. The most powerful houses and chiefs of each clan are the leading chiefs of the village, and, of these, the most powerful is considered the leading house and chief. There are minor variations in these arrangements among the Tsimshian, Nisga'a, and Gitksan. However, in all of the communities decision making is by consensus and involves all the chiefs and the matriarchs, who bring the other people into the discussion at various points in the process through clan meetings and informal consultations. The primary responsibility of the chief or matriarch is to manage the territory of the house, to provide for each of its members, and to meet the social and ceremonial obligations of the housegroup as a whole. While the position of chief and matriarch is inherited, a number of individuals may be eligible for any one position; a rigorous education system ensures that the one chosen will have the needed qualities of leadership and service. One metaphor that has been used to convey a chief's role is that the chief is married to his territory; although the chief holds power, he does so on behalf of his family, as well as its ancestors and descendants. The chief's wife is as important as the chief himself, and marriages were for a long time carefully arranged to ensure the well-being of the entire community.

Chieftainships have been strictly maintained and bear many responsibilities to their house and community. When the Nisga'a Land Committee was renamed the Nisga'a Tribal Council in 1955, the member communities decided to utilize the "common bowl philosophy," whereby decisions are made by the elected council as advised by the hereditary chiefs in concert with elected community officials (village governments). Among the Coast and Southern Tsimshian communities, the territories are sometimes identified with clan groups rather than with housegroups, but the underlying system is basically the same. The Tsimshian Tribal Council has undertaken an "umbrella" role to facilitate the pursuit of land rights by all of its member communities, and it is assisted in its activities by an advisory council of chiefs. Among the Gitksan, the housegroup system has retained the broadest functionality, and the house chiefs comprise the membership of the central organization.

The *adawx* is the charter of a housegroup. These family histories are private property, and the right to tell the history, and to show the symbols of its ownership, is exclusive to a set of relatives; this group may be quite large, and there may be branches in several different communities; many of the same *adawx* occur among the Gitksan, Tsimshian, and Nisga'a. The crests are symbols of ownership and are displayed at feasts and ceremonial events, and artists produce beautiful objects to dramatize these events. Totem poles are the best-known crest art, but housefront paintings, ceremonial robes and blankets, carved and painted boxes of cedar, frontlets, masks, jewellery, and tools and utensils are also created.

The feast, or potlatch, is a central social institution. Potlatch ceremonies include the highest forms of artistic and ritual expression and the distribution of the most treasured forms of wealth. At the feast the affiliations of each person and his or her connection with the whole community are acknowledged, and, at the same time, the continuance of the house and the ownership of its territories are ensured through the sharing of wealth. There are many types of feasts, marking, for example, a marriage, a death, or a totem-pole raising. In a modern death feast hosted by the Laxgibuu (wolf clan), the women of this group ensure that the food is prepared and contribute material goods. The men welcome and seat the guests and act as spokes-persons. Each person fulfils his or her responsibilities, and financial contributions are made by various categories of relatives in turn: wolf clan members, children of the wolf clan (members of other clans whose father's clan is wolf), the spouses of the wolf clan, and so on. The spouses of the wolf clan might dance or perform in a humorous manner as they donate their contributions to help to lighten the grief and sorrow of the family and to speed their healing. Payments are made by the wolf clan to each of the people and groups that provide services, including repayments of obligations owed by the deceased chief. The name of the chief is passed on to his nephew, designated by him before his death. Over the course of a year, everyone in a community may participate in many similar events hosted by each clan, a process that binds them together as a community.

Today, the socio-political system of the Nisga'a, Gitksan, and Tsimshian persists in spite of concerted efforts on the part of government agencies to undermine and replace it with the Euro-Canadian system. For example, although the Indian Act banned the potlatch in the nineteenth century, the Tsimshian peoples continued to feast. During the era of repression, defiance of the potlatch ban was relatively open in more remote communities in which agents of the state did not reside. In the communities where police, Indian agents, and missionaries resided, people feasted in their homes and in some places covered their windows to avoid detection if the feast lasted into the night. Some charges were laid under the anti-potlatch law, but they were not effective in ending the practice.

The efforts of missionaries had more impact. People in several communities voluntarily pledged to abandon feasting, and, in a few villages, ceremonial regalia was burned, sold, or surrendered at the instigation of the missionaries, some of whom amassed extensive personal collections of finely made objects in the process. Yet, even in those villages that gave up their regalia, the feast system was being used in the 1990s and in fact has experienced a great resurgence. There are some difficulties in maintaining the system today. The lack of recognition of native land rights in many areas is a major problem, since the ownership of land is the foundation of the potlatch tradition. As well, careful regulation of marriage partners to ensure clan exogamy – a crucial feature of the system in past times – is no longer practical; a creative practice of clan adoptions has sprung up as an adaptive substitute mechanism, with political control in the house maintained by those who are entitled by birth.

Culture and Religion

Euro-American interest in Tsimshian, Nisga'a, and Gitskan carving (done by men) and weaving and basketry (done by women) led to the development of a commercial industry in which new forms of artistic expression were created to supplement traditional ones. This industry waned in the first half of the twentieth century but revived in the 1970s. Northwest coast art is now in museums and art galleries and private collections throughout North America, Europe, and the Pacific rim. At the same time, artists continue to be commissioned by hereditary chiefs and others to create totem poles, ceremonial regalia, and other works of art for use in feasts and other public events. The former sexual division of labour in artistic production has been relaxed, and women as well as men now carve wood, design silkscreen prints, make jewellery, and weave.

Currently, young people join their elders in performing traditional songs, drumming, and dancing, both at ceremonial events within the community and in cross-community events ranging from theatrical performances to elders' gatherings. Literature, like the plastic arts, is inseparable from the rest of the culture. The *adawx*, together with totem-pole carvings and sacred songs, commemorate historic events and are akin to the classic epic poetry of the ancient peoples in other regions of the world. These *adawx* are now being incorporated into school and university programs to educate young people in their history and to foster the development of native scholarship. Most "literary" production is still in the form of speeches and oratory at ceremonial events, though there is a burgeoning interest in written publications. The Bookmakers at 'Ksan have published several volumes of stories and cultural materials; the Wilp Wilxo'oskwhl Nisga'a – a Nisga'a post-secondary institute – and School District 92 Nisga'a have also produced collections and curriculum resources; and the First Nations Resource Centre of School District 52 in Prince Rupert has put out several volumes in Sm'algyax and English. A small number of people from these groups are beginning to write poetry and stories in English, though few of their works have yet been published. One exciting example that appeared recently is Art Wilson's collection of original art and reflections on the struggles of indigenous people, with images ranging from the devastation of the landscape near his home community of Kispiox by unsound forestry practices to the execution of activist Ken Saro-Wiwa in Nigeria.

Northwest coast peoples do not separate religion from other aspects of their lives. The spiritual vitality and interconnectedness of creation – humans, animals, plant life, and the spirit world – are acknowledged in every aspect of life. Attitudes and practices that manifest respect for all living beings are instilled through education and extolled in the *adawx*. Spiritual beliefs and a value system based on them form the basis for the education of children, and they are especially emphasized throughout the lives of those destined to be leaders. The development of attitudes of respect begins at an early age and in the past was followed by specific spiritual training that empowered young adults to deal with the physical, social, and spiritual demands of life as an adult. Specific rituals were used for making contact with supernatural powers for healing and also for winter ceremonial dancing, for life-cycle rituals, and in preparation for hunting. Chiefs controlled some forms of spiritual powers, while shamans had access to others. There were many types of shamans, including healing shamans and divining shamans, as well as specialists who watched the sun and stars to predict the timing and bounty of the coming seasons.

When missionaries entered the area, it was often at the invitation of the communities to provide access to education, economic opportunities, and health care. Christian beliefs were chosen, adapted, and included in various ways in cultural practices. Each village first accepted a single denomination, and today the same denomination generally retains its pre-eminent position among Christian groups in that community. In some villages there is still only a single church, such as the United Church in Hartley Bay or the Salvation Army in Gitwinksihlkw. However, the proliferation of Protestant denominations and non-denominational groups has created considerable religious diversity.

The practices of the more long-established denominations have been incorporated into many public events such as weddings, funerals, and political gatherings. People do not see any inconsistency in holding firmly to pre-contact ideas such as reincarnation as well as to Christian doctrines. The role of church services varies by community; in some areas the most widely attended events, especially between the 1950s and 1970s, were the "revivals" conducted by travelling evangelical groups. Such groups often denounce drumming and traditional dancing as "heathen," whereas the mainstream denominations have apologized for their past behaviour and now accept indigenous practices as legitimate forms of spirituality.

Education, Language, and Communication

Traditionally, the education system drew on the resources of the extended family, with different members playing designated roles in the raising and educating of children. In their earliest years, children were cared for by their grandparents and their parents. Their grandparents taught the children practical skills, values, and proper behaviour. The chief or the matriarch of the housegroup instructed the children in their house's history – their *adawx* – and in the laws of the people.

As they grew older, children accompanied their parents and other family members throughout their territories, learning the names and boundaries of the land and assisting in the gathering and preparation of food and of all the other materials needed by the housegroup. At puberty, they entered the ceremonial life of the community and began the training that would allow them to take their place in the social and political functions of the village. At this point, aunts and uncles played a key role, assisting their nieces and nephews in various rites of passage and in their preparation for marriage and the adult responsibilities ahead.

This system of education was undermined by the church-sponsored shift to single-family homes, legislated schooling (especially residential schools), and participation in the mainstream economy by adult members of the extended family. From the beginning, there was both resistance to and acceptance of the idea of schooling. Those opposed saw it as an attempt to draw the younger generation away from their own society; others, who felt restricted by their inability to deal effectively with non-native institutions, saw it as an opportunity for the young to master the ways of the new socio-political systems in order to facilitate the long-term goal of re-establishing control over their lives. Both points of view continue today, with community-run schools in a number of villages, an immersion school in Gitwangak, and the establishment in the Nass valley in 1975 of School District 92, Nisga'a. There are increasing numbers of native university and college graduates in the fields of education, law, business administration, resource management, and social sciences, and, at the same time, non-native educational institutions are showing a growing awareness that teaching the languages, cultures, and histories of the Nisga'a, Gitksan, and Tsimshian not only will enrich their own programs but are essential for the education of people from these communities.

Since 1973 a number of locally controlled schools and school boards have been established. Among the Nisga'a, both School District 92 and the Wilp Wilxo'oskwhl Nisga'a have been successful in their areas of responsibility. In Gitksan communities, initiatives include the Gitksan-Wit'suwit'en Education Society and the Gitwangak Education Society, both of which offer immersion programs in Gitksan language and culture. Among the Tsimshian, there is a Tsimshian curriculum-development program attached to provincial School District 52 (where 47 percent of students are native); the North Coast Tribal Council Education Centre has offered a language-teacher education program through which two groups of students have already received their B.Ed. degrees; and the Northwest Band Social Workers Association, comprising students from numerous tribal areas, has a B.S.W. program in partnership with the University of Victoria.

The Nisga'a, Gitksan, and Tsimshian languages were initially used in the work of missionaries, and there are church liturgies and hymns in each that were developed a century ago. However, Skuuxs, the language of the Southern Tsimshian, is virtually extinct; today, only two people in Kitasoo (Klemtu) retain limited knowledge of its vocabulary. In the communities in which Southern Tsimshian was once spoken, it has been replaced by Coast Tsimshian. The languages of the Tsimshian,

Nisga'a, and Gitksan are still spoken by 25 to 30 percent of community members, and many children are now learning their language. Virtually all community members also speak English. Language-revitalization efforts have been undertaken in all communities, and the languages are now taught in immersion programs as well as being included in the curriculum of primary and secondary schools. Nisga'a was taught in the Indian Day Schools in the Nass valley in the 1970s. When School District 92 was established, a structured curriculum of Nisga'a reaching from kindergarten to grade 12 was instituted. The first school program in Coast Tsimshian began in Hartley Bay in 1972, and the language is now taught in all communities. There is currently an immersion primary school in Gitksan in Gitwangak.

In addition to these programs for school children, there have been a number of workshops over the past two decades to assist adults seeking to attain fluency or literacy in one of these languages. In 1994 a full-degree program in Nisga'a studies was established through a partnership between the University of Northern British Columbia and the Wilp Wilxo'oskwhl Nisga'a. University-credit courses offered since 1995 in Coast Tsimshian have drawn a large number of Tsimshian people into post-secondary classrooms. The Tsimshian, Gitksan, and Nisga'a use a common orthography and actively promote both the written and spoken forms of the language.

Since the Gitksan, Tsimshian, and Nisga'a form a large proportion of the regional population, First Nations issues receive extensive coverage in the local and regional media, though almost always from a non-native perspective. The Nisga'a newspaper *Hak'ak'a* (The Key), established in 1891 and now published by the Nisga'a Tribal Council, provides an alternative medium of communication that is available both inside and outside the communities. Additionally, there are publications such as the *Native Voice* (Vancouver, 1946–), published by the Native Brotherhood of British Columbia, as well as newsletters produced by all of the tribal councils. The latter have their own communication divisions, along with a presence on the Internet.

The practice of visiting always served to transmit information between villages, and recently CB radios, VHF radios, telephones, and now the Internet have added the ability to communicate beyond the local community. In the past two decades, each of the tribal councils has set up programs to facilitate internal communication as well as to present views to the external media. Community cable programs, hour-long documentaries aired on national networks, newsletters, annual conventions, informational brochures and posters, and coffee-table books have all been published under the auspices of these organizations. Northern Native Broadcasting offers both information and entertainment programs to communities throughout the northwest area and is linked to a national network.

The annual conventions held by each tribal council are especially effective venues for internal communication; these often attract large numbers of participants and include reports by all of the committees and agencies reporting to the council. There are also special education and health meetings held at various times of the year. The one occasion that brings together the most people from Gitksan, Nisga'a, and Tsimshian communities (as well as many other First Nations) is the All Native Basketball Tournament, started in 1947 and now held annually in Prince Rupert early each February. The feast system continues to facilitate political communication, and events have increased rapidly in frequency and size over the past decade, as communities revive traditions that were once suppressed. Feasts have been used in recent years to deal with the complex issue of overlapping land claims by different communities, and totem-pole raisings are once again events of public celebration across the region.

Politics

Until well into the nineteenth century, Tsimshian-speaking peoples regulated individual behaviour and conducted community affairs through the institution of the housegroup and through the leadership of hereditary chiefs and matriarchs. This system was challenged by the federal government's appointment of Indian agents and the imposition of a system of elected band councils in each community, with the number of councillors determined by population. Besides undermining local structures of self-government, the new arrangements placed control over all matters concerning relations with the federal and provincial governments in the hands of a few people (sometimes as few as three). At first, the communities simply adapted the system so that it perpetuated their own by electing one of the leading hereditary chiefs to the post of chief councillor; however, the chiefs were often forced to rely on individuals who were familiar with the procedures, politics, and bureaucracy of the Department of Indian Affairs, and the position of band manager was eventually created to fill this need. Ultimately, the interplay of the hereditary system, the elected system, and a local Indian agent with inordinate powers made routine decision making unnecessarily complicated and maximized the potential for divisions within each community and between communities, particularly since final approval of all decisions had to be granted by the federal government. Counterbalancing the forces of division were continuing respect for the role of the hereditary chiefs, matriarchs, and elders and perpetuation of the feast system.

In 1890 the Nisga'a organized a committee to fight for recognition of their land rights, and in 1913 they petitioned the Privy Council in England in pursuit of the same cause. Unsuccessful, they joined with the Coast Salish and other peoples to form the Allied Tribes of British Columbia in 1916, the first province-wide native organization. In 1926 the Allied Tribes presented its case to a joint Senate-House committee of the Canadian Parliament, only to have all of its arguments rejected. The committee recommended that, instead of treaty payments, B.C. natives should receive an annual grant of $100,000 (this recommendation was implemented, the grant becoming known as the "B.C. Special"), and another of its recommendations led to the passage of an amendment to the Indian Act making it illegal to raise funds to pursue land rights, a measure that was not repealed until 1951. The Allied Tribes folded soon after the report of the parliamentary committee, but in 1955 the Nisga'a reorganized their Land Committee into the Nisga'a Tribal Council (NTC).

The NTC's campaign for land rights culminated in the Supreme Court's ruling in the 1973 *Calder* case, named after the NTC president at the time. In a split decision, the court ruled that aboriginal title had existed in British Columbia; three judges concluded that such title still existed, three said that it had been extinguished by legislation, and the seventh did not express an opinion on the issue, ruling instead on a procedural matter. Following this decision, the federal government established the Office of Land Claims to negotiate settlements in all parts of the country not covered by treaty, including British Columbia. Talks between the goverment of Canada and the Nisga'a began in 1976; the B.C. government did not formally become a party to these negotiations until 1991. An agreement-in-principle was signed in 1996, and a formal treaty was achieved in August 1998. In return for abandoning future treaty claims and their tax-exempt status, the Nisga'a acquired control of almost 2,000 square kilometres of land, powers of self-government, resource rights, and $300 million in cash. This historic treaty, the first in British Columbia, will take effect on being formally ratified by the Nisga'a and the federal and provincial governments.

In the early 1970s the Gitksan formed a tribal council with their neighbours the Wet'suwet'en in order to defend themselves against the increasing incursions of multinational mineral and logging companies and the efforts of governments to restrict traditional native economic practices. The Department of Fisheries especially was a target for court action, since uniformed and armed fisheries officers routinely patrolled each housegroup's fishing sites, charging people and seizing their nets and fish for the infraction of laws of questionable legality. The success of these court actions and similar ones throughout the province laid the foundation for policy changes concerning the aboriginal fishery that are currently under way. The Gitksan and Wet'suwet'en also addressed the issue of their land rights with an extensive research project documenting every aspect of their claims. At the same time, First Nations across Canada were pressing the federal government for change. Yet by the early 1980s it had become clear that, in spite of constitutional debates, numerous commissions, and ongoing meetings with all levels of government, there had been no significant progress. Although the federal government had set up a process through which land claims could be negotiated, it had concerned itself so far only with the Nisga'a. As well, the B.C. government continued to refuse to acknowledge aboriginal title and to participate in negotiations.

It was in these circumstances that the Gitksan and Wet'suwet'en launched a lawsuit in 1984 in which they asked for acknowledgment of their ownership to and jurisdiction over about 58,000 square kilometres of their traditional lands, a territory – rich in natural resources – stretching along the Skeena, Nass, Bulkley, and Babine watersheds in northwestern British Columbia, about 700 kilometres north of Vancouver.

Known as *Delgamuukw*, after one of the fifty-one hereditary chiefs acting as plaintiffs, this case reached the British Columbia Court of Appeal in 1991. In a controversial judgment, Chief Justice Allan McEachern dismissed the claims of the Gitksan and Wet'suwet'en on the grounds that aboriginal title had been extinguished by the colony of British Columbia before Confederation, that the Royal Proclamation of 1763 was inapplicable to British Columbia, and that the Gitksan and Wet'suwet'en in pre-contact times were too primitive to have ever governed themselves in any meaningful sense. This decision was immediately appealed and was overturned by the Supreme Court in December 1997. In a unanimous judgment, the Supreme Court ruled that aboriginal title to lands not covered by treaty was not extinguished and that native people have a constitutional right to use these lands in whatever manner they see fit. Declaring that the Court of Appeal had erred in not taking native oral histories into account, the Supreme Court concluded that a new trial was necessary, though it added that a better outcome would be a negotiated settlement. At the time of writing, the federal and provincial governments have yet to announce their intentions.

For much of the 1980s the Gitksan were preoccupied with the *Delgamuukw* litigation. However, recently they have begun to focus more on other issues too, including the aboriginal fishery, education, health care, and devastation of the remaining Gitksan lands by logging. By 1992 the Tribal Council had changed its name to the Office of the Hereditary Chiefs to reflect its role as an integral part of the Gitksan system of governance.

The Tsimshian Tribal Council was formed in the 1980s. The member communities are considerably more disparate than are those of either of the other tribal councils in terms of remoteness, size, economic opportunities, and historical experiences. Achieving integration among them has been a priority for the leadership. Now that the Tsimshian Tribal Council is operating effectively, issues in resource management – especially fisheries, treaty negotiation, and education – are being addressed.

While the hereditary chiefs and matriarchs continue to exercise leadership in many contexts, each of the Tsimshian, Nisga'a, and Gitksan communities has an elected council which administers local services (with all decisions still approved by the federal government). There are no mainstream political parties within the villages; councillors and chief councillors are elected on the basis of their past record and community ties. In general, family connections are important factors in these elections, as might be anticipated in small communities. In some villages the same chief and council have been in place for lengthy periods, while in others it is not unusual to have the entire slate replaced at each election; in several villages there are slates which alternate in replacing each other at each new election, an arrangement indicative of two fairly large blocs of votes with a middle "swing" constituency.

The tribal councils also have annual elected positions such as president, vice-president, treasurer, and board members. These positions are often contested, and the choices are considered with grave deliberation, since the councils are responsible for land negotiations with the provincial and federal governments. The NTC is of the longest standing and manages the widest array of services. The Gitksan have a stable leadership and are expanding into new areas. The Tsimshian Tribal Council initially handled only land claims and resource-management issues, leaving capital works, education, and social services to the North Coast Tribal Council, an interim body established to assume the responsibilities of the local office of the Department of Indian Affairs. This body was phased out in 1996, and each village then assumed direct responsibility for its affairs.

All of the tribal councils are affiliated with the Canada-wide Assembly of First Nations and participate in its activities. The other major political body is the Native Brotherhood of British Columbia, which is both a fishing union and a political-action organization; members of the Tsimshian-speaking groups were prominent in this body when it was formed a half-century ago, and their continuing presence in large numbers in the Brotherhood is reflective of their significant role in the fishing industry. More than 50 percent of the Brotherhood's current executive is drawn from Nisga'a and Tsimshian communities.

Political relationships with nearby cities, regions, and the provincial and federal governments are generally managed through the tribal councils. Participation in provincial and federal politics is considerable, though variable. In some communities the right to vote is exercised with enthusiasm, while in others almost no one votes and the external political system is often rejected. Two Nisga'a leaders have been elected to the provincial legislature, Larry Guno and Frank Calder.

Intergroup Relations and Group Maintenance

One of the main institutions for managing intergroup relations for the Tsimshian, Gitksan, and Nisga'a is marriage. This was used to manage succession and inheritance, to establish trading partnerships, and to avert hostilities. Oral histories indicate that there were many marriages across these three groups and with the Haida and Tlingit as well; the clan systems of all three of these matrilineal groups were parallel and easily accommodated "international" marriages without disrupting community structures. When non-native traders came to the area, the same strategy was used with them; there were several marriages between prominent Nisga'a and Tsimshian families and HBC factors.

Arranged marriages being no longer possible, the management of relations with outsiders is sometimes now handled by clan adoptions, in which people are given status in a clan so that they can participate in local events. In some communities there is a feeling that this mechanism is being overused, and it has been informally agreed that such adoptions will take place only when someone is married into the community.

Beyond the local context, intergroup relations are formally managed mainly by the tribal councils.

Once non-native hegemony was in place, the provisions of the Indian Act and provincial policies and legislation established a repressive regime in which ceremonies such as feasts and political action to obtain land rights were outlawed (from 1887 to 1951) and Indians could not pre-empt or even purchase land. Indians could not vote provincially until 1949 and federally until 1960. Provincial laws that denied the rights of citizens to Indians led to separate education as well as health and social-service systems, and local authorities enforced such petty indignities as separately designated sections in theatres, restaurants, and hotels. Though these laws and local discriminatory practices are a thing of the past, a great deal of work remains to be done to eradicate the impact of generations of prejudice.

At the present time the identity and pride of the Gitksan, Nisga'a, and Tsimshian peoples are strong. During the first half of the twentieth century there was a period of low visibility and, for some, a loss of commitment, but in all communities since the 1960s and 1970s language, culture, feasts, and art have gained renewed prominence and are highly valued. People are now seeking creative new ways of expressing their identity and are working hard to revitalize their language skills and to exercise ownership of their resources.

One area of some difficulty is the expression of cultural commitment for people who reside outside the traditional territories. The Nisga'a have established urban locals that participate in their Tribal Council in a fashion similar to that of the villages. Among the Tsimshian there are "societies" for many of the villages in Prince Rupert; these are engaged in fund-raising and charitable works and are now seeking entry as active participants in the treaty process. Among the Gitksan, extraterritorial members are perhaps less of a concern, since Old Hazelton is the largest centre in their region and is also the site of a Gitksan reserve community, Gitanmaax.

Among people who live farther afield, a few who were raised outside the villages appear to focus less on their identity as members of any one housegroup or Tsimshian-speaking village than on a broader First Nations network of friends. Many more people have continuously maintained an attachment to their specific housegroup and village identity through periodic visits; frequent contributions to feasts via local relatives; gathering, preparation, and eating of traditional foods such as seaweed, smoked fish, and oolican grease; and use of traditional art in home decor and of distinctive items of ceremonial regalia and clothing, as well as by retaining the links of kinship and friendship with other members of their group. A number of communities are creating ways to maintain the links of kinship and community across great distances, and these expect their relationships with their clan sisters and brothers to continue for their great-grandchildren and beyond, to time immemorial.

FURTHER READING

Marjorie Halpin and Margaret Seguin (Anderson), "Tsimshian Peoples: Southern Tsimshian, Coast Tsimshian, Nishga and Gitksan," in Wayne Suttles, ed., *Handbook of North American Indians*, vol. 7 (Washington, D.C., 1990), 267–85, is the most authoritative published source on the identification of the Tsimshian groups. Franz Boas wrote several volumes on native mythology, technology, and social organization, including *Tsimshian Mythology* (Washington, D.C., 1916), which was based on texts collected by Henry Tate. Viola Garfield was a student of Boas's, who worked with the Tsimshian ethnographer William Beynon, and her study of Port Simpson in the 1930s, *Tsimshian Clan and Society* (Seattle, Wash., 1939), is a major source for this period and one of the few full ethnographic treatments of coastal groups. Stephen McNeary has contributed the only other comprehensive description of the Nisga'a, "Where Fire Came Down from: Social and Economic Life of the Niska" (Ph.D. thesis, Bryn Mawr College, 1976).

Marius Barbeau's long interest in the region yielded several volumes including *Totem Poles*, 2 vols. (Ottawa, 1950; repr. 1990), as well as an extensive collection of texts and documentation from people in the communities, housed at the Centre for Folk Culture Studies, Canadian Museum of Civilization, Hull. Wilson Duff's "Laws and Territories of the Kitwancool," in *Anthropology in British Columbia*, no. 4 (Victoria, 1965), is a major contribution based entirely on the accounts of members of that community. Duff's student, Marjorie Halpin, of the Museum of Anthropology at the University of British Columbia, has published extensively on art; especially worthy of mention is her "The Tsimshian Crest System: A Study Based on Museum Specimens and the Marius Barbeau and William Beynon Field Notes" (Ph.D. thesis, University of British Columbia, 1973). Jay Miller and Carol M. Eastman have edited a useful collection, *The Tsimshian and Their Neighbours of the North Pacific Coast* (Seattle, 1984).

The linguists who have published the greatest amount on languages in the Tsimshian language family include John Dunn (Coast and Southern Tsimshian), Bruce Rigsby (Gitksan), and Marie-Lucie Tarpent (Nisga'a). See especially Dunn's *A Practical Dictionary for the Coast Tsimshian Language* (Ottawa, 1978);

Lonnie Hindle and Bruce Rigsby's "A Short Practical Dictionary of the Gitskam Language," *Northwest Anthropological Research Notes*, vol. 7, no. 1 (1973), 1–61; and Tarpent's "A Grammar of the Nishga Language" (Ph.D. thesis, University of Victoria, 1989). On feasting, readers should consult Margaret (Seguin) Anderson's *Interpretive Contexts for Traditional and Current Coast Tsimshian Feasts* (Ottawa, 1985) and *The Tsimshian: Images of the Past, Views for the Present* (Vancouver, 1984).

Jim McDonald's "Trying to Make a Life: The Historical Political Economy of Kitsumkalum" (Ph.D. thesis, University of British Columbia, 1985) demonstrates that the economy of the region was built on the labour of the Tsimshian, Nisga'a, and Gitksan as well as on the resources found in their territories. The archaeology and prehistory of the region are topics of enduring interest, to which major contributions have been made by a number of long-term fieldworkers. See especially Richard Inglis and George MacDonald, *Skeena River Prehistory* (Ottawa, 1979); David Archer, "The North Coast Heritage Inventory Project: A Report on the 1990 Field Season," prepared for the province of British Columbia (1991); and Roy L. Carlson and Luke Dalla Bona, *Early Human Occupation in British Columbia* (Vancouver, 1995).

The link between oral histories and archaeological and historic evidence is discussed by Susan Marsden in "Evidence of Early Halocene Environments in Northwest Coast Oral Histories," *Canadian Archaeology Association, Papers* (1988), and "Defending the Mouth of the Skeena: Perspective on Tsimshian-Tlinglit Relations," *Canadian Archaeological Association, Proceedings* (1996). See also Neil Sterrit, Susan Marsden, Bob Galois, et al., *Tribal Boundaries in the Nass Watershed* (Vancouver, 1998), and Marsden and Galois, "The Tsimshian, the Hudson's Bay Company and the Geopolitics of the Northwest Coast Fur Trade, 1787–1840," *Canadian Geographer*, vol. 39, no. 2 (1995), 169–83.

As the Gitksan, Tsimshian, and Nisga'a peoples have shed their colonial legacies they have begun both to publish works and to sponsor publications by selected non-native authors. Gisday Wa and Delgam Uukw's *Spirit in the Land: Statements of the Gitksan and Wet'suwet'en Hereditary Chefs in the Supreme Court of British Columbia, 1987–90: Reflections* (Gabriola, B.C., 1992) presents the Gitksan and Wet'suwet'en perspective on their land rights; Daniel Raunet's *Without Surrender, without Consent: A History of Nishga Land Claims* (Vancouver, 1984) and the Nisga'a Tribal Council's *People of the Nass River* (Vancouver, 1993) recount the history of that group's struggle to claim its land.

There is not yet a parallel resource on the history of the Tsimshian people from their own perspective, but several valuable works exist. *Teachings of Our Grandfathers*, a series of beautiful volumes produced by School District 52 in 1992, includes clan histories, descriptions of social practices, and stories aimed at a school audience. Walter Wright's account of the ancient origins and history of his house was written down and published by local historian Will Robinson as *Men of Medeek* (Kitimat, B.C., 1962). Finally, the extensive material on the Tsimshian generated by the ethnographer William Beynon in a career spanning four decades is housed in the Centre for Folk Culture Studies, Canadian Museum of Civilization, and other archives. Selected texts published by John Love and George MacDonald can be found in *Tsimshian Narratives*, vols. 1–2 (Ottawa, 1987).

12

WAKASHANS

Alan McMillan

Identification

The various members of the Wakashan language family occupy the central mainland coast of British Columbia, along with northern and western Vancouver Island, extending as far south as the Olympic peninsula in Washington State. No common Wakashan identity exists; rather, the Wakashan label is a linguistic classification linking a number of related languages.

A major break separates the northern and southern branches of this language family. The northern Wakashans, once widely (although erroneously) referred to as the "Kwakiutl," consist of a number of politically separate groups speaking three distinct languages. In the north are the Haisla, today concentrated around the city of Kitimat. South of the Haisla are the Heiltsuk (formerly also known as the Bella Bella), whose traditional territories encompass a large area of the central B.C. coast. The Oweekeno of Rivers Inlet are a separate people, speaking a distinct dialect of the Heiltsuk language. To the south, on northern Vancouver Island and the adjacent mainland, are the speakers of the Kwakwala language, today known as the Kwakwaka'wakw (literally "speakers of Kwakwala"). Although the term Kwagiulth (or "Kwakiutl") is often applied to this group, it more correctly refers only to those who reside at the modern reserve community of Fort Rupert.

The southern Wakashans, once erroneously lumped together as the "Nootka," also encompass three separate languages. The most northerly are the Nuu-chah-nulth, who occupy most of the west coast of Vancouver Island. The southern portion of Vancouver Island's west coast is home to the Ditidaht. Across the Strait of Juan de Fuca, in Washington State, are their close relatives, the Makah.

Wakashan reserve communities today are almost invariably on the coastal waters, many in locations occupied by their ancestors for millennia. Others represent nineteenth- or early-twentieth-century movements around trading posts or other centres. Such communities offer modern economic and social facilities while also fostering a sense of identity with the Wakashans' cultural heritage. For many individuals, however, economic opportunities are greater in the outside world. Approximately 55 percent of Wakashan people now reside off-reserve, many in urban centres removed from their traditional lands.

The Wakashan population at the time of initial European contact is unknown. Conservative estimates suggest about 25,000 people in the northern branch and 10,000 in the southern; however, John Meares, an eighteenth-century European observer, calculated a population of 30,000 for the southern branch alone. Epidemic diseases following European contact greatly reduced Wakashan numbers. After a long period of recovery there are today about 9,500 northern Wakashans and 7,000 Nuu-chah-nulth and Ditidaht in Canada.

History

Archaeological discoveries in Heiltsuk and Kwakwaka'wakw territories indicate human occupation for over 9,000 years. On the west coast of Vancouver Island, Nuu-chah-nulth history has been traced back for about 4,000 years.

Wakashan peoples constructed large multi-family houses from the huge stands of cedar trees in the lush coastal rain forest. Split cedar planks, slung on a framework of posts and beams, could be removed and transported from place to place. Planks also covered the roof, being weighed down with poles and rocks as protection against the high winds of winter storms. Inside these large structures, heat and light came from several fires, which were also used for cooking, while boxes and baskets containing stored food supplies and ritual gear were stacked along the walls. Inner support posts might be carved with figures that were the inherited rights of the chiefly occupants.

Villages of such houses lined the beaches in protected areas along the coast. Hundreds of people gathered at winter villages, which consisted of one or more rows of houses facing the water. During other times of the year people were dispersed at resource camps, often taking with them the planks from their winter houses for temporary shelters. Some families owned house frames at several village sites, moving the planks between them.

Contact with Europeans began in the late eighteenth century. The 1774 encounter between a Spanish ship and several canoes of Nuu-chah-nulth on western Vancouver Island marks the initial contact in this area. Four years later, the arrival of Captain James Cook at Nootka Sound ushered in a period of more intensive contact. In the decades that followed, relations between natives and outsiders centred on trade, particularly for the soft pelts of the sea otter. A few ambitious and well-situated Nuu-chah-nulth chiefs, such as Muquinna in Nootka Sound and Wikinanish in Clayoquot Sound, greatly increased their personal and economic power through widespread trade monopolies. The northern Wakashans, away from the open coast, were less frequently visited by European traders.

Although the early trade period was generally peaceful, occasional hostilities did occur. In 1792, in reaction to a perceived plot against his ship, the American trader Robert Gray turned his cannons on one of Wikinanish's major villages, completely destroying it. A decade later, in 1803, Muquinna, likely a successor to the chief of the same name who greeted Cook, reacted to an insult from a ship's captain by seizing the ship and killing all but two of the crew.

This period of contact was short-lived, since by the end of the eighteenth century the sea otter had been hunted to local extinction. As the maritime trade declined, the Hudson's Bay Company (HBC) established permanent land-based trading posts. Fort McLoughlin was built in Heiltsuk territory in 1833, leading many Heiltsuk to relocate around it. Similarly, when Fort Rupert was established on northern Vancouver Island in 1849, four independent Kwakwaka'wakw groups joined together in its vicinity.

In the mid-nineteenth century, conflicts with colonial authorities led to the destruction of several Kwakwaka'wakw and Nuu-chah-nulth villages by the British navy. Epidemic diseases, such as measles and smallpox, also took a dreadful toll. One of the worst outbreaks began around Fort Victoria in 1862. Quickly spreading up the coast and far into the interior, it greatly reduced native populations and forced the abandonment of many villages. The modern Haisla, Heiltsuk, and Oweekeno were formed as several groups in each case coalesced at a single location. The number of politically separate villages among the Kwakwaka'wakw, Nuu-chah-nulth, and Ditidaht also was greatly reduced.

Great social and economic changes took place in the following decades. Christian missionaries were a major source of change, since many of them actively discouraged traditional practices. At the same time, declining populations continued to induce many Wakashans to amalgamate in villages around the missions or trading posts, a trend that further speeded the process of acculturation. Meanwhile, Euro-Canadian settlements increasingly sprang up on Wakashan lands, disrupting native life but providing new economic opportunities. Labour in Euro-Canadian ventures integrated some Wakashan groups into the commercial economy.

Except for a Hudson's Bay Company agreement at Fort Rupert, no treaty or other legal negotiations ceded Wakashan lands. Beginning in the 1880s, however, the federal government assigned reserves for all Wakashan groups, thereby reinforcing its claims to the Wakashans' remaining traditional territories. Today, each Wakashan First Nation holds a number of small, scattered reserves. Isolation from schools, roads, and jobs has prompted many families to move to nearby towns or more distant cities.

Economic Life

Fishing was the mainstay of the Wakashan economy. Salmon, caught on hooks, in nets, or in traps, were taken in huge numbers. Halibut, as important as salmon to the outer coast groups, were taken with hooks on long lines from offshore banks, often far out at sea. Lingcod, flounder, and rockfish offered welcome variety in the diet. Large schools of herring were taken during their spawning runs in nets or with an ingenious device termed a "herring rake" – a pole studded with sharp bone teeth which was swept through the water. Herring were also important for their roe, which was collected on evergreen boughs in the spawning beds. Another small fish, the eulachon, was highly valued for its oil, which was used as a sauce on a variety of foods. It was netted in quantity, allowed to "ripen" for a short period, and then cooked in large wooden vats to extract the oil. Many Kwakwaka'wakw groups congregated at the head of Knight Inlet for the spring eulachon fishery, as did the Oweekeno in Rivers Inlet, while other groups had to rely on trade for this important commodity.

Hunting also played a valuable economic role. Deer and elk were hunted throughout Wakashan territory, while mountain goats were important to more inland groups. It was the mammals of the sea, however, that were most prized. Seals, sea lions, and porpoises were hunted, generally by harpooning from canoes. Only the southern

Wakashans set out to sea in pursuit of whales, which also were harpooned. Success in such a venture required ritual preparation involving fasting and ceremonial bathing. In addition, small shrines containing human skulls or corpses were used in rituals to cause dead whales to drift ashore. Whales and other sea mammals provided a large part of the diet for the Nuu-chah-nulth and Ditidaht, a fact that enhanced the prestige of successful whaling chiefs.

Also essential to the coastal diet were various gathered foods. Clams, mussels, abalone, barnacles, sea urchins, and seaweeds were readily available in the intertidal zone. The deep deposits of crushed shells that mark ancient village sites throughout this area are testimony to the importance of such foods. Various roots, bulbs, and a wide range of berries also contributed to the diet.

To exploit resources throughout their territories, most Wakashan groups followed a seasonal pattern of movement. Critical locations such as salmon streams, herring spawning areas, clam beds, clover-root fields, and berry patches were the exclusive property of particular kin groups. Many resources were dried for later consumption, particularly during the winter months. Such preserved foodstuffs were stored in boxes or hung from the rafters in the houses.

European arrival and the maritime trade led to a new focus on hunting for furs. The collapse of the maritime trade left the Nuu-chah-nulth and Ditidaht in relative isolation, while the establishment of Hudson's Bay Company posts provided trade opportunities for the Heiltsuk and Kwakwaka'wakw. For the southern Wakashans, trade again picked up in the 1850s when they became major suppliers of dogfish oil, used as a lubricant in the logging industry.

The Wakashans were able to turn traditional skills to advantage in the new economy. Many men applied their knowledge of fishing for salmon to work as commercial fishermen, while large numbers of women found employment in the canneries which sprang up along the coast. Entire families moved seasonally as such jobs became available. In addition, many Nuu-chah-nulth and some Kwakwaka'wakw men turned to commercial fur-seal hunting. Sealing schooners took the hunters on lengthy expeditions across the Pacific in pursuit of the fur-seal herds. This lucrative enterprise continued well into the twentieth century, until it was halted by international treaty.

Economic change had visible architectural effects in Wakashan villages. The northern Wakashans, in particular, began to incorporate milled lumber, windows, and other European elements into their houses.

Such status indicators as free-standing carved poles outside the houses of important individuals also became more abundant in these late-nineteenth- and early-twentieth-century northern Wakashan villages.

Resource industries such as fishing and logging still dominate the economy throughout the Wakashan area. Fleets of native-owned fishing boats are a feature of many Wakashan communities, although government regulations and declining fish stocks have eroded the importance of the commercial fishery in recent years. The growth of nearby cities and towns has also added wider opportunities for wage labour. At the same time, Wakashan First Nations are taking the initiative in new economic ventures, many of which are related to tourism. The Nuu-chah-nulth operate whale-watching expeditions and heritage tours for visitors, and the Kwakwaka'wakw display their culture in two on-reserve museums. Modern hotels, run by a Nuu-chah-nulth group near Tofino and by the Kwakwaka'wakw at Cape Mudge, feature elements of native culture. In more isolated communities, however, the lack of economic opportunities has led many individuals and families to relocate off-reserve.

Kinship, Family, and Social Organization

The nature of the kinship units that made up Wakashan societies varied. The Haisla were divided into matrilineal clans, in the fashion of coastal groups farther north. Among the Kwakwaka'wakw, each community or "tribe" consisted of several kin groups known as *numayma*, meaning "one kind." The members of such social units were believed to descend from a common ancestor, frequently a supernatural being who had taken human form. The numayma held all the important group properties, including house sites, resource locations, ceremonial positions, songs, and names.

Wakashan nobility put great emphasis on their inheritance, keeping careful genealogies that extended back many generations. The Haisla followed the northern coast practice of tracing descent through the female line. The Heiltsuk, while not strictly matrilineal, tended to favour the mother's side. The Kwakwaka'wakw, Nuu-chah-nulth, and Ditidaht reckoned descent bilaterally. Kin terms distinguished between generations, but not between siblings and cousins. Kinship was basic to almost all social interaction, but even a remote relationship could be used to assert kin ties.

For high-ranking families, marriage was an alliance between groups.

After successfully negotiating the marriage, the groom's family might arrive at the bride's village in large canoes, several joined with planks to form a stage for masked dancing or other ceremonial display. The groom's family presented gifts, while the bride's group reciprocated with feasting and dancing, after which the bride generally went to live in the groom's village. She brought with her important prerogatives, such as names, dances, and rights to resource territories, that would eventually pass to her children.

Expectant mothers observed a variety of restrictions in diet and behaviour to ensure good health for their babies. They gave birth in temporary huts, assisted by their mothers or other female relatives, after which they were secluded for a number of days. The birth of twins, who were associated with spirits of the salmon, required much longer periods of seclusion for both parents and offspring. Infants had their ears pierced for ornaments, and gentle pressure while in the cradleboard produced the flattened forehead considered beautiful by most Wakashans. A name would be given, the first of a number of names the child might receive throughout his or her life.

Children of high-status families received careful instructions in correct modes of behaviour and on their traditions and inherited rights. Industry was encouraged; the first game killed by a boy and the first berries gathered by a girl were occasions for feasts. No specific observances marked puberty for a boy, but a girl's first menses required public acknowledgment. A period of seclusion and fasting ended with a feast, after which the young woman was eligible for marriage.

Marriages today characteristically occur in a church, with a Christian service. Frequently, however, this is followed by a feast or potlatch, often involving masked dancers. Traditional restrictions on eligible marital partners have largely been replaced with Euro-Canadian concepts. The close network of kin ties remains the basis for most Wakashan social life.

Social ranking characterized all Wakashan societies. Chiefs acted as heads of their kin groups, holding rights to important resource locations, ceremonial prerogatives, and names. Such positions were inherited, based on primogeniture in chiefly lines. Additional rights might be obtained through marriage. All such claims had to be validated publicly through potlatches. Management of the group's resources allowed chiefs to enhance their status by distributing food surpluses and material goods at feasts and potlatches. Commoners, who lacked inherited claims to titles or ceremonial privileges, provided the labour necessary to accumulate stores of food. Slaves, generally consisting of war captives, performed all menial tasks. Slaves were considered chattel and could be sold, given away at potlatches, or killed in mourning for a chief.

The potlatch was at the centre of Wakashan social and economic life. A high-status marriage, the birth of an heir, the transfer of an inherited name, or the raising of a carved pole were all occasions that required a potlatch. A chief recounted his family's history and then distributed gifts to all present to pay them as witnesses. The largest gifts went to other chiefs, whose own rank was thus recognized. Potlatches also served as occasions for masked dancers to display their ceremonial prerogatives. These could be lengthy events, lasting for days or weeks.

Declining populations in the late nineteenth century brought about changes in the potlatch, particularly among the Kwakwaka'wakw. Group amalgamation around the trading post at Fort Rupert stimulated competition between chiefs, and the great abundance of goods available from the post increased the scale of the potlatch. Hundreds of Hudson's Bay Company blankets, which became the standard unit of potlatch economics, were distributed at major events. As gestures of rivalry, chiefs also destroyed valuable items. Large canoes were hauled into the house and tossed onto the fire like beach logs, or valuable eulachon oil was poured on the fire in displays of chiefly wealth.

The decline in population also affected traditional status distinctions: more ranked positions became available than there were individuals with clear hereditary rights to fill them. In addition, new opportunities for wage labour meant that lower-ranked people could amass wealth and hold potlatches. This had the effect of allowing a wider range of individuals, both male and female, to acquire chiefly positions. Today, hereditary chiefs, although no longer holding ultimate political power, remain influential and respected in Wakashan societies. Assumption of a chiefly position still requires public validation through potlatching.

Religion

Religion was a vital part of traditional Wakashan culture. One of its central features was the lack of sharp divisions between animals and humans; when the bear returned to his cave he removed his coat and took human form. Salmon, seals, and killer whales lived much as humans did, in homes under the sea. It was essential to respect the animals, conducting rituals of welcoming before their flesh could be eaten. Even the cedar tree was thanked in prayer for its cloak of bark.

The sun and moon were important powers to which prayers were offered, while the Nuu-chah-nulth also prayed to the Four Chiefs, of the sky, horizon, land, and undersea.

During the winter months supernatural forces were believed to surround the Wakashan villages. This was a sacred time, when quarrels were forgotten and the people turned their attention to ceremonial activities. Dancers in elaborate costumes brought the supernatural presence into the human realm through their performances. A recurrent theme involved the capture of novice dancers by supernatural forces, the transfer of ceremonial privileges to them, and their reincorporation into human society. Ceremonies of the northern Wakashans featured a variety of supernatural beings, but the most important involved a "cannibal" dance. After a period of seclusion in the woods, the cannibal dancer burst into the house in a wild frenzy and was gradually "tamed." In southern Wakashan ceremonies, the wolf was the most important supernatural power. The elaborate masks, rattles, feast dishes, and painted dance screens used in these performances are among the greatest Wakashan artistic achievements.

Shamans were individuals who acquired supernatural power during long periods of solitary training in the woods. Such power generally came from a relationship with an animal spirit. The most important role of the shaman was in treating illness, often through public performances involving singing, shaking rattles, and sucking the disease-causing object out of the patient's body. Powerful shamans were feared, since they had the ability to inflict disease as well as to cure it.

Christian missionaries began arriving in the 1870s. Methodist missions were established among the Haisla and Heiltsuk, while the Kwakwaka'wakw were served by an Anglican mission. The Roman Catholics were first among the Nuu-chah-nulth, followed by the Presbyterians. The missionaries strongly opposed the shamans and ceremonial dancing. Many attempted to suppress all traditional native practices, including the potlatch, which they saw as a barrier to their goals of conversion and acculturation. After entreaties to the federal government, the potlatch became illegal in 1884. Most Wakashan groups ignored the ban, holding their potlatches in secret at isolated locations. In 1922, however, a group of Kwakwaka'wakw were prosecuted at Alert Bay, resulting in the incarceration of some individuals and the forced surrender of masks, rattles, and other potlatch goods. Legal prohibitions against the potlatch remained in effect until the Indian Act was rewritten in 1951.

In recent decades there has been a great expansion in Wakashan potlatching and ceremonial dancing. Big-houses in traditional form have been built for this purpose in such communities as Alert Bay and Fort Rupert, while community halls or gymnasiums are used in other villages. Modern artists are producing masks and other regalia for use in potlatch performances. In concession to modern needs, the once-lengthy potlatch now usually takes place in a single day.

Currently, the various Christian denominations are active in the regions where they were first established, and the Pentecostal church has made inroads into some Kwakwaka'wakw communities. Virtually all Wakashans are at least nominally Christians, and church events feature prominently in the lives of many individuals. Baptisms, marriages, and funerals typically take place in churches, but often these are followed by traditional dancing and feasting.

Education, Language, and Communication

Traditionally, native children learned by watching and imitating their older relatives. Boys accompanied their fathers or uncles on fishing and hunting expeditions, while girls helped in household activities. Grandparents provided invaluable counsel, teaching children family history and appropriate behaviour.

Since Confederation, native education has been the responsibility of the federal government, and it set up residential schools and on-reserve day schools. The residential schools, in communities such as Alert Bay and Port Alberni, housed children from more isolated locations. Removing children from their families interfered with traditional teaching and led to a loss of language and culture. This was exacerbated by a curriculum that stressed Euro-Canadian perspectives. Despite a legacy of social problems and educational failure, such schools operated among the Wakashans until the early 1970s.

Today, Wakashan children attend provincial schools, located off-reserve. In urban areas with substantial native populations, such as Port Alberni, some schools have instituted native language and culture programs. A few Wakashan communities, such as Alert Bay, have on-reserve band-run schools to provide education geared to the needs of their children; language and culture programs form an integral part of the curriculum at such schools. Levels of educational attainment have increased markedly in recent years. Substantial numbers of Wakashan students now attend colleges and universities, with many entering professions such as teaching and law.

The Wakashans, like other Canadian aboriginal cultures, lacked a written language. Instead, great emphasis was placed on oral traditions. Ceremonial oratory was greatly prized, and many chiefs had speakers to recount the history and inherited rights of their family at public gatherings.

Wakashan languages suffered great decline through their suppression in residential schools and elsewhere. Today, English is the dominant language in native communities. Many elders, however, retain their traditional speech; the 1991 census indicates that about 4,000 people can carry on a conversation in a Wakashan language. Of these, Nuu-chah-nulth has the largest number of speakers.

Determined efforts are being made to reverse the loss of Wakashan languages through school programs; phonetic scripts have been developed so that such tongues can be written down and taught. Language and culture programs, however, serve mainly to enhance native identity rather than to restore native languages to their former dominance.

The Nuu-chah-nulth Tribal Council publishes a newspaper, *Ha-Shilth-Sa*, which keeps its members aware of political and social developments. Except for a few words, this paper is written in English. The Nuu-chah-nulth and the Kwakwaka'wakw of Alert Bay have produced films to be used in educational programs and to communicate their history and culture to a wider audience.

Politics

For most Wakashans, the basic political unit was the group of people who resided together at a winter village. This might comprise a number of local groups which were scattered at other times of the year. The northern Nuu-chah-nulth developed complex confederacies that brought together large numbers of people at shared summer villages on the outer coast. Historic epidemics, by causing population decline and the abandonment of many villages, greatly reduced the number of separate political units.

Wakashan communities surviving into modern times have been incorporated as Indian bands under the Canadian Indian Act. Elected band councils operate much like municipal councils, administering such services as housing, water, sewers, and sanitation; in some areas they also take responsibility for health, welfare, and education. While many Wakashan groups elect their chiefs, among the Nuu-chah-nulth the hereditary chiefs frequently head the band councils.

Alliances of related groups into tribal councils have provided greater political influence on issues of common concern. The Nuu-chah-nulth and Ditidaht formed the West Coast Allied Tribes, later renamed the Nuu-chah-nulth Tribal Council, in 1958, one of the first such alliances in British Columbia. It now represents fourteen bands. The Kwakiutl District Council, today representing ten Kwakwaka'wakw bands, was established in 1974. Four bands around Kingcome Inlet, later joined by the people at Alert Bay, left in 1982 to form a separate alliance, the Musgamagw Tsawataineuk Tribal Council. The Oweekeno joined with their non-Wakashan neighbours to form the Oweekeno/Kitasoo Nuxalk Tribal Council. Wakashan First Nations that are not members of such political alliances are the Haisla, Heiltsuk, and Pacheedaht (the southernmost Ditidaht band).

Wakashan political struggles centre on demands for greater control of their own affairs and for settlement of long-standing grievances over ownership of lands and resources in their traditional territories. Most Wakashan First Nations, along with other aboriginal groups in British Columbia, have recently filed land claims with the British Columbia Treaty Commission and are actively negotiating with the federal and provincial governments. Settlements reached through this process will enhance Wakashan economic and political self-sufficiency.

Intergroup Relations and Group Maintenance

Since no overarching political identity existed, even among people speaking the same language, warfare was a common feature of traditional Wakashan life. Hostilities also occurred with non-Wakashans. Early in the historic period the Coastal Tsimshian forcefully displaced some of the northern Wakashans, while several groups of Kwakwaka'wakw expanded southward at the expense of the neighbouring Coast Salish.

Trade linked the Wakashan communities and their neighbours. Commodities such as eulachon oil, dentalium shells, and slaves were traded along the coast and far into the interior. When European items were introduced, they were rapidly distributed along indigenous trade routes. For example, when Vancouver's expedition reached northeastern Vancouver Island in 1792, it found the Kwakwaka'wakw already in possession of muskets, which they had acquired in overland trade with the Nuu-chah-nulth.

Social interaction fostered intermarriage, which in turn resulted in the transfer of names and ceremonial privileges between groups. The

Haisla intermarried with the Coastal Tsimshian, adopting from them the matrilineal clan system. The Heiltsuk were so intermarried with the Nuxalk (or Bella Coola) that some villages were bilingual. This led to considerable overlap in the traditional territories claimed by these groups today.

Wakashan individuals continue to interact with their neighbours, native and non-native. Many reserves are adjacent to non-native communities, and so there is extensive contact between them. Movement off-reserve has introduced many Wakashans to urban life and increased the likelihood of marriage with other cultural groups. Most individuals who choose to reside in towns or cities maintain close ties to their "home" reserves, making frequent visits for ceremonial or social occasions.

Although their languages and cultural practices were eroded by residential schools and the Indian Act, the Wakashan succeeded in maintaining much of their heritage and identity. Two museums demonstrate their cultural resiliency. In the late nineteenth century, legal suppression of the potlatch had resulted in forced surrender of many items used in such feasts. When the potlatch once again became legal, the Kwakwaka'wakw pressed the federal government for return of their lost treasures. By 1980 museums had been constructed in Alert Bay and Cape Mudge, with the newly returned artefacts forming the basis of their collections. These facilities serve today not just as static museum displays but as dynamic community cultural centres, promoting indigenous traditions and languages.

Wakashan artistic achievements also provide a highly visible source of cultural identity and pride. Poles, masks, silkscreen prints, and gold and silver jewellery are among the works produced by modern artists. Most pieces are purchased by non-native collectors and museums, but some are made for native use in potlatches and dances. Among many talented Kwakwaka'wakw artists, members of the Hunt family, particularly the brothers Tony and Richard Hunt, have achieved international reputations. Nuu-chah-nulth artists Joe David and Art Thompson have also received widespread recognition.

Though the challenges they face are formidable, the Wakashans are endeavouring – through educational programs, various forms of cultural expression, and political struggle – to ensure that their sense of identity as a people is strengthened and passed on intact to the next generation.

FURTHER READING

Franz Boas's long-term research with the northern Wakashans, particularly the Kwagiulth of Fort Rupert on northern Vancouver Island, has resulted in numerous scholarly publications. Perhaps the most useful general book is *Kwakiutl Ethnography*, edited by Helen Codere (Chicago, 1966). Ronald and Evelyn Rohner give a brief account of their work with the Kwakwaka'wakw, particularly at the community of Gilford Island, in *The Kwakiutl: Indians of British Columbia* (New York, 1970). A collection of papers on the Kwakwaka'wakw potlatch is available in a well-illustrated volume edited by Aldona Jonaitis, *Chiefly Feasts: The Enduring Kwakiutl Potlatch* (New York, 1991).

The primary ethnographic source on the Nuu-chah-nulth is Philip Drucker, *The Northern and Central Nootkan Tribes* (Washington, D.C., 1951). A more general book, dealing with all three southern Wakashan groups, is E.Y. Arima, *The West Coast (Nootka) People* (Victoria, B.C., 1983). The major Wakashan groups are covered in a popular illustrated book by Ruth Kirk entitled *Wisdom of the Elders: Native Traditions on the Northwest Coast, the Nuu-chah-nulth, Southern Kwakiutl, and Nuxalk* (Vancouver, 1986). Summary articles on all Wakashan peoples are available in the *Handbook of North American Indians*, vol. 7, *Northwest Coast*, edited by Wayne Suttles (Washington, D.C., 1990). In particular, see the articles "Nootkans of Vancouver Island" (E.Y. Arima and John Dewhirst), "Kwakiutl: Traditional Culture" (Helen Codere), "Haisla" (Charles Hamori-Torok), "Haihais, Bella Bella, and Oowekeeno" (Susanne Hilton), "Kwakiutl: Winter Ceremonies" (Bill Holm), and "Kwakiutl since 1980" (Gloria Webster).

CONTRIBUTORS

Margaret Seguin Anderson is a professor of First Nations Studies, University of Northern British Columbia.

Janet E. Chute is a historian in Halifax, Nova Scotia

Olive P. Dickason is professor emeritus, University of Alberta, and adjunct professor, University of Ottawa.

Louis-Jacques Dorais is a professor of anthropology, Université Laval.

Joan A. Lovisek is a historian in Unionville, Ontario.

Paul Robert Magocsi is a professor of history and political science, University of Toronto.

Mary C. Marino is an associate professor of languages and linguistics, University of Saskatchewan.

Susan Marsden is curator of the Museum of Northern British Columbia.

Alan McMillan is a professor of anthropology at Douglas College, New Westminster.

Bruce Granville Miller is an associate professor of anthropology, University of British Columbia.

J.R. Miller is a professor of history at the University of Saskatchewan.

Patrick Moore is First Nations Language Consultant with the Department of Education, Government of Yukon.

Deanna Nyce is Chief Executive Officer, Wilp Wilxo'oskwhl Nisga'a.

Alexander von Gernet is an adjunct professor of anthropology at University of Toronto (Erindale).

Eldon Yellowhorn is a lecturer with the Department of Archaeology at Simon Fraser University.